/3

How to Run a Limited Company

HOW TO RUN A LIMITED COMPANY

Nicholas Currie
with David Frederick

icsa.
Publishing

Published by
ICSA Information & Training Ltd
16 Park Crescent
London W1B 1AH

Typeset in 9½ on 12½ pt Kuenstler by Hands Fotoset, Woodthorpe, Nottingham
Printed in Great Britain by Hobbs the Printers Ltd, Totton, Hampshire

British Library Cataloguing in Publication Data
A catalogue record for this book is available from the British Library

ISBN 978-1-86072-452-7

Contents

Preface

This book is intended to be an up-to-date, practical guide to running a private company limited by shares. It has been written for directors, company secretaries, managers and any others who are new to running such a company or need to know more about it. It may also be of help to students and those training for professional qualifications, as well as being an accessible reference for established practitioners. However, that it is a guide should be emphasised. All companies differ in their individual circumstances and this book cannot be a substitute for expert advice. What it does aim to do is to give detailed information about the areas that are covered, to explain the law in a straightforward way and to highlight the key issues. It is hoped that this will enable directors, company secretaries and so on to go about their work and duties and to liaise with their professional advisers on any given issue, with a better understanding of the law and procedures involved.

The UK is split into three separate jurisdictions – England and Wales, Scotland and Northern Ireland. While much of the law applies equally to all UK companies regardless of where they are incorporated, there are some differences. This book is concerned with the law as it applies to private companies limited by shares incorporated in England and Wales.

It has taken a long time to bring the book to completion and I am very grateful to all of my friends, family and colleagues for their comments, suggestions and support. Thanks must also go to David Frederick for contributing chapters 13, 14, 17 and 18, without which the book would not exist in its current form.

All efforts have been made to ensure the accuracy of the information provided however neither the author nor the publisher can accept responsibility for any loss suffered by anyone relying solely on any of the information contained herein.

As to terminology, any references to the 'Companies Act' are to the Companies Act 2006 unless otherwise indicated and references to the 'Model Articles' are to the model articles for private companies limited by shares. The personal pronoun 'he' is used in most cases but its use includes both the male and female genders.

The law is stated as at 30 April 2013.

NICHOLAS CURRIE
June 2013

Acknowledgements

Appendix 8: Model articles for private companies limited by shares
© Crown Copyright 2009, reproduced with permission of the Controller of HMSO and the Queen's Printer for Scotland.

1 Business structures and the decision to incorporate

> ## ▓ In this chapter
>
> This chapter provides a general introduction to running a business as a limited company with regard to:
>
> - the other main types of business set ups – sole traders, partnerships and limited liability partnerships;
> - the separate legal personality of a limited company;
> - the relationship between the key players in a limited company – the directors and shareholders;
> - the different types of limited company that exist under UK law;
> - the potential advantages and disadvantages of running a business as a limited company; and
> - transferring an existing business into a limited company.

In today's world the limited liability company is part of the fabric of everyday life, but it was not always like this. In the great scheme of things, the limited liability company is a relatively recent phenomenon, only becoming freely available in the latter half of the nineteenth century. Prior to this, companies were only created by royal charter or by special acts of parliament. Although the exact figures vary, the number of limited companies that now come into existence each year in the United Kingdom is generally in the region of three to four hundred thousand. However, despite these numbers, the limited company is not the only (or the most popular) option for someone starting up a new business. There are in fact four main types of business structure. These are:

- sole trader;
- partnership;
- limited liability partnership; and
- limited company.

According to the Office for National Statistics, of the estimated 4.8 million private sector businesses in the United Kingdom, some 62.7% are sole traders,

9.3% are partnerships and 28% are limited companies. As such, the majority of businesses in the United Kingdom do not operate as a limited company but as a sole trader – the most straightforward of the four business structures. This is the form that most new businesses take when they begin their life.

Sole traders

The main attraction of operating as a sole trader is simplicity. Sole traders own and run their businesses, often starting up on their own, making products for sale or selling some kind of service. They are self-employed, so if they do undertake work for others they do so as a contractor and not as an employee. Any profits of a sole trader's business are theirs and are charged to income tax by filing a self-assessment tax return with HM Revenue and Customs (HMRC). When compared to a limited company, some of the main benefits of being a sole trader are to do with the relative lack of regulation and relative privacy that they enjoy. Starting a business in this way also gives the sole trader a chance to see whether their business is viable and likely to succeed in the long term, before considering any plans for growth or expansion.

The potential down side of being a sole trader lies with the fact that there is no separation between the sole trader and their business. They are one and the same thing. This means that if sole traders are unable to pay the debts of their business, their personal property is then at risk. By court order, their creditors can look to satisfy payment of the sums owed to them by seizing the sole trader's property. Only the tools of the sole trader's trade are safe, together with those items that are required to meet the essential needs of day-to-day living.

As well as this, if a sole trader wants to expand the business, they may find it difficult to raise the capital they need to do it. Loans from a bank or friends and family may be possible, but professional investors will usually look for an equity stake in the business (in the expectation that this will grow in value), which generally means taking shares in it. Because there is no separation between the sole trader and their business, there is nothing to take shares in. As a result, sole traders will often move their business forward by taking on a business partner and so the sole trader might become a partnership, or move straight to forming a limited company.

Partnerships

The law governing partnerships is contained in a very old piece of legislation – the Partnership Act 1890 – which still remains in force today. It defines a partnership as 'the relation which subsists between persons carrying on a business in common with a view to profit'. The effect of this definition is that people in business together can be deemed to be operating as a partnership (and thereby be subject to the provisions of the Partnership Act) whether it was their intention to operate as a partnership or not. There is no legal procedure that needs to be followed to form a partnership (which there is for forming a limited company), but for people going into partnership together it is a good idea to ask a professional to draw up a formal partnership agreement to regulate the way in which the partnership is run and to set out the rights and obligations of the individual partners. In the absence of a partnership agreement, or to the extent that a partnership agreement is silent on a given issue, the provisions of the Partnership Act will apply and this may produce outcomes that the partners do not want.

Partnerships enjoy similar benefits to sole traders in that the partners own and run the partnership, the partners' earnings (known as 'drawings') are charged to income tax and details of the partnership's internal affairs, including its accounts and the terms of any partnership agreement, are completely private and do not need to be placed on public record. The advantage that a partnership has over the sole trader structure is that the business benefits from the combined skills and experience of the individual partners and the fact that the risks of the business are shared. The flip side is that the principal drawback of being a sole trader is somewhat magnified in a partnership in that the partners are 'jointly and severally liable' for the debts of the business. This means that all of the partners are potentially liable for the business debts, whether they personally incurred those debts, or not. In a worst-case scenario a single partner could be left on their own by the other partners to deal with the partnership's creditors. Just as it is with a sole trader, each partner's personal property is at risk. This means that operating as a partnership requires a high degree of trust between the parties involved.

Limited liability partnerships

In basic terms, a limited liability partnership (LLP) is a cross between a limited company and a partnership. LLPs have many of the characteristics of a normal partnership but share one significant feature with limited companies, which is that an LLP is a separate legal entity. As such, they offer the flexibility of a normal partnership together with the benefits and advantages of a limited company. The concept of a 'separate legal entity' is explained below.

LLPs do not have partners, but have members who are the equivalent of the individual partners in a normal partnership. Each member of the LLP is usually required to contribute to the funds of the LLP on becoming a member and this represents the extent of their liability for the debts of the LLP in the event of a winding up (unless any circumstances exist which may give rise to personal liability, such as fraudulent trading or negligence).

LLPs are subject to regulation by the Companies Act (2006) (as applied to LLPs by the Limited Liability Partnerships Regulations 2001) and are required to file information about the LLP and its members with Companies House (the UK company registry) which means that there is a loss of privacy in operating as an LLP.

A significant difference between companies and LLPs is that LLPs are not taxed as limited companies, but are taxed in the same way as a partnership. This can make them more or less tax efficient, depending on the circumstances. However, as with any other kind of trading entity, proper advice should be taken as to whether an LLP is the appropriate structure to use for any given business.

The limited company

The key feature of a limited company that distinguishes it from the sole trader or partnership structure is that it is, in law, considered to be a separate legal entity. Companies have what is known as 'legal personality' and this opens up possibilities that have made companies one of the defining features of modern life. But what does 'legal personality' mean?

Legal personality

Legal personality means that a company is effectively a person. Not a real person, of course, but a *legal* person. While there is no separation between a sole trader and their business, and a partnership refers to a way of carrying on in business rather than to a thing in itself, the limited company exists separately from the people who run it and the people who own it. This principle was firmly established over a hundred years ago in the case of *Salomon v Salomon & Co Ltd*.

> ### Case example: *Salomon v Salomon & Co Ltd* (1897)
>
> Mr Salomon was a sole trader in business as a leather merchant. He decided to form a limited company and then to sell his business to the company which he would proceed to run as managing director. This was done, but the company soon got into financial difficulties and the case that followed involved a claim by the liquidator that the company set up was simply being used by Mr Salomon to avoid personal liability for the debts of his business. Overturning a decision of the Court of Appeal, the House of Lords ruled that the company had been properly formed in accordance with the legal requirements, that it was – as a result – a separate legal person and that Mr Salomon could not be made liable to pay its debts.

Because a company is a legal entity it can do things that real people can do. A company can:

- acquire property (including shares in another company);
- borrow money;
- employ people;
- buy goods and services;

- be a director or secretary of another company;
- sue other people or companies and be sued itself; and
- commit offences and be prosecuted for them.

In addition, because a company is a separate legal entity, its directors are not liable for the company's debts except if they have personally guaranteed them or in certain other circumstances if the company is in financial difficulties (see Chapter 7). However, this arises from the fact that the company is a separate legal person – the concept of limited liability actually applies to a company's shareholders, rather than its directors.

Limited liability

In company law terms, it is a company's shareholders who have limited liability, not the directors. The liability of a company's shareholders is limited to the amount paid up on their shares plus the amount, if any, that is unpaid on the shares held by them in the company. This means that if a company becomes insolvent a shareholder will only lose their original investment and be liable for paying to the company any money that remains owing on their shares. The shareholder will not be liable for the whole of the company's debts.

Example

Person A agrees to buy 100 shares of £1 each in Company X. Company X requires full payment before the shares are issued, so Person A pays £100 to the company and the company then allots the shares.

Three years later, Company X becomes insolvent and is wound up. Person A has no liability and contributes no money towards the assets of the company because the shares are paid for in full. However Person A may, of course, lose the £100 that they originally invested.

Creation

The process of creating a limited company is known as 'incorporation' and is sometimes also referred to as 'formation' or 'registration'. To incorporate a company in the United Kingdom, an application for incorporation must be submitted to Companies House which is an executive agency of the department for Business Innovation and Skills (BIS). If the application meets all of the requirements set out in the Companies Act and is in all other ways acceptable, the company will be incorporated. The exact procedure and requirements are explained in Chapter 2.

Management

As a separate legal entity, a company needs real people to act on its behalf. Companies have two distinct decision-making bodies – the board of directors and the shareholders. The people with responsibility for running a company are the company's directors. The authority to do this is given to them by the shareholders under the company's 'articles of association' – an important document which regulates the rights, powers and obligations of the directors and the shareholders in relation to the company. (The articles of association are discussed in detail in Chapter 3.) The role of a director will vary from one company to another. In a small owner-managed company there will be a single director who is also the company's sole shareholder and who probably deals with all aspects of the company's business, including its trading activities. At the other end of the scale are the directors of the United Kingdom's largest listed companies, men and women who may sit on the board of more than one company and who have made a career as professional directors and managers. The role of directors is explained in Chapter 6, their duties and liabilities in Chapter 7 and the procedures for directors' decision making in Chapter 8.

Ownership and control

A shareholder is a person who owns shares in a company. Shareholders are also 'members' of a company and can be referred to by that term because 'member' describes any person whose name is entered in a company's register of members. A member of a company enjoys the rights afforded to members by the Companies Act. However, not all companies have a share capital and where this is the case 'member' does not mean 'shareholder' and implies a different relationship with the company than in a company limited by shares (see 'private companies limited by guarantee' below).

Shares are a form of property and they confer certain rights in relation to a company. They also give shareholders a stake in the value of a company, which is why shares are sometimes referred to as 'equity'. Shareholders generally invest their money in a company in the expectation of receiving regular dividends (a share of the profits of the company) and in the hope that the value of their shares will increase over time. Having handed authority to the directors to run the company the shareholders are generally not expected to get involved in management decisions. They do, however, have to approve certain actions that the directors might want to take such as changing the articles of association, changing the company's name and making changes to the company's share capital, to name a few.

The directors' authority to run the company in any way that they want is restricted by the many rules and obligations set out in the Companies Act and other legislation. Although the powers of shareholders are fairly limited, they do have the inalienable right to remove a director by a formal vote in a shareholders' meeting. A director can be removed by a simple majority of votes in favour, meaning that a shareholder owning over 50% of a company's shares has a significant power.

Shareholders are the owners of a company, but a single shareholder holding a very small percentage of a company's shares may not experience much sense of this. At the same time, a shareholder holding 100% of a company's shares needs to remember that the company is a separate entity and any assets of the company, including any profit it makes, belong to the company and not to them. In the case of an owner-managed company this can be a particular challenge. Sole directors/shareholders must conduct themselves appropriately, depending on the capacity in which they act at any given time (i.e. that of director or shareholder).

Transferring ownership

Ownership, and thereby control, of a limited company is transferred by the transfer of shares. This is what happens when a company is sold. The business and assets of the company are owned by the company itself (and not the directors or shareholders), so a sale of the company is effected by a change of ownership of the company's shares. Once the new owner has voting control, they then have the power to remove and replace the existing directors if they so wish. Companies also have what is known in legal terms as 'perpetual succession'. Because shares are property, when an individual shareholder dies ownership of their shares will be transferred in accordance with their will or the rules of intestacy (subject to any restrictions on transfers in the company's articles of association). This means that companies can continue to operate, with shares being transferred as and when required until they are closed down by way of a formal winding-up process (see Chapter 17). For a sole trader this is obviously not the case. The sole trader's business simply ceases when they stop working for whatever reason. The lack of separate legal personality also means that partnerships do not benefit from perpetual succession and they may come to an end for a variety of different reasons.

▨ Different types of limited company

There are two main types of limited company – public limited companies and private limited companies. Public limited companies are always limited by shares (meaning that they must have a share capital and shareholders who hold the company's shares). Private companies can either be limited by shares or limited by guarantee.

Private companies limited by shares

The vast majority of companies in existence in the United Kingdom are private companies limited by shares. 'Limited by shares' means that a company has a share capital as opposed to a company limited by guarantee, which does not. Private companies limited by shares are prohibited from offering their shares for sale to the public and this is a key difference between private companies and public companies. Private companies can give shares to willing investors, but they cannot make a general invitation to the public to buy their shares. Because of this, private companies are more suited to small and medium-sized businesses and benefit from a lighter compliance regime when compared to public companies. As stated in the Preface, this book is about how to run a private company limited by shares.

Private companies limited by guarantee

Companies limited by guarantee are a type of private company which cannot issue shares. Instead the members of the company (equivalent to the shareholders in a company limited by shares – see earlier) agree to contribute a fixed amount of money towards settling the debts and liabilities of the company in the event that the company becomes insolvent and is wound up. The amount of money is usually quite small – as little as £1 for example – and this represents the extent of each member's liability for the company's debts. This sum is not paid on becoming a member, it only becomes payable in the event of a winding up.

Members of a company limited by guarantee also have the rights afforded to members by the Companies Act, but they are not shareholders. Where owning shares provides a means to participate in a company's profits or to realise value by a sale of the shares, companies limited by guarantee have no way of distributing profits to their members. This is what sets them apart from private companies limited by shares and dictates the kinds of organisations that they are suited to. For example, companies limited by guarantee are usually set up for specific purposes such as for clubs, societies, trade associations and other not-for-profit activities or functions. Flat-management companies have historically been limited by guarantee and charitable organisations that wish to operate as a limited company will also (in the vast majority of cases) form a company limited by guarantee in order to satisfy the registration requirements of the Charity Commission. The first members of a guarantee company are appointed on incorporation, but otherwise the route to becoming a member is normally by a written application to the directors who then decide whether to grant membership or not. As membership is not linked to holding shares in the company (since there are no shares) membership cannot be transferred as it can in companies with a share capital. The articles of association of a company limited by guarantee will usually state that membership is not transferable and consequently there is no need for the kind of complex provisions that place controls or restrictions on the transfer of membership as might be necessary in the case of a private company limited by shares. In addition, members who wish to terminate their membership are not in the (sometimes difficult) position that members of a company limited by shares are in, of having to find a buyer for their shares. Normally membership will simply be ended by notice in writing to the company, subject to any rules in the articles of association. Similarly, the articles will normally state that membership terminates on death.

As a form of private company, companies limited by guarantee are subject to the same regulation as private companies limited by shares, but with various differences mainly owing to the fact that they do not have shares. There are some specific rights afforded to guarantee companies such as the right to apply for exemption from using the word 'limited' at the end of the company's name and the right to use certain words in the name (such as association, federation and society) which cannot be used by other types of company. These are not automatic rights, however, and depend on certain conditions being met.

Companies limited by guarantee that have charitable status will also be subject to charity law. Charity law can be a difficult area. There is a wealth of information available to charities on the website of the Charity Commission (the regulator for charities registered in the United Kingdom), but for anyone considering setting up a charitable company advice from a professional who specialises in the regulation of charities is essential.

Public limited companies

Public companies are far less common than private companies. They have the same benefits of limited liability as private companies, but unlike private companies they can offer their shares for sale to the public. This gives them a means of raising finance that is not available to private companies; however, it also means that the level of regulation that applies to public companies is considerably higher. Public companies can also apply to have their shares and other securities listed on a recognised stock exchange. This opens up further avenues for raising capital, but also involves more regulation. Shares in companies with a listing on a recognised stock exchange are more attractive because of the relative ease with which they can be bought and sold. By comparison, shares in a private company can be difficult to sell, as there is usually no facility for trading them and there are often restrictions in the articles on how they may be transferred.

Public limited companies are generally only suited to larger profit-making organisations that wish to take advantage of these opportunities although some organisations may decide to incorporate as a public company for the enhanced status that such companies enjoy. Obtaining a listing for their shares is not a requirement for public companies, it is just a possibility. A comparison of private and public companies highlighting some of the main differences can be found in Appendix 1.

Other types of company

Falling under the heading of private companies limited by guarantee are two specific types of company. These are:

- right to manage companies; and
- commonhold associations.

Community interest companies are a further type of company which can be a private company limited by shares or by guarantee and can also be a public company.

Each of these forms of company are intended for specific purposes. Right to manage companies (RTM) are used by leaseholders (subject to the satisfaction of certain conditions) to take over their landlord's management functions by transferring them to the RTM company. Commonhold is a particular form of freehold ownership that provides an alternative to leasehold in multi-occupancy developments such as flats. Community interest companies are for use in social enterprises, with the assets and profits of the company being applied for the benefit of the community.

These companies would not be used for private and profit-making business pursuits and professional advice should always be taken in connection with setting up any of these types of company.

▣ Potential benefits of a limited company

The two main benefits of a limited company have already been highlighted – the fact the company is a legal entity in its own right (separate from the directors and shareholders) and that the liability of the shareholders is limited to any amount unpaid on their shares plus the loss of any amount already paid up on them. Another key reason for operating as a limited company is taxation.

Taxation

Many people who decide to form a limited company do so for tax reasons. This is because a general advantage that a limited company has over a sole trader or partnership is its tax efficiency. A sole trader with increasing taxable profits will pay tax at the basic rate of 20%, then dependent upon the level of the taxable profit, a higher rate of income tax at 40%, followed by an additional higher rate of income tax at 45%. The Chancellor of the Exchequer sets the thresholds for the payment of basic rate, higher rate and additional higher rate of income tax in the annual budget. Companies have a single rate of corporation tax, the only exception to this being small companies with an annual profit of under £300,000. The current corporation tax rate is 23% (as at 1 April 2013) and the small companies rate is 20%.

The basis for taxation for both a sole trader and a company is the accounting profit adjusted for any disallowable expenses less any capital allowances. A sole trader also has a deductible personal allowance, whereas a company does not receive such allowances. In addition, a sole trader will also be liable to pay class 4 national insurance based upon their profit if it exceeds the annual threshold set annually by the Chancellor. A limited company is not subject to class 4 national insurance contributions.

An example of the combination of these factors is shown in Table 1.1 for a sole trader and a limited company with the same accounting profit. The assumption

Table 1.1: Comparative income tax and corporation tax for a sole trader v a limited company

Sole trader		Ltd company
£		£
15,000	Accounting profit	15,000
0	*Add* back disallowable expenses	0
0	*Less* capital allowances	0
15,000	Adjusted profit	15,000
7,475	Personal allowance	0
7,525	Taxable profit	15,000
1,505	Tax @ 20%	
699	Class 4 NIC	
2,204	Tax and NIC Class 4	
	Salary	7,475
	Taxable profit	7,525
	Corporation tax @ 20%	1,505
	Savings	699

made for the limited company is that it will pay the sole director-employee a salary equal to the personal allowance. On a comparative basis, without any adjustment for higher professional fees for the limited company, the sole trader position is seen as less tax efficient.

However, a limited company presents its owners and directors with additional administrative responsibilities. A limited company has statutory responsibilities to HMRC and the Registrar of Companies (explained further below). Other additional responsibilities that a limited company is subjected to include the following:

- their annual accounts must comply with the requirements of the Companies Act;
- payment to a sole employee-director requires the registration of a payroll; and
- the company must account for tax credits when dividend payments are made.

The decision to run a business in the form of a limited company may also be driven by wider commercial factors excluding taxation. Any decision to trade as a limited liability company should not be made solely on the basis of actual or perceived tax efficiency, but with a holistic assessment and evaluation of the tax and non-tax drivers. Some of the other possible advantages of a limited company are set out below.

Access to finance

As mentioned earlier, a limited company may find it easier to raise finance than a sole trader. Operating as a limited company tends to imply a certain size, standing and reputation and makes limited companies a more attractive proposition for lending and investment than sole traders or partnerships. Chapter 13 explains the possible sources of finance for a limited company.

Perception and status

It is not only investors and lenders who may prefer to deal with a limited company, others may feel this way as well. Being a limited company conveys a certain credibility and companies are often perceived as being more stable than unincorporated businesses. Companies are heavily regulated and must make information about themselves available to the public via Companies House. Some companies will only do business with other incorporated companies.

Flexibility

The business form of a sole trader or a partnership may be perfectly adequate provided that the ownership and control structure are simple (i.e. a small number of people owning and contributing to the business in a straightforward way). However the company structure allows for more complex relationships to be created between the directors, company and shareholders. This means that the owner/founders can bring in external management to help grow the business and invest funds in return for an equity stake but still retain control financially and in terms of decision making. It also makes it easier to plan for the succession of the business (i.e. who takes over when the current owners and managers leave or die) and to give directors, employees and family members shares in the company, again without any loss of control.

Business continuance

Since companies have perpetual succession (as discussed earlier), a company remains in existence following the death of an owner-manager, or after a change of ownership or management. This means that, where a sole trader's business ceases to exist, a company can carry on and continue to benefit from the reputation and the 'goodwill' that it may have accrued over many years of trading.

Parents and subsidiaries

The fact that a company is a legal person allows it to acquire the shares of another company and this makes it possible to set companies up as a group. Indeed, this is what some of the largest and best-known companies are – huge multinational organisations consisting of a complex structure of companies across many countries all ultimately owned and controlled by a single company.

The circumstances in which one company will be considered to be the parent of another company are set out in the Companies Act. A company (known as a 'holding company') will be the parent of another company (known as its 'subsidiary') if it:

- holds a majority of the voting rights;
- is a member of the company and has the right to appoint or remove a majority of the board of directors; or
- is a member of the company and controls alone, by way of agreement with other members, a majority of the voting rights in it (Companies Act 2006, s. 1159).

One of the reasons why companies choose to operate as a group is to spread risk. Although a company can artificially separate one part of its activities from the others by creating a 'division' (e.g. a manufacturing division, a distribution division, a communications division etc) and even give that division a different name under which to trade and operate, it still remains part of the same company. In a group company set-up, each company in the group has some protection from the failure of the others. Since each company is a separate legal entity, the insolvency of one company does not mean the end for the others as well. Similarly, by separating different parts of the business in this way, the financial performance of each can be monitored more easily.

The other main reason for using a group structure relates to the issue of tax, because a group structure can be more tax efficient. That said, tax issues in a group set-up can be complex. Professional advice is, therefore, essential as to whether this is the right option and to provide guidance as to managing the group's tax affairs.

Name protection

Sometimes a company is incorporated purely for the purposes of protecting a particular name. Once a company has been incorporated, no other company can be incorporated with the same name. A sole trader trading under a business name could incorporate a company with that name to prevent anyone else from using it as the name of a limited company. The company then simply remains dormant, and the sole trader just has to make sure that the company complies with the minimal legal obligations required to keep it alive. A registered company that trades under a business name that is different from its registered name could also do the same thing. Issues concerning company names, business names and how to protect them are explained more fully in Chapter 2.

Limiting risk

Sometimes the scale and size of a business and the corresponding financial risks make the limited company structure the only feasible option. Similarly, in industries or businesses where litigation is common, operating as a limited company gives protection to the directors and shareholders as any legal claims will normally be made against the company.

Employee share schemes

Another advantage of a limited company is the relative ease (compared with other types of business structure) with which directors, management and employees can be given a stake in the business. Giving shares to employees can be an effective way to attract, retain and incentivise staff at all levels and this is something that the government is keen to encourage. Various different types of approved share schemes are available. Some have to be set up as 'all-employee' schemes that must be open to all staff and others are discretionary schemes that could, for example, be open only to directors and senior executives. The approved share schemes work in different ways but essentially allow employees either to acquire shares, or an option to buy shares with the benefit of specified tax breaks. Not surprisingly, there are detailed rules and eligibility criteria for these schemes. Professional advice should be taken about the most appropriate scheme for any given company (depending on what the company wants to achieve) as well as the applicable rules and eligibility criteria. Unapproved schemes can be used by companies that do not meet the criteria for an approved scheme but they do not provide the tax reliefs that approved schemes do. An unapproved scheme could also be used to 'top up' an approved scheme when its limits have been reached.

▨ Potential downsides and risks

Of course, using a limited company set-up is not all plain sailing. Some of the potential disadvantages and risks are discussed below.

Personal guarantees

A small or new company seeking to borrow money from a bank or other financial institution and which owns no major assets on which a loan can be secured, will most likely find that the lender in question will require the loan to be personally guaranteed by the directors of the company and/or the shareholders. The consequence of giving such a guarantee is that if the company defaults on the loan repayments, those persons who have guaranteed the loan will be personally liable for paying it back. The terms of the guarantee may well provide for interest at a penalty rate and the costs of enforcing the guarantee. Furthermore the lender may require security over the company's assets (known as a 'charge' – see Chapter 13) and/or the directors' personal assets, such as their homes. In this scenario, the directors and/or shareholders are in no better position than a sole trader and one of the key benefits of operating as a limited company is lost.

Publicity

One of the prices of limited liability is publicity. Companies are required to file information about their directors, shareholders, financial standing, and other matters including their articles of association with Companies House and this information is made available to the public. The rationale for this is that in return for the privilege of limited liability, companies have to give outsiders sufficient information to enable them to decide whether or not to deal with the company in the first place, and if they do, to decide whether or not to issue court proceedings for debt recovery (or any other cause of action) in the event of a default by the company. This loss of confidentiality and privacy may be a concern for some. Filing information at Companies House is not optional, which leads on to the next potential drawback.

Regulatory compliance

As well as any other legislation applicable to a particular business (such as financial services regulations, data protection law, employment law, health and safety law and so on) companies must comply with company law. Most of this is set out in the Companies Act, in regulations made under the Companies Act, and in other primary legislation such as the Insolvency Act 1986. In addition, as mentioned earlier, the relationship between the main players in a limited company (i.e. the directors and shareholders) is regulated further by the company's articles of association which will prescribe set procedures for directors' and shareholders' decision making, as well as a number of other matters. Companies must also prepare and file accounts at Companies House. These must comply with the requirements of the Companies Act, which may mean that the accounts have to be audited. In comparison, sole traders run their businesses relatively unencumbered by procedures and formalities.

Directors' liabilities

Failing to comply with company law can have consequences for directors. At the dark end of the spectrum is imprisonment and disqualification from acting as a director for up to 15 years. As well as this, in an insolvency situation directors can be made to contribute towards settling a company's debts under certain causes of action set out in the Insolvency Act. Directors therefore need to understand the regulatory environment in which they work. The personal risks that directors face for getting things wrong means that taking professional advice is often to be recommended and sometimes a necessity. Directors' liabilities are considered in more detail in Chapter 7 and insolvency in Chapter 17.

▧ The decision to incorporate

The decision to incorporate a business as a limited company should be made with the help and advice of a qualified accountant and/or qualified tax adviser. There is no general rule or set of conditions to satisfy before incorporating and the decision should address all of the relevant financial and non-financial drivers. The key determinants that a professional adviser will assess include:

- the nature of the business;
- its past and projected performance;
- the prevailing and future tax conditions; and
- the competency of the owner-management team.

Examples of the practical considerations that a professional adviser would examine prior to incorporation would include:

- the business accounting reference date;
- the business earnings growth;
- the value of any goodwill in the business;
- the business and corporation tax environment;
- the business owner's personal risk exposure;
- the current and non-current assets portfolio;
- the existence of any trading losses;
- the capital gains tax position; and
- the existence of any commercial property and its ownership within the business.

Transferring an existing business into a limited company

Transferring an unincorporated business into a limited company is essentially achieved by incorporating a new company which then proceeds to buy the business and assets of the existing sole trader structure. Of course, there are a great many issues to consider, and the transfer of an existing business into a limited company should not be undertaken without the advice and assistance of a qualified accountant or qualified tax adviser. Legal advice may also be required. Timing is important because there may be income tax to be paid on the cessation of the sole trader's business and unless the sole trader has sufficient cash available the extraction of cash from the limited company will give rise to an additional tax liability. A timetable for the transfer and a schedule of the tasks to be completed often provides for a smooth transition and minimises the risk of overlooking anything. Goodwill valuation of the business may be undertaken based upon the average profits for the last three years, less payment to the new owner multiplied by a factor of between 1 and 3. When the business is transferred to the limited company the transferred non-current assets are deemed to have been transferred or sold at the current market value, unless each item is valued at less than £6,000. Some consideration should be given to whether it is beneficial to pay any capital gains tax taking into account entrepreneurial relief to leave the cash transferred into the company tax free. An important consideration is the date when the sole trader commenced business, because if it was before 1 April 2002 the goodwill treatment is more restricted. A sole trader should avoid giving shares to family members when transferring from the sole trader structure into a limited company because HMRC may choose to tax the dividends as belonging to the former sole trader rather than the family shareholders.

Advice should be sought in relation to the level of cash holdings, its treatment and how to account for any property within the sole trader's business. The sole trader needs to notify HMRC and ensure that class 2 national insurance contributions are closed as they will be required to pay class 1 national insurance if they become an employed director of the newly incorporated company. The national insurance class 1 burden is much greater than class 2, and moreover, dependent upon the salary being paid the company will also be required to pay employer's national insurance contributions as well.

Summary

- The four main types of business structure are sole traders, partnerships, limited liability partnerships and limited companies.
- In law a company is a legal person, separate from its owners and those who manage it. As a legal person, a company can do many of the things that natural people do such as own property, borrow money and buy goods and services, among others.
- Companies are created by a formal process called incorporation. In the United Kingdom this process is administered and controlled by Companies House.
- The authority to run a limited company is delegated to its directors under the articles of association. The articles are a company's key constitutional document setting out the rights, duties and obligations of the directors and shareholders in relation to the company.
- The shareholders are not generally expected to get involved in managing a company's business. Certain significant decisions are reserved to them by the Companies Act, but their rights can be enhanced by suitable provisions in the articles of association or by way of a shareholders' agreement. The most important right and power of shareholders is to remove a director by a majority vote.
- There are various different types of company that can be created under UK law including private companies limited by shares, private companies limited by guarantee and public limited companies. The private limited company is by far the most common.
- As well as the benefits of having legal personality and limited liability, a limited company has other potential benefits which include tax efficiencies, possibly easier access to finance, perpetual succession and the relative ease with which employees (and others) can be given a stake in the business.

- In small companies or new start ups, banks and lenders may require directors and/or shareholders to personally guarantee loans to the company in which case the main benefit of separate financial liability is lost. Other possible disadvantages include publicity, regulatory compliance and directors' personal liabilities.
- The decision to incorporate should be made with the help and guidance of a professional and be based on a full and holistic assessment of the business.
- An existing business can transfer to a limited company structure by incorporating a new company which buys the business and its assets. Legal and tax advice is essential.

2 Forming a company

▨ In this chapter

This chapter explains the process for incorporating a limited company with particular regard to:

- the legal requirements for forming a limited company and explanations of key terminology;
- the incorporation process;
- using accountants, solicitors, chartered secretaries and formation agents;
- the rules on company names and business names;
- potential challenges and objections to a company's name; and
- the procedure for changing a company's name.

Incorporating a company in the United Kingdom is relatively straightforward. Chapter 1 touched on some of the features and components of a limited company, but what do you need to have in place to go ahead and incorporate a company?

▨ The requirements for forming a company

All private companies limited by shares formed in the United Kingdom must have:

- an acceptable name;
- at least one director;
- at least one shareholder;
- share capital consisting of at least one issued share; and
- a registered office

and must have a constitutional document known as:

- the articles of association

and another document known as:

- the memorandum of association.

They can also have, but are not required to have:

- a company secretary.

Company name

The choice of name for a company is restricted by a number of factors, including the availability of the name (has it already been registered by someone else?), restrictions on the characters that can be used in the name, restrictions on the use of certain words and expressions and issues concerning the rights of others. These issues are explained more fully later in this chapter.

Directors

The directors are responsible for the overall management of the company, setting its objectives and determining the appropriate strategies to achieve them. Private companies must have at least one director at all times, who must be at least 16 years old. If a company only has one director, that director must be a 'natural person'. This means a living, breathing human being as opposed to an artificial person that has legal personality, such as a company. A company that acts as director of another company is known as a 'corporate director'. Subject to a company's articles of association it can have as many corporate directors as it likes, as long as it has at least one natural director at all times. The directors of a company have many legal duties and responsibilities which are explained in Chapter 7.

Shareholders

All private companies limited by shares must have at least one shareholder who holds at least one share in the company. Shareholders can either be natural persons or corporate bodies, but should not be organisations that do not have legal personality. Shareholders are considered in more detail in Chapter 10.

Share capital

There is no minimum share capital requirement for a private company. All companies limited by shares must issue at least one share on incorporation which must have a fixed value known as its 'nominal value'. It is common for companies to issue just one or two shares on incorporation and to allot more shares afterwards if they need to, perhaps with different rights if required. Details about the shares allotted on incorporation are given by way of a 'statement of capital' in the incorporation application. See Chapter 9 for more about shares and Chapter 4 for more about statements of capital.

Registered office

Every company must have a 'registered office'. The registered office is a company's official address. It is placed on the public record and is therefore freely available to anyone who wants to know it. The registered office must be a physical location (not a PO box or a DX address – although a full PO box address with building number and street name is acceptable) at which any documents or notices sent to the company will be picked up and dealt with. Any formal legal documents are validly served on a company if delivered to its registered office. It is important that correspondence received at the registered office is opened and checked regularly because certain notices, such as a creditor's demand for payment, or other documents such as court papers, may need to be dealt with quickly. In addition, correspondence from Companies House will be sent to a company at its registered office which will include important notices and reminders.

A company's registered office address does not have to be the same as its trading address – the company's business can be carried on elsewhere at any number of other locations. For a variety of reasons some companies pay to use a different address for their registered office, such as their accountant's or solicitor's address. The registered office must be located in the part of the United Kingdom in which the company is incorporated – that is, England and Wales, Scotland or Northern Ireland. The registered office address can be changed but it cannot be moved outside the part of the United Kingdom in which the company is registered.

Memorandum of association

The memorandum of association is a simple document that confirms the wish of the company's first shareholder(s) to form a company, and states their agreement to take at least one share each in the company on incorporation. Once the company has been formed, the memorandum becomes an historical document that has no bearing on the management of the company's affairs from that point onwards. All matters of that sort are dealt with by the articles of association.

Articles of association

A company's articles of association (or just 'articles' for short) are its internal rule book. They set out rules and procedures for a variety of matters such as appointing directors, decision-making by directors, decision-making by shareholders, the payment of dividends, and the transfer and allotment of shares. The articles are an important document and they can be used to achieve a wide range of ends in terms of regulating the powers and rights of the directors and shareholders in relation to the company. In this respect, even greater flexibility can be achieved if the articles operate in conjunction with a shareholders' agreement.

Under powers conferred by the Companies Act, the Secretary of State prescribes three different sets of standard articles for use by – respectively – private companies limited by shares, private companies limited by guarantee and public limited companies. These standard articles are known as the 'model articles' and are adopted automatically by each type of company on incorporation, unless the company elects to exclude them and adopt its own.

The memorandum, articles of association and shareholders' agreements are considered in more detail in Chapter 3. As mentioned in the Preface, references in this book to the Model Articles (capitalised) are a reference to the model articles for private companies limited by shares.

The incorporation process

In the United Kingdom companies are incorporated by the UK company registry, Companies House. There is a separate office of Companies House in each part of the United Kingdom (England and Wales, Scotland and Northern Ireland) which deals with the incorporation of companies within that jurisdiction. Once it has been incorporated a company cannot re-register in another part of the United Kingdom, so for example, a company incorporated in England and Wales cannot become a Scottish-registered company. The one exception to this is that a company incorporated in England and Wales can change its jurisdiction to that of Wales alone and if desired can change back again to England and Wales. The significance of this is that a Welsh company can deliver documents to the Registrar of Companies in Welsh and use the Welsh equivalent of 'limited' at the end of the company's name.

To incorporate a company the required information and documents for the proposed company must be submitted to the appropriate office of Companies House together with the applicable fee. The details that have to be provided for private companies limited by shares are:

- the company's name;
- if the name contains any restricted or sensitive words or expressions that require the approval of a government department or other body (see later in this chapter), a statement to confirm that the approval of the appropriate department has been sought and a copy of their response;
- the company's type (e.g. 'private company limited by shares');
- the address of the company's registered office (and the part of the United Kingdom in which it is to be located);
- whether the company is adopting the Model Articles, the Model Articles with amendments, or an entirely bespoke set of articles;
- whether the articles are restricted (see the section on entrenched articles in Chapter 3);
- for each natural director – their name (and any former names used for business purposes in the last 20 years), date of birth, service address, residential address, nationality and business occupation;
- for each corporate director – in all cases the name and address of the corporate

body or firm; in the case of corporate body or firm registered in the European Economic Area (EEA), the country or state in which the body is registered and its registration number; in the case of a non-EEA corporate body or firm the legal form of the body, the law by which it is governed, and if applicable, the country/state in which it is registered and its registration number;

- for the company secretary (if a secretary is to be appointed) – their name (and any former names used for business purposes in the last 20 years) and service address;
- for a corporate secretary – in all cases the name and address of the corporate body or firm; in the case of corporate body or firm registered in the EEA, the country or state in which the body is registered and its registration number; in the case of a non-EEA corporate body or firm the legal form of the body, the law by which it is governed, and if applicable, the country/state in which it is registered and its registration number;
- a statement of capital showing the number, class and nominal value of the shares to be allotted on incorporation as well as details of the rights attaching to the shares in respect of voting, dividends, capital distributions and redemption (see Chapter 4 for more); and
- the names of the company's first shareholders and the number of shares that each has agreed to take.

The documents that have to be provided are:

- a copy of the company's memorandum of association, signed by the first shareholders and dated;
- in the case of a company adopting entirely bespoke articles of association, a copy of the bespoke articles; and
- in the case of a company adopting the model articles with amendments and/or additional articles, details of the additional articles and/or amendments.

In the case of a company adopting the model articles with no changes, no articles need to be provided.

Each director, secretary and shareholder must confirm their consent to be appointed or to take shares in the company, as the case may be and the application must also be accompanied by a 'statement of compliance'. This is a statement made by the first shareholders in which they must confirm that all the legal requirements for registering a company under the Companies Act have been complied with.

There are three possible ways of delivering the necessary information and documents to Companies House. These are:

- on paper;
- electronically, using the Companies House Web Incorporation Service; or
- electronically, by using approved software.

Submitting the incorporation application on paper

The application for incorporation is made by way of a Companies House form called a form IN01. This is a long form which captures all of the information required to incorporate a company, as well as the consent signatures and the statement of compliance referred to above. The completed form is sent to Companies House together with the company's signed and dated memorandum of association, its articles of association (as appropriate) and the required fee. Submitting the incorporation on paper is not usually the preferred option because:

- the fee for incorporating on paper is substantially higher than it is for an electronic incorporation;
- there is an increased chance that one or more items of information, or a required signature, will be missed which will result in the application being rejected; and
- applications made on paper generally take longer to process than those made electronically.

Submitting the incorporation application electronically

Incorporating a company electronically is faster, more efficient and incurs a lower fee than incorporating on paper. In most cases, an electronic incorporation is processed in around 24 hours. There is no need to fill out a lengthy form and no physical signatures are required from the first directors, secretary or shareholders. These are replaced by electronic signatures derived from items of information that are personal to each individual, such as the first three letters of their eye colour, or last three characters of their passport number. This can make things easier from a logistical point of view as it avoids the need for several people to add their signature to a single set of documents.

At present there are two possible options for incorporating electronically – using the Companies House website, or using approved software.

Using the Companies House web incorporation service

Companies House offers an incorporation service on its website that enables an application for the incorporation of a private company limited by shares to be submitted online. This is a purely web-based facility so no special software is needed to use it. The website takes the user through each stage of the process capturing all the required information. It is important to note the limitations of this service, which are that the company must be incorporated with the Model Articles and the proposed company name cannot include any words or expressions that require special permissions (see further below). This means that this option is only really suitable for completely standard incorporations. However, if this method is used, changes can be made to the name and articles of the company after it has been incorporated, if required.

Using approved software

Approved software packages are able to deal with the incorporation of all types of companies with no restrictions affecting the choice of name or the type of articles that can be adopted. However, most people will not have access to an approved software package except through the services of a company formation agent, company secretarial provider, accountant or solicitor.

■ Formation agents, company secretarial providers, accountants and solicitors

The main advantage of using a formation agent or a professional such as a company secretarial provider, solicitor or accountant is that they will have a good deal of experience in setting up companies, and should be up to date with all legal and regulatory requirements. This can ensure that the incorporation is accepted first time around and also means that there is someone on hand to provide help and advice in relation to any queries or questions that may arise.

There are many, many providers who can assist with carrying out company incorporations and entering the words 'company formations' into an internet search engine will produce a large number of results. Electronic incorporations are generally the norm although some providers will still keep a stock of ready-made companies known as 'shelf companies' that are available to buy. Sometimes there are reasons for using a shelf company (e.g. if a company that has already been registered for VAT is needed), but otherwise it is preferable to form a company from scratch, and usually cheaper and faster. Done that way, the company is brand new, has no history and the proper directors and shareholders are in place from the point of incorporation.

Most providers offer fixed-price packages for company incorporations. Costs can vary greatly and are usually determined by what is included in the package and the level of service provided. The efficiencies of incorporating electronically enable formation agents to offer company formations at a very low cost. However with a low-cost formation, the agent may just supply the company itself and give only minimal advice in response to any queries or questions. Some providers offer different levels of service. For instance, the incorporation package may include a set of statutory books and records and a company seal and this may command a higher fee. It all depends on what you need, so shop around. Compared with other countries, it is relatively easy to incorporate a company in the United Kingdom, so if the fees seem too high then they probably are. As a benchmark, check the current fee for a 'do-it-yourself' incorporation using the Companies House web incorporation service (see above).

What happens next?

However the incorporation application is submitted, Companies House will examine the information and documents and if everything is in order, the company will be incorporated. The incorporation details are placed on the public record and the company is issued with a certificate of incorporation showing its name, registered number (a unique identifier that does not change), the part of the United Kingdom in which it is incorporated and the date of incorporation. The effect of incorporation, as per s. 16 of the Companies Act, is that:

- the subscribers to the memorandum become a body corporate by the name stated in the certificate of incorporation;
- that body corporate is capable of exercising all the functions of an incorporated company;
- the legal status and registered office are as stated in the application for incorporation;
- the subscribers become holders of the shares specified in the application; and
- the persons named as the first directors and secretary (if the company has a secretary) are deemed to have been appointed as such.

In short, the company now exists as a separate legal person and can proceed with the next steps towards starting up its business. On the other hand, if any issues have been identified which prevent the application from being accepted, Companies House will contact the presenter of the application to advise them that it has been rejected and the reason(s) why.

Helpful hints: common reasons why an incorporation might be rejected

1 There is a problem with the company name. The name is the same as or too similar to another name on the company index, or it contains sensitive words or expressions that need approval (see below).

2 The registered office address is not acceptable. If the address appears to be incomplete in some way, or is a bare PO box address, the application may be rejected.

3 Similarly, if a director's or secretary's service address or residential address appears to be incomplete Companies House may hold up the incorporation to query it.

4 One or more required items of information have been omitted – a director's date of birth, for example, or any of the information required in the statement of capital. Using the Companies House web incorporation service or a formation agent/professional should prevent this from happening.

5 The memorandum of association is not in the prescribed form or one or more signatures are missing. Again, using the Companies House web incorporation service or a formation agent/professional should prevent this.

Company names and business names

Company names and business names are not the same thing. While all companies must have a name that is registered at Companies House, they do not have to trade under that name. If a company carries on business under a name that is different from its registered name, that name is known as a business name. Some companies may have more than one business name which they use to identify different divisions of the company's business. If a sole trader uses a name other than their surname, and if a partnership trades under a name other than the names of the partners, those names are also business names. There are rules in the Companies Act that restrict the names that companies can adopt as their registered name, and also restrict the names that they (and any other trading entities) can use as a business name.

Choosing a company name

For most companies, choosing the right name is very important. However, as well as finding a name that presents the business in the desired way, there are a number of other issues to consider. For reasons that are explained below it may not always be possible or advisable for a company to use its preferred choice.

Rules and restrictions in the Companies Act

There are rules in the Companies Act that dictate:

- how long a company name can be, and the characters that can be used in a name;
- the word that has to be used at the end of the name to indicate the company's legal status;
- when one company name is regarded as being the same as another one; and
- that certain words or expressions can only be used if specified conditions are met.

In addition, a company name must not:

- give a misleading impression of the company's activities;
- be offensive; or
- constitute a criminal offence.

Length of names and permitted characters

A company name cannot be more that 160 characters in length and for these purposes a blank space is treated as being a character. The characters that a company can use in its name are specified in the Company and Business Names (Miscellaneous Provisions) Regulations 2009 (SI 2009/1085). These are largely as would be expected and include all the letters of the English alphabet (in upper case, however, not lower case), common punctuation, various brackets, inverted commas and symbols such as @, &, £, $ and €. Accents and diacritical marks such as those used in other languages are not allowed. Symbols such as %, #, = and + can be used but not as one of the first three characters of a name.

Indication of legal status

The word at the end of a company name tells the world what its legal status is. The ending 'limited' or its abbreviation 'ltd' indicates a private company limited by shares or limited by guarantee whereas, for example, the abbreviation 'plc' indicates a public limited company. All companies must use the word(s) or abbreviation that correctly describe their legal status and must not use words or abbreviations that give a misleading impression of their legal status. This means that a private company has to use the word 'limited' or its abbreviation 'ltd' at the end of its name (private companies that elect to have their registered office in Wales can use the Welsh equivalents). Whichever version a company is registered with is the version that needs to be used in any documentation, stationary or signage in which the company name appears. Private companies limited by guarantee can apply for exemption from using the word 'limited' (or 'ltd') at the end of their name, provided they meet certain conditions. There is no such exemption for private companies limited by shares.

The 'same-as' rules

The Registrar will not register a company with a name that is the same as another company already on the index. 'Same as' means identical but it also means 'is treated as being the same as' due to the fact that certain words and symbols are ignored when one name is compared to another. There are a number of different filters that are applied in a specific order that effectively remove certain words and symbols from a proposed company name. Whatever is left afterwards is then assessed against the names on the index (also with the relevant words and symbols disregarded) to see whether there are any identical matches.

Some of the words that are disregarded are:

- the word that describes the company's legal status (e.g. 'limited' or the abbreviation 'ltd'); and
- words appearing at the end of a company's name where the word follows a blank space, a full stop or the @ symbol such as: co.uk, com, company, GB, group, holdings, international, services and uk.

When preceded and followed by a blank space, or when appearing at the start of a name and followed by a blank space, the following words and symbols are regarded as being the same:

- words and symbols such as 'and' and '&', 'plus' or '+';
- any numerals and their written equivalents; and
- the symbols £, $, €, ¥, % and @ or their written equivalents.

As a result, careful checks need to be made to ensure that the proposed name for a company is not the same as, or will not be treated as being the same as, a name that is already on the index of company names.

Helpful hints: checking the availability of names

Take for example the name Clothing Limited. By operation of the same-as rules, this name would be treated as being the same as:

- C. Lothing Limited
- Clothing UK Limited
- Clothing plc
- Clothing.co.uk Limited

and all of these names would be treated as being the same as each other. The existence of any one of these names on the index would prevent registration of any of the others.

To help people to check whether a name that they want to register is available and is not the same as any other name on the index, there is a search facility on the Companies House website. This can be found on the webCHeck search screen. Instead of searching on the alphabetical index, select the 'company name availability search' option. This will then show any names that are the same as, or are treated as being the same as, the name that is being searched against.

There is an exemption to the same-as rules (in the Company and Business Names (Miscellaneous Provisions) Regulations 2009 (SI 2009/1085)) which allows a company to register a name that is the same as another company name if:

- the company whose name is already on the index of names consents to the registration of the proposed name; and
- the companies are or will be part of the same group of companies.

So, in the case of a proposed new company that will be a subsidiary or parent of another company, it is possible to give the new company a name that is the same as the name of that other company. It has to be noted however that when talking about one name being the same as another in this context, what is meant is that the names are treated as being the same by operation of the same-as rules – for example Clothing Limited and Clothing Services Limited. Two absolutely identical names are not permitted in any circumstances.

To take advantage of this exemption, a letter from the company whose name is already on the index must be submitted with the incorporation application, providing a statement confirming the details set out above.

Sensitive words

Some words and expressions cannot be used unless the company has obtained special permissions or unless certain conditions or criteria have been or will be met by the company. These are known as 'sensitive words'. The general idea in making certain words sensitive is to prevent companies from using a name that gives a misleading impression of itself in terms of its status, activities, business pre-eminence or anything else.

There is a wide range of words and expressions that are restricted in this way. Words that imply national or international pre-eminence such as 'British', 'Great Britain', 'United Kingdom', 'European' and 'international' are all sensitive. Words that imply that a company is a parent company or a subsidiary company, namely 'group' and 'holdings' are also sensitive. It is common for companies to want to use these words and the conditions that have to be met in each case – as specified by the Companies House guidance – are set out below. There are many words that imply specific functions such as 'bank' or 'dental' and words that imply representative status such as 'association', 'federation', 'council' and 'society' which are all also sensitive. As well as this, any words that imply a connection to a government department, a devolved administration (the Northern Irish, Scottish or Welsh Governments), or a public authority are also sensitive. This includes words such as 'assembly', 'commissioner' and 'health and safety'.

In some cases, use of a sensitive word will be granted on the basis of an assurance or confirmation from a director of the proposed company, or the company's professional advisors, that the company meets the relevant conditions or criteria for using it. In other cases, it may be necessary to obtain a letter of non-objection from a particular body or authority. The Companies House guidance booklet 'Incorporation and Names' (Reference: GP1) contains full lists of all the restricted words and expressions and the circumstances in which their use will be permitted. If in any doubt, speak to the Companies House contact centre who should be able to clarify any queries. If using a formation agent or other professional services provider then they should also be able to give appropriate advice.

If within five years of incorporation it comes to light that misleading information was provided to Companies House concerning a company's eligibility to use a sensitive word in its name, or an assurance given by a company turns out to be false, the Secretary of State can order the company to change its name.

Restricted names

Some words are protected by specific regulations. 'Architect', 'chemist', 'Olympic', 'optician' and 'vet' are just some examples of words whose use is restricted by law. Generally, it is an offence to use such words without written permission from a relevant regulatory body. The written permission will need to be submitted to Companies House with the application for incorporation and if it is not then the application will be rejected. As such, there is little chance of a company using one of these words unknowingly and hence committing an offence. A list of the words

Helpful hints: commonly used sensitive words and the conditions that have to be met in order to use them

British, Britain, Great Britain	If use implies a connection with a government department or body or a local or specified authority then a letter or e-mail of non-objection is needed from the body in question. If no such connection is implied, and if used at the start of the name or if used as 'of Britain' or 'of Great Britain' anywhere in the name, the company must show that it is pre-eminent or very substantial in its field by providing independent support from a representative body, trade association or other relevant body. If use of the word is desired because it is a surname and no connection with a government department etc is implied, approval will normally be given if the company name includes forenames or initials.
United Kingdom	If use implies a connection with a government department or body or a local or specified authority then a letter or e-mail of non-objection is needed from the body in question. If no such connection is implied and if used at the start of the name the company must show that it is pre-eminent or very substantial in its field by providing independent support from a representative body, trade association or other relevant body. If no such connection is implied and if not used at the start of the name, approval will normally be given. 'UK' is not sensitive and does not require approval unless it implies a connection with government.
European	If use implies a connection with official bodies of the European Union then a letter or e-mail of non-objection is required from the relevant body.
International	If used at the start of a name, the company must show at the time of registration that a significant part of the company's activities is in trading overseas. The country or countries in which the company trades must be stated. If used elsewhere in a name, the company must confirm that it trades overseas in at least one country stating the country or countries in question.
Group	The company must show that it is in a parent/subsidiary relationship with at least two other companies. This condition must be satisfied at the time of registration of the name by identifying the relevant companies. If the name clearly shows that the purpose of the company is to promote the interests of a group of individuals then use will normally be approved.
Holdings	Can only be used if the company is a holding company within the definition in s. 1159 of the Companies Act (see Chapter 1). This condition must be met on or within three months of registration and the name of at least one subsidiary company must be provided. If not met on registration, the company must confirm that it will meet it within three months.

can be found in the Companies House guidance booklet GP1 mentioned above. Particular care needs to be taken if using any of these words in a business name, as explained below.

Misleading company names

The Secretary of State also has power to direct a company to change its name if it gives so misleading an impression of the company's activities that it could be likely to cause harm to the public.

Offensive names

Any name that the Secretary of State deems to be offensive will not be permitted. For example, this could include names that imply involvement in criminal activities.

▨ Choosing a business name

Many of the same rules and restrictions that apply to company names also apply to business names. However, a fundamental difference between business names and company names is that there is no registry of business names in the United Kingdom. Whereas a company name will be examined and assessed for acceptability by Companies House, there is no central agency that controls the use of business names. Companies, sole traders, partnerships and others using business names therefore need to make sure that their business name does not contravene any of the rules and restrictions in the Companies Act.

Business names:

- must not include words that give a misleading impression of the legal status of the business (e.g. a private company cannot describe itself as a 'plc');
- cannot include any sensitive words unless permission from the relevant persons or authorities has been obtained;
- must not be offensive; and
- must not constitute a criminal offence.

Where a business name includes a word that needs approval, permission to use that word must be obtained from Companies House. As such a letter needs to be sent to Companies House providing whatever evidence or information is required to meet the relevant conditions. Using the name without having done this is an offence.

▨ Challenges and objections

A trading name, whether it is a company name or a business name, is a valuable asset and their owners will seek to protect them. There are two main ways in which a company name can be challenged:

- by complaint to Companies House that the name is 'too like' another name already on the index; or

- by complaint to a company names adjudicator.

Both company names and business names can also infringe the rights of others and may give rise to:

- an action for 'passing off'; or
- an action for registered trade mark infringement.

'Too like' objections

As explained earlier, a company name will be rejected if it is exactly the same as another name on the index. However, what if the name is not identical to another name but is very similar? The answer is that the Secretary of State has power to direct a company to change its name where it has been registered with a name that is 'too like' another name on the index.

This power is exercised by Companies House, usually on receipt of a complaint, which must be made within 12 months of the offending name being registered. In considering whether one name is 'too like' another, Companies House will make a comparison of the two names based on how each name looks and sounds. Issues such as the activities of the companies, their geographical location and disputes over other rights in the names are not taken into account. If the difference is so trivial as to be likely to result in the public being confused as to which company is which, or could lead the public to assume that the companies are related, the complaint is likely to be upheld.

Because of this it is essential to make careful checks of the index of company names using the Companies House webCHeck facility – not just for identical names but for names that are too close to the proposed name in how they look and sound. Among others, this means thinking about how the proposed name might be spelt differently but in a way that it sounds exactly the same. For example, the word 'fish' sounds the same as 'phish' but the latter will not appear in the results of a search against the former. If using a solicitor or other service provider, this additional layer of checking is something that they could be asked to do (although it may incur a higher fee). Most service providers will check whether a proposed name is available (i.e that it is not identical to another name that has already been registered), but more detailed checks are required to flush out any names that are potentially too similar. As such it is advisable to ask for confirmation as to what level of checks will be carried out as standard.

Company names adjudicators

Under s. 69 of the Companies Act, a person can object to a company name registered on the index of names at Companies House on the grounds that:

- it is the same as a name associated with the person raising the objection, in which they have goodwill; or
- it is sufficiently similar to that name that its use in the United Kingdom

would be likely to mislead by suggesting a connection between the offending company and that person.

These objections are dealt with by the company names tribunal. The difference between 'too like' objections made to Companies House and objections made to the company names tribunal is as follows. The 'too like' objections made to Companies House concern similarities between two company names registered on the index of names at Companies House. Complaints made to the Tribunal can be made by anybody that has goodwill in a particular name which under s. 69 includes reputation of any description. The name does not have to be the name of another limited company; it can be a name used by a sole trader or partnership, for example. So, a sole trader operating under the name Peak Building Services could raise an objection to a company that is registered at Companies House under the name Peak Building Services Limited.

Once an objection has been lodged, the subsequent proceedings are presided over by the company names adjudicators and there are rules that govern the way in which a case goes forward. If the grounds for raising an objection are established to the adjudicators' satisfaction (as described above), the objection will be upheld unless the offending company can raise one or more of the defences listed in the Companies Act. Among the defences that can be raised are:

- that the name was registered before the applicant commenced the activities on which they are relying to show that they have goodwill in the name;
- that the company is operating under the name, or is proposing to do so and has incurred substantial start-up costs, or used to operate under the name but is now dormant; or
- that the name was adopted in good faith.

What the defences show is that the company names tribunal is generally concerned with cases where a company name has been registered in bad faith – so as to sell the name back to the person who has goodwill in it for example, or to suggest a connection between the offending name and the person making the objection.

If an application is successful, the adjudicators will order the offending company to change its name within a specified time. If it fails to do so, the adjudicators will instruct Companies House to change the company name to a name determined by them. It should be noted that applications to the tribunal are not free and if an application is unsuccessful, this can result in an order to pay the costs of the other side.

The provisions of s. 69 are applied strictly. If the offending party can show a defence which is accepted by the adjudicators, the objection will fail. Similarly, if the objector cannot or does not establish that they have goodwill in the name in question, the objection will fail. Issues concerning registered trade mark infringement or the common law tort of passing off do not come within the ambit of the adjudicators.

Passing off

The common law tort of passing off provides a way of preventing one person from trading in a manner that causes damage to the business or goodwill of another. Specifically, passing off prevents a person from misrepresenting that their goods and services are those of another business or misrepresenting that their goods or services are associated with another business. This would typically involve a new or less well-known business trading in a way that could cause their business to be confused with, or appear to be associated with, a more established, better known business thereby attempting to benefit from its reputation and goodwill. This could be the case for example, if a small, independent fast food restaurant presented itself in a similar way to a larger and better known rival. The way in which a business might do this could include using the same or a similar name, presenting the name in a similar way by using the same type face or style of lettering and the same colours, using a similar logo or using similar packaging.

If a court found that passing off had taken place, the remedies the court could award include damages, an account of profits (if the profits made as a result of the passing off exceed the damage done, the claimant could choose this option), an injunction to prevent further passing off and delivery up or destruction of any offending material. There are a number of factors that the court will consider in deciding whether to grant a remedy for passing off including whether the claimant has goodwill or a reputation in the name, logo, packaging etc in question and whether the actions of the defendant amount to a misrepresentation. Court proceedings can be costly and success will depend on the particular circumstances of each case and is by no means guaranteed. Having said that, the possibility of a passing-off action should not be discounted when choosing a company name.

Passing off is normally the chosen course of action to prevent the unauthorised use of unregistered trade marks. Where a trade mark has been registered at the UK Intellectual Property Office, other remedies are available to a claimant (see below).

Sensible precautions

The difficulty with a complaint to the company names tribunal and a potential claim for passing off is that either can arise from someone who is using a business name that is similar to or the same as the name chosen for your company. Businesses that take brand protection seriously (and many do) can pay service providers to monitor the index of company names for any new names that might be a risk to their own (of course, new companies might consider doing this themselves). Being forced to change a company's name can incur a great deal of inconvenience and expense, so this is something best avoided if at all possible. As noted above, there is no central registry of business names in the United Kingdom which means that not only does a proposed company name need to be checked against the index of company names at Companies House, but that it is also necessary to do whatever is possible to search for other businesses in the same industry using the same or a similar name as a business name. This can be done by looking in the phone books for the local area, checking trade journals, using internet search engines and generally staying alert and keeping your ears and eyes open. In addition to all of this, you also need to be sure that your proposed company name will not infringe someone else's registered trade mark.

Registered trade mark infringement

Trade marks are all around us and are used by businesses and other organisations on products and services that we see every day. The UK Intellectual Property Office defines a trade mark as:

> any sign which can distinguish the goods and services of one trader from those of another.

If certain statutory criteria are met, a trade mark can be registered at the UK Intellectual Property Office, giving rise to a registered trade mark. Registered trade marks can take various forms including names, logos, slogans, letters, numbers or even a particular kind of packaging. They are a valuable asset which, in the case of trade marks that are very well known, can bring instant recognition of a particular brand, company or business.

Registered trade marks have to be registered against specific classes of goods and services which gives the owner the exclusive right to use the trade mark in respect of the goods and services for which it is registered. A registered trade mark also gives the owner the right to prevent the use of the same or a similar mark in respect of the same or similar goods and services for which it is registered where this is likely to give rise to confusion.

When choosing a company name, care needs to be taken to avoid inadvertently using a word or phrase (either identical or similar) to a word or phrase that has been registered as a trade mark against the same or similar goods or services that the company will be providing. If a claimant brought a successful action for registered trade mark infringement, the remedies the court could award include damages, an account of profits (if the profits made as a result of the infringement exceed the damage done, the claimant could choose this option), an injunction to prevent further infringement and delivery up or destruction of any offending material. A business does not have to be operating as a limited company in order to register a trade mark. They can be registered by sole traders, partnerships and any other kind of trading entity.

When Companies House receives an application to incorporate a new company, the examiners do not check whether the proposed company name could infringe a registered trade mark, so you need to make these checks yourself.

The UK trade mark registry can be searched online at the website of the UK Intellectual Property Office (www.ipo.gov.uk) however, since trade marks are registered against one or more classes of goods and services, searching can be difficult and if a search uncovers something that might cause a problem it can be tricky to assess what the risks are. For this reason you may wish to ask a professional such as a trade mark attorney to help.

Looking at this from the opposite point of view, an effective trade mark can help to make a company's goods and products stand out in the market place, give assurance of a certain quality, build brand loyalty and ultimately become a valuable asset. In considering a name for a new company, or a business name that the company intends to trade under, it may be worth giving thought to whether or not it can be registered as a trade mark. A trade mark does not have to be registered to be recognised as a trade mark and, as explained above, the unauthorised use of an unregistered trade mark has some protection in the common law tort of passing off. However, it is far easier to make out the requirements for an action for registered trade mark infringement than it is for passing off.

Not all names, slogans and so on are capable of registration. This is because registered trade marks have to be distinctive for the goods and services they relate to and not merely descriptive of those goods or services. For example the phrase 'delicious hot catering' is unlikely to be accepted as a mark for registration by an outside catering company because these are words that are commonly used in the catering industry – they are descriptive and not distinctive. If it were possible to protect this phrase as a registered trade mark, that would prevent anyone else from using it. Put another way, such descriptive words are not capable of distinguishing the goods and services of one trader from those of another.

On the other hand, a made up word that is catchy and memorable, or a word that is not normally associated with the goods or services in question, can make a successful trade mark. Words of this sort are not a requirement, but may help to avoid problems with the mark being too descriptive.

Once it has been registered, a trade mark can be renewed indefinitely provided that the required fees are paid when they become due, and provided that the mark is not revoked for non-use (a mark can be revoked by application if it has not been used for a period of five years). Trade marks can be registered in countries throughout the world so if a company intends to operate or sell its goods and services in any overseas countries, registration of the company's trade mark in those countries should also be considered.

In all aspects of creating and registering a trade mark, professional advice from a trade mark agent or attorney is strongly recommended as this is a specialist area. For general background knowledge a great deal of information about trade marks can be found on the UK Intellectual Property Office website and on the website of the Institute of Trade Mark Attorneys (www.itma.org.uk). The latter can also be used to find a trade mark agent or attorney in your local area.

▋ Website domain names

Having a presence on the internet is now almost an essential way of reaching potential customers so it is also advisable to check whether the proposed name for a company and/or a proposed business name, brand name or trade mark can be registered as a domain name. Owning an internet domain name does not in itself give rise to any rights of action (in the way that owning a registered trade mark does), but domain names are registered on a first come first served basis so it is essential to check whether the name you want is available. Nominet, which manages the registry of .uk domain names (as in .co.uk, for example) has a search facility on its website which can be used to check for domain names that end in .uk (www.nominet.org.uk). Other countries have their own separate registries and domain names ending in .com can be checked on the InterNIC website (www.internic.net). It may be prudent for a company to consider registering more than one domain name so as to maximise traffic to its website and also to prevent anyone else from registering names that might divert business away from the company. The availability of an appropriate domain name can therefore be a significant issue to consider in choosing a company name.

Domain names can be registered through an accredited Internet Service Provider (ISP). For registration of a .uk domain name a list of accredited ISPs can be obtained from the Nominet website. However, as usual, this is another area where care needs to be taken. Any decision about domain names should be informed by all the enquiries referred to earlier, including trade mark searches. Registering and using a domain name which infringes the rights of others could give rise to the difficulties referred to above and could also lead to the domain name being assigned to the other party. Professional advice is to be recommended.

▋ Changing a company's name

Section 77 of the Companies Act states that a company can change its name either by a special resolution of the company's members, or by other means provided for by the company's articles. The Act does not specify what such 'other means' might be but allows companies to determine their own rules and procedures. However, in the absence of any alternative procedure, the rules in the Act will apply and this is the case for companies with the Model Articles unamended.

All of the same careful checks that need to be made when choosing a company's first name need to be made again whenever a change of name is considered. Bear in mind that once the company's name has been changed, the original name immediately becomes available for registration by someone else. Some companies choose to transfer an old name to another company which then sits dormant purely for the purpose of protecting that name and preventing anyone else from using it as a registered company name. Companies with a name that was registered before the implementation of the current Companies Act need to take great care. This is because the 'same as' rules referred to earlier were different before the current Act came into force and a name that could be registered then without any problem might now be considered to be the same as another name on the index. If an attempt is made to try and 'move' that name to another company while immediately re-naming the company that it came from (which can be done by way of a simultaneous name change), the original name can be lost. Check very carefully and use the company name availability search on the Companies House website, mentioned earlier.

Procedurally, unless there is any alternative procedure specified in the company's articles, a decision to change a company's name needs to begin with a meeting of the company's directors who propose the special resolution to change the name either by way of a written resolution of the company's shareholders or a general meeting (see Chapters 12 and 11, respectively). Once the shareholders have approved the change of name, this needs to be notified to the Registrar of Companies by submitting:

- a notice that the special resolution has been passed;
- the applicable Companies House form (see below); and
- the appropriate fee, depending on whether the standard or same-day service is used (see the Companies House website for details of the current fees).

If everything is in order, Companies House will register the new name and issue a certificate to show that the company's name has been changed. This certificate is known as a 'certificate of incorporation on change of name' and should be kept somewhere safe and secure. Legally the change of name is effective from the date on which the new certificate is issued (s. 81(1)).

It is important to make sure that the correct Companies House form is sent, together with the notice of passing of the special resolution. If this is not provided then the change of name will not be processed. These forms all have the prefix 'NM'. In most cases the applicable form is the form NM01 which is a notice of change of name by resolution. If the new name contains a word or expression that needs the consent of a government department or other body then a form NM06 is also required, as well as the letter of response from the relevant department or body. The other NM forms are for use in less common situations such as a change of name that is conditional on a certain event taking place (NM02 and NM03), notice of a change of name by means provided for in the articles (NM04) and notice of change of name by the directors, as would be required if they were directed to change their company's name by the Secretary of State, for example (NM05). If unsure as to which forms are required check with the Companies House contact centre.

If the new company name contains no sensitive words then notice of the change can be submitted electronically using the Companies House WebFiling facility. In any other case the submission must be on paper (including any case where an exemption from the 'same-as' rules is being claimed).

Once a change of name becomes effective all relevant parties must be notified (the company's bank, HMRC, insurers and professional advisors as well as amending any official documentation relating to the company's property – title deeds, trade mark registrations, share certificates and so on) and all necessary changes to the company's signage and stationary need to be made to comply with the trading disclosure regulations made under the Companies Act. The requirements imposed by these regulations are explained in Chapter 4.

▓ Summary

- In the United Kingdom companies are incorporated by Companies House. The United Kingdom is divided into three jurisdictions each with its own office of Companies House – England and Wales, Scotland and Northern Ireland. Each office keeps the records of companies incorporated in its part of the United Kingdom.
- The requirements for incorporation are set out in the Companies Act. These requirements have to be met or the application for incorporation will be rejected.
- The application for incorporation consists of a form IN01, a memorandum of association and articles of association. The Companies Act prescribes standard articles known as the Model Articles which are automatically adopted in full on incorporation unless amended or excluded.
- The application can be submitted on paper, or in electronic format using either the Companies House Web Incorporation Service or approved software. The Companies House web incorporation service can only be used for companies adopting the Model Articles with no sensitive words in the company's name. Approved software packages are used by formation agents, solicitors, accountants and other service providers.
- If using a formation agent or other service provider carefully review what is included in the fee and be sure to shop around.
- Once it has been incorporated, a company is given a unique company number and is issued with a certificate of incorporation. The company can change its name any number of times but its registered number stays the same.
- Shortly after incorporation the company's name, number, registered office, details of its officers and its constitutional documents are placed on the public record.
- Careful checks need to be made to ensure that a proposed name is available, will not be regarded as being the same as any other name on the index of company names and will not potentially infringe the rights or goodwill of any other companies or businesses. Time spent on this can avoid costly problems later – if in doubt take professional advice.

- It is also important to check whether a proposed company name contains any sensitive words and if it does to assess whether the company will meet the conditions and requirements for using them.
- Company names and business names are not the same thing – a company name is the name that a company is registered with at Companies House. A business name is any name that a company trades under which is different from its registered name.
- A company's name and/or business name can infringe another person's registered trade mark or give rise to an action in the tort of passing off.
- A company's name and trade marks, and the reputation and goodwill that attaches to them are valuable assets which are worth protecting. Professional advice should be sought on the best way to do that.

3 The company's constitution (and shareholders' agreements)

■ **In this chapter**

This chapter considers a company's constitution, specifically:

■ the documents that make up a company's constitution;
■ the old and new style memorandum of association;
■ a company's objects;
■ the articles of association and the model articles;
■ the relationship between the articles and the Companies Act;
■ tailoring the articles to suit a company's needs; and
■ shareholders' agreements.

In the context of a company, the term 'constitution' means much the same thing as it does in relation to a country. It refers to the various rules, regulations and authorities that determine how the company is run, the powers of those who run it (the directors) and the rights and obligations of its members (the shareholders). The majority of these rules and regulations are contained in the articles, but the company's constitution also includes any special (and some ordinary) resolutions of the company's members (to the extent that they are not incorporated into the company's articles) as well as any agreements that would not otherwise be effective unless they had been passed as a special resolution of the members (ss. 17 and 29). This latter provision could potentially capture a shareholders' agreement but in most cases a shareholders' agreement will not form part of a company's constitution. Notwithstanding this, shareholders' agreements usually have a significant bearing on the way a company's affairs are conducted and are considered in more detail at the end of this chapter.

It was noted in Chapter 2, that as well as the articles of association, an application for incorporation of a company has to include a memorandum of association. There is no reference to the memorandum in ss. 17 and 29 of the Companies Act and as such it does not form part of a company's constitution. However this is a significant change from how things used to be before the Companies Act came into force. The old-style memorandum was very different to the memorandum that we have now and was an important constitutional document. All of the matters dealt with in the old-style memorandum are now dealt with elsewhere with the exception that one has disappeared entirely (the authorised capital clause) and another is now optional (the objects clause). This is explained below.

■ The old-style memorandum of association

Prior to the implementation of the Companies Act the memorandum of a private company limited by shares had to include six clauses. These were:

- a name clause;
- a registered office clause;
- an objects clause;
- an authorised capital clause;
- a limited liability clause; and
- a subscription clause.

Of these clauses, only the subscription clause survives in the new memorandum. The contents of the new memorandum are explained further below but first we consider what the other clauses were and what has happened to them.

The name clause

The name clause was simply a statement of what the company's name was (e.g.'the name of the company is X Limited'). If a company changed its name it was usual to update the memorandum to show the new name of the company and with an explanatory note to say when the name was changed. The form IN01 (mentioned in Chapter 2) has to include a statement of a proposed company's first name, but there is no requirement to have a name clause in what is now the main constitutional document, the articles of association.

The registered office clause

This was not a statement of the address of a company's registered office but a statement of the part of the United Kingdom in which the company's registered office was situated (i.e. England and Wales, Scotland or Northern Ireland). As such this clause was sometimes referred to as the 'domicile clause'. Since a company's registered office had to be situated in the part of the United Kingdom in which the company was incorporated, this clause effectively specified whether the company was based in England, Wales, Scotland or Northern Ireland. This statement is now made in the form IN01, as is the statement of the location of the company's first registered office. A company's 'domicile' is unchangeable, just as it was under previous Companies Acts, with one exception which is explained in Chapter 2.

The objects clause

The objects clause was a statement about what the purpose of the company was – it set out what the company was authorised to do. The objects clause has a long and slightly troubled history, but as a concept it is still relevant to companies formed under the new Act and can still be a significant aspect of a company's constitution. For this reason the objects clause is considered separately below.

The authorised share capital clause

The authorised share capital clause set the maximum number of shares that a company was allowed to issue. It was normally expressed as a total monetary amount divided into shares of a fixed value (known as their 'nominal' value). For example, a company might be formed with an authorised share capital of £100 divided into 100 shares of £1 each. The authorised share capital consisted of both issued and unissued shares – the shares that the company had actually issued and the shares that the company had not issued, but was authorised to issue. The authorised share capital therefore placed a limit on the number of shares that a company could issue. The directors would need a separate authority of their own to be able to exercise the power of the company to issue shares, but this authority could not exceed the upper limit set by the authorised share capital. If all of the shares comprised in the authorised share capital had been issued and the directors wanted to issue more shares, the authorised capital would need to be increased by a resolution of the company's shareholders approving the creation of more unissued shares. Another resolution might also then be needed to give the directors' authority to allot the new shares.

If this sounds confusing it may be a relief to know that the concept of authorised share capital has no meaning in the Companies Act 2006. Instead, what we are now concerned with is only whether the directors have an authority to allot shares or not and what the extent of that authority is. That authority can be stated in a company's articles or in a resolution of the company's shareholders. This is explained in Chapter 9. If a company so wished, it could include a provision in its articles to set a limit on the amount of shares that the company can issue but there is no obligation to do this and there is no such limit in the Model Articles.

The limited liability clause

Just as it sounds, this was a statement that the liability of the company's members is limited. In a company limited by shares, the liability of the shareholders is limited to any amount that is unpaid on the shares held by them. This obviously important statement now has to be included in the articles of association.

▉ The new memorandum of association

As can be seen from the above, the memorandum used to be an active and significant part of a company's constitution. Under the new Act, the memorandum is a greatly simplified document. It consists merely of a statement signed by the company's first shareholders (known in the Companies Act as the 'subscribers') to confirm that they wish to form a company and agree to take at least one share in it each. Even this is a slight change from the subscription clause in the old-style memorandum, since it is no longer necessary for the first shareholders to state the number of shares that they agree to take. Again, this is now dealt with in the form IN01. Once a company has been incorporated, the memorandum is now only of historical significance – it has no part to play in the ongoing governance of the company.

The Companies (Registration) Regulations 2008 (SI 2008/3014) prescribe a set form that the memorandum has to take. It is important that the memorandum follows this prescribed form because if it does not this is reason enough for Companies House to reject the application for incorporation. This is only an issue if applying to incorporate a company in paper format. If incorporating electronically using the Companies House website, the correct form of memorandum will automatically be generated on submission to the Registrar. Similarly, formation agents, company secretarial providers and solicitors will use their own standard form documents that comply with the regulations.

Prescribed form of the memorandum for a company limited by shares

COMPANY HAVING A SHARE CAPITAL

MEMORANDUM OF ASSOCIATION OF ....

Each subscriber to this memorandum of association wishes to form a company under the Companies Act 2006 and agrees to become a member of the company and to take at least one share.

Name of each subscriber	Authentication by each subscriber

Dated

A company's objects

As mentioned earlier the objects clause in the old-style memorandum was a statement that said what a company can do. The requirement for a company to state its purpose in its constitution goes back to the earliest companies which were formed by charters from the Crown and Parliament. Whatever the company's constitution said the company was for, that was what the company had to stick to. For example, the purpose of a company might have been to construct a railway or to set up a mining operation. When the government eventually enabled companies to be created by a procedure that was freely available to anyone, the requirement to include an objects clause in the constitution remained. The rationale for this was that anyone investing in or dealing with a company should know what the company does. Someone who had invested in a company that makes hats, for example, might not be happy if the company suddenly decided to change tack and do something else instead. If a company did anything that was beyond what it was permitted to do by its objects, on the face of it that act was void. This is known as 'ultra vires' – literally 'beyond powers'. The *ultra vires* principle applies to any person (natural or artificial) whose powers are restricted in some way such that any act they perform that is beyond the limits of their powers is void. From the point of view of an outsider dealing with a company this could be harsh as any contract or agreement that they entered into that was beyond the company's powers was simply null and void. But it could also be restricting for the company as well. A company could change its objects by resolution of the company's shareholders in certain circumstances, but it was not until amendments made by the Companies Act 1989 that a company could freely alter its objects clause. In any event, changing the objects clause by resolution would take time and was therefore not always practical in a fast-moving commercial environment.

To try and get around the *ultra vires* problem, companies started to draft their objects clauses in the widest conceivable terms to give them as much freedom as possible. The objects clause would be headed up by statements about the company's main purpose which would be backed up by any number of sub clauses listing all the things that the company could do in pursuit of its main objects. These were the company's 'powers' and would usually cover things like buying and holding property, mortgaging, charging or leasing any of the company's property or rights and borrowing money being just some among many others.

The Companies Act 1989 sought to alleviate this issue by permitting companies to have an objects clause simply stating that the company was a 'general commercial company' thus (theoretically) allowing the company to do anything that this might entail. However, there was still uncertainty as to what such an objects clause would or would not allow a company to do and many companies continued to err on the side of caution and adopt lengthy objects clauses trying to cover all bases.

A company's objects under the Companies Act 2006

Fast forward through various other changes to the law which also sought to alleviate the problem of trying to draft all-encompassing objects clauses and the operation of the *ultra vires* rule and we get to the current Act which says (in s. 31) that:

unless a company's articles specifically restrict the objects of the company, its objects are unrestricted.

What this means is that if a company wants to restrict itself in terms of its objects, it needs to include an appropriate statement in its articles saying what the company's objects are. For most companies this will not be appropriate but there are companies – charitable companies being one example – that do need to restrict their objects. If a company's articles are silent about what the objects of the company are, the objects are unrestricted and the company can do anything. The standard articles used by formation agents, solicitors and others will generally not include any provisions to restrict a company's objects and there are also no such restrictions in the Model Articles.

The position for outsiders

For outsiders dealing with a company there have always been two main issues to be concerned about:

- does the company have the power to perform the act that is being proposed; and
- do the directors have the authority to perform that act on behalf of the company?

This might seem confusing but the power of the company to do something, and the authority of the directors to do that something on behalf of the company are two separate things. A company's constitution might allow it do something, but might place restrictions on the director's ability to exercise that power on behalf of the company.

There are two important provisions in the Companies Act that deal with this. First, we have s. 39 which says that:

the validity of an act done by a company shall not be called into question on the ground of lack of capacity by reason of anything in the company's constitution.

In other words, anything that a company does is valid regardless of whether that act was in fact beyond the powers of the company. This effectively removes the problem of *ultra vires*.

Secondly, we have s. 40(1) which says that:

in favour of a person dealing with a company in good faith, the power of the directors to bind the company, or authorise others to do so, is deemed to be free from any limitation under the company's constitution.

Under s. 40(2) 'dealing with a company' means someone who is a party to any transaction or other act to which the company is a party. A person dealing with a company:

- is not required to enquire about any limitations on the powers of the directors to bind the company or to authorise others to do so;
- is presumed to have acted in good faith unless the contrary is proved; and
- will not be regarded as acting in bad faith because they know that an act is beyond the powers of the directors.

Together these sections have the effect that an outsider dealing with a company, provided that they act in good faith, does not have to be concerned about either the capacity of the company to perform a particular act, or whether the directors of the company have the authority to perform that act on behalf of the company. Regardless of whether or not the directors had the authority, the company will be bound.

However, it is important to note that 'directors' here is in the plural which means that we are talking about the board of directors acting together as a whole. It is also important to note that this does not mean that the directors can do whatever they like. If they exceed their powers they can be liable to the company and its shareholders.

Where a director acts on their own, the position for outsiders can be different. In a company with only one director (a 'single director company'), the company's articles should authorise that director to exercise all the powers of the company. But in a company with more than one director each director may or may not have individual authority to bind the company, depending on the powers that the company has given them, and on any direct authority bestowed on them by the board. A company can still be bound by an individual director who acts beyond their powers but this depends on a number of factors and the principles of a particular area of law known as 'agency law'. This is explained in Chapter 8.

Changing the objects clause

In the case of companies that do have a statement of objects in their articles, a change to the objects constitutes a change to the articles and therefore requires a special resolution of the company's members. Once the resolution has been passed, a filing copy of the resolution must be submitted to Companies House, together with an updated version of the company's articles and a form CC04. The CC04 is a simple form to notify how the objects have changed – whether by an addition or alteration, or by removal. It is important to file the form CC04 as the change to the objects does not take effect until it has been registered at Companies House (s. 31(2)(c)).

Companies with an old-style memorandum

In the instance of companies that were formed under an earlier Companies Act and that still have an old-style memorandum, all of the provisions of the memorandum are treated as provisions of the articles (s. 28). Various transitional regulations were brought in at the same time as the Companies Act to enable these companies to function under the new law and there is no legal obligation for them to change their constitutional documents. For example, the author-ised share capital (since this concept does not exist in the new Act) now takes effect as a provision of the articles that sets a limit on the amount of shares that a company can issue in terms of their aggregate nominal value and a company can choose whether to amend or revoke this by a resolution of the company's shareholders.

While companies incorporated under an earlier Companies Act are under no obligation to update their constitutional documents it is worth considering getting them reviewed by a professional who can give advice about what to do. For older companies it is not unusual to find that they are operating with articles of association based on standard articles from the first half of the twentieth century. The articles of most companies incorporated before the current Companies Act will have at least some provisions that are inconsistent with it. Circumstances may force a company into making changes, for example, if its objects clause does not permit the company to do something it needs to do, like borrowing money. Due to the uncertainties of how to alter an objects clause in an old-style memorandum a legal adviser is likely to recommend a complete overhaul of the constitutional documents, removing the memorandum and adopting a new set of articles in their place. Updating the articles in this way will ensure that they work effectively in and, do not conflict with, the new legal framework.

The articles of association

As mentioned previously, the articles are a company's rule book that set out how the internal business of the company is to be conducted. All companies must have articles of association which have to be contained in a single document and divided into paragraphs numbered consecutively (s. 18). The content of the company's articles of association will be decided by the company's first share-holders and many companies simply adopt the Model Articles for this purpose (see below), but whether the Model Articles are appropriate requires careful consideration. The articles can contain virtually any rules and provisions that the shareholders want provided that they are not illegal or do not conflict with the Companies Act or any other legislation. In most cases the Act will override the articles (and a provision of the articles that is inconsistent with the Act will be void), but that is not always the case. This point is considered in more detail below.

The articles are a public document. A company's first articles have to be filed with the Registrar of Companies as part of the application for incorporation, and any subsequent alterations have to be notified to the Registrar together with a copy of the updated articles. Any interested parties can obtain a copy on payment of a small fee. This might include anyone doing business with the company, banks and lenders, prospective investors, or anyone else with an interest in the company's internal governance.

The articles as a contract

Section 33 of the Companies Act says that the provisions of a company's constitution (the main part of which is the articles of association) bind the company and its members to the same extent as if there were covenants on the part of the company and of each member to observe those provisions. The articles are therefore a kind of contract, but as contracts go it is an unusual one. Normally, an alteration to a contract requires the agreement of all those people who are a party to it, but the articles can be altered by a majority of 75% of the company's shareholders. In addition, while the articles may be devised and agreed by the company's first shareholders, any person becoming a member of the company thereafter will also be bound by the articles, despite not having had any say about their contents. As well as this, many of the common law principles that would apply to an ordinary contract do not apply to a company's articles.

As a contract the articles can be enforceable by the company against a member and by a member against the company but there are situations where this is not possible. Similarly, the courts will allow one member to enforce a provision of the articles against another member but only in certain circumstances. This is a difficult area where professional advice is needed. Issues to do with enforceability can be overcome by a shareholders' agreement which is one of the reasons why such agreements are common.

Contents of the articles

The articles need to deal with any and all matters necessary to facilitate the functioning of the company. There are a range of things that this could include. Some of the matters most commonly dealt with by the articles are:

- the liability of the company's shareholders;
- the directors' power to run the company and any limitations on that power;
- the appointment and termination of appointment of directors;
- directors' decision making;
- shareholders' decision making;
- organisation and conduct of general meetings;
- share allotments;
- share certificates and replacing missing share certificates;
- transfers of shares;
- dividends and capital distributions;
- company communications; and
- directors' indemnities and insurance.

These are among the basic provisions that all companies need in their articles to be able to conduct their internal business effectively. It is not uncommon for

companies to go further and to tailor their articles to the company's own particular circumstances. More is said about this later.

The Model Articles

Since 1856 each major Companies Act has prescribed a set of standard articles for
use by companies incorporated under that Act. The standard articles prescribed
by the current Act are known as the 'model articles'. There are three different
sets of model articles – one for private companies limited by shares, one for
private companies limited by guarantee and one for public limited companies.
Throughout this book any references to the Model Articles (capitalised) means
the model articles for private companies limited by shares.

The important point to note about the model articles is that the relevant
model articles apply to a company to the extent that they have not been excluded
or varied (s. 20). Most companies formed under the Companies Act have articles
that are based on the model articles. They will generally either:

- incorporate some provisions of the relevant model articles (with or without
  modifications) and then add in other provisions that are not included in the
  model articles; or
- exclude the model articles entirely and set out a complete set of bespoke
  articles.

Even if the latter is the case, the articles will still usually be based on the model
articles and replicate many of the provisions that they contain. Solicitors,
company secretarial advisers, accountants and formation agents will all usually
have their own standard articles, based on the model articles, which they use for
straightforward company formations. The application and/or exclusion of the
model articles is usually dealt in the very first provision and will either say something along the lines of:

> The model articles for private companies limited by shares contained
> in Schedule 1 of The Companies (Model Articles) Regulations 2008 (SI
> 2009/3229) shall not apply to the company,

which means that the model articles are completely excluded and the articles
are entirely bespoke (although they will probably resemble or even duplicate the
model articles in a number of areas); or

> The model articles for private companies limited by shares contained
> in Schedule 1 of The Companies (Model Articles) Regulations 2008 (SI
> 2009/3229) shall apply to the company except in so far as they are modi-
> fied or excluded by, or are inconsistent with these articles,

which means that the Model Articles have been adopted with amendments, some
provisions of the Model Articles will apply, some will not and some will have
been modified.

The Model Articles differ from the standard articles prescribed by previous Companies Acts in that they are:

- a good deal shorter, and
- written in plain language rather than the legalese that sometimes made the previous standard articles difficult to understand.

This does mean that the Model Articles or articles based on the Model Articles will not be suitable for all companies. The government's approach in drafting the Model Articles was to 'think small first'. As such they may be perfectly adequate for a small owner-managed company but not for a larger company. For example, the Model Articles assume that all shares that the company issues (apart from the shares issued to the subscribers to the memorandum of association) will be issued as fully paid. This means that a company with the Model Articles unamended cannot issue partly paid shares. To be able to issue partly paid shares, the articles would have to be changed so as to permit this, to include provisions to set out the procedure for calling in any monies due from a shareholder to the company, and rules that say what happens if the shareholder does not pay.

Whether a standard set of articles will be suitable for a company or not is one of the issues to consider when setting up the company. If using a formation agent the form and quality of the standard articles will vary from one agent to another but there is nothing to prevent a company from using a standard set of articles for the purposes of the incorporation, and then engaging the services of a professional to adopt a more suitable set of articles later on. Consideration should also be given to whether any aspects of the directors' and shareholders' relationship with the company should be addressed by a shareholders' agreement (see later).

Helpful hints: amendments to the Model Articles

The Model Articles (as well as the model articles for guarantee companies and public companies) were amended on 28 April 2013 by the Mental Health (Discrimination) Act 2013. Section 3 of this Act removes article 18(e) of the Model Articles which relates to the automatic termination of a director's appointment on the grounds of mental health. The provisions of the original version of the Model Articles continue to apply to companies incorporated before 28 April 2013 to the extent that they have not excluded or varied them. The provisions of the amended version apply to companies formed on or after 28 April 2013, again to the extent that they have not excluded or varied them. See Chapter 6 for more.

The articles and the Companies Act

It is important to understand the relationship between the Companies Act and a company's articles. The Act is very long and very detailed but it does not provide rules and procedures to govern every aspect of a company's internal business. This is where the articles come in. Anything not regulated by the Act needs to be dealt with in the articles and the company has freedom (within the restraints of the Act and the wider law) to determine what its rules and procedures will be. For example, there is nothing in the Companies Act that says how directors are to go about making their decisions – this has to be set out in the articles. Most of the rules in the Companies Act override the articles of association in the event of a conflict but in some cases the Act allows companies to alter or vary the position set out in the Act, whatever that may be. A particular section of the Companies Act might say specifically how it can be varied by the articles, or might just say that it takes effect 'subject to any provision of the company's articles' meaning that if the articles say something different, the articles prevail.

A consequence of the separation of regulations between the articles and the Companies Act is that anyone involved in the management of a company needs to know where to look for a particular rule or procedure – in other words, is it in the articles or is it in the Act? To make life easier, a company might try to make its articles as comprehensive as possible so that the rules in the Act that have a regular application to the company are reproduced in the company's articles. The directors can then see those rules in the articles and do not have to refer back to the Companies Act.

Previous versions of the government's standard articles did just that but the Model Articles do not – they do not duplicate any rules that are set out in the Act. As such there are some important matters which you might expect to find in the Model Articles but which are actually dealt with by the Companies Act. Some examples of these are:

- the number of shareholders that have to be present at a general meeting in order for the meeting to be 'quorate' (s. 318 – see Chapter 13);
- the voting rights of shareholders (s. 284);
- the authority for subdivision or consolidation of a company's shares (s. 618); and
- the directors' authority to allot shares (s. 550).

All of these rules could be altered by a company's articles in one way or another, but because they are not mentioned in the Model Articles they apply to a company with the Model Articles by default. So, to take the example of holding and running a general meeting, some of the procedural aspects are set out in the Model Articles (arrangements for attending a meeting, adjourning a meeting, appointing a chairman, and who has the right to attend and speak, for example) but other rules, the rules about quorum and shareholder voting rights being just two examples, are set out in the Companies Act.

Companies incorporated by a formation agent, solicitor or other professional are likely to have adopted a set of articles that are based on but which modify the Model Articles. They may follow the Model Articles example of not duplicating rules set out in the Companies Act, or they may not. The key point to note is that no matter how detailed a company's articles are they always have to be viewed within the wider context of the Companies Act and any other relevant laws and regulations. This means that anyone involved in running a company needs to be familiar with the company's articles as well as the rules and regulations set out in the Act. Unfortunately there is no short cut to achieving this and there are many occasions when professional advice may be needed.

As a non-exhaustive guide Appendix 2 sets out a checklist indicating whether certain common matters are dealt with by the Model Articles or dealt with by the Act and if they are in the Act, whether the rules can be modified or varied by the articles.

Altering the articles

A company's articles can be amended by a special resolution of the company's shareholders (s. 21). As such any alteration to a company's articles requires the agreement of at least 75% of the company's shareholders (or such higher percentage as may be specified in the articles) although in practice the company's ability to change its articles could be restricted by the terms of a shareholders' agreement. The articles can be altered by way of small changes, such as inserting one or two new articles, or deleting an article that is no longer needed. Alternatively a company can adopt a whole new set of articles to replace its current articles in their entirety.

There is no restriction on the changes that a company can make to its articles except that:

- the amendments must be lawful;
- an amendment cannot increase the liability of any member unless the member agrees in writing, before or after the amendment has taken place (s. 25);
- if the amendment varies the rights of a class of shareholders then the procedure for variation of class rights must also be followed (see Chapter 9); and
- the amendments must be bona fide for the benefit of the company as a whole.

The process of amending a company's articles or adopting new articles usually commences with a decision of the directors. The directors must agree the proposed changes and then resolve to put them to a vote of the company's shareholders either by way of a written resolution or at a general meeting (see Chapters 12 and 11 respectively). Whatever method is used, the proposed changes must be set out fully and accurately in the text of the special resolution. If it is proposed that a whole new set of articles be adopted, then a copy of the new articles should be sent to each shareholder with the written resolution or notice of general meeting, as the case may be.

Once the resolution has been passed by the members, a filing copy of the resolution must be submitted to Companies House within 15 days, together with a print of the amended or new articles. It is important to remember to file a copy of the articles because:

- failure to do so is an offence; and
- Companies House has the power to issue the company with a notice to file them which can be enforced by way of a £200 fine.

Entrenchment

Section 22 of the Companies Act enables a company to state in its articles that certain provisions can only be changed if a specified percentage of shareholders agree, such percentage being higher than the percentage required to pass a special resolution (i.e. higher than 75%). Such a provision is known as a 'provision for entrenchment'. The effect of this is to make it more difficult for the entrenched article to be changed. If a company entrenches any of its articles it must send notice to the Registrar of Companies on form CC01. If the articles are amended in accordance with the provision for entrenchment then a statement of compliance must be provided on form CC03. If a provision for entrenchment is removed, this must be notified on form CC02. It should be noted that at the far end of the scale the most that can be done is to require unanimous agreement in order for a particular article to be changed – complete entrenchment so as to make an article immovable is not permitted.

Tailoring the articles

While the Model Articles cover all the essential matters that the articles of a small private company need to deal with, one size does not fit all. It is important to consider whether the articles need to be adapted to fit the company's particular situation. For small companies a key concern is often for the founder members to retain control of the company both as directors and shareholders, but also to have a clean exit should they wish to sell their stake in the company and move on. For companies with more than one shareholder (or that anticipate having more than one shareholder), it is certainly to be recommended that a discussion with a professional adviser is had at the outset to ensure that the company's articles are fit to deal with the kind of events that may not seem important at the beginning of a business venture, but which can cause problems at a later stage. Carefully drafted articles can be used in conjunction with a shareholders' agreement to create the desired balance of rights and obligations.

Some common issues to think about are set out below.

Share classes

Many companies function with just one class of shares, but there may be reasons why a company needs to differentiate the rights of the shareholders. This can be done by creating different classes of shares, with each class having rights that are specified in the company's articles. See Chapter 9 for more on share classes and share rights.

Directors' powers

Just as it is possible to create different classes of shareholders, it is also possible to give particular rights or powers to certain directors by designating them as, for example, an 'A Director' or a 'B Director'. The articles can state the rights or powers that the A Director or B director has. For example, the articles might require that an A Director has to be present at a directors' meeting in order for the meeting to be quorate or that certain decisions require the consent of an A Director. This means that no business can be transacted without the A Director being involved. A set up of this sort might be appropriate in the case of a joint venture company where the articles give the investor shareholder the right to appoint a person of their choosing as an A Director or where a majority shareholder wishes to retain board control.

Removal of directors

The Companies Act sets out a procedure for the removal of a director by ordinary resolution of the shareholders. The articles cannot exclude this but can, if so desired, provide for an easier way to remove a director. This is often seen in the articles of a subsidiary company which might allow the majority shareholder to remove (or appoint) a director by way of a notice in writing deposited at the company's registered office. A small owner-managed company could also implement a similar mechanism.

On the other hand, a founder director can protect their position (such as by way of designation as an A Director as above) with an article giving them enhanced voting rights on a resolution to remove them that are sufficient to enable them to out-vote all of the other shareholders. If the articles give a minority shareholder or investor the right to appoint a director then the articles will normally provide that such a director can only be removed by the person or persons who appointed him.

Share allotments

The Model Articles do not include any articles dealing with the directors' authority to allot shares, which means that for as long as a company with the Model Articles has only one class of shares, the directors have unlimited authority to allot shares of that class (s. 550 – see Chapter 9). The directors' authority under s. 550 can be excluded and a limited authority put in its place.

Share transfers

It may be appropriate or desirable to place restrictions on who a company's shareholders can transfer their shares to. This can be done either by way of a specific limitation in the articles such as one stipulating that shares may only be transferred to a shareholder's immediate family (or other connected party), or by general rights of pre-emption that give existing shareholders a right of first refusal whenever a shareholder wishes to transfer any of their shares. This can work well in conjunction with a share structure made up of different share classes to ensure that shares never pass into the hands of someone that the founders of the company do not approve of.

Shareholders' decision-making

In the same way that a founder director may want to ensure that no decisions can be taken without them, a majority shareholder may wish to ensure that a general meeting cannot proceed unless they are present. This can be done by overriding the quorum provision in the Companies Act and setting a quorum requirement of, for example, two shareholders holding between them a specified percentage of the voting rights in the company.

Provisions to deal with a sale of the company

In a sale situation a buyer of a company will often want to obtain full control of the company by acquiring its entire issued share capital. If one or more minority shareholders do not want to sell their shares it could prevent the sale from going ahead. To deal with this, companies can include 'drag along' provisions in their articles. If a buyer acquires a specified percentage of the shares in the company sufficient to give them a controlling interest (which could be anything over 50% to over 90%) the drag along provisions will enable the selling majority to require the remaining shareholders to sell their shares to the buyer on the same terms.

The reverse situation, where a buyer may not wish to acquire the entire issued share capital, can be dealt with by 'tag along' provisions. In the event that a buyer does not acquire all of a company's shares the minority shareholders can be left with a new majority shareholder who they do not want to be in business with. Tag along provisions work in a similar way to drag along provisions in that where a buyer acquires a specified percentage of the shares in the company the sellers must procure that the buyer acquires the shares of the company's other shareholders on the same terms as their own. This will essentially prevent a sale from going ahead unless the buyer agrees to buy all of the shares in the company, thereby ensuring that all shareholders have an exit. It can be difficult to exercise these rights in practice, but they provide good protection to minorities in terms of involving them in exit plans and maintaining the value of their shares.

Standard provisions not included in the Model Articles

As mentioned earlier, the Model Articles do not allow and therefore do not include any provisions to deal with partly paid shares. Similarly, they do not include any provisions to allow the appointment of what are known as 'alternate directors'. Articles dealing with these matters are included as standard in the model articles for public limited companies but they may also be appropriate or necessary for larger private companies.

Making changes to the articles to tailor them to the company's needs is some-thing on which professional advice should be taken. Many solicitors, company secretarial advisers and other professional advisors have considerable experience of drafting bespoke articles and will be able to help you to achieve the desired outcome.

Shareholders' agreements

For some companies, the rights and obligations of shareholders and directors can be adequately established by way of suitable provisions in the articles of association supported by the rights and protections given to shareholders (and the restrictions placed on directors) by the Companies Act. However, in other cases there are reasons why the use of a shareholders' agreement may be considered. As mentioned previously this might be to do with issues of enforceability, confidentiality or because some matters can be regulated more effectively in a shareholders' agreement than they can in the articles. These points are explained in more detail below.

What are shareholders' agreements?

A shareholders' agreement is essentially a contract entered into by the shareholders of a company. It may be entered into when a company is first set up but can be created and entered into at any time in the life of a company. As mentioned at the start of this chapter, a shareholders' agreement can potentially form part of a company's constitution but in the majority of cases this will not be the intention. One of the attractions of a shareholders' agreement is that – provided it stays on the right side of the line from a constitutional point of view – it does not need to be filed with the Registrar of Companies. In that case the terms of the agreement remain private and confidential as between the parties.

Enforceability

It was mentioned earlier that although the articles of association are a statutory contract, there can be doubt about who the rights in the articles can be enforced by, and who they can be enforced against. There are no such problems with a shareholders' agreement. It is a contract and as such it is subject to ordinary contract law and principles. Any one party to the agreement can enforce it against any of the others (provided that they are prepared to take the matter to court).

The only area where care needs to be taken is if the company is also a party to the agreement, because the courts have held that a company cannot contract out of any rights that are given to it in law. Where a shareholders' agreement contains provisions that would have this effect, careful drafting is required to ensure that the shareholders can still enforce the relevant right against each other, even if a court would find that it is unenforceable against the company.

Entering into a shareholders' agreement

Any person who becomes a member of a company is automatically bound by the articles but that person will not automatically be bound by an existing shareholders' agreement. As a private contract, the new shareholder will only be bound by the agreement if they specifically agree to be. To deal with this a shareholders' agreement will normally make it a condition of any share transfer that the existing shareholder must procure that the new shareholder signs up to the agreement. This is done by way of a document called a 'deed of adherence'.

Who uses shareholders' agreements?

Shareholders' agreements are common in small private companies and particularly in companies where there are only a few shareholders, some or all of whom are also directors of the company. This is because a shareholders' agreement allows the parties to it to regulate their relationship in a way that may not be possible or desirable to do by way of provisions in the articles of association. Shareholders' agreements are also used as a matter of course in a number of common business transactions such as joint ventures.

Contents of a shareholders' agreement

Many of the standard terms of a shareholders' agreement could be included as provisions in a company's articles although there are some things that can be achieved with a shareholders' agreement that cannot be done in any other way. A shareholders' agreement can work alongside a company's articles so that some rights and obligations of shareholders and directors are set out in the articles and others in the shareholders' agreement. For example, any issues that need to be kept confidential can be dealt with in the agreement. Some of the matters commonly dealt with in a shareholders' agreement are described in the table below.

Table 3.1 Matters commonly dealt with in a shareholders' agreement

Matters requiring shareholder consent	A company's articles will normally give the directors complete authority to exercise all of the powers of the company. However, a shareholders' agreement can (confidentially) alter this position by setting out a schedule of matters that require the prior approval of the company's shareholders. This is all about protecting each shareholder's rights and their entitlement to be involved in the way that the company is run. Examples might include issuing new shares, giving loans or issuing loan capital, selling or disposing of any part of the business or making changes to the remuneration packages of any senior employees among many others. The list is potentially endless and a professional advisor will be able to suggest a wide range of issues that it may or may not be desirable to reserve to shareholders in this way.

Table 3.1 *continued*

Positive obligations	A shareholders' agreement might give shareholders rights that they would not otherwise have in their capacity as shareholders. This might include the right to be involved in any changes to the company's business plan or in the recruitment of senior management and staff. It may also include the right to receive financial information such as the monthly management accounts and details of company expenditure.
Restricted and permitted share transfers	As mentioned earlier provisions of this sort are often seen in articles of association but might also be included in a shareholders' agreement. The aim here is to restrict share transfers so that for example, one shareholder cannot increase their shareholding and their control over the company by acquiring more shares, or so that shares cannot be transferred into the hands of outsiders. This is normally done by giving the shareholders rights of pre-emption (a right of first refusal) on all share transfers. On the other hand certain types of transfers may be permitted, such as transfers by a shareholder to a nominee or to a family trust.
Compulsory transfers	Linked to the above, share transfers may be made compulsory in certain circumstances such as the insolvency or bankruptcy of a shareholder or in the event that a shareholder materially breaches the shareholders' agreement or leaves the company (see Leavers section below).
Class rights	The rights attaching to different share classes are usually set out in the articles but a shareholders' agreement can be used to give one or more class of shareholders additional rights over particular issues, such rights being kept private by virtue of being in the agreement as opposed to the articles.
Financing policy	How a company obtains finance can adversely affect existing shareholders. If achieved by issuing shares to a new investor, the existing shareholders will find that their respective stakes in the company are diluted. The shareholders' agreement might therefore include provisions to protect against this.
Dividend policy	A shareholders' agreement can set out what the company should do with its profits. It may stipulate that profits should be re-invested into the business perhaps for a specified number of years. On the other hand if dividends are to be paid the agreement can specify what percentage of profit is to be paid each year or any restrictions or conditions on paying dividends.
Exit	Provisions to give all shareholders an exit from the business in the event of sale may be included in the form of drag along and tag along provisions of the sort referred to earlier in relation to the articles.

Table 3.1 *continued*

Leavers	Provisions to deal with leavers can set out what will happen to the shares held by a director or employee when that person leaves the company. Usually this will trigger a compulsory transfer but the agreement can stipulate how the value of the leaver's shares will be calculated. This can be made more elaborate by defining some leavers as 'good' and others as 'bad' – a good leaver receiving market value for their shares and a bad leaver receiving a reduced, perhaps only nominal, value. For example a bad leaver could be someone who leaves their employment with the company before the expiration of a stated period of time.
Deadlock	Disagreements between directors and/or shareholders could result in a deadlock where the company is unable to move forward. In normal circumstances this could result in a dispute being taken to court (with the associated costs, stress and disruption) or in the company being wound up, neither outcome being ideal. A shareholders' agreement can include terms to say how disputes will be resolved so that issues can be settled in a more orderly way, perhaps through mediation with a third party, or by one shareholder buying out the other.
Confidentiality and restrictive covenants	When a director or senior employee leaves a company, the shareholders' agreement may place restrictions on them requiring them to keep sensitive business information and know-how confidential, to refrain from contacting significant clients or customers, and to refrain from setting up a competing business within a specified distance from the company or within a specified time period.

Do I need a shareholders' agreement?

In small companies with more than one shareholder most solicitors would always recommend a shareholders' agreement where there are matters that need regulating which would not normally appear on public record. The above examples of provisions often found in shareholders' agreements illustrate the flexibility and the protections that they can afford. The value of a shareholders' agreement is in setting up mechanisms to deal with problems that the parties may not envisage or entertain at the beginning of their relationship. Provisions to deal with disputes and deadlock are particularly important in this context as these provide a detailed agenda for what must happen if the working relationship breaks down. An ongoing dispute will often cause the value of the company to fall and a buyer, investor or bank would rarely want to support a business where the key players are at odds with each other. As a note of caution, professional advice should always be taken in regard to drawing up such an agreement; it is not something to attempt on your own. The cost of a solicitor or other professional may be off-putting but it can be money well spent in the long run.

▨ Summary

- A company's constitution consists of its articles of association, any special resolutions of the company's members and any other agreements that would not be effective unless passed as a special resolution.

- The memorandum of association, whilst formally a significant part of a company's constitution, is now a greatly simplified document that has only historical significance once a company has been incorporated.

- A company is no longer required to state what its objects are. If a company does include a statement of its objects in its articles then its activities and powers will be restricted to whatever is included in that statement. If a company does not state what its objects are then its objects are unrestricted.

- A company's main constitutional document is its articles of association. The articles are the company's rule book and they determine how a wide range of matters relating to the company's internal business and management are to be conducted.

- The articles form a contract between the company and its members, and between one member and another but enforcement can be uncertain. Because of this important matters may be dealt with in a shareholders' agreement which can be enforced more easily.

- The Companies Act provides for the Secretary of State to prescribe standard form articles which are known as the 'model articles'. Each type of company will automatically adopt the relevant model articles on incorporation except to the extent that they are amended or excluded.

- A company's articles of association have to be read in conjunction with the Companies Act. Some matters are dealt with solely in the articles, some in the Act, and some matters are dealt with partly by the Act and partly by the articles.

- Unless they state otherwise the articles can be altered by a special resolution of a company's shareholders. This could take the form of specific, ad hoc changes, or a whole new set of provisions to replace the existing articles in their entirety.

- The Model Articles and standard form articles used by solicitors, formation agents and other providers may not be suitable for all companies, particularly as they grow and develop. The articles can and should be tailored to suit a company's own particular circumstances – professional advice is needed.

- The rights and authorities set out in the articles can be supplemented by a shareholders' agreement. A shareholders' agreement is a private contract which in most cases does not form part of a company's constitution.

4 After incorporation

▣ In this chapter

This chapter details the main issues that a company may need to deal with once it has been incorporated and during its first year, including:

- trading disclosures;
- statutory registers;
- the rules on inspection and location of a company's statutory registers and other records;
- other practical matters such as changing the registered office address, changing the accounting reference date and opening a bank account;
- filing the annual return; and
- completing a statement of capital.

In previous years, when many companies were formed from ready-made or 'shelf' companies, there would be a number of changes that would have to be made to the company in order to 'transfer' it to the person purchasing it. The nominee directors would have to approve and action at least the following:

- the appointment of the new directors;
- the transfer of the company's issued share(s) from the nominee shareholder to the purchaser's shareholder;
- the change of the company's registered office address; and
- the termination of their own appointments.

Most companies are now formed electronically with the proper directors and shareholders in place from the start, but there may still be changes that need to be made once the company has been incorporated. Among other things the company may need to appoint one or more new directors, allot additional shares or change the company's registered office address as well as dealing with other more routine matters that need to be dealt with in order to enable the company to begin trading, such as opening a bank account. If the company has been incorporated to acquire the business and assets of a partnership or sole trader (i.e. a sole trader or partnership has decided to incorporate) then the transfer of the business into the new company can now be progressed, as outlined in Chapter 1. In addition, there are a number of matters that all new companies need to deal with in order to comply with the requirements of the Companies Act, like writing up its statutory registers and making sure that the company complies with the rules on 'trading disclosures'.

This chapter looks at the requirements in the Companies Act that apply as soon as a new company has been incorporated, other matters that commonly need attention immediately after incorporation and then looking a little further ahead, at statements of capital and annual returns.

■ Trading disclosures

All companies must make certain information about themselves known and visible to the outside world. These are referred to as trading disclosures and they are set out in the Companies (Trading Disclosures) Regulations 2008 (SI 2008/495) as amended by the Companies (Trading Disclosures) (Amendment) Regulations 2009 (SI 2009/218). The aim of the regulations is to ensure that anyone dealing with a company is provided with the company's name (as registered at Companies House), its limited liability status and the place where the company's records can be inspected. To achieve this, the Regulations lay down requirements as to where and how a company's name must be displayed and the information that must be included on a company's website, letterheads and other business stationery.

Display of the company name

Unless a company has been dormant since incorporation, the company's name must be displayed at the company's registered office and any location at which it keeps its records available for inspection (this is known as a 'single alternative inspection location' – see further below). The name must be displayed in characters that can be read by the naked eye and must be positioned so as to be easily seen by any visitor to that location even outside office hours. The company name must also be displayed at any location at which it carries on business except where:

- that location is primarily used for living accommodation; and
- except in the case of a company where each of the company's directors has been granted an exemption under s. 243 of the Companies Act in respect of the disclosure of their residential address to credit reference agencies (see Chapter 6).

So, if a company's business is carried on at the usual residential address of one of the company's directors, the company's name does not need to be displayed there. Similarly, the name does not need to be displayed if all of a company's directors have the benefit of a s. 243 exemption, whether the locations at which the company carries on its business are residential addresses of the company's directors or not.

Where six or more companies share the same registered office address, inspection location or business location and they display their names by electronic means (such as with an electronic sign that displays one company name at a time), each company name must be displayed for at least 15-second intervals every three minutes. This could apply if a company's registered office is located in a large office building along with a number of other companies.

Disclosure of the company name in communications and on websites

The company's name (in addition to any business name it may be using) must also be disclosed in its communications whether these are in hard copy, electronic or any other form. So, for example, this includes communications sent by e-mail.

'Communications' breaks down into:

- business letters, notices and other official publications;
- bills of exchange, promissory notes, endorsements and order forms;
- cheques purporting to be signed by or on behalf of the company;
- orders for money, goods or services purporting to be signed by or on behalf of the company;
- bills of parcels, invoices and other demands for payment, receipts and letters of credit;
- applications for licences to carry on a trade or activity; and
- all other forms of business correspondence and documentation.

As well as the above, the company's name must also appear on its website. This does not mean that the name has to appear on every page – many companies have one specific page on their website where legal and other information about the company is provided.

Further details required to be disclosed in business letters, order forms and websites

The following details must also be disclosed in a company's business letters, order forms and on its website. As with the requirement to disclose the company's name, this applies whether the business letters and order forms are sent in hard copy, by electronic means or in any other form and again, this includes e-mail. The details that must be disclosed for all companies are:

- the part of the United Kingdom in which the company is registered;
- the company's registered number; and
- the address of the company's registered office.

Any communication that could be regarded as a 'business letter' should include these details, which would arguably include invoices and other demands for payment as well as receipts and letters of credit. In addition, there are two further requirements to be aware of that apply in the following specific circumstances:

- where a company discloses its share capital in its business letters, order forms or websites then it is the company's paid-up share capital that must be referred to; and
- where a company's business letter includes the name of a director of the company (other than in the text of the letter or as a signatory), the letter must disclose the name of every director of the company.

Table 4.1 summarises the trading disclosure requirements.

Table 4.1: Trading disclosure requirements

Location or document	Information that must be disclosed
Registered office	The company's name, as registered with Companies House.
Alternative inspection location	
Place at which the company carries on business	
Websites	The company's name, as registered with Companies House and any trading name. The part of the United Kingdom in which the company is registered (i.e. England and Wales, Wales, Northern Ireland or Scotland).
Business letters	
Order forms	
Invoices and other demands for payment, receipts and letters of credit	The company's registered number. The company's registered office address.
Bills of exchange, promissory notes and endorsements	The company's name, as registered with Companies House.
Cheques purporting to be signed by or on behalf of the company	
Notices and other official publications	
Applications for licences to carry on a trade or activity	
All other forms of business correspondence and documentation	

It should be noted that additional requirements apply to charities, companies that are exempt from using the word 'limited' at the end of the company's name, and investment companies.

Updating company signage and stationery

When a company changes its name, it must update all of its signage and business stationery as soon as it can once the company's new name has been registered at Companies House. There is no specific time limit for doing this in the Companies Act but if the company does not make the required changes and uses stationary that shows the incorrect company name (for example) this will be an offence. Logistically this can be a challenge. As mentioned in Chapter 2, the special resolution approving a change of name has to be filed with the Registrar of Companies within 15 days of being passed. This gives the company some breathing room to sort out the necessary changes however it needs to be remembered that the change of name does not become legally effective until it has been registered by Companies House and that company names cannot be reserved. As such, the company's new name could be taken by another company right up until the moment before it is registered. As a precaution some companies may decide to incorporate another company with the new name in order to protect it pending approval and registration of the change of name. Once the company is ready to register the new name, this can be done by way of a simultaneous name swap.

Otherwise it is advisable to choose a date when the company intends its name change to become effective and then use the Companies House 'same day' service to ensure that the new name is legally adopted on the desired date. The company can then make the necessary preparations so that the new signage and stationery is ready for use as soon as possible thereafter.

■ Statutory registers

All companies must keep formal records relating to their directors, secretaries (if any), members and any mortgages or charges over the company's assets. These details must be kept in the form of registers known as 'statutory registers' – they are referred to as 'statutory' because they are a requirement of the Companies Act.

Private companies must have and maintain the following registers:

- a register of directors;
- a register of directors' residential addresses;
- a register of secretaries;
- a register of members; and
- a register of charges (in respect of charges created on or before 5 April 2013).

In the case of companies formed by a formation agent, solicitor or other service provider then the formation package may include a set of statutory registers which have been written up to reflect the first director appointments and the allotments of the subscriber shares. If not then this is something that the directors need to arrange to be done or otherwise do it themselves. Failure to maintain the required registers is an offence on the part of the company and every officer of the company who is in default. Blank sets of registers can be obtained from legal stationers and some of the larger formation agents. They can also be kept in electronic form (so that a company could create its own registers using a computer) provided that they are capable of being reproduced in hard copy (s. 1135). Where a company keeps its records otherwise than in bound books, the Companies Act requires that adequate precautions be taken to guard against falsification of the records and to facilitate the discovery of falsification (s. 1138).

The information that has to be included in each register is stipulated in the Companies Act. As well as the statutory registers listed above, most companies limited by shares will also keep and maintain two non-statutory registers which are:

■ a register of allotments; and
■ a register of transfers.

Although these are not required by the Companies Act, they are both very useful in keeping track of a company's issued share capital. The contents of each statutory and non-statutory register are explained in the appropriate chapters relating to directors, secretaries, members and charges. An example of what each of the statutory and non-statutory registers would typically look like can be found in Appendix 4.

It is important that the statutory registers are kept properly. Whenever a new director is appointed or a current director resigns, or whenever new shares are issued or existing shareholders transfer their shares, the appropriate registers must be updated to reflect the changes that have taken place. Essentially, a company's statutory registers, together with the records of directors' and shareholders' decisions and copies of all documents filed at Companies House should enable someone unfamiliar with the company to achieve a clear picture of the company's history, from the point of incorporation to the present day. While these tasks may seem a little onerous and time consuming (and do not appear to advance the more immediate concerns of running the business) there are good reasons why directors should make the effort to keep on top of them. First among these is the fact that failure to properly maintain the statutory registers is an offence. Second (and on a more practical level) lenders, investors and potential buyers will, as part of their own due diligence processes, wish to inspect the company's registers to ensure that they are accurate and up to date. When time is short, the directors may have no choice but to ask a professional to put the registers in order. Depending on the company's history it can be a time-consuming job and, consequently, expensive.

Location and inspection of company records

As well as dictating what records a company has to keep, the Companies Act also has rules about where to keep them. There are only two possible options which are:

- the company's registered office; and/or
- the company's single alternative inspection location, or 'SAIL' for short.

A SAIL is what it sounds like – it is a location other than the registered office at which some or all of the company's records are located and can be made available for inspection. If a company has a SAIL then it must be a physical location situated in the same part of the United Kingdom in which the company is registered. For example, a company registered in England and Wales cannot have a SAIL address in Scotland and vice versa. Each company can only have one SAIL address and notification of the address must be given to Companies House using form AD02. If a company moves any record or document to the SAIL or from the SAIL back to the registered office, notification must be given on forms AD03 and AD04 respectively. It should be stressed that a company can have only one SAIL, not one for each class of record or document.

The different records and documents that a private company must either keep at the company's registered office or at the SAIL are set out in the Companies Act as follows:

- register of members;
- register of directors;
- directors' service contracts;
- directors' indemnities;
- register of secretaries;
- records of resolutions;
- contracts relating to any purchases of a company's own shares;
- documents relating to any purchases of own shares out of capital by a private company;
- register of debenture holders; and
- instruments creating charges and register of charges.

As far as 'records of resolutions' are concerned the requirement is to keep copies of all resolutions of members passed otherwise than at general meetings (e.g. written resolutions), minutes of all proceedings of general meetings, and records of decisions of a sole member.

Disclosure of location of company records

Under the Companies (Trading Disclosures) Regulations 2008 (SI 2008/495), any person that a company deals with in the course of its business may make a written request to the company for information regarding the address of its registered office, the address of a SAIL at which it keeps any of its records and the type of company records which are kept at each. The company must respond with the information within five working days of receiving the request, thus informing the person as to where they can inspect the records in which they are interested.

Inspection of company records

In general a company's records must be open to inspection by a company's shareholders free of charge and by any other person on payment of the prescribed fee (the records that can be inspected, who can inspect them and the applicable fees are set out in Table 4.2 below). Private companies must make their records available to anyone that has requested to inspect them on a day chosen by them, provided that the day in question is a working day and that the person has given the company the correct period of notice. If the company has given notice of a forthcoming general meeting or a meeting of a particular class of members, or has circulated a written resolution (see Chapters 11 and 12 for all of these) then the notice required is at least two working days. Otherwise, at least ten working days' notice has to be given. Any person making such a request must also specify the time on their chosen day at which they wish to commence the inspection and this must be a time between 9.00 am and 3.00 pm. The company records must be made available for a period of two hours starting from the specified time.

In addition to the above:

- there is no obligation for a company to present its records in a different order, form or structure from the way they are normally kept; and
- anyone inspecting a company record is entitled to make a copy of the whole or any part of that record, but this must be done at the location where the record is kept and the company is not obliged to help in any way.

However if the company receives a request for a copy of a record in hard copy form then it must provide it. Similarly, if requested to provide a copy in electronic form then the company must do this but not if the record in question is only kept in hard copy form. All of the above rules can be found in the Companies (Company Records) Regulations 2008 (SI 2008/3006).

Fees for inspection of company records and for providing copies

A company is entitled to charge a fee for allowing inspection of its records and for providing copies, although it may choose not to. These fees are prescribed by the Companies (Fees for Inspection of Company Records) Regulations 2008 (SI 2008/3007) and the Companies (Fees for Inspection and Copying of Company Records) Regulations 2007 (SI 2007/2612).

Table 4.2 sets out the records that can be inspected, the fees that can be charged and the respective inspection rights of members and non-members. Any form of record not mentioned in the table does not have to be made available for inspection. These would include minutes of directors' meetings, records of directors' decisions taken otherwise than in a meeting, accounting records, the register of directors' residential addresses and non-statutory registers such as the register of allotments and register of transfers. When a company receives a request for a hard copy of a particular record, the copy does not have to be provided until the relevant fee has been paid.

Table 4.2: Records available for inspection and fees for inspection/copies

Record	Fee for inspection	Fee for providing a copy
Register of members*	Free to members £3.50 per hour or part thereof for non-members	£1 for each of the first five entries; £30 for the next 95 entries or part thereof; £30 for the next 900 entries or part thereof; £30 for the next 99,000 entries or part thereof; and £30 for any remaining entries plus the reasonable costs of delivering the copy to the person who has requested it.
Register of directors	Free to members	There is no obligation to provide a copy of these records.
Register of secretaries	£3.50 per hour or part thereof for non-members	
Instruments creating charges and register of charges	Free to members and creditors £3.50 per hour or part thereof for non-members	
Directors' service contracts**	Free to members Non-members have no right of inspection	For members: – 10 pence per 500 words copied or part thereof; and – the reasonable costs incurred of delivering the copy to the person who has requested it. Non-members have no right to request a copy.

*   The right to inspect or request copies of a company's register of members is subject to the important controls in s. 116 of the Companies Act (see Chapter 10).
** Copies of directors' service contracts must be provided within seven days.

■ Other practical matters

It was noted at the start of this chapter that many companies will need no further changes in terms of their directors or shareholders once the company has been incorporated. However, if any changes are needed, these are usually dealt with at the company's first board meeting. In company law there are procedures for almost everything, so anyone new to running a limited company needs to make sure they know what they are doing before going ahead and if need be, take professional advice. If a company set-up goes beyond that of a simple owner-manager then the directors and/or shareholders (as the case may be) may take professional advice at an early stage about the appropriate share structure, tailoring the articles of association and perhaps entering into a shareholders' agreement. If that is the case then the professional advisors will most likely deal with any director appointments and share allotments as well. Some of the other, more practical matters that companies commonly deal with in the first board meeting are set out below.

Changing the registered office address

The registered office address of a company can be changed at any time by a resolution of the directors – shareholder approval is not needed. The same rules about the location and nature of a registered office address that apply to a company's first registered office (see Chapter 2) still apply on any subsequent change. Notice of a change of the registered office address must be given to the Registrar of Companies on form AD01 which can be (and in the case of companies signed up to the PROOF scheme has to be) filed electronically.

A change of registered office address becomes effective on the date that it is registered by Companies House but documents may still be validly served on the company at the previous registered office address for up to 14 days after the new address has been registered (s. 87(2)). During this 14-day period, the directors must make any arrangements with regard to the disclosure of the registered office address in its business stationery and on its website and must also deal with relocating any documents or registers that are kept at the company's registered office to the new address. All relevant parties should be notified of the change such as the company's bank, HM Revenue & Customs (HMRC), solicitors, auditors and so on.

Appointing accountants or auditors

All companies must keep accounting records that comply with the requirements of the Companies Act. This is specifically the duty of a company's directors. However, if the directors decide to do so they can engage the services of an accountant to deal with this for them. It is important to note, however, that if this task is delegated to another, the responsibility for preparing the accounts stays with the directors. If the directors decide to appoint an accountant, this will often be formally approved in the company's first board meeting.

Not all private companies have to appoint an auditor. The Companies Act sets out whether a company's accounts can be exempted from audit and also contains detailed rules about when and how an auditor should be appointed. If audited accounts are unlikely to be required then the directors can resolve not to appoint an auditor (s. 485). If there is any doubt speak to a professional.

Changing the company's accounting reference date

All companies whether active or dormant are required by the Companies Act to prepare accounts for submission to Companies House. Private companies must submit their accounts within nine months of the end of their accounting period. The date on which a company's accounting period ends is known as the accounting reference date. For example, a company with an accounting reference date of 31 December must make up accounts for the period from 1 January to 31 December. The accounting reference date of a new company is automatically set as the last day of the month in which the company was incorporated. Sometimes this date will not be appropriate. For example, if the company forms part of a group of companies the directors may want to bring the accounting reference date in line with the other companies in the group. The accounting reference date is changed by a resolution of the directors (shareholder approval is not needed), either by shortening or extending the company's current accounting period. For a new private company this is subject to the restriction that the company's first accounting period cannot be less than six months and cannot be longer than 18 months, starting with the date of incorporation.

The Companies Act imposes a general restriction on all companies which is that an accounting period can only be extended once in any five-year period and no accounting period can be longer than 18 months. By way of exception, an accounting period can be extended more than once in a five-year period if:

■ the company is in administration;
■ the Secretary of State has approved the extension; or
■ the company is aligning its accounting reference date with a parent or subsidiary company in the United Kingdom or another state in the European Economic Area.

Note that no change can be made to the end date of a particular accounting period once the accounts for that period are overdue. Once approved by the directors, notice of the change of accounting reference date must be given to Companies House on form AA01 which can be filed electronically.

Bank account

If a company is going to trade then it will need to open a bank account. It is important to remember that even in the case of a company with a sole director/ shareholder, the money that the company earns does not belong to that person and must be kept separate from their own. The directors can resolve to open a bank account at the bank of their choosing in the company's first board meeting. Banks go through various standard due diligence checks which will usually involve verifying the identity of the company's directors, checking that the directors' appointments have been notified to the Registrar of Companies and they will probably also wish to see the company's certificate of incorporation (or a certified copy of it) and possibly also confirmation of the identity of the company's shareholders. A mandate naming authorised signatories will also need to be approved and submitted to the bank for processing. Opening a company bank account can be a lengthy process involving a good deal of paperwork.

Adopting a company seal

A seal is a kind of stamp that is engraved with a company's name and, rather than using ink, leaves an impression of the company's name on paper documents as a kind of signature. Affixing the company's seal to a document is a way of 'executing' that document on behalf of the company. 'Execution' is a legal term which refers to the way in which a person formally enters into an agreement either by signing it or affixing a seal. There is no requirement for a company to have a seal and for many small private companies it is not a necessity. Directors can execute documents on behalf of a company under the execution provisions set out in s. 44 of the Companies Act (see Chapter 8). The use of seals is more common in overseas jurisdictions, so some companies do have a seal for use in any business transactions with parties based overseas. If the directors decide that the company will have a seal then it should be formally adopted by resolution. Use of the seal is governed by the articles – see article 49 of the Model Articles.

Relevant insurances

Once a company has been incorporated, the directors should give some thought to the insurance cover that the company might need. There are some types of insurance that are compulsory in certain circumstances (employer's liability insurance being one example) and many others which might be advisable. The kinds of insurances that might be considered could include:

- property insurances such as fire and material damage, business interruption and theft;
- liability insurances such as employers' liability (compulsory if a company employs staff), public liability, product liability, employment law protection insurance (to provide cover in connection with employment law disputes) and environmental damage insurance;
- other personal liability insurances such as professional indemnity insurance (compulsory for some professionals) and directors' and officers' liability insurance;
- motor insurance – most standard insurance policies do not cover use of a vehicle for work purposes – and travel insurance (where relevant); and

- goods in transit insurance to cover the movement of goods by rail, road or by post or any other means.

The kinds of insurance that might be advisable will depend on the company's activities and the risks that it is subject to. Take advice from an insurance specialist.

Tax matters

A company's profits and chargeable gains are subject to corporation tax. Companies House notifies HMRC when a new company has been incorporated and in turn HMRC will write to the company at its registered office to advise the directors of the information that must be supplied following the commencement of the company's first accounting period (essentially when the company becomes active and starts trading). Based on the information provided, HMRC will fix dates for the filing of a corporation tax return. Accordingly, the directors need to put arrangements and systems in place for the maintenance of proper accounting records, the preparation of statutory accounts and the calculation of the company's corporation tax liabilities. As mentioned earlier, the directors may decide to engage the services of an accountant to assist with these.

In addition, the directors should consider whether the company will need to register for VAT (or if it would be advantageous to do so) and to set up a payroll system for PAYE and National Insurance purposes in respect of directors and employees' salaries and other benefits. See Chapter 14 for more.

The annual return

The annual return is a standard Companies House form which provides a snapshot of a company in terms of its registered office address, directors, shareholders and various other details. All companies have to file an annual return in each 12-month period whether the company has traded or not and whether or not there have been any changes to the company's directors or shareholders. It should not be confused with the company's accounts, or the annual report that forms part of a company's accounts.

Filing deadlines and the made-up date

As a snapshot of information, the details provided in the annual return have to be accurate at a specific date in time. This date is known as the annual return's 'made-up date'. A company's first annual return has to be made up to the date which is the anniversary of the company's date of incorporation. For example, for a company incorporated on 1 May 2013, the first annual return must be made-up to 1 May 2014. All annual returns have to be filed within 28 days of the made-up date or an offence is committed by the company and every director, secretary (if there is one) and any other officer who is in default. If a company does not make good the default, the Registrar of Companies may initiate a dissolution of the company or/and commence proceedings for prosecution (see Chapter 5 for more). The made-up date of the annual return should not be confused with a company's accounting reference date. The former determines the snapshot date for the details shown in the annual return; the latter determines the period-end date of the company's statutory accounts.

After the first annual return, the next annual return will be due on and must be made-up to the same date in the next year. If the company files another annual return in the intervening period then the due date of the next one will change to the date that is 12 months after the made-up date of that additional or premature annual return. In this way, the anniversary of the made-up date of the last annual return becomes the due date of the next one. A company can file as many annual returns as it likes provided that it files at least one every 12 months. There are no events which trigger a requirement to file an annual return other than the anniversary of the made-up date of the previous return, but sometimes a company will file an additional annual return to try and clarify information about the company on the public record. There are other more effective ways of correcting company information which should be considered before filing an additional annual return in this way (see Chapter 5).

It is important to pay attention to the made-up date when preparing and submitting the annual return. For example, if a company makes any changes prior to the made-up date that require a notification to be sent to the Registrar of Companies (such as the appointment of a new director) that information needs to be filed at Companies House before or at the same time as the annual return (the Companies House WebFiling facility allows changes to be submitted online at the same time). With the exception of shareholder details, if the company's filing record is up to date, then the annual return should just reflect the information already held on Companies House records.

Submitting the annual return

The prescribed Companies House form for the annual return is the AR01, but it can be filed electronically and in most cases this is the easier (and cheaper) option – the vast majority of companies file their annual return this way and companies signed up to the PROOF scheme must do so. The only issue for companies using the Companies House WebFiling facility is that the system has some limitations in terms of the information that can be submitted concerning a company's share capital and shareholders which in some cases can mean that a company is unable to use the WebFiling option. This is explained further below.

Contents

The details that have to be provided in the annual return of a private company limited by shares are:

- the company's name and registered number;
- the made-up date of the annual return;
- the company's principal business activities;
- the company's legal status (e.g. private company limited by shares);
- the registered office address;
- the company's SAIL address (if it has one) and the company records that are kept there;
- details of the company's directors;
- details of the company's secretary (if there is one);
- details of the company's issued share capital (known as a 'statement of capital'); and
- details of the company's shareholders.

Completing the annual return

If completing an annual return using the WebFiling facility the presenter is first asked to confirm whether or not any of the company's shares were admitted for trading on a market during the period to which the annual return relates. A 'market' basically means an investment exchange (otherwise known by the more familiar term 'stock exchange') recognised by the FSA, or a market established under the rules of a recognised investment exchange. For the vast majority of private companies the answer to this question will be no. The reason for asking is that companies whose shares are traded on a regulated market have to provide different information about their shareholders to companies whose shares are not traded on a regulated market.

After this the system guides the user through the form, in each section showing the information that is currently held by Companies House on the company's record. As such, there is no need to worry about getting the company's name, number and legal status right – this information will be populated into the form automatically. Similarly, the registered office address, SAIL address and records held there (if applicable), names and other details of the company's directors and secretary (if there is one) will all be drawn from Companies House records. What does need to be done is to check that all of this information is correct and accurate as at the made-up date. For example, have any of the directors changed their service address, or has the company appointed a new director but notice of that appointment has not yet been submitted to the Registrar? Has the company moved any records to or from the SAIL address?

If any of the pre-populated details need to be changed then the system will ask for a date of change and this will then generate a separate return of information of the appropriate form type which will be submitted electronically at the same time as the annual return. If filing on paper, any changes that occurred during the 12 months prior to the made-up date that have not yet been notified to the Registrar must be submitted before the annual return is filed – the paper version of the annual return cannot be used to notify any changes.

If at any point during the WebFiling process it is necessary to stop and log out, the system will save any changes that have been made. When logging back into WebFiling the process can be resumed by selecting the option to continue with the part-completed annual return.

Principal business activities

In this section of the annual return, the company has to provide details about its main business activities. This is done by stating one or more of the Standard Industrial Classification (SIC) codes from the list issued by the Office of National Statistics. The full list can be viewed on the Companies House website (the contact centre can help to locate it). These codes cover a wide range of business activities grouped by sector – the code or codes which best describe what the company does should be selected. These codes then appear on the company's record and can be seen on the company details screen on the Companies House website. The SIC codes can be changed on subsequent annual returns if the company's activities change.

Statement of capital

Each annual return has to provide details about the company's issued share capital as at the made-up date. The annual return is not the only Companies House form that has to include a statement of capital and so these are explained in more detail below. The statement of capital in the annual return should agree with the statement of capital that the company has filed most recently, unless a change has been made that does not trigger a requirement to file a statement of capital (i.e. a re-designation of shares – see below). In general though, if changes need to be made to the pre-populated information in the WebFiling system the presenter should check whether there are any events that have not been notified to Registrar.

Shareholder details

As well as the company's issued share capital, the annual return has to provide details about the company's shareholders, specifically:

- the name of each shareholder of the company at the made-up date, and the number of shares held of each class;
- the name of each person who has ceased to be a shareholder since the made-up date of the last annual return (or since incorporation in the case of a company's first annual return);
- the number of shares transferred by each shareholder or former shareholder since the made-up date of the last annual return (or since incorporation); and
- the dates on which the transfers of shares were registered in the company's register of members.

The shareholder details provided on the annual return constitute the only publicly available information about who a company's shareholders are and any shares that they have transferred or otherwise disposed of during the period since the last annual return, or since the company's incorporation, as the case may be. This is because there is no requirement to provide the names of shareholders who have taken shares in a notice of a share allotment (form SH01) and there is no requirement to notify the Registrar of share transfers, other than on the annual return. As such it is important to get this part of the annual return right. Unfortunately, at present the WebFiling facility is limited in that it only allows presenters to update the company's shareholder list in terms of changes to a shareholder's name, or removing a joint shareholder who has died or to report share transfers. If any shares have been disposed of in another way – such as by way of a buy-back of shares by the company, for example – there is no separate option for this. In addition, in a complicated re-organisation of share capital where there might be one or more subdivisions of shares, various re-designations and multiple share transfers, a complete and accurate representation of the changes may simply not be possible either using the WebFiling service or the paper form AR01. In these circumstances professional advice may be required to ensure that the company provides the most appropriate picture of what has happened.

A company's very first annual return must give a full list of the company's shareholders, details of all share transfers and details of any persons that have ceased to be shareholders since the company was incorporated. In each of the next two annual returns, the company has the option to only give details of share transfers and of people who have ceased to be members (i.e. a full list of all shareholders is not required). This means that in practice, starting with a company's second annual return, the company must give a full list of shareholders plus all changes, on every third annual return submitted to the Registrar of Companies. However, having said that, if the WebFiling facility is used a full list of shareholders will automatically be generated for each annual return.

Payment

The annual return is one of the few returns of information that has to be accompanied by a fee. If filing on paper it is important to remember to send payment or the annual return will not be accepted – it will not have been 'properly delivered' (see Chapter 5). If filing using WebFiling the system requires payment to be made at the point of submission. As Companies House operates on a cost-recovery basis (i.e. it is non profit-making) any and all filing fees are reviewed periodically and can change to reflect actual costs incurred. An up-to-date list of fees can be found on the Companies House website. Whatever the fees may be it is now always substantially more expensive to file an annual return on paper than it is to file one electronically.

Statements of capital

A statement of capital is a snap shot of a company's share capital at a given date. As noted earlier, the annual return has to include a statement of capital which must accurately reflect the company's issued share capital as at the made-up date of the return. Other occasions when a company has to submit a statement of capital to Companies House include:

- an allotment of shares by a company (form SH01);
- a subdivision, consolidation or redemption of shares (form SH02);
- a cancellation of shares (following a buy-back, for example – form SH06); and
- a reduction of capital (SH19).

Essentially, any action by a company that affects the number of shares that it has in issue triggers a requirement to submit a statement of capital. The statement of capital is usually incorporated into the applicable Companies House form. For example, in the case of an allotment of shares, the statement of capital is included as part of the form SH01; on a subdivision, consolidation or redemption of shares it is in the form SH02. The one occasion where a statement of capital is not required (although you might expect it to be) is when a company gives notification of a re-designation of some or all of its shares. This is notified by a form SH08 which does not contain a statement of capital.

Completing a statement of capital

The information that has to be given in a statement of capital is specified in the Companies Act. For each class of shares that the company has issued the following details are required:

- the name of the class of shares (e.g. ordinary, preference, redeemable);
- the amount that has been paid for the shares and any amount that is unpaid (as to both the nominal value and any premium);
- the number of shares of that class in issue; and
- the aggregate nominal value of the shares of that class.

Many private limited companies have simple share capital structures with only one class of shares where the shares will have been issued at their nominal value with no premium attached. Table 4.3 is an example of how a statement of capital would look for a company that has issued 100 ordinary shares of £1 each, and where each share was issued at its nominal value.

Table 4.3: Example statement of capital

Class of shares	Amount paid up on each share	Amount (if any) unpaid on each share	Number of shares	Aggregate nominal value
Ordinary	£1.00		100	£100
Totals			100	£100

If the same company had issued half of the shares at their nominal value and half at a premium of £9 per share then the statement of capital would look different. Two separate entries would be needed – one for the shares issued at their nominal value, and one for the shares issued at a premium. For the shares issued at a premium, the 'amount paid' box would need to state the amount paid for each individual share including both the nominal value of the shares and the share premium, which in this case would amount to £10. The statement of capital would appear as in Table 4.4:

Table 4.4: Example statement of capital with shares issued at a premium

Class of shares	Amount paid up on each share	Amount (if any) unpaid on each share	Number of shares	Aggregate nominal value
Ordinary	£1.00		50	£50
Ordinary	£10.00		50	£50
Totals			100	£100

Note that the totals at the bottom of the table refer to the total number of shares and their aggregate *nominal* value and that these have therefore not changed – it is only the amount paid for the shares that is different. Someone looking at this statement of capital may wonder whether these two entries represent classes of shares with different nominal values. The answer to this lies with the aggregate nominal value column. Divide the aggregate nominal value by the number of shares in issue to arrive at the nominal value of each share – in this case £1.

Companies with multiple 'amounts paid' within the same share class

In the above example, the company has one class of shares but some of the shares have been issued at their nominal value and the other shares at a premium. A company in this position is not able to submit a statement of capital to Companies House using the WebFiling facility. This is because the system, at present, is not set up to capture this kind of information. Consequently, these companies cannot use WebFiling to file any of the prescribed Companies House forms that contain a statement of capital, including the annual return. The approved software systems (mentioned in Chapter 2) can deal with this, but most smaller companies will only have access to such software through the services of a solicitor, company secretarial adviser, accountant or other professional.

There are some other limitations specific to filing annual returns which will not affect most private companies or if they do so then only rarely. These relate to the amount of data that can be captured which is limited to (among others):

■ a maximum of 1,000 individual and joint shareholders;

- a maximum of 30 individual share transfers per class of shares; and
- a maximum of 10 joint shareholders per shareholding.

Problems with statements of capital

When statements of capital were introduced by the current Companies Act it caused something of a stir. The reason for this is that the requirement for companies to state the amount paid or unpaid on each share is entirely new and was not required under any previous Companies Acts. For companies with a long share allotment history, putting together an accurate statement of capital could be difficult and in some cases not possible. Even for new companies there are problems that might be encountered in preparing a statement of capital. Where a company with shares of one class that have been allotted for different prices subdivides those shares or consolidates them, the 'amount paid up per share' information in the statement of capital needs to be adjusted accordingly which will involve some careful calculations. But what if the shares are re-designated into two different classes at the same time as the subdivision or consolidation? Again, whoever prepares the statement of capital will have to track which shares carrying which premium have been re-designated as shares of which class. This can be time-consuming and difficult.

The best advice is that the statement of capital should give an accurate (or as accurate as possible) picture of the company's issued share capital as at the date of the return of information being made to Companies House, even if this means re-distributing share premiums (somewhat artificially) among shares which have been subdivided, re-designated and so on. Keep careful records, proper board minutes and ensure the register of members records all of the amounts paid per share and the company should always have the information that it needs. If in doubt take professional advice.

Prescribed particulars

The numerical information provided in the statement of capital has to be accompanied by narrative information setting out the rights attaching to each class of shares in the company's issued share capital. These are known as the 'prescribed particulars' and (under art. 2(3) of the Companies (Shares and Share Capital) Order 2009 (SI 2009/388)) must comprise details of:

- voting rights, including rights that only arise in certain circumstances;
- rights to participate in a dividend;
- rights to participate in a capital distribution (including on a winding up); and
- any rights of redemption.

There is one exception to this which is the statement of capital in the annual return – this need only provide details of the voting rights attaching to each class of shares. In any other statement of capital all the above details are required in full. If a company has more than one class of shares, the rights attaching to each class will normally be set out in the articles of association (but could be set out in a shareholder resolution). Although these rights can sometimes be quite complicated they still need to be provided in the statement of capital, but only in so far as they relate to the prescribed particulars listed above. Details of any other rights attaching to the shares do not need to be provided. Share rights are often dealt with in a section of provisions near the start of the articles but if not then look under the headings of voting rights, dividend rights and so on. If in doubt seek professional advice. Once a suitable and accurate narrative has been produced it can be re-used for each subsequent statement of capital until or unless any of the rights change.

In the case of a company with just one class of ordinary shares in issue, the shares will have full voting, dividend and capital distribution rights and should not be redeemable (as this would contravene the Companies Act – see Chapter 9). As such a fairly simple narrative statement can be given. For the annual return Companies House suggests wording along the lines of 'each share is entitled to one vote in any circumstances'. For any other statements of capital this could be extended to say 'each share has full dividend and capital distribution (including on a winding up) rights and is not redeemable'. A bare statement such as 'all shares rank equally', 'all shares rank pari passu' or 'as per the company's articles of association' is not acceptable because it does not comply with the requirements of the Companies Act and could result in the information being rejected by Companies House. For more about share classes and share rights, see Chapter 9.

Summary

- Most new companies are incorporated with the intended directors and shareholders in place at the outset but may still need to make additional changes such as appointing additional directors or allotting further shares. Whatever a company does it is essential that the correct procedures are always followed.
- A company must disclose certain details about itself at its places of business, in its business communications and on its websites. These are known as trading disclosures.
- Certain information about a company's directors, secretary, members and charges must be kept in the form of 'statutory registers' prescribed by the Companies Act. Although not required by the Act, it is normal practice to keep additional registers of share allotments and share transfers.
- A company's records have to be kept either at the registered office address, or at its single alternative inspection location, or a mixture of the two. The single alternative inspection location must be in the same part of the United Kingdom in which the company is incorporated. Any movement of any company records between the SAIL and the registered office must be notified to Companies House.
- A company's records can be inspected by its shareholders and in some cases by

members of the public. This is regulated by rules made under the Companies Act.

■ Other practical matters that a company might need to deal with following incorporation include changing the registered office address, appointing an accountant and auditor, changing the accounting reference date, opening a bank account, and obtaining appropriate insurance.

■ A company must file an annual return with the Registrar of Companies within each 12-month period. The annual return is a snapshot of a company as to its directors, shareholders and other matters as at a particular date known as the 'made-up' date. Failure to file an annual return is an offence.

■ Some of the standard Companies House forms must include a statement of capital. A statement of capital is a summary of a company's issued share capital at a particular point in time.

■ Each statement of capital must include information about the rights attaching to the company's issued shares known as the 'prescribed particulars'.

5 Companies House and company law compliance

▦ In this chapter

This chapter explains the role of Companies House and the Companies Act filing regime, in particular:

- the role and functions of Companies House;
- the obligation to file information and the public record;
- filing information in hard copy and filing electronically;
- protecting against corporate identity theft; and
- the powers and duties of the Registrar of Companies including examination of documents, rectification of the register and enforcement.

▦ Companies House

We have already touched on the role that Companies House plays in incorporating limited companies but what exactly is Companies House and what else does it do? Companies House is an Executive Agency of the Department for Business Innovation and Skills (BIS). It is the government body responsible for maintaining a register of information for every company (and other entities such as LLPs) incorporated in England and Wales, Scotland and Northern Ireland.

According to its website, Companies House has three main functions. These are to:

- incorporate and dissolve limited companies;
- examine and store company information delivered under the Companies Act and other related legislation; and
- make this information available to the public.

Companies House is headed up by a single 'Registrar of Companies' who has overall responsibility for the running and operation of the agency. When the Companies Act sets out an obligation to file information at Companies House, it is always phrased in terms of delivering that information to the Registrar. In reality, however, Companies House is a huge organisation with many staff that are responsible for exercising the powers and duties that are ascribed to the Registrar.

The incorporation of a new company marks the beginning of a relationship with Companies House that continues until the company is dissolved. A key responsibility for directors is to make sure that they are aware of and observe the requirement to file information about their company with the Registrar at the appropriate times.

The obligation to file information

The obligation to file information at Companies House is imposed by provisions in the Companies Act and other legislation and arises in numerous situations. Generally, failure to comply with an obligation to supply information to the Registrar within the time limits specified in the Companies Act is an offence which could result in prosecution and fines for the company's officers. As well as this, Companies House has the power to remove a company from the UK register (to 'dissolve' it) if it does not respond to requests to bring its filing record up to date when it is in default of its obligations. As such, it is important to get into the habit of thinking about the information that needs to be submitted to Companies House and the events or occasions that trigger the obligation to supply it. Some information has to be filed on a yearly basis, while other information has to be filed as a result of specific things that the company has done.

Annual filing requirements

All companies have to file at least two documents at Companies House each year:

- the company's annual return (see Chapter 4); and
- the company's accounts (see Chapter 14).

As soon as a company has been incorporated, the deadlines for submission of these two documents are set. Out of all of the returns of information that a company might be required to make to Companies House during its first year and each subsequent year, these are the two documents that the Registrar knows to expect. As such, the Registrar's powers of enforcement are most often exercised in connection with companies that fail to file them. (See 'Powers and Duties of the Registrar' later in this chapter.)

Other filing requirements

There are many other occasions where a return of information has to be made. These are not regular or annual requirements but are reactive, event-driven requirements that arise in relation to an act or decision of the company's directors or shareholders. The allotment of new shares, the adoption of new articles of association and the appointment, or removal, of a director are just a few examples. A table listing common events that trigger the requirement to file information with the Registrar, together with the time limits for filing it, can be found in Appendix 3.

■ The public record

Every item of information that a company sends to the Registrar is placed on the public record. The only exceptions to this are:

- directors' residential addresses;
- the fact that a director's service address is the same as his residential address;
- letters sent by a company to Companies House to change the company's 'authentication code' (see below); and
- supporting evidence in respect of the conditions that need to be met to use sensitive words and expressions (see Chapter 2).

All other information can be inspected by members of the public. Some information, such as a company's name, registered number, registered office address and the names and service addresses of its directors are available free of charge. Other information, such as details of mortgages and charges over the company's assets, are available for a small fee, as are copies of the specific forms and documents that a company has filed with the Registrar. All of this information can be obtained from the Companies House website, by using the WebCHeck facility (follow the link for 'Find Company Information' from the home page). Copies of the forms and documents that a company has filed can be downloaded from the website, obtained by attending Companies House in person, or can be ordered over the telephone for delivery by post.

Viewing a company's filing record

To see a list of all the information that has been filed by a company, first locate the company's record in WebCHeck and then click on the 'order information on this company' option on the right hand side of the screen. When viewing a company's filing record, the details are presented in chronological order, with the information or document that the company has filed most recently at the top of the list. Each document is dated with the date on which it was registered by Companies House, which may not necessarily be the same as the date of the event that has been reported. Documents that have been filed most recently may not be available for download. If this is the case they are highlighted in red. Many older documents pre-dating the electronic register will not have been converted into electronic form (and will be marked with a cross through them) but can still be obtained on a 'scan on demand' basis. An electronic image of such a document is generally provided, on request, within two hours. CDs containing a complete set of the archived documents for a company can be obtained for a fee (currently £20.00).

It is a straightforward process to obtain information from the Companies House website but there are many service providers who can help with this such as solicitors, company secretarial advisers, accountants and company formation agents.

The purpose of making all of this information available to the public is to enable anyone dealing with a limited company to obtain any details about the company that they may need. They may want to confirm that someone they have had contact with is named as a director of the company, for example, or they may want to know who the company's shareholders are or review the company's latest financial statements. This is the element of publicity integral to running a limited company that was mentioned in Chapter 1. At the same time, this publicly available information is a resource that a company should use both to carry out its own due diligence in relation to the company's corporate customers and suppliers and to keep an eye on its competitors. Since it is likely that interested parties will also examine a company's records in this way, it makes it all the more important to file the right information at the right time to keep the company's records up to date.

■ Filing information

For many of the events in a company's life that have to be reported to the Registrar there is a prescribed form that must be used for the purpose. For other events there is no prescribed form. These events, such as the adoption of new articles of association, are reported by submitting the documents stipulated by the relevant provisions of the Companies Act.

There are two possible ways of submitting information to the Registrar – in paper form or by electronic filing. At the present time, not all returns of information to the Registrar can be made electronically but Companies House is gradually moving towards electronic filing for all but the least-used forms and documents.

Filing in hard copy

At one time, paper filing was the only means of providing information to the Registrar, but with the continuing expansion of electronic filing, it is now used less frequently. However, as not all returns of information can be made electronically, paper filing is still necessary in some cases. Furthermore, electronic filing is not yet mandatory and there is nothing to prevent a company from filing on paper even though the electronic option is available.

Paper forms can be downloaded from the Companies House website free of charge or can be obtained from legal stationers for a fee. Any forms or documents sent in hard copy must be clear, legible and capable of being reproduced as an electronic image as Companies House has to scan them to create an electronic image. The original document is stored and the electronic version is attached to the company's filing history available for download. Information not provided using a prescribed form, such as a notice of passing of a special resolution, must be provided on white A4 paper with a good margin and must always include the company's name and registered number. Almost all information submitted to the Registrar on paper has to be signed by an authorised person, either a director, or the company secretary if there is one. In all cases it is the original signed version of a paper document that needs to be sent and not a copy. It is important to make sure that hard copy forms and documents are of acceptable quality; if they are not, they may be rejected.

Companies incorporated in England and Wales must submit their information to the Cardiff office of Companies House, for Scottish companies, the Edinburgh office and for companies incorporated in Northern Ireland, the Belfast office. Each office will re-route documents to the appropriate registry but this will delay registration and increase the risk of something going missing. All forms of delivery can be used including courier and DX. To meet the filing deadlines specified in the Companies Act, information must be received by Companies House on or before the relevant date.

When filing information in hard copy:

- make sure all the required information has been provided – most of the prescribed forms include a short checklist to assist with this;
- keep a copy of everything being sent, including any cheques or postal orders;
- request confirmation of receipt – if a copy of the covering letter and a stamped addressed (or pre-paid) envelope is included, Companies House will place a barcode label on the letter stating the date of receipt and return it; and
- check the company's filing history a few days later to make sure that the information has been filed correctly (if using Monitor, an e-mail notification will follow automatically – see below).

Electronic filing

Electronic filing is a faster and more secure way of filing. No special software is needed as any company can file electronically using the WebFiling service on the Companies House website. There are company secretarial software packages commercially available that can help companies manage their compliance and administration (including electronic filing of forms and documents) but for most small companies the WebFiling service is perfectly adequate. It should be noted, however, that not all Companies House forms can be filed using WebFiling and there are also some limitations in the system which will prevent some companies from using it to file certain forms. An up-to-date list of the forms that can be filed using WebFiling (or approved software) can be found on the Companies House website.

To gain access to the WebFiling service, a presenter first needs to register by following one of the links to WebFiling from the homepage of the Companies House website and selecting the 'register' option on the log-in screen. Once registration is complete, Companies House will send an e-mail to the address provided during registration. The e-mail will include a link which allows the user to create a password for the sign-in process. This password connects to and identifies the e-mail address of the person making the electronic filing.

At the same time, an 'authentication code' is automatically issued to the company and is sent by letter to the company's registered office. (A further such letter can be requested at any time by selecting the 'Don't have your authentication code' option on the company sign-in screen.) All authentication codes are made up of six alpha-numeric characters and take the place of a director's or secretary's signature for the purpose of authenticating any forms or documents that are filed electronically. As such, it is a highly sensitive piece of data that should be kept secure and should not be disclosed to anyone unless that person is authorised to file documents electronically for the company. Once set up, the presenter signs into WebFiling using their e-mail address, the password that is linked to it and the number and authentication code for the company they are intending to file information for.

The WebFiling service is simple to use and has several advantages over filing on paper. The system guides the user through the completion of each form or document and flags any missing information. Once submitted, an acknowledgement of receipt is sent by e-mail, followed by another e-mail to confirm whether the information has been accepted or rejected. Where a fee is charged for processing particular forms or documents (such as the annual return) it is lower when filed electronically than it is when filed on paper.

Appointments and terminations of directors and secretaries, changes to a director's or secretary's personal details, changes of registered office or SAIL address, change of accounting reference date and returns of allotment of shares can all be filed electronically, as can the annual return, form DCA (dormant accounts), and audit-exempt small or abbreviated accounts. It is also possible to file notice of a change of name.

Where a document must be accompanied by a fee (such as an annual return), payment of the fee is made prior to submission by credit or debit card. Alternatively users who make ten or more chargeable transactions over the course of a year can apply for a credit account. In this case, payment is not taken at the point of submission and instead the user receives a monthly invoice. The application form for a credit account can be downloaded from the Companies House website.

■ Protecting against corporate identity theft

Just as identity theft is an issue for us as individuals, corporate identity theft is a risk to companies. The fact that information about a company can be submitted to Companies House on paper makes it possible for someone unconnected with a company to file false information about it (e.g. changing its registered office address, or changing its directors). By doing this, a perpetrator can create the illusion that they are running the company, apply for credit cards or loans and order goods in the company's name. Corporate identity theft can have severe consequences for a company leaving it with huge debts and a ruined credit rating. To help companies guard against this, Companies House operates two schemes known as 'PROOF' and 'Monitor'.

PROOF

A company that signs up to the PROtected Online Filing (PROOF) scheme agrees to file certain critical returns of information to Companies House electronically. Under PROOF, the following information must be filed electronically:

- notice of the appointment or termination of appointment of a director or secretary;
- notice of a change of a director's or secretary's details;
- notice of a change of registered office address; and
- the annual return.

If any of the above information is filed on paper, Companies House will reject it unless accompanied by a completed form PR03 which must state the company's authentication code. The idea is that because only someone who has access to the company's authentication code can file information electronically, this should dramatically reduce the risk of false information being filed.

To sign up to the PROOF scheme, click on this option after logging into the company's details in WebFiling.

Monitor

The monitor service does exactly what it says – it enables a person to monitor the information that is filed for their company, or for any other company on the UK company index. Each time a form or document is filed for a company that is being monitored, Companies House will send an e-mail notification to the person monitoring it. This should mean that any fraudulent filings become quickly apparent. This service is also helpful in ensuring that any information that a company has submitted itself has been correctly filed. There is no limit to the number of companies that one person can monitor, which means that it is possible to keep watch over any companies that are key to your business, whether customers, suppliers or competitors.

To monitor a company, locate the company's details in WebCHeck and click on the 'monitor this company' option on the right hand side of the screen.

Helpful hints: protecting against corporate identity theft

- Register for electronic filing and sign up to the PROOF and Monitor schemes.
- Keep your company's authentication code safe and do not disclose it to anyone unless you want them to file information for your company.
- Change your authentication code periodically and always after someone who knows the code leaves the company.

- Protect sensitive information about your company such as bank account details and passwords and ensure that your IT system is secure.
- Take steps to ensure the security of your premises, keep important information in locked cabinets or in a safe.
- Dispose of any documents containing sensitive information using a confidential waste disposal service.

Powers and duties of the Registrar

In processing and registering the information that companies submit, the Registrar is bound by the duties and powers that are conferred on him by the Companies Act. The main powers and duties of the Registrar relate to:

- the examination of documents;
- inconsistency notices;
- rectification of the register;
- removal of companies; and
- enforcement.

It is a good idea to have an understanding of these powers and duties as it helps to explain why Companies House does what it does – particularly as it relates to rejecting information that has been received, or dealing with errors in information that has been accepted and registered.

Examination of documents

The Registrar must examine any information that a company submits and decide whether to accept that information and place it on the register, or to reject it.

Whether the information can be accepted or not will depend on whether it meets the requirements for 'proper delivery'. It was mentioned earlier that forms and documents sent to Companies House have to meet certain standards – they should be legible, of A4 size and be completed in black ink. This is one of the requirements for proper delivery. Another requirement is that the form or document should contain all the information required by the Companies Act. Yet another requirement is that forms and documents must be authenticated, either by way of a physical signature (if filing on paper) or by way of the company's authentication code (if filing electronically). In addition, if the Companies Act or any other regulations say that the form or document must be accompanied by a fee, then the fee must be provided. Failure to tick any of these boxes will mean that the requirements for proper delivery have not been met and the Registrar must reject the information provided. If this happens, Companies House will send an appropriate communication to the company either by e-mail or letter (depending on whether the form or document was filed electronically or on paper) giving the reasons for the rejection.

On the other hand, if a form or document does meet the requirements for proper delivery, the Registrar must accept it and place the relevant information on the register.

Inconsistency notices

If a company supplies information that is inconsistent with other information that has previously been provided (e.g. if a company files a notice of termination of appointment of a director where that director's appointment had never been notified in the first place) the Registrar must accept it (provided that it has been properly delivered) but will then try to resolve the inconsistency. In the first instance the Registrar will usually write to the company to explain the situation and ask for the appropriate information. If this does not meet with a response, the Registrar will issue the company with an 'inconsistency notice' – a formal request to rectify the situation. It is important not to ignore an inconsistency notice. Failure to comply is an offence (punishable by a fine) and the Registrar can annotate the company's record to highlight the inconsistency, which could potentially cause problems for the company in its dealings with outsiders. If you ever receive such a notice and are not sure why it has been issued or how to put things right, then contact Companies House for more information or take professional advice.

Rectification of the register

Once the Registrar has placed an item of information on a company's record it can be – depending on what the information relates to – fairly difficult to correct or remove it. If a mistake does happen there are three possible ways of dealing with it:

- file the information again (known as a 'second filing');
- apply to the Registrar to have the information removed; or
- apply to Court to have the information removed.

Each of these options is different, either in terms of the information that can be corrected, the way that the information is corrected and the procedure involved.

Second filing

Second filing provides a straightforward way for companies to file an amended version of a form to correct an error contained in an earlier version that has been accepted by the Registrar and placed on the company's record. This is a very useful way of dealing with an error, but is limited in that it can only be used in respect of the forms set out in Table 5.1.

If the error is in respect of information provided on any other form or document, the second filing option cannot be used.

To make a second filing, the form containing the incorrect information needs to be reproduced (with the mistake corrected), signed in the normal way and submitted to the Registrar together with a completed form, RP04. This must

Table 5.1 Forms that can be second-filed

Form	Description
AP01	Appointment of director
AP02	Appointment of corporate director
AP03	Appointment of secretary
AP04	Appointment of corporate secretary
CH01	Change of director's details
CH02	Change of corporate director's details
CH03	Change of secretary's details
CH04	Change of corporate secretary's details
TM01	Termination of appointment of director
TM02	Termination of appointment of secretary
SH01	Return of allotment of shares
AR01	Annual return

identify the original form and the date that it was registered by the Registrar. When filed, the corrected document will appear on the company's record as a 'second filing' and the Registrar will place an annotation next to the original document to say that a second version of it has been filed. Note that the original information remains on the company's record. In the case of a company that wants to have information removed from the register, it is necessary to check whether this can be done by the Registrar or whether a court order is required.

Removal of information by the Registrar
The Registrar has the power to remove information from the register in respect of information that:

- is invalid or ineffective;
- was submitted without the authority of the company; or
- is either factually inaccurate, or is derived from something factually inaccurate or forged;

in as far as the information relates to:

- a change of registered office address;
- the appointment or termination of appointment of a director or secretary; and
- details of the company's first director(s) and secretary as stated in the application for incorporation.

A successful application for rectification will result in the information being removed, as if it had never been filed in the first place. This power of the Registrar to remove information is mainly intended for use in dealing with fraudulent filings; however since it also applies to information that is factually inaccurate, it can be used to deal with errors and mistakes. Note, though, that the scope of information that can be removed is narrower than the information that can be amended by a second filing (e.g. it is not possible to remove information relating to an allotment of shares).

An application for rectification is made using form RP02A. On receipt of the form, the Registrar will assess whether the application can proceed and, if so, he writes to all interested parties to invite any objections to it (namely the company's directors and secretary (if there is one), the presenter of the form and any other person that the information relates to). If no objections are received after a period of 28 days has elapsed, then the information will be removed from the register.

Anyone considering making an application for rectification may wish to speak to Companies House to make sure that the information that they want to remove falls within the scope of the Registrar's power and to make sure that the application is completed correctly. If in doubt, take professional advice.

Removal of information by order of the court

If it is not possible to deal with an error by way of a second filing, or by applying to the Registrar to have the information removed, then the only other option is to obtain a court order. The court can order the removal of any information that:

- is invalid or ineffective;
- was submitted without the authority of the company; or
- is factually inaccurate, or derived from something factually inaccurate or forged.

However, whereas the Registrar's power is limited to certain types of information, the court can order the removal of any information. This is subject to one exception. Information having a 'legal effect' such as information relating to a company's incorporation, a change of name, or a reduction of capital can only be removed if:

- the presence of the information on the register has caused or may cause damage to the company; and
- the company's interest in removing the information outweighs the interest of any other person in keeping it on the register.

Obtaining a court order for the removal of information is a last resort and is likely to involve time and expense. Anyone in a position where this seems to be the only option should take professional advice.

Removal of companies from the index (dissolution)

Under s. 1000 of the Companies Act, the Registrar has the power to remove a company from the index if he believes that the company is no longer carrying on business or in operation. The two most common situations in which the Registrar uses this power are when a company fails to file its annual return or fails to file its annual accounts. The Registrar will send an initial letter of enquiry, stating that the company appears to be inactive and that he will take steps to strike the company from the index within one month unless the company files the required information or contacts the Registrar to confirm that the company is still required. If no such reply is received, or the required information is not filed, a second similar letter is sent. If the second letter also meets with no reply, a formal notice is placed in the *Gazette* stating that, unless cause is shown to the contrary, the company will be struck off after the expiration of three months from the date of the notice.

If this happens to you then do not ignore these warnings – they are not empty threats. This is an efficient process which will result in the company being struck off, its bank account being frozen and any assets of the company passing automatically to the crown. In order to regain access to its funds, a dissolved company needs to be restored to the register. This will usually require the services of a solicitor. As well as the disruption to the business and potential loss of trade and goodwill, this will incur costs and delays that are best avoided. If the Registrar is proposing to remove your company and you are not sure why, then get in touch with Companies House or take professional advice.

Enforcement

As well as the ability to remove companies from the index, Companies House has other powers of enforcement. The most commonly used of these is the power to issue fines for the late filing of accounts. Private companies can face a fine of £1,500 for accounts which are filed over six months late and if accounts are filed late two years in a row, the fine in the second year is doubled. As well as this, Companies House can initiate criminal proceedings against directors personally for failing to deliver accounts and annual returns on time, or for not delivering them at all. In the event of a successful prosecution, a director will incur an additional fine (for which they are personally liable), a criminal conviction and potentially – in severe cases of repeated offences – disqualification from acting as a director.

For the most part, however, the Registrar cannot know what the many thousands of companies on the register are doing and what returns of information they should be making. If a company defaults on its obligations, the Registrar is dependent on someone bringing it to his attention. If the Registrar does becomes aware that a company has failed to provide information required by the Companies Act, he is empowered to instruct the company to make good the default. If the company fails to take the necessary action, the Registrar can apply to court for an order directing the company to deliver the required information. Repeated defaults are grounds for disqualification (see Chapter 7).

That said, the Registrar's overriding aim is to encourage compliance rather than enforce it. In reality, the onus is on directors to be aware of their responsibility to deliver information when the Companies Act requires it in the light and knowledge of the legal and commercial consequences that could follow if they fail to do so.

Summary

- Companies House is the registry for companies incorporated in England and Wales, Scotland and Northern Ireland, each of these parts of the UK having its own office.
- All companies must make returns of information to the Registrar of Companies on the occurrence of certain events. Companies incorporated in England and Wales must submit their returns to the Cardiff office of Companies House.
- All companies must file accounts and an annual return at Companies House each year, irrespective of whether the company has traded, or whether there have been any changes in the company's directors or shareholders.
- The majority of information that a company files with the Registrar is placed on the public record. Some can be viewed free of charge and some on payment of a fee.
- Information filed with the Registrar can be presented in paper format using the standard Companies House forms, available from the website. The most common returns of information can be filed electronically using the Companies House WebFiling facility or by using approved software.
- Once information has been placed on the public record it can only be removed or corrected in certain circumstances
- Companies House operates two schemes to help companies protect themselves against corporate identity theft, known as PROOF and Monitor. Companies that sign up to the PROOF scheme agree to make certain returns of information electronically.
- The office of the Registrar of Companies is created by the Companies Act. The Registrar has overall responsibility for the running and operation of Companies House.
- When the Companies Act sets out a requirement to file information with Companies House, this is expressed in terms of notifying the Registrar. In reality, the great many returns made to the Registrar each day are processed by the staff working in the various sections of Companies House.
- The Registrar has various powers and duties under the Companies Act. The principle powers and duties relate to examination of documents, inconsistency notices, rectification of the register, removal of companies and enforcement.

- The Registrar has limited powers of enforcement although prosecutions are regularly brought against directors for failure to file accounts and for failure to file annual returns.
- Directors need to be aware of their responsibility to file information with the Registrar as and when it is required. Repeated failure to make returns is grounds for disqualification under the Company Directors' Disqualification Act 1986 (see Chapter 7).

6 Introduction to directors

In this chapter

This chapter provides an introduction to the office of director including:

- the role and purpose of directors;
- notable features of the office of director including directors' powers and duties and different types of directors;
- the procedure for appointing a director;
- related issues such as protecting a director's residential address, practical matters to deal with following an appointment and directors' service contracts;
- termination of the appointment of a director under the articles of association and removal under the Companies Act;
- practical matters to deal with following a termination of appointment; and
- the register of directors and register of directors' residential addresses.

What are directors?

In broad terms, a company's directors are responsible for the overall management and governance of a company. Directors can face heavy responsibilities and the higher the profile of a particular company, the more likely it is that the company's directors may – from time to time – feel the glare of the public eye. In recent years, for example, the directors of some of the UK's largest banks have come under intense scrutiny in connection with the perceived failings that came to light in the wake of the UK (and global) financial crisis. Most limited companies are nowhere near as large as companies like these, but whether the company is a huge multi-national organisation, or a small family-run business, one fact remains the same – the buck for the way in which the company is run stops with the directors.

Helpful hints: Director's knowledge and supervision

The office of director carries responsibilities that must be taken seriously. In one of the court cases that followed the collapse of Barings Bank in 1995, it was stressed that directors must inform themselves of the affairs of the company and join in with the other directors in supervising those affairs (*Secretary of State for Trade and Industry v Baker (No. 5)* (1999)). Barings Bank collapsed following the revelation of huge losses that had been incurred by one of its Singapore traders, Nick Leeson. The directors were held culpable for failing to adequately monitor the activities of the Bank's traders.

Not all cases that come before the courts are as high profile or involve the same degree of scandal as the *Barings* case. However, the principle that a director must know about the activities of their company and must monitor and supervise those activities applies to all companies, large and small.

It may seem odd, then, that the Companies Act 2006 does not set out what a director's role should be and what directors are actually supposed to do. In practice, the remit of a particular director will vary greatly depending on the size and type of organisation that they work for and their specific role within it. For example, an individual running a painting and decorating company of which he is the sole director and shareholder will probably have to deal with everything from simple administration to book-keeping and financial matters, as well as providing the services for which the company gets paid. In larger organisations, the role of a director is different. Here the directors are usually professionals and run the company like the captains of a large vessel. They have a leadership role which encompasses but is not limited to:

- setting the company's objectives and strategy;
- determining how the company's financing needs should be met;
- serving the interests of the company's shareholders and other stakeholders; and
- ensuring that all aspects of the company's operations are run properly and in accordance with best practice and the law.

In a large company with a public listing the board has (or should have) a more clearly defined role. Although some individual directors will have executive and managerial responsibilities, within the day-to-day to day running of the company, the board as a whole does not. By comparison, in a small owner-managed company – like our painter-decorator – the roles may not be so delineated; indeed the owner-director needs to be careful that the lines between his various roles do not become blurred or lost.

While the Companies Act is not particularly helpful in illuminating the role of the board and of individual directors, it does place a great many obligations on directors, sets limitations on what they can do and spells out the specific duties to which they are subject. In addition, principles of good governance set standards for best practice which also shape the role and responsibilities of directors. We consider the duties and liabilities of directors in the next chapter. Corporate governance issues are considered in Chapter 16.

Features of the role of director

Directors as fiduciaries

Although a company is a separate legal person, it is an artificial person and has no means of making decisions or taking action by itself. It is the directors who are responsible for acting on the company's behalf. They have stewardship of the funds that have been invested into the business by the company's shareholders and others, as well as the funds generated by the company's activities and any of its assets. This puts them in a 'fiduciary' relationship with the company. This is rather like the relationship between a trustee and the property which is subject to the trust that the trustee must administer – a trustee must always be endeavouring to maximise the value of the trust property, but must make no personal gain from doing it. Directors are not trustees, but they do occupy a position of trust with regard to the company and its assets. These assets belong to the company, not to the directors, but they are nevertheless under the directors' control and accordingly it is the directors who have the power to decide what use to make of them. The various duties that the law places on directors (explained in the next chapter) have come about as a result of their fiduciary relationship with the company.

Directors' powers

Directors take their authority to run the company from the articles. Most articles will include a provision similar to article 3 of the Model Articles which states that:

> Subject to the articles, the directors are responsible for the management of the company's business, for which purpose they may exercise all the powers of the company.

Directors, therefore, have discretion to exercise their powers in whatever way they see fit, subject to:

- any specific restrictions and limitations in the articles of association;
- any specific restrictions and limitations in the Companies Act (and other laws and regulations);
- the rules in the Companies Act that require certain decisions to be approved by shareholders;

■ any directions given to the directors by the shareholders to do or refrain from doing specified acts (this is an established right of shareholders but is nevertheless set out in article 4 of the Model Articles); and

■ any rules or restrictions contained in another agreement, such as a shareholders' agreement.

Making decisions

It is important to recognise that the word 'directors' in article 3 of the Model Articles is in the plural, not the singular form and that this is for a reason. Directors, as a general rule, must exercise their powers collectively. Subject to the company's articles and the Companies Act, the directors can delegate their powers to individual directors, senior management and others (and indeed must do this if the company is to function effectively) but, as a principle of good governance, significant and major decisions should be taken by the board as a whole. The board must decide what decisions it will reserve to itself, what powers can be delegated and how those delegated powers will be monitored and controlled. More is said about this in Chapter 8.

Binding the company

Linked to this is the question of what authority individual directors have to bind the company. Providing it acts within its powers and any applicable rules and restrictions, the board of directors, acting together as a whole, can bind the company in any way it sees fit. However the authority of an individual director might be subject to specified limitations. As long as a director acts within the limits of his authority all is well, but if he exceeds his authority things become tricky. This is because for outsiders dealing with the company, a director has any authority that is reasonably implied by that title and any authority that the company holds him out as having. As a result, a director can still bind the company even though he has acted beyond the limits of his authority. This is also explained in more detail in Chapter 8.

Executive and non-executive directors

It was mentioned earlier that the board of directors has a role that is distinct from the day-to-day management of the company. A company director who is also an employee of the company with an executive or senior management role is known as an 'executive director'. Examples would include finance director, marketing director and director of operations among others.

The term 'non-executive director' denotes someone who is a director of a company but who does not have an executive role within the company. In corporate governance terms, non-executive directors are expected to have a monitoring role, bringing independence and objectivity to the board and acting as a check on the executive directors. While usually to be found on the board of listed public companies, some small private companies do appoint non-executive directors as a means of bringing skills, experience and expertise to the board that may help the company grow and develop. Where executive directors have a full-time role within a company, non-executive directors do not and are not required to make the same time commitment as their executive counterparts.

However, it is important to note that the Companies Act makes no distinction between executive and non-executive directors. Any person appointed as a director, whether executive or non-executive, will be subject to the same duties, responsibilities and liabilities that the office of director carries with it. At the same time, it is also important to note that having a job title which includes the word 'director' does not in itself mean that a person is a director of a company. This title might be given to senior executives as a means of enhancing their status, but it does not make them a director in law. A person can only become a director by formal appointment in accordance with the relevant provisions of the company's articles of association.

De facto directors and shadow directors

The Companies Act defines a director as 'any person occupying the position of director, by whatever name called' (s. 250). This is a broad, almost circular, definition but it is drafted deliberately so that anyone acting with the power and authority of a director – whether that person has been formally appointed or not – can be made subject to the duties and liabilities imposed on directors by the Companies Act and any other laws and regulations. A person holding himself out as a director and acting as a director without having been formally appointed is known as a *de facto* director. The significance of this is that a person found to be a *de facto* director can be caught by any of the provisions of the Act or any other legislation that applies to directors whether in terms of duties, obligations or offences.

A shadow director is defined in s. 251(1) of the Companies Act as 'a person in accordance with whose directions or instructions the directors of the company are accustomed to act'. The difference between a shadow director and a *de facto* director lies in the shadow director's intention of avoiding the legal duties and responsibilities of being a director, or of having any apparent connection with the affairs of the company (although the courts have said that the element of deception or lurking in the shadows is not necessarily a prerequisite). Shadow directors compromise a company's transparency and integrity, as anyone dealing with the company may not be aware of their existence and their influence over the company's business. As with *de facto* directors, a person judged to be a shadow director is subject to the same provisions of the Companies Act (and any other applicable legislation) as a director who has been properly appointed. For clarity, s. 251(2) states that people giving advice to directors in a professional capacity (e.g. a solicitor or an accountant) will not be regarded as shadow directors. However, care needs to be taken to ensure that advisors do not exceed their remit and place themselves in a position where they are at risk of being held to be a shadow director.

Whether a person will be found to be a *de facto* director or a shadow director depends on a number of factors and the circumstances of each case. A shareholder in a company could be a *de facto* or shadow director if they involve themselves in the running of the company and give directions to the company's directors which the directors then follow. A key issue is whether the person in question has real power and/or influence with regard to the way in which the company is governed.

Case example – *Gemma Limited (In Liquidation)* v *Davies* (2008)

In this case proceedings were brought against a director and his wife, who was company secretary of his company, for the misappropriation of company funds. The claimants had sought an order against the director's wife (as well as the director himself) for the repayment of the funds in question. The success of the claim would depend on whether the director's wife could be considered to be a *de facto* director. In the circumstances, the court found that the wife's role as company secretary was purely clerical in nature and involved no decision making. She had no influence over the way in which the company was run, therefore could neither be a *de facto* director nor in breach of any duty to the company with regard to the company's funds.

Natural directors and corporate directors

Under s. 155 of the Companies Act, all companies are required to have at least one director who is a 'natural director'. A natural director means a real, living, breathing person as opposed to a 'corporate director' which is a director that is itself a company. Provided that a company has at least one natural director, it can (subject to the articles) have as many corporate directors as it likes. Corporate directors can be used to avoid some of the liabilities that the office of director carries with it. By operating through a corporate director, an individual can still have a voice in board discussions and decisions while the risks and liabilities of being a director rest with the corporate director. In recent years, cases have come to court in which it has been claimed that a sole director of a corporate director is a *de facto* director of the company in which the corporate director holds office. At present, the position seems to be that as long as the sole director has at all times acted only in his capacity as a director of the corporate director, he will not be a *de facto* director of the company in question. That said, anyone seeking to limit their risk exposure in this way should take professional advice.

Qualification

No formal qualifications are needed to hold office as a director. However the following categories of persons are prohibited from being appointed as directors:

- undischarged bankrupts (this is a specific prohibition in the Company Directors' Disqualification Act 1986);
- persons under the age of 16;
- persons disqualified from being a director under the Company Directors' Disqualification Act 1986; and furthermore
- a company's auditor may not also be a director of that company.

In addition, a company's articles may prevent a person from being appointed as a director in certain circumstances, or may cause an existing appointment to cease – see later under Termination of Appointment. While there is no requirement for a director to hold any formal qualifications, all directors are subject to a duty to act with reasonable skill and care. This is one of the directors' duties set out in the Companies Act and is explained in more detail in the next chapter. It is for each individual director to ensure that they have the skills and knowledge that they need to be able to fulfil their duties to the company. This would include updating and refreshing skills and knowledge as and when appropriate. There are providers that offer training for directors and a professional qualification is available from the Institute of Directors.

Remuneration

The position of director is an 'office' which carries various duties but does not confer the right to receive any remuneration. The specific services that a director is expected to provide to the company will be set out in either their service contract (in the case of directors with a full-time executive role in the company) or in a letter of appointment (in the case of a non-executive director). Directors can only be paid for these services if the articles allow or if the shareholders specifically approve it. Most articles will permit the directors to determine their own remuneration – see article 19 of the Model Articles. In some cases, such as in a subsidiary company, the parent company may wish to retain control over the directors' pay and the articles may say that any proposed remuneration has to be approved by the shareholders.

Appointing a director

A company's first directors are those persons named as directors on the application to form the company (see Chapter 2). The appointments become effective as soon as the company has been incorporated, by operation of s. 16 of the Companies Act. There are no other provisions in the Companies Act that deal with the appointment of directors and although shareholders have a common law power to appoint directors by ordinary resolution in a general meeting, it is usual to specify rules for appointing directors in the articles of association. There are normally two options.

Appointment by resolution of the board

An article of this sort will allow the directors of the company to appoint another director by board resolution. In the Model Articles, article 17 provides for this, enabling a director to be appointed by 'a decision of the directors'. For companies that have adopted the Model Articles with amendments, or a bespoke set of articles based on the Model Articles (or an earlier set of standard articles) it should not be assumed that they contain such a provision – always check.

Appointment by resolution of the shareholders

Most companies will also have a provision in their articles that allows for a director to be appointed by a resolution of the members. The relevant article for this in the Model Articles is also article 17, which simply states that a director can be appointed by ordinary resolution. Articles that pre-date the Model Articles may have slightly more complicated provisions and require notice of the proposed appointment to be given to the company within a specified time frame from the date of the general meeting. Again, always check what the articles actually say. If the articles are silent, then the right of the shareholders to appoint a director by ordinary resolution will be inferred by the common law.

Of the two methods on offer in the Model Articles, it is generally faster and easier for a director to be appointed by a decision of the existing directors. Nevertheless, the power of the company's members to appoint a director by ordinary resolution is still an important one which can come into play for example if the members exercise their right to remove one or more of the directors and appoint replacements of their own choosing – see further below.

Other methods

The two basic means of appointment set out in the Model Articles can be varied or supplemented by additional provisions in the articles or in a shareholders' agreement. For example, it may be appropriate for a particular shareholder (e.g. an investor) to have the right to appoint a director of their choice. In a company that is a subsidiary of another company (see Chapter 1) it is not uncommon for the articles to give the shareholder or shareholders holding a majority of the shares the right to appoint or remove a director by written notice to the company at its registered office. The right to appoint and remove directors is one of the issues to consider in tailoring the articles to meet a company's particular needs and circumstances.

Maximum and minimum numbers of directors

Some articles of association may stipulate a maximum and a minimum number of directors that the company can have at any one time. When considering the appointment of a new director it is important to check for this and make sure that any stated maximum will not be exceeded by making the new appointment. If the upper limit will be breached, then it will need to be increased before the appointment goes ahead. Normally, the articles will say that this can be done by ordinary resolution of the shareholders.

The opposite also applies in that when a director resigns, the articles need to be checked to ascertain whether the number of directors left in office has fallen below any stated minimum. If so, the remaining directors will have no right to continue to act unless there is a provision in the articles that permits them to do so. Even when there is such a provision, if the number of directors is less than the number required to form a quorum (see Chapter 8) the articles will usually state that they can take no action in relation to the company other than to appoint additional directors or to convene a general meeting of the shareholders so that the shareholders can do likewise.

For companies with the Model Articles this is not an issue as they do not stipulate a minimum or maximum number of directors. A company with the Model Articles can operate with a single director (provided that the sole director is a natural person) or as many directors as the company wishes to appoint. For more on sole directors see Chapter 8.

Death of an owner-manager

A particular problem can arise in a small owner-managed company when the owner-manager dies. This is because neither of the company's decision-making bodies are able to function, so the company is left in a position where it cannot appoint a new director and process the transfer of the deceased owner-manager's shares. To pre-empt this situation, most standard articles will usually include a provision that allows the personal representatives of the deceased owner-manager (his shares in the company forming part of his estate) to appoint a director by notice in writing to the company. Once in office, the new director can deal with the transfer of the deceased owner-managers' shares and the company can continue to function (see article 17 of the Model Articles).

Notifying the registrar of companies

The appointment of a natural director must be notified to the Registrar of Companies on form AP01 and the appointment of a corporate director on form AP02, in either case within 14 days of the date of appointment. It is a common misconception that the validity of an appointment is dependent on notice being submitted to the Registrar – it isn't. The appointment of a director is effective from the date of the board or shareholders' resolution by which the director was appointed, or such date specified in the resolution if the appointment is not to take effect immediately. However, failure to file the form AP01/AP02 is an offence under the Companies Act on the part of the company and any officer of the company in default.

To notify the appointment of a natural director, the Registrar must be provided with the director's:

- full name;
- any previous names used for business purposes in the last 20 years;
- service address;
- residential address;
- date of birth;
- nationality; and
- business occupation.

For a corporate director, the following details are needed:

- the name of the corporate body or firm;
- the registered office address;
- for companies registered within the European Economic Area (EEA) the country/state where the company is registered and its registration number; and
- for non-EEA companies, the legal form of the company or firm, the law by which it is governed and, if applicable, the country/state in which it is registered and its registration number.

The notification can be sent on paper or in electronic form (either using approved software or the Companies House web-filing service). For companies signed up to the PROOF scheme, this is one of the notifications that must be made electronically or, if filed on paper, must be accompanied by a completed form PR03 (blank PR03 forms are available from Companies House).

Directors' service and residential addresses

As noted above, all directors must provide the Registrar of Companies with both a service address and a residential address. A director's service address will appear on the public record, but the residential address will not. This means that a director can keep his residential address private by filing a service address that is different to his home address. If a director files a service address that is the same as his residential address, the fact that the two addresses are the same will not be apparent from the public record. Both the residential address and (if applicable) the fact that the residential address is the same as the service address are protected information (see further below).

A director can use the company's registered office as a service address. If filing on paper, this should be done by stating 'the company's registered office'. If using web-filing, the option to link the service address to the registered office should be selected. Doing this will have the effect that whenever the company's registered office address changes, the director's service address will simply go with it and there will be no need to notify Companies House separately of any change of the service address.

Any address can be used as a service address as long as it is the full address of a building or location at which someone will be available to accept service of any documents addressed to the director in question. A bare PO box address or a

DX address is not acceptable. The service address does not need to be within the United Kingdom and can be anywhere in the world (this is also true of a director's residential address – there is no requirement for a director of a UK company to be resident in the UK).

Any change in a director's service address or their residential address must be notified to Companies House using form CH01. In the case of a corporate director changing its service address, the notification is made using form CH02. These notifications must be made within 14 days of the date of the change.

Section 243 exemption

The Registrar of Companies cannot disclose a director's residential address (or the fact that the director's residential address and service address are the same) except:

- to certain public bodies specified in the Companies (Disclosure of Address) Regulations 2009 (SI 2009/214);
- under the order of a court; or
- to credit reference agencies.

The Registrar's power to disclose a director's residential address to any of the specified public bodies, or on order of a court are immoveable. However, for directors who consider that they (or someone that lives with them) may be at serious risk of violence or intimidation because of the activities of a company of which they are a director, it is possible to make an application to the Registrar under s. 243 of the Companies Act to prevent their residential address from being released to credit reference agencies. Applications must be made in writing using the appropriate prescribed form which can be obtained from Companies House – note, however, that these forms are not available on the website and must be requested over the telephone. The grounds for an application will be satisfied if the director has previously worked for GCHQ, MI6, MI5 or the police. Otherwise an application must be accompanied by documentation that supports the director's claim that he is at risk. Ideally this should be in the form of a letter from the police, so any relevant incidents or occurrences should be reported. For more information see the Companies House guidance booklet 'Restricting the disclosure of your address' available from the 'Guidance' section of the website.

Other practical matters

Once the appointment of a new director has been made the other practical matters that need to be considered and dealt with include the following.

Record of the decision

Whether the appointment was made by a resolution of the board or of the shareholders, appropriate evidence of the decision should be drawn up, authenticated and then stored safely.

Bank mandate

If the new director is to be authorised to sign cheques for the company, then the company's bank mandate will need to be updated – this should be formally approved by a resolution of the directors.

Information and induction

The new director should be provided with a copy of the company's articles of association, a copy of the latest and any previous financial statements and should be given an induction appropriate to their role along with guidance on their duties and responsibilities. The ICSA guidance note 'Induction of directors' (available on the ICSA website) provides detailed advice on this.

Declarations of interest

The new director should be asked to disclose any direct or indirect interests that they have in the company's contracts or other arrangements and should also disclose any matters that either give rise, or could potentially give rise to, a conflict of interest on their part (see Chapter 7).

Register of directors

The appointment must be recorded in the company's register of directors (see further below).

Directors' service contracts

It is usual for directors in an executive role to have contracts with the company which set out the terms of their employment. Section 227 of the Companies Act defines a service contract as a contract under which a director of the company undertakes personally to perform services (as director or otherwise) for the company, or for a subsidiary of the company. Many of the issues that will be dealt with in a director's service contract are similar to those that would be covered by a standard contract of employment (e.g. pay, holiday entitlement, pension rights, entitlement to sick pay). It will probably also cover such matters as the director's specific duties and responsibilities within the company, restrictive covenants, confidentiality, intellectual property and termination.

An important difference between a director's service contract and a normal employment contract is that directors' service contracts are subject to specific rules in the Companies Act. These concern provisions in a service contract relating to a fixed term of employment and the notice period required to be given on termination. There has been considerable coverage in the media in recent years concerning director's service contracts and, in particular, the costs that a company might incur in removing a director. The rules in the Companies Act go some way to addressing this by requiring shareholder approval for provisions for fixed terms and notice periods that exceed certain specified limits. As such it is advisable to have service contracts drawn up by a professional. See also the ICSA guidance note 'Directors' Service Contracts' (available on the ICSA website) for more information.

Disclosure of directors' service contracts

As a further check on directors and to ensure transparency regarding the terms of a director's service contract, ss. 228 and 229 of the Companies Act require that copies of directors' service contracts must be kept available for inspection by shareholders either at the company's registered office or at the company's single alternative inspection location (see Chapter 4). If a service contract is not in writing, then a 'memorandum' setting out the terms of the contract must be kept instead. Copies of service contracts or any memoranda must be kept for a period of at least one year from the date of termination or expiry of the contract in question. Shareholders are also entitled to be provided with a copy of a director's service contract or the memorandum of its terms on payment of the prescribed fee. A company must comply with such a request within seven days.

▓ Termination of appointment

It is normal for the articles of association to specify certain circumstances in which a director's appointment will automatically terminate. Article 18 of the Model Articles sets out five situations in which a directors' appointment will cease:

- the director ceases to be a director by virtue of any provision of the Companies Act or is prohibited from being a director by law – this would include disqualification under the Company Directors' Disqualification Act 1986;
- a bankruptcy order is made against the director (as per the Company Directors' Disqualification Act 1986);
- a composition is made with the director's creditors generally in satisfaction of the director's debts;
- a registered medical practitioner who is treating the director gives a written opinion to the company stating that the director has become physically or mentally incapable of acting as a director and may remain so for more than three months; and
- notification is received by the company from the director that the director is resigning from office, and such resignation has taken effect in accordance with its terms.

Of these situations the most common to occur is a director's resignation, the effect of which will be governed by the terms of the director's service contract. However it is a good idea to be aware of the other four circumstances, so that any situations that are developing which may result in the automatic termination of a director's appointment are identified and kept under review. Of course, a director's appointment also terminates automatically on death.

It should be noted that article 18 of the Model Articles was amended on 28 April 2013 by the Mental Health (Discrimination) Act 2013 which deleted article 18(e). Article 18(e) provided for the automatic termination of a director's appointment in the event that:

> by reason of the director's mental health, a court makes an order which wholly or partly prevents the director from personally exercising any powers or rights which he would otherwise have.

The articles contained in the previous version of the Model Articles will continue to apply to companies incorporated under the Companies Act before 28 April 2013, to the extent that they have not excluded or varied them. There is no obligation for companies with articles that incorporate article 18(e) to remove it, but they may wish to consider doing so, particularly given that the article does not confer a discretionary power but has automatic effect. Take professional advice.

Removal of a director

Most articles do not allow the directors to terminate the appointment of one of their number by board resolution and this is the case with the Model Articles. However, just as bespoke provisions in the articles can confer rights on certain individuals or groups of individuals to appoint a director, so the articles may confer specific rights of removal as well. Accordingly, this should always be checked.

If a director cannot be removed under provisions set out in the company's articles a mechanism for removal is set out in ss. 168 and 169 of the Companies Act. This allows a director's appointment to be terminated by an ordinary resolution of the company's shareholders at any time before the expiration of the director's period of office. The procedure to be followed involves the following:

- 'special notice' of the proposed resolution to remove the director must be given to the company by the shareholders at least 28 days before the date on which the meeting will be held;
- on receipt of the special notice the company must send a copy to the director in question;
- the director can make 'representations in writing' to the company and require these to be circulated to each shareholder to whom notice of the general meeting is sent. The company must comply unless it is too late to do so or unless a court orders that the director is abusing this right. If it is too late to comply, or the company defaults in complying, the director can require that the representations are read out at the general meeting; and
- the director has the right to attend the meeting and to speak on his proposed removal.

The process may be instigated either by the directors or the shareholders. If the latter, then the shareholders will utilise their right under s. 303 of the Companies

Act to requisition a general meeting (see Chapter 11). Sometimes the articles (or a shareholders' agreement) may give a director what is known as 'weighted voting rights' in relation to any decision to remove him. Such provisions are legal in private limited companies and effectively enable the director concerned to outvote all others. thereby defeating the resolution.

In general, directors or shareholders who wish to instigate the removal of a director should take professional advice. If the procedure in the Companies Act is to be used then it must be followed carefully and in all cases there can be employment law issues that will need to be addressed (such as the potential for a constructive and/or unfair dismissal). The removal of a director under ss. 168 and 169 does not deprive the director of any rights they may have to compensation for loss of office.

Practical matters

Practical matters that need to be considered following the termination of appointment of a director include the following.

Notifying the Registrar of Companies

Notification of the termination of appointment must be filed at Companies House using form TM01 within 14 days of the date of termination. Failure to file this form is an offence, although the act of filing the form does not itself terminate a director's appointment. The appointment must have firstly been terminated by way of resignation, automatic termination, removal under the Companies Act, or by any other means set out in the articles of association (or a shareholders' agreement).

Letter of resignation

Often overlooked, it is important that a director who is resigning their office provides the company with a letter of resignation. If the departing director does not do this, then technically, their directorship will not have ceased.

Record the decision or circumstances

The termination and the reasons for it, or the circumstances in which it has taken place, should be recorded. This could be done at the company's next board meeting, or at a meeting specifically called for the purpose, depending on the situation. The record and any related documentation should be kept safe for future reference. In any case other than a straightforward resignation, professional advice should be taken so that the company follows the correct procedures and takes the appropriate actions.

Bank mandate

Any necessary amendments to the company's bank mandate should be approved and put in place.

Documents and property
All company documents and property should be returned.

Register of directors
The termination of directorship must be recorded in the company's register of directors.

▪ Register of directors

Section 162 of the Companies Act requires all companies to keep a register of directors.

The information that must be entered into the register of directors is the same as the information that is supplied to Companies House on the form AP01 in the case of a natural director, or AP02 in the case of a corporate director (see earlier in this chapter). In either case, the register should also record the date on which the director was appointed, and in the event that the appointment terminates, the date of termination. The register of directors must be open to inspection by any member of the company without charge, and by any other person on payment of the required fee. See Chapter 4 for details.

Register of directors' residential addresses
In addition to the register of directors, all companies must also keep a register of directors' residential addresses. This is required by s. 165 of the Companies Act but, unlike the register of directors, this is a completely confidential register that must not be made available for public inspection.

The register must state the usual residential address of each of the company's directors. If a director's residential address is the same as their service address, then an entry to this effect can be made in the register (but not if the service address has been given as 'the company's registered office' – in that case the full address must be stated).

Failure to keep a properly maintained register of directors or register of directors' residential addresses is an offence on the part of the company and of every officer of the company in default.

See Appendix 4 for an example of a register of directors, and a register of directors' residential addresses.

▪ Company secretary

The Companies Act does not say what the responsibilities of a company secretary are, but in practice the secretary has a very different role to that of the company's directors. Where the directors are responsible for the overall running of the company, the company secretary would not normally be involved in making decisions affecting the management or governance of the company. The secretary is more of an advisor to the board and to the chairman in particular, assisting the board in its decision-making process by providing information and guidance and facilitating the implementation of the board's decisions and strategy. As well as this, the company secretary will usually be responsible for dealing with many of the administrative matters that arise in the course of running a company. The role of company secretary can be very broad in scope and can differ from one company to another but will usually encompass at least the following:

- organising meetings of the directors and meetings of the shareholders (and/ or written resolutions), attending such meetings and ensuring that the proper procedures are followed. The secretary would normally be responsible for preparing minutes of all board meetings and shareholder meetings;
- maintaining the company's statutory registers;
- administering the company's registered office and directing any mail received to the appropriate people;
- ensuring that the company complies with the requirements on trading disclosures;
- dealing with share transfers and any other changes to the register of members such as new share allotments, the death or bankruptcy of a shareholder or a shareholder's change of address;
- assisting with the preparation of the annual report and accounts;
- overseeing and being responsible for communications with shareholders (and being the first point of contact for shareholders);
- ensuring that the company complies with the Companies Act and any other relevant legislation;
- making appropriate returns of information to the Registrar of Companies when required by the Companies Act (e.g. appointment/resignations of directors, allotments of shares, change of registered office and so on);
- preparing and filing the company's annual return each year;
- ensuring that the directors act in accordance with the company's articles of association; and
- acting as adviser to the directors on corporate governance best practice and changes in legislation.

For more on the role and the typical responsibilities of a company secretary, see the ICSA guidance note 'Duties of a Company Secretary' available on the ICSA's website.

The company secretary as an officer of the company

Section 1173 of the Companies Act says that a company secretary is an officer of the company. This means that the company secretary can be liable as an 'officer in default' with regard to any breaches of the provisions of the Act (see Chapter 7). As an officer of the company, the company secretary can sign the majority of forms that must be filed with the Registrar of Companies and can also be a signatory to company documents where the signatures of two officers are required. It would also be usual for the secretary to be on the company's bank mandate. However, the scope of the secretary's authority is much narrower than that of the directors and the secretary needs to know where the limits are and be careful not to exceed them (see Chapter 8).

Appointing a company secretary

Prior to the implementation of the current Companies Act, all companies were required to appoint a company secretary and a company's articles would normally include a provision giving the directors the power to do this. However, private companies are no longer obliged to appoint a secretary (unless specifically required to do so by their articles) so the government took the decision not to include an article of this sort in the Model Articles. This was based on their view that most small private companies will choose not to appoint one. Most solicitors and formation agents still include a suitable provision in their standard articles for the appointment of a secretary. Companies with the Model Articles will need to formally change them by adding a new article, such as that in the model articles for public limited companies.

Fling requirements and register of secretaries

Notice of the appointment of a company secretary must be given to the Registrar of Companies on form AP02 (AP03 for a corporate secretary) within 14 days of the date of appointment (s. 276). For a 'natural' secretary, only the secretary's name, any former names used for business purposes in the last 20 years and a service address need to be provided. Company secretaries do not need to provide their residential address to the Registrar. In the case of a corporate secretary, the details required are the same as those required for a corporate director and are set out earlier in this chapter. If a company secretary's details change at any time (e.g. such as a change of service address) this must be notified to the Registrar on form CH03.

Section 275 of the Companies Act requires all companies to keep a register of secretaries. In the case of a 'natural' secretary, the register must include the secretary's name, former names and service address. For corporate secretaries, the details to be included are the same as those required to be sent to the Registrar. Although not required by the Act, it is also advisable to include the date of appointment and date of termination of appointment of each secretary. An example of a register of secretaries can be found in Appendix 4.

The register of secretaries must be kept open to inspection by any member of the company free of charge and any other person on payment of the prescribed fee (see the table in Chapter 4 for details).

Does my company need a company secretary?

It is very much at the discretion of a company's directors to decide whether or not to appoint a company secretary. When looking at the list of responsibilities set out earlier, it may seem unlikely that these tasks alone will justify the full-time appointment of a company secretary in a small company and the role is often combined with other executive duties. However, as companies grow their needs can change. A company secretary can have a wide variety of additional duties such as administration of the company's insurance policies, pension arrangements, employee share schemes and intellectual property. In addition, a company secretary might be responsible for buildings and facilities management, personnel administration, financial management, credit control and data protection. There are no hard and fast rules; it all very much depends on the needs of the company. For directors of a new company, one of the main concerns should be to ensure that the company complies with its legal obligations. So, if the company does not intend to appoint a company secretary, the directors need to decide who will take care of the basic tasks that a company secretary would otherwise deal with. One possible answer to this might be to outsource the company secretarial function to a professional.

■ Checklist – appointing a director and termination of appointment of a director

Appointing a director

✓ Ensure that there are no legal impediments to the appointment (e.g. check that the proposed director is not an undischarged bankrupt).

✓ Check the company's articles of association for the means by which a director can be appointed. If the company's articles specify a maximum number of directors that the company can have, then check whether this limit will be exceeded by the proposed appointment.

✓ Appoint the new director in accordance with the provisions set out in the articles. Ensure that appropriate documentation to record the decision to appoint the director is prepared, authenticated and stored safely.

✓ Send notification of the appointment to Companies House within 14 days using form AP01 or the WebFiling facility. If filing on paper, then the new director must sign the form to confirm their consent to the appointment. If filing electronically, then the director's consent is given by way of three items of information that are personal to the director.

✓ Enter the required details of the new director into the company's register of directors. Enter the director's residential address into the register of directors' residential addresses.

✓ Deal with any practical matters (including updating the company's bank mandate and providing the director with an appropriate induction so that they fully understand what is required of them), a copy of the company's articles of association, latest financial statements and so on.

✓ Any subsequent change of the director's details including change of service address or change of residential address must be notified to Companies House on form CH01 (or form CH02 for a corporate director) and must also be recorded in the register of directors and/or register of directors' service addresses.

Termination of appointment of a director

✓ If the appointment has terminated by way of resignation, ensure that the director has signed a letter of resignation.

✓ Record or evidence the fact of the termination and the reasons for it in a formal board minute.

✓ File notice of the termination with the Registrar of Companies on form TM01 within 14 days of the date of termination.

✓ Deal with any practical matters (including updating the company's bank mandate and the return of any company property).

✓ Enter the date of termination in the company's register of directors.

✓ Check whether the remaining directors are sufficient in number to form a quorate board meeting in accordance with the articles.

✓ Check that the company still has at least one director who is a natural person.

✓ If in doubt, take professional advice – particularly in the case of removal by shareholder resolution.

Summary

■ The role of directors is not defined in law and will vary from one company to another.

■ Directors have a fiduciary relationship with the company which gives rise to the duties to which they are subject.

■ The directors' authority to run the company and exercise its powers is derived from the articles of association. They can delegate their powers to others, but must make important or significant decisions collectively.

■ Executive directors have a full-time executive role in a company, non-executive directors do not. Both are subject to the same duties and liabilities.

■ A person who has not been formally appointed as a director, but who nevertheless occupies that role, could be found to be either a *de facto* director or a shadow director.

■ Directors do not need any formal qualifications but must make sure that they have the requisite skill and knowledge to be able to fulfil their duties to the company. The law prohibits some categories of people from being appointed as a director.

- The means by which a director can be appointed are set out in the articles of association. The appointment of a director must be notified to the Registrar of Companies within 14 days.

- Companies must keep and maintain a register of directors and a register of directors' residential addresses.

- It is usual for executive directors to have a service contract setting out the terms of their appointment. Certain matters relating to service contracts are regulated by the Companies Act.

- The articles of association usually provide for situations in which a director's appointment will terminate automatically. Otherwise a director can be removed by an ordinary resolution of the shareholders, in accordance with the procedure set out in the Companies Act.

- The termination of appointment of a director must be notified to the Registrar of Companies within 14 days.

- Private limited companies are not required to appoint a company secretary. If the directors decide not to appoint a secretary they must ensure that the matters for which a company secretary would normally be responsible are dealt with by someone else.

7 Directors' duties and liabilities

■ **In this chapter**

This chapter considers the duties and liabilities of directors in particular:

- the seven codified duties in the Companies Act;
- the possible consequences of breach of duty by a director including derivative claims and claims for unfair prejudice;
- specific restrictions on directors in relation to loans and substantial property transactions;
- situations in which a director could be personally liable for a company's debts;
- offences under the Companies Act, the risk of prosecution, and disqualification under the Company Directors' Disqualification Act 1986;
- obligations under other laws and regulations; and
- indemnities and insurance.

■ Directors' duties

Prior to the implementation of the current Companies Act the duties to which directors are subject were not to be found in any Act of Parliament or Regulation. Directors' duties existed only in common law as a result of principles developed by the courts over a great many years. The Companies Act has attempted to codify these principles into a succinct list that – it is hoped – is clearer and easier to understand both for directors and for those advising them.

Directors owe their duties to the company and not to the company's shareholders or to anyone else (except if the company becomes insolvent – see Chapter 17). The duties arise as a result of the fiduciary relationship that directors have with the company and essentially require directors to act with honesty and in a way that reflects their position as stewards of the company's business, assets and its future prosperity. It should be noted that the duties codified in the Act are general duties. As such, the list of duties that we see in the Act is not exhaustive and there are many other obligations that directors are subject to which are set out throughout the Companies Act and in other legislation.

There are seven general duties set out in the Act which require directors to:

1   Act within the limits of the company's constitution.
2   Promote the success of the company for the benefit of its members as a whole.
3   Always use their own judgement.
4   Exercise the level of skill, care and diligence that is expected of them.
5   Avoid conflicts of interest and not divert business opportunities away from the company for their own benefit.
6   Not except gifts or benefits from third parties.
7   Declare any interests they may have in company transactions.

Most of the duties have been transplanted from the common law with little or no change. The two notable exceptions to this are the duty to promote the success of the company, and the duty to avoid conflicts of interest, both of which expand on and alter the scope of the pre-existing common law. The Act tells us that the codified duties are to be applied and interpreted in the same way as the common law rules and principles that they are based on. This means that the application and interpretation of the duties will continue to evolve through the decisions of the courts in the same way that it has done for many years. The duties are not mutually exclusive and two or more of the duties may apply at any one time (s. 179). Each of the codified duties is considered in more detail below.

Duty to act within powers (s. 171)

As explained in the previous chapter, the power to run a company is delegated to the directors by an appropriate provision in the articles of association which usually authorises them to exercise all the powers of the company. What s. 171 says is that directors must not exceed those powers that are given to them. This means that they must act in accordance with the articles of association and any resolutions of the company's shareholders. An example of this is the power to allot shares. The directors can only exercise the company's power to allot shares if they are given the authority to do so by the articles, by a resolution of the company's shareholders, or if they have authority under s. 550 of the Companies Act (see Chapter 9). If the directors were to allot shares without having the proper authority to do so, they would be in breach of the duty to act within their powers. Acts of directors which exceed their powers may be open to challenge.

Section 171 also encompasses a related common law rule which is that directors must not exercise their powers for an improper purpose. What this means is that directors must exercise their powers for the purposes for which those powers are intended (e.g. the directors' power to allot shares should generally be exercised to raise capital for the company). Exercising the power for a different purpose, such as to change the balance of voting control among the company's shareholders would most likely be an improper use of this power. An improper use of powers may arguably also involve a breach of the next duty in the Act – the duty to promote the success of the company.

Duty to promote the success of the company (s. 172)

Section 172 is derived from the common law rule that directors must act in a way that they believe in good faith is in the interests of the company and its shareholders as a whole. In codifying this common law rule, the government decided to try and broaden its scope to influence the behaviour of directors in a particular way. Section 172 states that directors must act in a way that they consider, in good faith, would be most likely to promote the success of the company for the benefit of its members as a whole. In doing this, the Act says that directors must 'have regard' to the following factors 'amongst other matters':

- the likely consequences of any decision in the long term;
- the interests of the company's employees;
- the need to foster the company's business relationships with suppliers, customers and others;
- the impact of the company's activities on the community and the environment;
- the desirability of the company maintaining a reputation for high standards of business conduct; and
- the need to act fairly as between the members of the company.

Accordingly, a director's primary duty under this section is to promote the success of the company for the benefit of its shareholders, but in doing that, they must have regard to the various factors listed above. From the explanatory notes to the Companies Act it can be seen that this is a deliberate attempt by the government to codify the accepted norms of responsible business practice. Prior to the implementation of the Companies Act, the department for Business, Innovation and Skills (formerly known as the Department for Trade and Industry) released selections from the parliamentary discussions on the formulation of this duty. From these extracts we can see that:

- the wording of the duty is intended to enshrine in statute the principle of 'enlightened shareholder value' – that directors are more likely to achieve long-term sustainable success for the benefit of their shareholders if their companies pay attention to a wider range of matters;
- 'success' means the aims that the shareholders collectively want the company to achieve; for a commercial company, this will normally mean a long-term increase in value;
- directors must promote the success of the company for the members as a whole – not for the benefit of a majority shareholder, a particular group of shareholders or for the benefit of directors who may hold shares themselves;
- the words 'amongst other matters' in relation to the list of factors that

directors must take into account are there to clarify that the list is not exhaustive;

- the words 'have regard to' mean 'think about' or 'give proper consideration to' – a box-ticking approach is not acceptable; and
- consideration of the factors should be an integral part of the duty to promote the success of the company.

In making their decisions, directors must, therefore, balance all the factors listed in the Act (as well as any other factors that are relevant) and decide how much weight to give to each one. In this way, directors have to take account of the potential effects of the company's activities in the widest context. However, the requirement to have regard to all relevant factors is not intended to tie directors up in knots. For example, although the Act says that directors have to consider the interests of the company's employees, the DTI extracts recognise that at times it will be necessary to make redundancies to ensure the long-term success of the company.

On some occasions, the process of evaluating the factors relevant to a proposed action may be straightforward. However, where a particular decision may negatively affect one or more stakeholder groups, the directors may need to take time to properly evaluate what those effects will be (e.g. if there could be a potential environmental impact). The more significant a decision is, the more important it is that the directors keep proper records of how they have arrived at it – both in the form of minutes and any relevant reports, supporting documentation or materials that were used or considered in the decision-making process.

Duty to exercise independent judgement (s. 173)

Directors must not compromise their ability to exercise complete discretion in their decision making. This means that a director must not make an agreement with a third party as to how he will exercise his judgement or discretion at some future date or with regard to a particular matter, or act so as to favour the concerns or interests of one group of persons over another. Taken in conjunction with the duty to promote the success of the company, it is clear that if a director gives up his ability to exercise independent judgement, it is quite likely that he will be unable to act in the company's best interests. Of course this does not prevent a director from taking appropriate advice when it is needed, but any such advice must not be followed blindly and the director's ultimate decision must be his own.

Duty to exercise reasonable skill, care and diligence (s. 174)

This section of the Companies Act sets out the level of skill and care that is expected of a director. The Act requires that a director acts with the care, skill and diligence that would be expected of a reasonably diligent person with:

- the general knowledge, skill and experience that may reasonably be expected of a person carrying out the functions carried out by the director in relation to the company; and

■ the general knowledge, skill and experience that the director has.

This formulation therefore contains two elements: an objective element with regard to the director's role within the company and a subjective element which considers the actual knowledge, skill and experience that the director has. The overall effect is cumulative because if a director has skills or expertise in a particular area (perhaps by way of a professional qualification) the level of skill, care and diligence expected of that director will be higher than the level that would be expected of another director in the same role who did not have the same expertise. In other words, if directors have particular skills or knowledge they will be judged by a higher standard, so they must use and apply them in order to fulfil their duty to the company. It should be noted, however, that just because one director in a company does have expertise in a particular area (e.g. accounting and finance) that does not absolve the other directors of responsibility for those matters. Directors have a collective and individual responsibility for the overall management of the company's affairs.

Case example: *Queens Moat Houses plc v Bairstow, Hersey, Marcus and Porter* (2004)

A company published accounts which significantly overstated its profits causing the company's shareholders, bankers and others to be misled as to its financial position. The defendant director argued that he could not be held responsible as he had no accounting expertise and had relied on others with regard to the production and audit of the financial statements. Applying the *Barings* case, the court held that while the defendant had no duty to check functions that were within the expertise of an accountant, the irregularities in the financial statements should have been apparent to him. The misleading accounts would not have been published had he exercised his duties properly.

Directors must make many decisions in the course of implementing the company's strategy and seeking to achieve its objectives. The courts will not generally hold a director to account for what, in hindsight, may turn out to have been an error of judgment. Neither will the court try to substitute its own views for those of the company's directors. However, inactivity, ignorance or incompetence will not be a defence if a director has failed to act with reasonable skill, care and diligence.

Duty to avoid conflicts of interest (s. 175)

Section 175 says that directors must avoid situations in which they have, or can have, a direct or indirect interest that conflicts, or possibly may conflict, with the interests of the company. This applies, in particular, to the exploitation of any property, information or opportunity whether the company could take advantage of it or not. This codifies the common law principle that a director should be loyal to the company and should not take advantage of any opportunities that may be presented to him, whether privately or in his capacity as a director, unless permitted by the company to do so. This rule is applied strictly so that it doesn't matter whether or not the company could take advantage of the opportunity. The duty also applies to a director after he has left the company. If a director resigns his appointment to pursue an opportunity, he will still be in breach of this duty unless the company's shareholders have given their approval.

Case example: *Bhullar Bros Ltd v Bhullar* (2003)

The defendant directors privately purchased a property adjacent to a property owned by the company without disclosing the purchase to the company's other directors.

The court held that the directors were in breach of their fiduciary duty to the company. The fact that the premises were available for purchase should have been communicated to the other directors and the company. Whether the company either would or could have taken advantage of the opportunity was not relevant. The directors were ordered by the court to transfer the property to the company at the purchase price.

However, in its new codified form, the duty is not only concerned with the exploitation of business opportunities but also with the more general concept of a director's conflict of interest and conflict of duties. For example, a typical situation where a conflict of interest can arise is where a director is a significant shareholder in his company. The director must act in the best interests of the company but, on occasions, his interests as a shareholder may be at odds with his duties as a director. Similarly, where a director holds more than one director-ship, it is possible that his duties to one company will conflict with his duties to another.

Having a conflict of interest is not the end of the line for a director because the Act stipulates that the duty will not be infringed in two distinct cases. The first is if the situation cannot be regarded as being likely to give rise to a conflict of interest. This allows the directors to assess whether a particular situation gives rise to a conflict of interest or not (i.e having a particular interest doesn't always have to mean that the director is in conflict). Of course, such situations should be kept under review in case the circumstances change and a conflict either becomes a possibility or an actuality. Note that the prohibition on conflicts includes situations that 'possibly may' conflict with the interests of the company. If there is any doubt professional advice should be taken.

The second possibility is for the conflict to be authorised by the other directors. This is done by way of a board resolution. If the conflict is approved then the director will not be in breach of his duty under s. 175 and any transaction or arrangement to which it relates will not be liable to be set aside. It is important to note that the director who has the conflict of interest cannot take part in the vote (s. 175(6)) and neither can any other interested director. In a situation where there are insufficient uninterested directors to form a quorum, the decision must go to the company's shareholders.

Companies may want to consider including provisions in their articles to deal with the approval of conflicts in order to formalise their procedures. For example, the articles may require details of all conflict authorisations to be recorded in writing and allow for authorisations to be conditional –a typical condition would be that that the director absents himself from discussions relating to the matter that gives rise to his conflict. The model articles do not contain any provisions of this sort. Solicitors can provide standard articles for authorising conflicts which may be perfectly adequate as they are or could be adapted to suit a particular company's needs. It should also be pointed out that the directors of private limited companies incorporated before s. 175 came into force (1 October 2008) do not have any automatic right to authorise directors' conflicts – their power must first be 'activated' by an ordinary resolution of the company's shareholders. This is one of the few ordinary resolutions that must be filed with the Registrar of Companies. Directors of private limited companies incorporated under the current Companies Act can authorise conflicts unless the articles say otherwise.

When considering whether or not to authorise a director's conflict, the other directors must keep in mind the other duties that they are subject to. They should ask themselves whether, in authorising a director's conflict, they are acting in a way that is consistent with the fulfilment of their duties to the company (e.g. will authorising the conflict promote the success of the company for the benefit of its members as a whole?).

The duty under s. 175 to avoid conflict of interest does not apply to any interest that a director has in a transaction with the company – this is covered by s. 177 and is explained further below.

Duty not to accept benefits from third parties (s. 176)

A director must not accept a benefit from a third party which is conferred by reason of his being a director, or his doing or not doing anything as a director. The aim of this duty is to prevent directors from compromising their independence, or from exploiting their position for personal profit. It does not, of course, apply to benefits received from the company in which he holds office. Many companies have internal policies that govern the acceptance of benefits and provide guidance to directors and employees on when a gift can be accepted and when it cannot. Companies may also establish an internal procedure for directors (and others) to report benefits to central management. These kinds of measures have become particularly important since the implementation of the Bribery Act 2010 (see Chapter 16). The duty is not infringed where the acceptance of the benefit cannot reasonably be regarded as likely to give rise to a conflict of interest, but care should be taken over this. If there is any doubt, then the matter should be brought to the attention of the board as soon as possible and legal advice may need to be taken. Like the duty to avoid conflicts of interest, this duty also continues to apply to a director after he has left a company, for similar reasons.

Duty to declare interest in a proposed transaction or arrangement (s. 177)

Directors must disclose the nature and extent of any interest that they have, whether direct or indirect, in any proposed transaction or arrangement with the company. For example if the company is proposing to enter into a contract for the supply of goods or services from a supplier in which a particular director has an interest (perhaps because he is a director or significant shareholder of that company) then the director must declare his interest to the other directors. The declarations under s. 177 enable the other directors to make an informed decision about whether or not to continue with the transaction. If they do decide to continue with it, appropriate measures can be put in place to protect the company's interests.

The declaration has to be made before the transaction has been entered into and can be made either at a meeting of the directors, or by way of a notice in writing. A written notice must be sent to the other directors and, once given, is deemed to form part of the proceedings at the directors' next meeting. It is important to note that the duty to disclose interests is an ongoing one and, should any previous declaration prove to be, or become, incomplete or inaccurate, then a further declaration will need to be made.

Connected persons

A director's interest in a transaction may arise not because he is interested personally but because he is 'connected' with a company, firm or an individual who is. The Companies Act provides specific rules that determine when a director will be regarded as being 'connected with' another party in this way. Among others a director's connected persons include:

- a director's spouse or civil partner;
- any other person with whom the director lives as partner in an enduring family relationship;
- the director's children or step children; and

- a company in which the director has (or has together with his connected persons) an interest in 20% of the equity share capital.

So, for example, if a director's spouse is a director of a company and the director's company is considering entering into a transaction with this company that will constitute an interest on his part and must be disclosed. These rules can be found in ss. 252, 253 and 254.

A director can give a general notice under s. 185 that he has an interest in a specified company or firm and is to be regarded as being interested in any transaction or arrangement that may, after the date of the notice, be made with that company or firm. Similarly, a general notice can be given that the director is connected with a specified person (other than a company or a firm) and is to be regarded as interested in any transaction or arrangement that may, after the date of the notice, be made with that person.

Exceptions

A director will not be required to declare an interest:

- if the director is not aware of the interest, or of the transaction or arrangement in question (a director will be treated as being aware of any matters that he ought reasonably to be aware of);
- if the director's interest cannot reasonably be regarded as giving rise to a conflict of interest;
- if, or to the extent that, the other directors are already aware of it (to this end directors will be treated as being aware of anything that they ought reasonably to be aware of); or
- if, or to the extent that it concerns the terms of his service contract which has been or are to be considered.

In addition, since directors are required to disclose their interests 'to the other directors' the better view is that a sole director does not have to declare any interests because there is nobody for him to declare them to. However, this will only be the case if the company's articles permit the company to function with a sole director. It should also be noted that where a director is also the sole member of the same company and the company enters into a contract with him in his capacity as the sole member which is not in the course of the company's ordinary business, there is an additional record keeping requirement under s. 231 of the Companies Act. This is intended to focus the director's attention on separating the interests of the company from his own interests as shareholder and is explained in Chapter 12.

Interests in existing transactions

It is possible that a director could find that he has an interest in a transaction that the company has already entered into. This might happen if the company entered into the transaction before the director was appointed or if the director becomes interested in it at some point afterwards. This is dealt with by s. 182, which requires directors to declare the nature and extent of any direct or indirect interest that they have in an *existing* transaction or arrangement with the company. Such declarations can be made in the same way as declarations made under s. 177 and must be made 'as soon as is reasonably practicable' (s. 182(4)).

It is important to note that s. 182 does not constitute one of the general duties of directors. Failure to comply with s. 182 is a criminal offence, but is not a breach of a director's fiduciary duties to the company.

Provisions in a company's articles

It is common for a company's articles to contain provisions relating to the directors' declarations of interest and these should be reviewed to ascertain what effect they have. In the model articles, declarations of interest are dealt with in article 14. This article comes under the heading of 'conflicts of interest' which may suggest that it deals with the situational conflicts of interest caught by s. 175 of the Companies Act but it does in fact relate to declarations of interest in transactions with the company under s.177.

The position under Model Article 14 is that a director cannot vote or form part of the quorum at a meeting in respect of a transaction in which he has an interest unless:

- this prohibition is disapplied by ordinary resolution of the company's members; or
- the director's interest cannot reasonably be regarded to give rise to a conflict of interest; or
- the director's conflict of interest arises from a 'permitted cause'.

The permitted causes are:

- the giving of a guarantee to or by the director;
- the subscription by the director for shares or other securities in the company, or to underwrite, sub-underwrite, or guarantee subscription for any such shares or securities; and
- arrangements by which benefits are made available to employees and directors (or former employees and directors) which do not provide special benefits for directors or former directors.

Overall, Model Article 14 provides for fairly limited circumstances in which an interested director will automatically be able to participate in a meeting for quorum and voting purposes. It is common in small private companies (particularly where the directors and shareholders are the same people), for the articles to allow directors to participate provided that the necessary declarations of interest have been made. This avoids a situation where the directors have to revert to the shareholders for authorisation when the directors and shareholders are the same people. The standard articles used by solicitors and formation agents usually have provisions to this effect.

Breach of duty

An obvious question that arises from a discussion of the seven codified directors' duties is what happens if a director breaches one of them? Section 178 of the Companies Act states that the consequence for a breach (or a threatened breach) of any of the duties is the same as would apply to a breach of the common law rule or equitable principle that the relevant duty is derived from. As such, the remedies that a court might grant will depend on the circumstances of each case but could either be:

- an 'injunction' to prevent the director from taking or continuing to take a specified action, or alternatively requiring the director to take a specified action;
- the 'setting aside' of a relevant transaction (un-doing the transaction);
- an order requiring the director to make an 'account of profits' to the company (handing over to the company a sum equal to the profit the director has made in breach of his duties); or
- an order requiring the director to restore property to the company.

Who can bring a claim for breach of the statutory duties?

A director owes his duty to the company, which means that when a director breaches any of them, it is the company that is wronged and therefore the company that must take action. Of course, the company has no means of acting on its own, so any action the company takes would need to be instigated by the directors themselves. The directors may be prepared to bring a claim against one of their number, but if the directors as a whole are in breach it is unlikely that they will bring a claim against themselves. Accordingly the law provides two possible avenues for aggrieved shareholders to seek redress. These are a 'derivative claim' and a claim for 'unfair prejudice'.

Derivative claims

A derivative claim is defined in s. 260 of the Companies Act as 'a claim brought by a member of a company in respect of a cause of action vested in the company, and seeking relief on behalf of the company'. Such claims can be brought in respect of an actual or proposed act or omission involving negligence, default, breach of duty or breach of trust by a director. There is no qualification requirement that the member holds a certain percentage of shares in the company or holds a certain percentage of the voting rights – a derivative claim can be brought by any shareholder of the company. It also doesn't matter if the cause of action arose before that person actually became a shareholder of the company.

The procedure for bringing a derivative claim involves an initial vetting process where the court must consider whether to allow the claim to go ahead. The shareholder must be refused permission to continue if:

- a person acting in accordance with s. 172 of the Act (duty to promote the success of the company) would not seek to continue the claim; or
- where the cause of action arises from an act or omission that is yet to occur, that act or omission has been authorised by the company; or
- where the cause of action arises from an act or omission that has already occurred, that the act or omission was authorised by the company before it occurred, or has been 'ratified' by the company after it occurred.

Helpful hints: ratification

Ratification is the retrospective approval or validation of the acts of a company's directors. Ratification of an act of a director amounting to negligence, default, breach of duty or breach of trust in relation to the company must be carried out in accordance with s. 239 of the Companies Act. Under s. 239, ratification requires an ordinary resolution of the company's shareholders. If the director whose act is to be ratified is also a shareholder of the company, then he will not be permitted to vote on the resolution to ratify it; neither will any shareholder who is connected with him. Where a director's act has been ratified by the company, this will prevent a derivative claim from being brought in respect of that act.

The Companies Act sets out a list of factors that the court must have particular regard to in considering whether to allow a derivative claim, including whether:

- the member is acting in good faith;
- the act or omission in question could, or is likely to be, approved or ratified by the company; and
- whether the member could pursue the claim in their own right rather than on behalf of the company.

If the member succeeds in establishing a *prima facie* case, the court will then consider the evidence of both the shareholder and the company before deciding whether to allow the claim to continue. This vetting process is intended to prevent time and money being spent on frivolous or vexatious claims or claims that have no chance of success and to date appears to be working effectively.

Unfair prejudice

Section 994 of the Companies Act provides a mechanism by which a shareholder can apply to court for an order that the company's affairs either are being, or have been, conducted in a manner that is unfairly prejudicial to the interests of the company's shareholders generally, or some part of its shareholders, including, at least, the shareholder making the application. Unfair prejudice is not defined in the Act, but examples of where the courts have upheld claims of unfair prejudice include the range of possible breaches of directors' fiduciary duties such as:

- misappropriation of company assets;
- improper use of directors' powers;
- making secret profits; and
- taking advantage of a corporate opportunity without disclosing it to the company.

A key difference between a derivative claim and a claim for unfair prejudice is that derivative claims are brought by a shareholder for and on behalf of the company. Claims for unfair prejudice are brought by shareholders in their own right. The remedies that a court can grant are set out in s. 996(1) and include:

- an order requiring the company to do, or refrain from doing, a specified act;
- an order authorising civil proceedings to be brought in the name of the company by such persons or persons and on such terms as the court directs; and
- an order for purchase of the shares of any shareholders of the company by other shareholders or by the company itself. (This is the most common outcome.)

Other restrictions on directors

Aside from the seven codified duties there are two other important restrictions on directors in the Companies Act that arise from their fiduciary relationship with the company. These relate to loans by a company to a director and certain transactions known as 'substantial property transactions'.

Loans to directors

A loan by a company to a director could expose the company to financial risk or could result in a loss to the company if the terms of the loan are too favourable. The Companies Act places a general prohibition on loans to directors unless the loan (and its terms) has been approved by the company's shareholders. This also applies to a guarantee or security given by the company in respect of a loan made to a director by a third party. If the director is a director of the company's holding company, then a resolution of the holding company's shareholders is also required. Before the resolution is passed, details about the loan must be made available to the shareholders in the form of a memorandum. This must set out:

- the nature of the transaction;
- the amount of the loan and the purpose for which it is required; and

- the extent of the company's liability under any transaction connected with the loan.

If the resolution is proposed by way of a resolution in writing, the memorandum must be sent to each shareholder entitled to vote on it either before, or at the same time as, the written resolution. If the resolution is to be proposed at a general meeting, the memorandum must be made available for inspection at the company's registered office for a period of at least 15 days ending with the date of the meeting and be available for inspection at the meeting itself.

The Companies Act also includes similar rules in relation to 'quasi-loans' made to directors and 'credit transactions' with directors which also apply to a director's connected persons. A quasi loan refers to an arrangement whereby the company agrees to pay a director's creditor on the basis that the director will repay the company at some later date. These rules will only apply to a private company if it is associated with a public company. For this purpose two companies are associated if one is a subsidiary of the other, or if both are subsidiaries of the same holding company.

Exceptions
Shareholder approval is not needed in the case of:

- a loan that does not exceed £10,000;
- funds advanced to a director in respect of expenditure incurred (or that will be incurred) for the purposes of the company or for enabling him to perform his duties (up to a maximum amount of £50,000);
- a loan made by a company to a director in the ordinary course of the company's business on the same terms as would be offered to a person of the same financial standing who is unconnected with the company.

Approval is also not needed for a company to lend money to a director to fund his defence of any criminal or civil claim brought against him in connection with any alleged negligence, default, breach of duty or breach of trust by him in relation to the company. This is on the condition that the terms of the loan require the director to repay the company in the event that the defence is unsuccessful.

If a loan that requires shareholder approval is not so approved, then subject to certain limitations, the company has the right to treat the loan as void. Whether the company decides to void the loan or not, the director who received the loan and any other director of the company who authorised it are liable to account to the company for any gain made directly or indirectly as a result of the transaction.

Substantial property transactions
The rules on substantial property transactions are concerned with the acquisition of non-cash assets by a director from the company, or the acquisition by the company of non-cash assets from a director. Their aim is to prevent transfers of assets for less than their fair value or more than their fair value, depending

on whether the asset is being sold to, or by, the company. The relevant provisions are set out in ss. 190 to 196 of the Companies Act. The general rule is that a company cannot enter into an agreement for the sale of a substantial non-cash asset to a director, or the acquisition of a substantial non-cash asset from a director unless:

- the company's shareholders have passed an ordinary resolution to approve it; or
- the arrangement is conditional on such approval being obtained.

The possibility for the arrangement to be entered into on condition of shareholder approval allows the parties to go ahead when time is of the essence. As the word 'substantial' implies, minor transactions do not come within the scope of the rules and a transaction will only be substantial if the value of the asset:

- exceeds 10% of the company's asset value, such percentage being more than £5,000; or
- exceeds £100,000.

The rules also apply to arrangements with any person who is connected with a director of a company and arrangements between a company and a director of its holding company, or any person connected with a director of its holding company. However a transaction between a company and a director in his capacity as a shareholder of the company is excluded, as is a transaction between a holding company and its wholly-owned subsidiary and two wholly-owned subsidiaries of the same holding company.

A 'non-cash asset' means property of any kind so it is important to consider whether the rules apply whenever any transaction between a director and the company is being contemplated. That said, the rules do not apply to any entitlements a director has under his service contract or any payments for loss of office (the latter also requiring shareholder approval in certain circumstances). If shareholder approval for a substantial property transaction is not obtained then, subject to certain exceptions, the company has the right to treat the transaction as void. In any event, the director or connected person is liable to account to the company for any gain that they have made and to indemnify the company for any loss or damage that it has suffered. This could be relevant, for example, in an insolvency situation where the liquidator seeks to enforce any rights or claims that the insolvent company has against its directors.

Personal liability for a company's debts

One of the main advantages of running a business as a limited company is that the debts of the business are the company's debts. Hence, most of the time, the directors of a company should not face any personal liability for them. However, there are two main situations in which this may not be the case – first, if a director has personally guaranteed a loan or any debt of the company, and second, in certain circumstances when a company has become insolvent.

Personal guarantees

If a director personally guarantees a debt, then provided the guarantee is enforceable, the director will be liable under its terms should the company be unable to satisfy the repayment on its own. See the more detailed explanation in Chapter 1.

Liabilities on insolvency

The Insolvency Act 1986 creates two causes of action by which a director can be made to contribute to the assets of an insolvent company. These are:

- wrongful trading; and
- fraudulent trading.

In addition, a director can be liable to a company for any act coming under the general heading of 'misfeasance'.

These are explained in Chapter 17.

Officers in default

As mentioned elsewhere in this chapter, the Companies Act places numerous obligations on companies and their directors and, in the majority of cases, failure to comply with such obligations is a criminal offence on the part of the company and any officer who is 'in default'. Section 1121 of the Act sets out what this means. An officer is 'in default' in respect of a contravention of a rule or obligation in the Act if:

he authorises or permits, participates in, or fails to take all reasonable steps to prevent, the contravention.

An officer includes any director, manager or secretary and any person who is to be treated as an officer of the company for the purposes of the provision in question. Although most of the offences attach to the company and every officer in default, some offences, such as the failure to file accounts with the Registrar of Companies apply to the directors alone.

At the time that the Companies Act was given Royal Assent it was the longest piece of legislation ever to have passed through parliament. This gives some clue as to the number of criminal offences that it contains. For almost every obligation created by the Act there is a corresponding offence for officers in default. Below are just a small number of the requirements in the Act where failure to comply is an offence:

- keep adequate accounting records;
- file an Annual Return with the Registrar of Companies during each 12-month period;

- keep and maintain registers with details of the company's directors, directors' residential addresses, members and any charges over the company's assets;
- maintain other company records including members' resolutions and records of directors' decisions;
- keep all company records available for inspection and comply with any proper requests to inspect or to be provided with copies;
- make proper trading disclosures;
- comply with all requirements to make returns of information to the Registrar of Companies such as on appointment or resignation of a director or secretary, allotment of shares, change of registered office address, alteration of share capital, adoption or amendment of articles of association and so on; and
- comply with procedural requirements regarding meetings of the company's shareholders and written resolutions.

The risk of prosecution

What is the likelihood of being prosecuted for committing any of the Companies Act offences? More prosecutions are brought against directors for the failure to file accounts than for any other offence, closely followed by the failure to file annual returns. Prosecutions for these offences are instigated by Companies House and are more common than might be thought. Companies House releases statistics each year on its website that show the number of prosecutions brought in the previous year and the number of these that were successful. The issue of proceedings does not mean that a conviction is certain and all directors have the chance to put their case to the court. Needless to say, professional advice in this situation is highly advisable.

What about some of the other offences? If a company fails to keep a register of directors, how is anyone going to know this, or complain about it and how could that lead to a prosecution? This is a fair question and the answer is that a prosecution for an individual offence of this sort is unlikely to be brought by either Companies House or the other main enforcing body, the Department for Business Innovation and Skills (BIS). If a prosecution is brought it would be more likely to be a private prosecution instigated by an aggrieved shareholder. Although the fines for transgression of the smaller and more technical requirements of the Companies Act may not be particularly significant, the more damaging consequence for a director is the stigma of a criminal conviction. In addition, the failure to comply with any of the (seemingly) lesser obligations in the Act could add weight to a claim for breach of one of the codified duties such as the duty to act with reasonable skill, care and diligence. It can also be a contributory factor in action being taken against a director for disqualification – see further below.

Bringing breaches to light

The ways in which the conduct of a company's directors can be brought to light include the following.

Complaints to Companies House

Where a company is in default of an obligation to file a document with the Registrar of Companies, s. 1113 of the Companies Act provides that a member or creditor of the company, or the Registrar of Companies himself, can issue a notice to the company requiring it to make good the default. If the company fails to comply within 14 days, the Registrar, member or creditor can apply to the court for an order directing the company or a specified officer of the company to take the appropriate corrective action within a specified time frame. Orders of this sort are treated as a failure to comply with an obligation to file information with the Registrar, for the purposes of s. 3 of the Company Directors' Disqualification Act 1986 – see below.

Insolvent companies

The question of whether a director generally complies with his obligations under the Companies Act can become an issue if a company becomes insolvent. When an insolvency practitioner is appointed as the liquidator or administrator of an insolvent company, he or she has a duty to report on the conduct of the company's directors to the Secretary of State. This would include reporting on the extent to which the directors have breached any of the codified duties and have failed to comply with their obligations under the Act. Investigation following insolvency is the most common way for a director's conduct to receive the attentions of the enforcing authorities.

Company investigations

Broader still, where a company behaves dishonestly or incompetently towards its customers, or appears to be in serious breach of the Companies Act or any other legislation, it may result in an enquiry into the company's affairs by the Companies Investigation Branch (CIB) of BIS. The CIB has power to investigate companies where it considers an investigation to be in the public interest. This might be as a result of information received from the general public, the police, Trading Standards or from another regulator. Although relatively uncommon (when compared with the number of complaints that the CIB actually receives) investigations by the CIB can result in the company being made subject to a compulsory winding-up order, or in proceedings being brought by other regulatory bodies against the company's directors.

Disqualification

It has long been the case that, as a matter of principle and public policy, the law should not allow reckless or dishonest directors to abuse the privilege of limited liability. This is enshrined in law in the Company Directors' Disqualification Act 1986 (CDDA). Disqualification is a key sanction against directors and enables a person to be prevented from acting as a director for a specified period of time.

Under s. 1 of the CDDA, the effect of a disqualification order is to prohibit a person from:

- being a director of a company;
- acting as a receiver of a company's property; and
- in any way, whether directly or indirectly, being concerned or taking part in the promotion, formation or management of a company,

except with the leave of the court. A disqualification order also prohibits the person from acting as an insolvency practitioner (with no possibility of relief from the court). The CDDA sets out the circumstances in which a disqualification order can be made. In some cases disqualification is compulsory and in others it is discretionary.

Compulsory disqualification

The court must make a disqualification order in the following situations:

- where a person has been a director of a company which has become insolvent and the court is satisfied that his conduct as a director of that company makes him unfit to be concerned in the management of a company (s. 6); and
- where a person is a director of a company which commits a breach of competition law and the court considers that his conduct as a director makes him unfit to be concerned in the management of a company (s. 9A).

Where a director is found to be unfit as a result of his conduct in relation to an insolvent company, the minimum period of disqualification is two years and the maximum period is 15 years. For unfitness in relation to a company that has breached competition law, there is no minimum period of disqualification, with the maximum also being 15 years. The question of how a court determines whether a director is 'unfit' is explained further below.

Discretionary disqualification

The court has the power to make a disqualification order in the following circumstances but is not necessarily obliged to do so.

Indictable offences (s. 2)

This section applies where a person is convicted of an indictable offence in connection with the promotion, formation, management, liquidation or striking off of a company, or with the receivership or management of a company's property. An indictable offence is one that has to be tried by jury in a crown court. The maximum period of disqualification is 15 years.

Failure to file information (s. 3)

Where it appears to a court that a person has been persistently in default in relation to any provisions of company law requiring returns, accounts, other documents or notice of any matter to be filed with the Registrar of Companies, he can be disqualified for a period of up to five years. Although it can be proved in any other way, the requirements of this section are satisfied by showing that in the previous five years, the person has been adjudged guilty of three or more defaults. Defaults include any convictions and any default orders such as those made under s. 1113 of the Companies Act, explained earlier.

Fraud (s. 4)
Where a person has been guilty of the offence of fraudulent trading (whether or not he has been convicted) under s. 993 of the Companies Act, or has otherwise been guilty of any fraud in relation to the company or any breach of his duty, he can be disqualified for up to 15 years.

Summary offences (s. 5)
This section applies to summary offences for the contravention of any provision of company law requiring returns, accounts, other documents or notice of any matter to be filed with the Registrar of Companies. A summary offence is an offence that can normally only be tried in a magistrates' court. Where a person is convicted of an offence caught by this section the court can make an order for disqualification if the person has had made against him, or has been convicted of, in total, not less than three default orders and other such summary offences. Disqualification under this section can be for a period of up to five years.

Conduct uncovered on investigation (s. 8)
This section is concerned with the conduct of a director of a company that is revealed by the exercise of specified powers of investigation. Where the court is satisfied that the conduct makes the person unfit to be concerned in the management of a company, the court can disqualify him for a period of up to 15 years.

Wrongful trading and fraudulent trading (s. 10)
Where a court makes a declaration that a person is liable to contribute to a company's assets in connection with the offence of fraudulent trading or wrongful trading (under ss. 213 or 214 of the Insolvency Act 1986) the court can make an order for disqualification of that person for a maximum period of 15 years.

Determining 'unfitness'
When considering whether a person should be disqualified on the grounds of unfitness, the CDDA sets out specific matters that a court must have regard to. Among others, the matters that apply to unfitness under s. 6 (compulsory disqualification for conduct in relation to an insolvent company) and unfitness under s. 8 (discretionary disqualification for conduct uncovered in the course of an investigation) include:

- any misfeasance or breach of any fiduciary or other duty including the codified duties set out in the Companies Act;
- the extent of the director's responsibility for any failure by the company to comply with specified provisions of the Companies Act which include those relating to the requirements to keep statutory registers, to file annual returns and to notify the Registrar of Companies of changes to directors and secretaries; and
- the extent of the director's responsibility for any failure by the directors of the company to prepare and approve annual accounts and for the accounts to include the name of the person signing the balance sheet and directors' report.

The Act also sets out additional matters that must be considered in relation to determining unfitness under s. 6, among which are:

- the extent of the director's responsibility for the causes of the company becoming insolvent;
- the extent of the director's responsibility for any failure by the company to supply any goods or services which have been paid for in whole or in part; and
- any failure by the director to comply with specified provisions of the Insolvency Act 1986.

Unfitness in relation to breaches of competition law is determined by the criteria set out in s. 9A(6) which concern the director's contribution to, or knowledge of, the breach.

Undischarged bankrupts

In addition to the provisions relating to disqualification, the CDDA also makes it a criminal offence for a person to act as a director of a company or to directly or indirectly take part in or be concerned in the promotion, formation or management of a company without the leave of the court at a time when:

- he is an undischarged bankrupt;
- a moratorium under a debt relief order applies in relation to him; or
- a bankruptcy restrictions order or a debt relief restrictions order is in force in respect of him.

Breach of a disqualification order

A director who acts in contravention of a disqualification order is liable to imprisonment of up to two years and/or a fine. Furthermore, he is also personally liable for any debts of the company incurred during the period in which he was involved in the management of the company. Any person who acts on the instructions of the disqualified director (knowing them to be disqualified) is also liable for any debts of the company incurred during the period in which he was so acting.

Disqualification undertakings

If the Secretary of State believes that it is expedient and in the public interest to do so, he can accept a 'disqualification undertaking' from a director instead of seeking a disqualification order from the court. The effect of a disqualification undertaking is the same as that of a disqualification order and the consequences of contravention are also the same. The option for the Secretary of State to accept a disqualification undertaking is not available in all cases, only in relation to disqualification under the following sections of the CDDA:

- s. 6 – unfitness in relation to an insolvent company;
- s. 8 – unfitness based on conduct uncovered in the course of an investigation; and
- s. 9A – unfitness in relation to a breach of competition law.

The Secretary of State is required to maintain a central register of those persons who are disqualified under the CDDA, either by way of a disqualification order or a disqualification undertaking. This record is kept by Companies House and can be searched from the WebCheck section of the website.

▦ Obligations under other legislation

Directors must be aware of the application of a wide range of other laws and regulations including (but not limited to):

- health and safety;
- employment matters such as the national minimum wage, working hours, and discrimination;
- data protection;
- environmental protection;
- competition;
- tax;
- financial services;
- consumer credit;
- consumer rights; and
- bribery and corruption.

One of the challenges for directors is to make themselves aware of the regulations that apply to their business and take the appropriate steps to ensure compliance. This is a risk-management issue and is something that should be addressed by a company's risk-management system. Health and safety regulations are discussed in Chapter 15, but as regards any of the other areas of law mentioned above (and any that aren't mentioned) the question arises as to how a director will know what rules and regulations apply to his company and what rules are out there that he may not be aware of. Unfortunately there are no short cuts to achieving this. There are many books on the subject of business law and, in addition, an internet search will reveal a number of training providers who run courses for company directors. A professional can help with any areas of specific concern or can carry out a more general 'health check' to ascertain whether the company is complying with its various obligations. Alternatively, or in addition, smaller businesses may wish to consider joining the Federation for Small Businesses, which offers support and a range of services to its members including legal news and updates on changes in employment, taxation and business law (see the FSB website at www.fsb.org.uk). Some other possible support frameworks for a company and its directors are considered in Chapter 18.

■ Indemnities and insurance

With the range of duties and liabilities that they are subject to directors may want to look at the ways in which they can protect themselves against their financial liabilities. There are two possible options: an indemnity from the company and a form of insurance known as directors and officers' liability insurance. The articles of association of most companies will allow the company to provide directors with indemnities and will allow the company to purchase insurance for them. Articles 52 and 53 in the Model Articles deal with these matters respectively. However, note the use of the word 'may' in article 52 – a director 'may' be indemnified out of the company's assets – meaning that the company is not obliged to provide an indemnity.

Indemnities

An indemnity by a company is a kind of insurance in which the company agrees to settle certain liabilities of a director in the event of a claim against him. However a company cannot indemnify a director in respect of their liability to the company, but only in respect of their liability to third parties. Even then, the company is not permitted to indemnify the director in respect of:

- a fine imposed in criminal proceedings;
- a penalty imposed by a regulatory authority;
- the costs of defending criminal proceedings which result in the director being convicted;
- the costs of defending civil proceedings brought by the company in which judgement is given against the director; and
- certain procedures in the Companies Act that allow a director to apply to court for relief from liability.

Indemnities need to be approached carefully, both in terms of their drafting and the general policy considerations involved in deciding whether to grant them. Details of indemnities are required to be disclosed in a company's annual report and they must also be available for inspection by shareholders. Professional advice is essential.

Directors and officers' liability insurance

The Companies Act permits a company to buy and maintain insurance for its directors with no restrictions on the liabilities that can be covered. In practice, however, policies of this sort will not usually cover fines and penalties in criminal proceedings or liabilities where the director is found guilty of fraud or dishonesty, among other matters. As with any form of insurance careful attention needs to be paid to the exclusions and the extent of cover provided. Professional advice is needed.

Helpful hints: advice for directors

The ministerial statements released by the DTI in June 2007 (in relation to the codified duties of directors in the Companies Act) included this very good advice for directors.

- Act in the company's best interests, taking everything you think relevant into account.
- Obey the company's constitution and decisions taken under it.
- Be honest, and remember that the company's property belongs to it and not to you or to its shareholders.
- Be diligent, careful and well informed about the company's affairs. If you have any special skills or experience, use them.
- Make sure the company keeps records of your decisions.
- Remember that you remain responsible for the work you give to others.
- Avoid situations where your interests conflict with those of the company. When in doubt disclose potential conflicts quickly.
- Seek external advice where necessary, particularly if the company is in financial difficulty.

Summary

- The Companies Act codifies seven general duties of directors that previously existed only in the common law.
- Directors must act in accordance with the codified duties and more than one duty may apply in any given situation.
- The Companies Act states that the consequences of breaching a duty are the same as they would be for breaching the common law rule on which each duty is based and could include an injunction, an account of profits and the setting aside of a particular transaction.
- In the event of a breach it is the company that is wronged. A shareholder can bring a claim against the directors on behalf of the company. This is known as a derivative claim.

- If the actions of the directors amount to conduct that is unfairly prejudicial, an aggrieved shareholder may bring a claim for unfair prejudice.
- Substantial transactions between a director and a company and loans from a company to a director above a specified amount are subject to approval by shareholders.
- Directors are not normally liable for a company's debts, but can be liable in certain circumstances (i.e. if they have personally guaranteed a loan, or in respect of certain offences under insolvency law).
- The Companies Act places many obligations on directors and in most cases failure to comply is an offence.
- Prosecutions for any of the more technical obligations in the Companies Act may be relatively rare but breaches of the Act can become relevant in other situations.
- A key sanction against directors is disqualification under the Company Directors' Disqualification Act 1986. Disqualification is either compulsory or discretionary, depending on the circumstances.
- Besides the Companies Act and the Insolvency Act, directors have responsibilities for ensuring compliance with a wide range of other legislation.
- Directors can protect themselves against some of the financial implications of a claim against them by way of an indemnity from the company or under a directors and officers' liability insurance policy.

8 Decision-making by directors

In this chapter

This chapter explains the rules and procedures for decision-making by directors with regard to:

- collective decision making;
- the procedure for holding a directors' meeting, including quorum, voting and directors' interests;
- decisions by unanimous agreement;
- decision making by a sole director;
- minutes and records of directors' decisions;
- the power of the board and others to bind the company in contracts and transactions; and
- executing contracts and other documents on behalf of the company.

Directors' decision-making

It was noted in both Chapter 1 and Chapter 6 that the directors take their authority to run the company from the company's articles. It is important to understand that the authority that the articles give to the directors is bestowed upon them not as individuals but as a unit. Directors must exercise their decision-making powers *collectively*. The directors can (provided the company's articles allow) delegate their powers and functions to a board committee, an individual director or such other persons as they see fit, but such delegation needs to be appropriate and considered. As a principle of good governance, the directors should always take important or major decisions together and no one director should have unfettered powers. Delegation by directors is explained later in this chapter in relation to the power of directors and others to bind a company.

There is no law or regulation that sets out how often the directors of a company must meet in a full board meeting; this will vary from one company to another. Arrangements in larger companies are likely to be more structured, in smaller companies they may be less so. In larger companies, the directors may fix dates in advance for their meetings (e.g. the first Tuesday of each month). Directors of smaller private companies may just hold meetings as and when they need to. It is not the case that directors must always take their decisions at formal board meetings and the Model Articles allow for alternative methods that better reflect what many small companies actually do. Nevertheless, board meetings have a key role in enabling directors to keep abreast of and discuss matters concerning the company, particularly its financial position, which is essential if they are to fulfil their duties to the company.

▇ Rules for directors' decision making

The rules on how directors must make their decisions are not set out in the Companies Act, so have to be included in a company's articles of association. The Model Articles provide for two methods by which directors can make decisions. These are:

- by a majority decision at a meeting; or
- by a unanimous decision in accordance with Model Article 8.

The articles set out the relevant rules and procedure in each case. Subject to these rules, Model Article 16 provides that the directors can make any rule which they think fit about how they take decisions, and about how such rules are to be recorded or communicated to directors. This means that directors must follow the rules in the articles, but are free to make any additional rules that they want and to decide how any additional rules are recorded and communicated (e.g. by way of a meetings handbook).

▇ Meetings

It is important that board meetings are held in accordance with the rules set out in whatever articles a company has adopted. For most companies, the procedure will be similar and for companies that have adopted the Model Articles without amendment, the procedure for calling and holding a board meeting is as follows.

Calling a board meeting

Calling a board meeting is sometimes referred to as 'convening' a board meeting. Model Article 9 states that any director can call a directors' meeting by giving notice to the directors or by authorising the company secretary (if there is one) to give such notice. Any notice must give the proposed date and time of the meeting, the location where it is to take place and if the directors will not be in the same place, the means by which the directors will communicate with each other during the meeting. Although it should probably go without saying, Model Article 9(3) states that the notice must be given to each director. Such notice need not be in writing but if it is, it may make it easier to address any later disputes as to whether the notice was actually given.

The Model Articles do not say how much notice has to be given of a board meeting. Is three or four days sufficient for example, or should at least a week's notice be given? The common law requires that notice be 'reasonable'. What is or is not reasonable will depend on the circumstances and on the established practice of a particular company. It is important to bear in mind that, since directors' decision-making should be collective, a director's ability to attend a board meeting should not be impeded by giving unreasonably short notice.

Helpful hints: communications with directors

The Model Articles specify that any notice or document to be sent or supplied to a director in connection with any decision making by directors can be sent or supplied by any means by which the director has asked to be sent or supplied with such notices or documents (article 48(2)). This means that directors are free to stipulate how they want to receive information and documents sent by the company in connection with decisions of the board. When a director asks to be provided with notices or documents in a particular way, article 48(3) allows the director and the company to agree when any such communications will be deemed to have been received by him, which can be less than 48 hours from the time of sending. This therefore allows for alteration of the default position on deemed delivery set out in s. 1147 of the Companies Act, in relation to documents or information sent to that director (for more on the 'deemed delivery' rules and company communications in general see Chapter 12).

It is prudent for directors to agree on the means of communication that they will use, both in the company's communications with them and in their communications with each other. In small companies, this can be done with little need for formality. In larger companies, it may be desirable to have a written policy.

Agenda

Although not required by the Companies Act or by the Model Articles, it is good practice to send an agenda setting out the items of business to be considered at the meeting together with the notice. The agenda should be accompanied by any papers or documentation that the directors need to read in advance. As well as enabling the directors to participate fully in discussions at the meeting, this should also alert them to any interests they may have in the proposed business that they need to declare in accordance with s. 177 of the Companies Act (see Chapter 7).

Participating in a board meeting

It may not always be possible for directors to be in the same place for the purposes of holding a board meeting. For this reason, Model Article 10 clarifies when a director will be considered to be participating in a directors' meeting. This is important because a certain number of directors must participate in a meeting in order for the meeting to be *quorate* (see below).

Under Model Article 10(1), directors participate in a board meeting when the meeting has been properly convened in accordance with the articles and the directors can each communicate to the others any information or opinions they have on any particular item of the business of the meeting. Model Article 10(2) adds that it is irrelevant where any director is or how they communicate with each other. This means that a director can attend a board meeting by way of telephone conference, video link or any other means of communication. The key point is that the director must be able to hear and be heard by the other directors so as to be able to effectively take part in the meeting.

Quorum

A 'quorum' is the minimum number of directors that must participate in a board meeting in order for any decisions taken at the meeting to be valid. The quorum is always specified in the articles of association and may vary from company to company but can never be less than two (as far as the common law is concerned, a meeting with just one director present cannot be a meeting except for companies with a sole director – see further below). Model Article 11(2) states that:

- the quorum for directors' meetings may be fixed from time to time by a decision of the directors;
- it cannot be less than two; and
- unless the directors decide otherwise, it is two.

So, for companies with the Model Articles unamended, the quorum for board meetings is two directors, but this can be changed by a decision of the directors (i.e. at a properly convened board meeting or by unanimous agreement under Model Article 8). If it is changed, then it would be advisable to record this in any 'meetings handbook' issued to directors under Model Article 16. You may note here that the directors are permitted to change the quorum without changing the articles of association. This means that there will be no public notice of the change and the directors should notify their professional advisors or they will be unaware of it.

Whether or not a quorum is present remains relevant throughout the whole length of any board meeting (e.g. if one director has to leave the meeting and the number of remaining directors is less than the quorum, then the meeting cannot continue). Similarly, issues can arise if a particular director is not eligible to vote on a certain item of business to be considered. This might be the case if a director has a conflict of interest of the sort contemplated by s. 175 of the Companies Act

which, although it has been authorised by the other directors, has been authorised on the condition that the director cannot either participate in or form part of
the quorum of any meeting, or part of any meeting, at which that item of business
is discussed. If a quorum is not present for a particular item of business then any
decision taken on it will not be valid.

If the company's total number of directors falls below the quorum required for
a board meeting (e.g. as a result of the resignation of director) then Model Article
11(3) says that the directors must not take any decision other than a decision to
appoint further directors or to call a general meeting so as to enable the shareholders to appoint further directors.

Chairman

As with any formal meeting, it is normal for the proceedings of a directors'
meeting to be conducted by a chairman. Model Article 12(1) states that the directors may appoint a director to chair their meetings and Model Article 12(3) states
that the chairman's appointment may be terminated by the directors at any time.

The chairman's role is to conduct the board meeting in an orderly manner
and to take the meeting through each item to be discussed or considered. On each
item requiring the board's approval, the chairman should formally propose a resolution to the meeting, record the votes for and against and declare the resolution
as being carried or defeated.

The chairman has a position of power since Model Article 13 gives the
chairman a casting vote if the numbers of votes for and against a particular
proposal are equal. Under Model Article 13(2), if the person chairing a meeting is
not eligible to be counted in the quorum for voting purposes in respect of a particular item of business, then they will not have a casting vote. For this reason it is
important to be clear about who the chairman is at any one time. The appointment, termination or resignation of the chairman should always be properly
recorded in the minutes of the relevant board meeting (see below for more about
minutes).

Under Model Article 12(4), if the chairman is not participating in a board
meeting within ten minutes of the start time, then the other participating directors must appoint one director from among them to chair it.

Voting

Decisions of the board are known as 'resolutions'. Subject to the articles, a resolution is passed at a formal meeting of the directors when a majority of directors
vote in favour of it. Each director has one vote, apart from the chairman who
has a casting vote when the number of votes for and against a resolution is equal
(provided that the chairman is eligible to vote on the resolution himself). It is
important to remember that only the directors can vote. A company secretary or a
professional advisor, if not also a director, cannot vote.

It is also important to bear in mind that sometimes a director may not be eligible to vote on a particular matter because they have a direct or indirect interest in it. At the commencement of each board meeting the directors should each declare whether they have any interest in the business to be considered at the meeting that they have not previously declared, and should update any previous declarations they have made if they are no longer accurate. This is in accordance with their duty under s. 177 of the Companies Act which is explained in Chapter 7. The company's articles must be checked for provisions relating to directors' interests in transactions because, for example, article 14 of the Model Articles states that if a director has an interest in a transaction he will not be able to participate in the decision-making except in certain limited circumstances or unless shareholder approval has been given. In addition, if a director has a situational conflict of interest of the sort contemplated by s. 175 of the Act and which the other directors have authorised, the terms of the authorisation may require that director to refrain from participating in meetings or such part of a meeting that concerns the matter giving rise to his conflict. See Chapter 7 for more.

■ Written resolutions and decisions by unanimous agreement

The articles of association of most companies will allow the directors to take decisions by way of 'resolutions in writing' (also known as 'written resolutions'). A written resolution is a document setting out matters that are proposed to be resolved by the directors which is then circulated to all of the directors for each director to sign, thereby confirming their agreement. The resolutions are passed when all directors have signed. Written resolutions can be useful because they allow the directors to make decisions without actually having to convene and hold a formal board meeting.

Model Article 8 expands on the concept of a written resolution by broadening it to encompass any and all 'unanimous decisions' of the directors. A decision of the directors is taken in accordance with Model Article 8 'when all eligible directors indicate to each other by any means that they share a common view on a matter'. The 'any means' referred to can include a resolution in writing (as specified in Model Article 8(2)) but could also include e-mail and potentially even a text message.

It is advisable for the directors to determine, utilising their power under Model Article 16, by what means unanimous decisions can be taken and also to determine the mechanics of how each director's agreement to the proposed resolutions is to be communicated to the others. For example, if a unanimous decision were to be proposed by e-mail, each director could reply with their response, copying in each of the company's other directors.

It is important to remember that decisions taken in this way must be unanimous and also that the same rules concerning a director's eligibility to vote that apply to formal board meetings also apply to unanimous decisions. Proper records of such decisions must also be kept – see further below. Model Article 8(3) states that references to 'eligible directors' means directors who would have been entitled to vote on the matter had it been proposed as a resolution at a directors' meeting. Therefore, a director who would be excluded from voting on a particular resolution at a board meeting because of a conflict of interest or for any other reason, would also be excluded from voting on the same resolution if proposed by way of a unanimous decision. If the number of directors eligible to vote on a unanimous decision would not have formed a quorum at a formal board meeting then the decision cannot be taken, or if taken, will be invalid.

When is a unanimous decision actually taken?

The Model Articles do not say explicitly when a resolution proposed in accordance with article 8 will actually have been passed (e.g. if a decision is proposed by way of a resolution in writing, there may be a delay of a few days before all eligible directors respond). Since decisions under article 8 must be unanimous, a resolution proposed in this way will not be passed until the last eligible director has indicated their agreement. As well as determining how they are to communicate their agreement to a unanimous decision (using their power under Model Article 16) the directors may also wish to clarify to whom it should be communicated (e.g. in a company with a company secretary, it might fall to the company secretary to co-ordinate unanimous decisions and to then confirm to the directors when the resolution has been passed).

Sole directors

As private companies are only required to have one director it follows that a sole director should be able to act on his own; in practice this depends on the articles. The articles will state the number of directors that must be present at a board meeting to form a quorum, the standard requirement being two. Unless the articles qualify this provision and permit a sole director to act on his own, then he may not do so and will normally be restricted to taking action only to appoint further directors. Article 7(2) of the Model Articles states that if the company has only one director and no provision of the articles requires it to have more than one director, the sole director may take decisions without regard to any of the provisions of the articles relating to directors' decision making. Since the Model Articles do not require a company to have more than one director, this means that the rules on directors decision making that are set out in the Model Articles do not apply to a sole director, including the quorum requirement. However, it should be noted that a sole director must still act in accordance with the duties and other obligations set out in Companies Act. Similarly, a sole director should also keep a record of his decisions and, if appropriate, the reasons for making them.

▉ Minutes and records

Section 248 of the Companies Act says that all companies must maintain a record of all proceedings at meetings of the company's directors and that such records must be kept for at least ten years from the date of the meeting to which they relate. Details of the proceedings at directors' meetings are normally kept in the form of 'minutes'.

There are no hard-and-fast rules as to how minutes should be written, but generally they take the form of numbered paragraphs (with appropriate sub-sections as required), with each paragraph dealing with a new item of business. In terms of content, minutes of directors' meetings should record at least the following matters:

■ the name of the company and its registered number;
■ the date, time and location of the meeting;
■ the names of the directors participating in the meeting;
■ the means by which any directors not physically present are participating (e.g. by telephone conference);
■ the name of the director chairing the meeting;
■ the names of any other persons in attendance, such as the company secretary or a professional advisor;
■ confirmation that a quorum was present;
■ any declarations of interest made by the directors participating in the meeting;
■ a summary of each matter that was discussed;
■ details of decisions/resolutions proposed to the meeting; and
■ whether such decisions/resolutions were passed.

If any directors or non-directors join or leave the meeting at any point then this should be recorded in the minutes. As mentioned above, this can affect whether a quorum is present in respect of any decisions that are proposed.

Section 249 states that a set of minutes which are authenticated by the chairman of the meeting, or by the chairman of the next directors' meeting, are (until the contrary is proved) evidence of the proceedings at the meeting. It is good practice for a draft set of minutes to be prepared and circulated to all the directors for their comments and then for a final set of minutes to be prepared for signature by the chairman. Once they have been signed the minutes should be kept securely. As a precaution against loss or damage, an electronic copy of all minutes can be kept, although access to them should be restricted to authorised persons.

It is important that minutes of directors' meetings are clear and accurate. They do not need to take the form of a verbatim transcript, but should clearly evidence decisions that the directors have made and the basis on which they made them. This can be particularly important in the event of a dispute between directors or between directors and shareholders and is also important in circumstances where a company might be approaching an insolvency situation. If this happens, the directors must consider whether or not the company can continue to trade and their decisions may ultimately come under the scrutiny of a liquidator (see Chapter 17). Since decisions at a directors' meeting are by majority, it may be the case that one or more directors disagree with a particular resolution or course of action. This should also be recorded in the minutes.

Records of unanimous decisions

The Companies Act does not set out any obligation to keep records of unanimous decisions of the sort made in accordance with Model Article 8. However Model Article 15 states that the directors must ensure that the company keeps a record in writing of every unanimous or majority decision taken by the directors and those records must be kept for at least 10 years from the date of the decision recorded. This, therefore, covers decisions taken at either a traditional board meeting, or unanimous decisions taken in accordance with Model Article 8. For decisions taken under Model Article 8, there is no guidance as to what form the record of the decisions should take. However, the same general principles that apply to board minutes should also apply to records of unanimous decisions, which should therefore record:

- the company name and number;
- the date on which the unanimous decision was taken;
- the names of the directors that were eligible to vote on each proposal;
- confirmation that the eligible directors would have formed a quorum at a directors' meeting in respect of each resolution;
- details of each resolution passed; and
- the means by which the directors communicated their agreement to each other.

In the case of a unanimous decision taken by a resolution in writing (see above), the resolution in writing is itself a sufficient record of the decisions taken. If the directors have signed separate copies of the resolution in writing, then all copies must be retained. Similarly, if the directors have taken a decision by e-mail, it would be advisable to keep a copy of the relevant e-mails together with the formal record of the unanimous decision.

Inspection of records of directors' decisions

Shareholders and members of the public do not have any right to inspect minutes and records of directors' meetings or unanimous decisions.

▨ Follow-up actions

Decisions taken at a directors' meeting or by unanimous agreement may trigger an obligation to update the company's statutory records or to file forms and documents at Companies House. In a company with a company secretary, the secretary will usually be instructed to deal with these matters. In a company without a secretary, the directors must ensure that someone takes responsibility for maintaining and updating the company's records and submitting the appropriate forms or documents to the Registrar of Companies for filing. In addition, any follow-up actions agreed at a meeting should be dealt with by the relevant persons, with a progress review at the next meeting. It can be helpful to include a schedule of any follow-up actions at the end of the minutes.

Company contracts – binding the company

Most contracts that are made in the course of running a business will be made either in the name of the company or on behalf of the company, so that it is the company that enters into the contract and not the directors or anyone else (at least, this should be the intention). This is one advantage of setting up a separate legal entity in comparison to operating as a sole trader (who must always contract in his or her own name). The directors may be responsible for ensuring that the company does or doesn't do certain things under the terms of a particular contract and for complying with their duties to the company as directors, but ultimate liability under a contract rests with the company itself, unless the terms of the contract (or any other side documents) say otherwise.

Contracts and agreements can take many forms. There are contracts that a company may enter into fairly regularly (e.g. for the supply of materials, goods or services that are necessary for the company's business). These will not necessarily be in writing. Then there are contracts and agreements that a company may enter into less often – in respect of a loan or investment, or perhaps the acquisition of the whole or part of another business. In these cases the written agreements are likely to be long and detailed so as to clearly set out all the terms that have been agreed.

When we are thinking about a company entering into a contract, however large or small, there are two main questions to consider:

- does the company have the power to enter into the contract; and if so,
- who has the authority to enter into it on the company's behalf?

The company's authority to enter contracts and agreements

As explained in Chapter 3, the power of a company is governed by the statement of its objects; anything that is not covered by the objects is beyond the powers of the company. So what if the directors commit the company to a contract that is beyond what it is authorised to do? It used to be the case that the contract would be voidable and the company could choose to void the contract but the law has long since recognised how harsh this is from the point of view of a third party. The law changed the position and this change has been carried forward by ss. 39 and 40 of the Companies Act.

The effect of these two sections is to prevent a company from voiding a contract on the grounds that the company or the directors did not have the power to enter into it. Section 39 states that the capacity of the company to do something cannot be challenged by reason of anything in the company's constitution. Of course, most companies formed under the current Companies Act do not have an objects clause and their objects are unrestricted. However, the directors can be restricted in their exercise of the company's powers (e.g. by the company's articles). In this case, s. 40 states that, from the point of view of a third party acting in good faith, the authority of the directors to bind the company, or to authorise others to do so, is deemed to be free of any restriction imposed by the articles, any resolutions of the company's shareholders or any other agreements that form part of the constitution. This means that, generally speaking, a third party dealing with the company does not have to worry about whether an act of the company is beyond its powers or whether the directors are exceeding their authority in committing the company to perform that act. There may be restrictions that the directors should observe, but if they fail to do so, the company will generally still be bound by a party that has contracted with it in good faith and provided that the relevant directors had actual or apparent authority (see below).

This doesn't mean that the restrictions and limitations have no relevance – they do. If the directors act beyond any restrictions placed on the company or placed on them, the company and its shareholders can seek redress from the director concerned.

Who can bind the company? The authority of the board of directors

The board of directors sits at the top of the decision-making hierarchy in any company. As noted earlier, the directors' power to run the company vests in the board as a whole. As such, provided that they act within any restrictions placed on them and act in accordance with their duties and in accordance with the law, the power of the board (acting as a whole) to bind the company in contracts and other agreements is largely unassailable. But does the board have to approve every contract in order for the company to be bound by it?

Delegation

If the articles of association allow, the board can delegate its authority to others. This is essential because it is simply not practical or necessary for every business decision to be made by the board. Article 5 of the Model Articles permits the board of directors to delegate its authority to:

- such persons or committee;
- by such means (including by power of attorney);
- to such an extent;
- in relation to such matters or territories; and
- on such terms and conditions,

as the board sees fit. This means that the board can create one or more committees to deal with certain aspects of the company's business and can delegate specific powers and authorities to individual directors, senior managers, employees or anyone else so that the company can be run in an efficient manner. Each person's role confers on them the powers and authorities that the board wants them to have and in this way, the delegated powers of the board filter down through the company's management chain. The reality is that third parties can and will reasonably expect individual directors, the company secretary, senior managers and employees to be able to contract with them on behalf of the company and for the company to be bound by those contracts. Whether or not a person acting for the company does, in fact, have the authority to bind the company is determined by the principles of agency law.

Agency law

An agent is a person who is authorised by another person – the agent's 'principal' – to act on that person's behalf and to bind them in contracts or agreements with third parties. Agency law is concerned with how and when a principal will be bound by the acts of their agent and this comes down to a question of authority. There are two main types of authority that an agent can have – actual authority or apparent authority.

Actual authority

If a principal specifically authorises an agent to carry out certain tasks or duties, this is known as actual authority. As well as being express, actual authority can also be implied by the agent's position. An example of this is when the board appoints one of their number as 'managing director'. The position of managing director carries with it a wide range of powers and authority that are implicit in that role. Whenever an agent performs an act that is within the ambit of their actual authority (express or implied), the principal will be bound by it. But what if the agent does something that exceeds the authority that has been given to them? This is where the second type of authority comes in.

Apparent authority

Where an agent performs an act that is beyond his actual authority, the law may decide that the principal is still bound because the agent had apparent authority to perform it. Apparent authority can arise in different ways and can be categorised into different types but generally, for an agent to have apparent authority, there must be some kind of representation by the principal that leads a third party to conclude that the agent has the authority to carry out the act that the agent is purporting to perform. The courts take a very broad view of the kind of representations that are sufficient to do this. Things said or done (or not said or done) by the principal, previous dealings that the third party has had with the agent or a person's job title can all give rise to apparent authority. These representations are sometimes referred to as 'holding out'.

If an agent's act comes within the ambit of their apparent authority, the principal will be bound by it unless it can be shown that the third party was aware of a restriction on the agent's authority or if the circumstances were such that they should have put the third party on notice that something was amiss. Actual authority, implied actual authority and the different types of apparent authority can overlap in ways that makes it difficult to distinguish between them. Placed in the context of running a company it all boils down to one key point: people can bind the company even though they haven't been given any actual authority to do so.

The authority of individual directors

Most directors are likely to have a mixture of both actual and apparent authority to bind the company. Actual authority can be bestowed by the company's articles or by resolutions of the board. More usually, a director's authority will be implied by their role or office, if not explicitly set out in their service agreement. All directors have apparent authority to bind the company in respect of contracts or agreements that come within the scope of their particular function within the company. If a director's powers are narrower than might normally be expected of a director in a particular position (because the company has limited them), they may still bind the company (due to having apparent authority) despite the fact that they have exceeded their actual authority to do so.

The authority of the company secretary

The company secretary does not have the same level of authority as the directors but does have authority to bind the company in matters relating to the administrative side of the company's business. Whether a company secretary will be found to have bound the company, despite exceeding their actual authority, will depend on the circumstances and any way in which they have been held out.

The authority of managers and employees

Senior managers, managers and employees (in a similar way to directors) will each have the authority that is specifically given to them (the authority that the company wants them to have – their actual authority) and the authority that may be implied from their position in the company, their job title, any previous dealings they have had with third parties or any way in which the company holds them out, knowingly or unknowingly (their apparent authority).

In all cases, whether a director or non-director will be found to have bound the company, despite having exceeded their actual authority, will depend on the specific circumstances. Someone with the job title 'Head of IT' could be reasonably expected to have authority to order the items and services that an IT department would need on a day-to-day basis. This is likely to come within his actual authority. But what about ordering a suite of ten brand new PC's? This might be beyond the authority that the company has given him, but if that was the case, would it be within the apparent authority of a person with that job title? This would depend on many factors including the supplier's knowledge about the company, the nature of his previous dealings with it and any other ways in which the Head of IT has been held out.

Keeping control

It is essential that everyone within a company, from the directors down to the most junior employees, knows and understands the limits on their authority.

Defining the limits

The limits on each person's authority can be specified in their job description, their contract of employment or in an office handbook. Each person should be briefed on the limits of their authority as part of their induction. As far as the board of directors is concerned, the directors should formally agree on the decisions that can only be taken by the board acting together – in other words, the decisions that cannot be delegated. The ICSA guidance note 'Matters Reserved for the Board' sets out a specimen list of this sort. Although it is aimed at public companies (and therefore includes matters that will not be relevant to smaller private companies) it is a valuable guide for companies of all sizes. Some decisions require the approval of the board by virtue of the wording of the Companies Act; in other cases it is a question of common sense and good business practice. As an additional measure, the directors may also wish to adopt a policy on signing documents that specifies the person or persons who can sign particular types of contracts, or contracts over a certain value. The ICSA guidance note is available for download from www.icsaglobal.com.

Staying informed

Establishing clear and effective reporting lines is also essential so that senior managers can update the board on contracts and agreements that the company has entered into, but which the directors may not all be aware of. Maintaining a central record of contracts entered into by the company is another useful control. Although directors can delegate their powers, they remain responsible for how those powers are (or are not) exercised so it is crucial that directors actively keep on top of what is happening in the company. Directors are ultimately responsible for overseeing the company's affairs and retaining control of its finances. This is a recurring theme in cases on directors' disqualification. The kind of controls described above should form part of a company's internal risk management system. Maintaining such a system is a principle of good corporate governance – see Chapter 16.

What if an individual director, manager or employee exceeds their authority?

If the company is bound, then it must fulfil its obligations under the contract or agreement in question, but may be entitled to seek compensation for any financial losses from the person at fault. Whether this is a realistic course of action or not will depend on the circumstances. In any event, such conduct should be subject to internal disciplinary procedures. If the company is not bound, because the director, manager or employee has no actual or apparent authority, the individual at fault may be personally liable to the third party. This makes it all the more important to ensure that everyone within the company understands the potential consequences of going beyond the limits of their authority.

Execution of contracts and documents

When a contract, agreement or other document is signed it is known as 'execution'. As noted earlier, not all contracts or agreements will be in writing, but there are many instances where written agreements will be made either because it is essential to have clarity about the matters that have been agreed, or because the law requires the agreement to be in writing (such as transfers of land). If you are ever unsure as to the formalities of entering into a particular contract or transaction it is vital to take advice. Similarly, if a third party presents you with a written agreement and you are not sure whether the terms are fair or acceptable then a solicitor specialising in commercial contracts will be able to advise you.

Written agreements or contracts need to be signed by the company or by someone acting on the company's behalf. It is very important that documents are signed in the right way so that the execution is effective and the individual signing them does not unwittingly commit themselves to the transaction personally, instead of committing the company. In addition, failure to execute a contract correctly has the potential to cause problems later if the company needs to rely on or to enforce any of its terms.

Execution by the company

When we are talking about execution by the company we are talking about execution by the company itself, as opposed to execution by an authorised person acting on the company's behalf. In agency terms, it can be thought of as signature by the principal rather than by the principal's agent. Execution by the company is not required all that often. The documents that have to be executed by the company are:

- documents known as 'deeds' (a formal type of document required in certain specific circumstances); and
- some documents that are not deeds but which have to be or generally are executed by the company due to other specific requirements.

Examples of documents that have to be signed as deeds include mortgages and charges, land transfers, leases and powers of attorney. An example of a document that is not a deed but which still needs to be executed by the company is the standard form of stock transfer form prescribed by the Stock Transfer Act 1963. Even when execution by the company is not specifically required, the other party to a transaction may still insist on it. This is because it provides stronger evidence of the company's intention to be bound by the contract or agreement in question. Similarly, a third party may insist on a document being signed as a deed because of issues concerning enforceability that can arise in relation to some types of agreements. If unsure of your position, take legal advice.

The Companies Act sets out rules that determine when a document is deemed to have been signed by a company. Section 44 states that, for companies incorporated in England, Wales and Northern Ireland, a document is validly executed by the company if:

- the company affixes its seal to it;
- it is signed by either two authorised signatories; or
- it is signed by a director in the presence of a witness who attests the signature.

These methods are explained below.

Execution under seal

A seal is a sort of stamp that, when applied to a paper document, impresses the company's name into it (and also the company's registered number if included on the seal). There is no legal requirement for companies to have a seal and most private companies will not need one. The use of seals is more common in other jurisdictions around the world and for UK companies this is sometimes where the need for a seal arises. The use of the seal is normally regulated by provisions in the company's articles; in the case of the Model Articles this is dealt with in article 49. When the seal is applied to a document, article 49 requires that the document is also signed by at least one authorised person in the presence of a witness who attests the signature. For these purposes an authorised person is a director, the company secretary (if the company has one), or any person authorised by the directors to sign documents to which the seal is applied.

The appropriate wording to add to a document to show that the company has executed it under its seal (with one authorised signatory signing in the presence of a witness) would be as follows, although note that this would not be adequate for a document that must be signed as a deed:

Executed by affixing the common seal of .... Limited in the

presence of .... Director/Secretary/Authorised Person

Witness signature ....

Witness name ....

Witness address ....

Execution by two authorised signatories

Section 40 of the Companies Act says that execution by two authorised signatories, as long as it is expressed to be execution by the company, has the same effect as if the execution was under seal. For these purposes, an authorised signatory is any director of the company or the company secretary, if the company has one. The signature clause for this form of execution should be as follows, although again, this is not suitable for a deed:

Executed by .... Limited acting by

.... Director

.... Director/Secretary

Execution by one director in the presence of a witness

Where a company only has one director and no company secretary, valid execution by the company requires the signature of the sole director in the presence of a witness who attests the signature. Again, this has the same legal effect as if the execution was under seal. The role of the witness in 'attesting' the signature is to confirm that he has witnessed the director's signature. The witness evidences this by signing the document and stating their name and address. The witness does not have to be independent – they can be connected to the company or to the director in some way, but it is preferable that they are not. It is worth noting that this form of execution is not specifically reserved for companies with a single director, it is a valid form of execution for all companies regardless of how many directors the company has. A standard form of signature clause for executing a document in this way is shown below. As before, this clause would need to be amended for a deed.

Executed by .... Limited acting by

.... Director

in the presence of

Witness signature ....

Witness name ....

Witness address ....

Execution on behalf of the company

Simple contracts and other documents that are not required to be executed by the company can be signed by an authorised person. The Companies Act does not say who is or who is not an authorised person for this purpose – whether a person has authority or not will depend on the principles of agency discussed earlier. Where a single person is signing on behalf of a company it is important that the signature clause makes this clear. The appropriate form of wording would be as follows.

Signed by...for and on behalf of

.... Limited.

Signature...

In the case of a contract or agreement signed by an authorised signatory, it may sometimes be reasonable for a third party to make enquiries to ensure that the person signing has the necessary authority to do so. If you are the one in this position and need to confirm the authority of someone that you are dealing with, you may wish to request a certified copy of a board minute showing that the contract has been approved by the board and that the signatory has been specifically authorised to sign it. If you need to confirm the identity of a company's directors, this can be done by obtaining information from Companies House, as explained in Chapter 5. The larger the transaction, the more care that needs to be taken. If in doubt, speak to a professional.

Summary

- Calling and holding a directors' meeting (for companies with the Model Articles, un-amended)

Calling a directors' meeting
- Any director can call a directors' meeting by giving reasonable notice to all of the directors, or by authorising the company secretary to give such notice.
- The notice must state the date, time and location of the meeting, but need not be in writing.
- There is no requirement for an agenda to be provided in advance of the meeting but it is good practice to do so.

At the beginning of the meeting
- If the chairman is not present within 10 minutes, the other directors must appoint one of themselves to chair the meeting (Model Article 12(4)).
- Each director present must declare any interest that they have in the business to be considered that they have not previously declared, or update any previous declarations if they are no longer accurate due to change of circumstances. Consider whether any interests declared by a director prevent him

or her from participating in the meeting under Model Article 14. If a dispute arises, the chairman's ruling is final (Model Article 14(6)).

- If applicable, ensure that the remaining eligible directors form a quorum.
- If the remaining directors do not form a quorum, the relevant provisions of Model Article 14 must be disapplied by ordinary resolution of the company's shareholders to enable any ineligible directors to participate.

During the meeting

- The chairman conducts the meeting and takes the directors through each item to be considered.
- If any director leaves the meeting, ensure that the remaining directors still form a quorum.
- If a consensus on any matter is not reached then a formal vote is to be taken. Each director has one vote (unless the articles have been amended to say otherwise) and resolutions are passed by a simple majority (Model Article 7). In the event of an equality of votes for and against a particular matter, the chairman has a casting vote provided he is eligible to vote on the matter in his own right (Model Article 13).

After the meeting

- Make any necessary updates to the company's statutory books. File any forms or documents with the Registrar of Companies that need to be filed. Address action points agreed and review progress at the next meeting.
- Prepare a draft set of minutes and circulate to the directors for their comments.
- Present the minutes at the next directors' meeting. The chairman should highlight any amendments that have been made and if there are no further comments or queries, the minutes should be signed by the chairman.

Binding the company

- Contracts and agreements can take many forms and may not always be in writing. The two key questions for a company entering into a contract are: (i) Does the company have the power to enter into the contract? If so, (ii) Who has the authority to enter into it on the company's behalf?
- A company's objects can place restrictions on what the company can do. Even if the objects are unrestricted, a company's articles (and other constitutional agreements) can restrict the directors' exercise of the company's powers. However, by virtue of ss. 39 and 40 of the Companies Act, a person dealing with the company in good faith does not generally have to be concerned with restrictions on the powers of the company, or any limits on the directors' authority in the company's constitution.
- The board of directors, acting as a collective, sits at the top of the decision-making hierarchy in any company. Provided the articles allow, the board

can delegate its authority to others and this is a practical and commercial necessity.

■ The true authority of each individual within the company will depend on the authority that has been delegated to them. This is known as their actual authority. However a person can still bind a company if they have apparent authority. This is the authority that the company holds them out as having.

■ It is essential for the directors to set clear limits on each person's authority. This can be done by way of job descriptions or role profiles, contracts of employment or the office handbook.

■ Appropriate procedures and reporting lines can help the board to maintain control and should form part of a company's internal risk management system. See Chapter 16 for more on internal controls.

■ The act of signing a contract or agreement so as to give it legal effect is known as execution. A company can execute a contract by affixing its seal, by the signature of two directors, by the signature of one director and the company secretary, or by signature of one director in the presence of a witness.

9 Shares

In this chapter

This chapter provides an introduction to shares and share capital with regard to:

- what shares are and a company's initial capital;
- basic rules about shares;
- different types of shares and class rights;
- the directors' authority to allot shares;
- shareholders' rights of pre-emption on allotment;
- the procedure for allotting shares; and
- share buy-backs, consolidations, subdivisions and reduction of capital.

What are shares?

Academics may diverge in their views about what shares are, but essentially, shares are a form of personal property which confer certain rights on the person who owns them in relation to the company that has issued them. These rights are set out in the Companies Act and a company's articles. Additional rights and entitlements may be set out in a shareholders' agreement. However, it is important to recognise that in most cases a shareholders' agreement is a private contract that gives rights to the parties only in their *capacity* as shareholders. This is in contrast to rights set out in a company's articles which attach to the shares themselves and not to the person who holds them. By way of example, if a shareholder who is a party to a shareholders' agreement were to transfer his shares to someone else, that person would not have the benefit of the rights set out in the shareholders' agreement unless he agreed to be bound by it. On the other hand, he would be entitled to enjoy the rights set out in the articles and in the Companies Act as soon as his name had been entered in the company's register of members.

In the case of listed companies, the usual reason why someone buys shares is the expectation of dividends (a regular share in the profits of the company) and in the hope that the value of the shares will increase over time. However shares are a risky form of investment. Neither dividends nor an increase in value are guaranteed and in the event of an insolvency, ordinary shareholders rank last in the pecking order for payment out of the company's assets. In addition, although such shareholders will have the benefit of the rights set out in the company's articles of association and the Companies Act, their shareholdings are often too small for them to be able to exert any real influence over the company's affairs.

In private companies the position tends to be different in that the shareholders are not usually remote investors but people who are closely linked with the company and its directors or are directors themselves. The split of the company's shares between the various shareholders and the rights that attach to those shares are of great significance in determining the balance of power and control in the company and the respective rights of shareholders to dividends and to payments out of the assets in the event of a winding up. More is said about this later.

Initial capital

A company limited by shares must have at least one shareholder who holds at least one share in the company. The first shares in a company are issued to those people who are the subscribers to the company's memorandum of association. In signing the memorandum the subscribers confirm their wish to be formed into a company and to take at least one share each. The exact number of shares that they take is set out in the application for incorporation (form IN01 – see Chapter 2). By operation of s. 16 of the Companies Act, the subscribers become members and become the holders of the shares that they have agreed to take as soon as the company is incorporated.

The majority of private companies are incorporated with just one or two shares being taken by the subscribers. Issuing further shares can be used as a way to raise finance for the company but professional advice should be taken (without exception) and there are other options to consider – see Chapter 13 on sources of finance.

Basic rules about shares

The Companies Act sets out various basic rules about shares as follows.

Nominal value

Shares must have a fixed value known as the 'nominal value' (s. 542) which is also sometimes referred to as the 'par value'. This means that a company cannot issue shares that have no monetary worth. When the shares are issued, the nominal value is the minimum that must be paid for them, although subject to the articles and at the directors' discretion they can be partly paid with the balance due later. The nominal value can be small, such as £0.10, £0.01 or £0.001 – any value is acceptable, as long as the shares have a set value.

Denomination

The nominal value of a share can be denominated in any currency (e.g. euros, dollars or Japanese yen). This is not particularly common, however and most UK registered private companies denominate their shares in pounds sterling.

Share premium

If a person taking (or 'subscribing') for shares in a company pays the company more than the nominal value for each share, the difference in price between the nominal value and the amount paid is known as a 'share premium'. This reflects the value of the shares over and above their nominal value, in relation to the overall worth of the company. For accounting purposes, funds acquired by way of a share premium must be allocated to a 'share premium account' and must be shown separately on a company's balance sheet. Share premiums form part of a company's share capital and are therefore non-distributable, but s. 610 of the Companies Act confirms that they can be used to:

- pay up the issue of new shares as bonus shares;
- write off the expenses of issuing the shares to which the premium is attached; and
- to write off any commission paid on the issue of those shares.

The total amount paid for a share, as to both its nominal value and any premium, must be disclosed in any statement of capital that a company is required to file with the Registrar of Companies. If a company has allotted some shares at a premium (and/or for different premiums) and some shares at their nominal value, the different amounts paid per share in each case must be stated which could mean making multiple entries for each class of shares (see Chapter 4).

Discount

Shares must not be allotted at a discount (s. 580). In addition, it is not possible to allot a fraction of a share, such as half or quarter – shares must be allotted as whole units, although they can be allotted partly paid as mentioned above. See also 'Payment for shares' later on in this chapter.

Distinguishing numbers

Section 543 of the Companies Act requires that each share in a company that has a share capital must be distinguished by a number. This means that if a company has issued 100 shares, then each share would have to be numbered consecutively from 1 to 100 and the company would have to keep a record of the distinguishing numbers of the shares. There are two exceptions when shares will not need to be numbered in this way which are:

- all the issued shares in the company are fully paid up and rank equally in terms of the rights attached to them; and

- all the shares of a particular class in the company are fully paid up and rank equally in terms of the rights attached to them.

It is quite rare for a company's shares to have distinguishing numbers.

Different types of shares

Section 629 of the Companies Act states that shares are of one class if the rights attached to them are in all respects uniform. Different share classes are therefore set apart by the rights that attach to the shares. In this respect there are, broadly, four main types of shares.

Ordinary shares

Ordinary shares are the most common type of shares with no special rights attached to them other than the right to vote, the right to participate in a capital distribution and the right to receive a dividend. As noted earlier, ordinary shares usually have no guaranteed right to a dividend and rank last for payment in the event of a winding up. Ordinary shares are the basic building block of a company's share capital.

Preference shares

Shares which are designated as 'preference shares' carry certain preferential rights in relation to other classes of shares (e.g. they usually carry the right to a fixed yearly dividend). If the shares are 'cumulative' preference shares then the amount of any fixed dividend which is not paid in a given year will roll over to the next year. Preference shares normally rank above other classes of shares for a return of capital in the event of a winding up, but often have restricted or no voting rights.

Redeemable shares

Redeemable shares are shares which can be bought-back by the company that issued them. While it is possible for a company to purchase and cancel any shares that it has issued (in accordance with the rules set out in the Companies Act) redeemable shares carry the specific right to be redeemed, either at the option of the company or the shareholder, depending on the terms on which the shares were issued. The power to issue redeemable shares is conferred by s. 684 of the Companies Act, but is subject to any restrictions in a company's articles. If the articles are silent on the matter of redeemable shares (as is the case with the Model Articles) the power in s. 684 will apply. A company's issued share capital cannot consist only of redeemable shares (and no shares of any other class), because if all the redeemable shares were redeemed, the company would be left with no share capital and no shareholders. Shares that are issued as non-redeemable cannot be converted to redeemable shares at some later date. The detailed rules on redeemable shares are contained in Chapter 3 of Part 18 of the Act.

Convertible shares

Convertible shares are shares which can be converted into shares of another class. For example, a company may issue preference shares which can be converted into ordinary shares on terms specified in the company's articles.

Class rights

In many cases it will be perfectly sufficient for a new company to issue shares of one class: ordinary shares. One ordinary share of (for example) £1.00 nominal value will meet the requirement in the Companies Act for a company to have at least one shareholder holding at least one share. All shares of this class that the company issues will rank equally in terms of voting, dividends and capital distribution. So, if there is more than one shareholder, the shareholders will all have equal rights

Of course, there may come a stage when it may not be appropriate for all shareholders in the company to have equal rights. If so, this can be addressed by creating different classes of shares. The main variations in share rights are usually in terms of:

- voting;
- dividends;
- capital distributions; and
- rights to a return of capital on a winding up.

For example, voting may be restricted so as to only allow voting on certain issues of particular concern to that class of shareholder or the shares may confer no voting rights at all. Rights to dividends and capital distributions may be enhanced or reduced and may be structured to produce an order of priority as to who gets paid first. However, class rights can also encompass other matters such as the right to appoint or remove a director, the right to transfer shares in certain circumstances (where transfers are otherwise subject to strict controls) and the power to block certain decisions that fall to the company's shareholders. The latter can be achieved by providing that certain decisions require the consent of a particular class of shareholders or that certain decisions will constitute a variation of the rights attaching to that class of shareholders which then invokes the procedure for a variation of class rights (see below).

The different rights that should be attached to different classes of shares will be determined by the circumstances and what the company is trying to achieve. For example, an investor will usually look to secure rights that protect his investment and ensure the best possible return. This may necessitate the creation of several new classes of shares. An owner-managed company may wish to allot shares to family members so that they can participate in dividends and hold an equity stake in the company. This may involve creating two classes of ordinary shares designated as, say, A ordinary shares and B ordinary shares, where the A shares give the owner-manager full voting control and all other rights in relation to the company and the B ordinary shares confer only the right to a dividend. The range of possibilities is vast. In some private companies, the financing and other arrangements can become highly complicated, necessitating an equally complex share structure utilising a combination of different share classes. Regardless of how complex or straightforward the circumstances are, professional advice in relation to these matters (on both the legal and tax aspects) is always essential. However many classes of shares a company has in issue, details of the rights attaching to each class must be set out in the prescribed particulars section of every statement of capital that the company files with the Registrar of Companies (see Chapter 4).

Variation of class rights

Section 630 of the Companies Act states that the rights attached to a class of shares can only be varied:

- in accordance with provisions in the company's articles for the variation of those rights; or
- if there are no such provisions in the articles, if the holders of shares of that class consent to the variation.

If the articles are silent then it is the procedure in the Companies Act that needs to be followed. Under the Act, consent has to be obtained in one of two ways, either:

- by way of consent in writing from the holders of at least three-quarters in nominal value of the shares of that class; or
- by a special resolution at a general meeting of the holders of that class – such a meeting being known as a 'class meeting'.

A variation of class rights will normally involve making changes to the articles of association in which case the procedure will also necessitate a special resolution of the company's shareholders as a whole.

A variation might be clear and obvious like a change to voting or dividend rights. However, in other situations, it may not be clear cut as to whether a proposed alteration will constitute a variation of class rights or not. When drafting articles that set out the rights of different classes of shares, it is not uncommon to also specify certain matters that will constitute a variation of those rights. The desired effect can be to either give the holders of that class a right of veto over certain matters (e.g. such as any change to the articles, or a change of name of the company) or to simply achieve certainty. A professional will be able to advise whether or not a proposed course of action will constitute a variation of class rights and professional advice in this area would be recommended in general. Even if consent to a variation is obtained, s. 633 of the Companies Act sets out a procedure for dissenting shareholders of the relevant class to object to the variation by applying to court. The court may disallow the variation if it is satisfied that it would unfairly prejudice the shareholders of the class in question. Notice of a variation of the rights of a class of shares has to be given to the Registrar of Companies on form SH10.

Allotting new shares

When issuing shares it is very important that the correct rules and procedures are followed. As well as the legalities there can also be tax implications to consider and professional advice should always be taken before going ahead. The next part of this chapter explains the main rules that directors need to be aware of and sets out the procedure involved.

'Allotment' and 'issue' – what is the difference?

According to s. 558 of the Companies Act, shares are 'allotted' when a person acquires the unconditional right to be included in the company's register of members in respect of the shares. The shares are 'issued' when the necessary details of the allotment have been entered in the company's register of members. This is a subtle distinction and quite often these words are used interchangeably to mean the same thing; this is the case in this book. However, it is worth noting that a person does not become a member of a company until their name has been entered in the register of members.

Directors' authority to allot shares

To issue new shares the directors of a company must have the authority to do so. Section 549 of the Companies Act states that directors must not exercise any power to allot shares in the company except in accordance with ss. 550 or 551. These provide two possible sources of the directors' authority to allot shares.

Private companies with one class of shares – s. 550

Under s. 550, directors of private limited companies that have only one class of share can exercise any power of the company to allot shares of that class, except to the extent that they are prohibited from doing so by the company's articles. This means that if a company has only one class of shares (e.g. ordinary shares) and there are no provisions in the company's articles to place any limits on the directors' authority to allot shares, the directors' authority will be unlimited.

This is the position for companies that have adopted the Model Articles without any amendments since the Model Articles place no restrictions on the directors' authority to allot shares. It should be remembered, however, that if the company creates a new class of shares this authority will cease. In addition, the authority only relates to shares of the one class in existence (i.e. if the directors want to issue shares of a different class, they will need a specific authority from the company's shareholders in order to do this). Such authorities are given under s. 551.

Authorisation by the company – s. 551

Under s. 551, a company's directors can allot shares in the company if they are authorised to do so either by the company's articles or by resolution of the company's shareholders. Any such authorisation has to comply with the terms of s. 551 which are that it must:

- state the maximum amount of shares that the directors can allot; and
- specify the date on which the authority will expire which must be in no more than five years.

If the authority is included in the company's articles at the time that the company is incorporated then the authority cannot last for longer than five years from the date of incorporation. If the authority is given by way of a shareholders' resolution then it cannot last for longer than five years from the date on which the resolution is passed. The directors' authority can be renewed (or revoked) at any time but any renewed authority may also not exceed five years.

An authority under s. 551 can be expressed to be for just one specific share allotment, or can be a general authority. It can also be subject to conditions or can be unconditional. If the authority is intended to allow the directors to allot shares of different classes then this should be made clear in the wording of the authority. For clarity, it should also state the aggregate nominal value of shares of each class that the directors are authorised to allot.

A resolution of the company's shareholders granting or renewing the directors' authority to allot shares can be passed as an ordinary resolution (i.e. by simple majority). This is still the case even if the authority is contained in the company's articles where, ordinarily, a special resolution would be required to make an amendment. Whenever the directors' authority is granted, renewed (or revoked) by resolution of the members, a copy of the resolution must be filed at Companies House within 15 days (s. 551(9)).

Shareholders resolution to authorise directors to allot shares

THAT the directors be and are generally and unconditionally hereby authorised, for the purposes of section 551 of the Companies Act 2006, to exercise any power of the company to offer or allot or to grant rights to subscribe for any ordinary shares of £0.01 each in the company to any person, at any time and subject to any terms and conditions as the directors think proper. The authority:

(a) shall be limited to a maximum nominal amount of £_____;
(b) shall apply insofar as the company has not renewed, waived or revoked it by ordinary resolution; and
(c) may only be exercised for a period of five years commencing on the date of the passing of this resolution.

Shareholders' rights of pre-emption

As well as establishing whether the directors have the necessary authority to allot shares, the rights of 'pre-emption' of the existing shareholders also need to be considered. Shareholders' pre-emption rights on allotment are enshrined in s. 561 of the Companies Act. This section says that a company cannot allot ordinary shares to anyone unless it has first offered those shares to existing holders of ordinary shares, in proportion to the number of shares that they already hold in the company. In this context, 'ordinary shares' means:

> shares other than shares that as respects dividends and capital carry a right to participate only up to a specified amount in a distribution (s. 560(1)).

This essentially gives the existing holders of ordinary shares a right of first refusal on the new ordinary shares. Section 562 sets out how pre-emption offers have to be communicated to existing shareholders, including a minimum time limit on how long the offer has to be open for. The purpose of pre-emption rights is to prevent existing ordinary shareholders from having their shareholding diluted as a result of the company issuing more shares.

Example

Mr A holds 10 ordinary shares of £1.00 in company X, which has a total issued share capital of 100 ordinary shares of £1.00. Mr A therefore holds 10% of the company's issued share capital.

If the company were to allot 20 new ordinary shares of £1.00 to a new shareholder, Mr B, the company's issued share capital would increase to 120 ordinary shares of £1.00 each and Mr A's holding would be reduced to just over 8%.

Not only does this affect Mr A's voting power but it also means that in the event that the company pays a dividend, the amount paid per share will be reduced because there are more shares in issue for the dividend to be paid on. The pre-emption rights in s. 561 are intended to prevent this from happening. However, for private limited companies there are different ways in which these rights can be excluded or disapplied.

Dealing with pre-emption rights

In the case of a private company, the provisions of ss. 561 and 562 can either be:

- completely excluded by the company's articles; or
- disapplied in relation to the directors' authority to allot shares.

This is an area where professional advice is essential. If the directors allot shares in contravention of the existing shareholders' rights of pre-emption, then the company and every officer in default are jointly and severally liable to each share-holder to whom an offer should have been made for any loss, damage, costs or expenses which that shareholder has sustained or incurred by reason of the contravention.

General exclusion by the company's articles

Under s. 567 of the Companies Act, a private company can exclude ss. 561 and 562 by a provision in its articles. This can be either a general exclusion or an exclusion in relation to particular allotments. A general exclusion amounts to a permanent and unlimited shutting out of the rights in ss. 561 and 562, which will cease only if the relevant provision in the articles is removed.

Companies with one class of shares

If a company has only one class of shares (and the directors of the company thereby have unlimited authority to allot shares of that class under s. 550) then s. 569 provides that the company's articles can give the directors power to allot shares of that class as if s. 561 does not apply. This differs from the general exclusion under s. 567 in that it is a disapplication of pre-emption rights in relation to allotments of the one class of shares that are in issue, rather than a complete exclusion in relation to any and all allotments. However, it could be unlimited because the directors' authority to allot shares does not expire (except as mentioned above) and so the disapplication of s. 561 need not have an expiration date either.

Companies with one class of shares can also disapply s. 561 by passing a special resolution to that effect. Again, this would disapply pre-emption rights in connection with the directors' authority to allot shares under s. 550 and can be unlimited. So, if a company's articles do not disapply s. 561 (in relation to the allotment of shares under s. 550) it is not necessary to go through the process of amending them, the same result can be achieved by passing an appropriate special resolution instead.

It is important to note, however, that if the company ceases to have just one class of shares, then not only will the directors' authority to allot shares under s. 550 be extinguished but any associated disapplication of pre-emption rights will also terminate.

Companies with authority to allot shares under s. 551

If the directors of a company do not have authority to allot shares under s. 550, then they will need an authority under the terms of s. 551 as explained above. If the directors have an authority to allot shares under s. 551, s. 570 provides that the directors can be given power either by the company's articles, or by a special resolution, to allot shares as if s. 561 did not apply.

The important point to note about this is that any disapplication of pre-emption rights under s. 570 is linked directly to the directors' authority under

s. 551. This means that it can only apply to the allotment of shares of whichever classes the directors have been authorised to allot under that section. When the directors' authority expires (either because the maximum number of shares have been allotted or because it has lapsed due to the passage of time) the associated disapplication of pre-emption rights will also expire. If the authority is renewed, the disapplication of s. 561 can also be renewed, but must still be restricted to the terms of the renewed authority.

Ad hoc disapplications

If, for whatever reason, the company does not wish to use any of the above methods to disapply pre-emption rights (either a general exclusion in the articles or a disapplication linked to the directors' authority to allot shares) then they can be disapplied in connection with a specific or one-off allotment of shares by passing a special resolution. The procedure for doing this is set out in s. 571. Generally, this is a less popular way of dealing with pre-emption rights because a special resolution cannot be passed under this section unless it is (i) recommended by the directors; and (ii) the directors have complied with the requirement to circulate a written statement setting out:

- their reasons for making the recommendation;
- the amount to be paid to the company in respect of the shares to be allotted; and
- the directors' justification of that amount.

This creates additional administration but the greater concern lies in the fact that the directors are liable (under s. 572) for any false, misleading or deceptive material provided in their statement and on conviction can face imprisonment, a fine, or both.

Letters of waiver

A final option for dealing with pre-emption rights is to request that each shareholder specifically waives their rights of pre-emption in relation to a particular allotment by signing a letter of waiver. In practical terms, this may be no less onerous than arranging for the passing of a special resolution and could be problematic because in order to be effective, *all* of a company's existing shareholders have to sign one. Compared to a special resolution which requires the agreement of 75% of shareholders, this amounts to dis-application by unanimous agreement. Take professional advice.

Filing requirements

Whenever a company passes a special resolution to disapply the rights of preemption set out in s. 561, notice of the resolution must be filed at Companies House within 15 days of the date on which the resolution was passed.

Helpful hints

The Model Articles do not contain any provisions to exclude pre-emption rights. So in a company that has adopted the Model Articles without amendment, the statutory pre-emption rights will apply to any allotment of shares that the directors propose to make. The directors then have to decide whether to follow the procedure for offering any such shares to the company's existing shareholders, or take appropriate action to disapply or exclude the pre-emption provisions. Professional advice is needed. However it should be noted that pre-emption rights do not apply to:

- shares taken by the subscribers to a company's memorandum of association (s. 577);
- shares allotted wholly or partly for non-cash consideration (s. 565);
- shares allotted pursuant to an employee share scheme (s. 566);
- an allotment of bonus shares (s. 564); and
- any shareholder other than holders of ordinary shares, as defined by s. 560(1) (s. 561(1)(a)).

The allotment procedure

Having settled questions regarding the directors' authority to allot shares and the shareholders' rights of pre-emption, the procedure for allotting shares is fairly straightforward. The following are the steps that typically need to be followed.

Subscription letters

It is normal practice to apply for the allotment of shares in a company by a letter of subscription. This does not usually need to be a complicated document and should just confirm the agreement to take the shares in the company, to pay the sum required to be paid for them and to be bound by the company's articles of association. A letter of subscription can help to address any doubts or questions about the allotment that might arise at a later date. At this stage any issues over the capacity of the applicants to acquire and hold shares in the company should be considered – these are described in Chapter 10 in relation to a company's register of members.

Board meeting/decision of the directors

The board of directors should meet to discuss the proposed allotments and to review the letters of subscription. The board should note whether the correct subscription monies have been received by the company (the amount agreed to be paid for the shares) and if so can then approve the allotments and resolve to carry out any and all necessary actions to put them into effect. This would include filing a form SH01 at Companies House, entering details of the allotments in the company's registers and issuing share certificates.

Form SH01

Notice of the share allotments must be delivered to the Registrar of Companies on form SH01. This form can be filed either on paper or electronically. Details of the number of shares of each class that have been allotted need to be provided, together with an up-to-date statement of capital. The statement of capital should set out the company's issued share capital following the allotments reported on the form (see Chapter 4 for guidance on completing a statement of capital). The date on which the allotments took place must be stated on the first page of the form and the form must be filed within one month of that date (s. 555).

If the shares were allotted for non-cash consideration (see further below) then a narrative description of the non-cash consideration must be given in the box at the bottom of the first page. It was formerly a requirement that a copy of any agreement relating to the non-cash consideration be provided to the Registrar of Companies but this is no longer the case.

Register of allotments

Details of the shares that have been allotted should be entered into the company's register of allotments. This register is not required to be kept by law, but it is good practice to maintain one as it can be helpful in terms of cross-referencing with the register of members if any questions arise concerning the company's share allotments in future. Usually the register of allotments will record:

■ the date of allotment;
■ the name and address of the applicant/allottee;
■ the number of shares allotted;
■ the price per share;
■ the total amount paid; and
■ the number of the share certificate issued pursuant to the allotment.

Each allotment should be numbered sequentially and this reference number can then be entered in the register of members for cross-referencing purposes. An example of a register of allotments can be found in Appendix 5. Original copies of the subscription letters can be kept with this register but it should be remembered that these are not public documents and neither is the register of allotments which means that shareholders and third parties do not have any right to inspect them.

Register of members

Details of the share allotments must be also be entered in the company's register of members. Section 554 of the Companies Act stipulates that this must be done 'as soon as practicable' and at most within two months of the date of allotment of the shares. As usual, failure to comply with this is an offence on the part of the company and every officer in default. Unlike the register of allotments, all companies are required to keep a register of members by law. The register of members is an important legal document as it gives the definitive position as to who the company's shareholders are and the number of shares that they hold. It is important that the register of members is maintained correctly and advice on how to do this is given in the next chapter.

Share certificates

The company must issue each shareholder with a share certificate within two months of the date of allotment (s. 769). The Companies Act says that a share certificate is *prima facie* evidence of a shareholding. This means 'at first sight' and is essentially saying that a share certificate is proof of a shareholding but there is the chance that it could, on further investigation, turn out to be invalid or inaccurate.

The Act does not set out what information has to be included in a share certificate but the Model Articles do. Article 24 of the Model Articles states that a share certificate must be issued free of charge and must specify:

- the class and number of shares in respect of which it is issued;
- the nominal value of those shares;
- that the shares are fully paid; and
- any distinguishing numbers assigned to them.

Of course, it should also state the name and address of the shareholder and the name and registered number of the company issuing it. It is also a good idea for share certificates to be numbered and for the number of the certificate to be recorded in the register of allotments and register of members alongside the relevant entries for the shareholder in question. This can help to keep track of which certificates are valid and to identify certificates as genuine when a shareholder deposits them with the company in connection with a transfer of some or all of their shares. A separate share certificate should be issued for each different class of shares. So, for example, one share certificate should not represent a shareholder's holding of both ordinary and preference shares (see article 24(3) of the Model Articles). In addition, where shares are held by more than one person jointly, article 24(4) of the Model Articles states that those people are only entitled to one share certificate in respect of those shares.

Share certificates must be executed formally by the company which means that they must be signed by either:

- two directors; or
- one director and the company secretary; or
- one director in the presence of a witness who attests the signature.

A share certificate can also be executed under the company's common seal if it has one (see Chapter 8 for more on the execution of documents). Blank share certificates are normally included in the company books available from legal stationers and formation agents or can be purchased separately. They do not have to be bought-in however and a company could create them by computer using any appropriate software. For guidance on what to do when a shareholder reports their share certificate as lost or missing, see the section in the next chapter dealing with transfers of shares

Payment for shares

Article 21 of the Model Articles says that no share can be issued for less than the aggregate of its nominal value and any premium. In other words, if a company has adopted the model articles without amendment, then all shares allotted by the company have to be allotted fully paid (apart from the first shares taken on incorporation). The government took this approach in drafting the Model Articles because shares in small private companies are usually issued as fully paid. However, this will not always be the case and a company that intends to allot shares as partly paid or nil-paid will need to check that its articles do not prevent it from doing this. Where a company allots partly-paid or nil-paid shares, provisions are also needed in the articles to deal with making demands for payment of monies due to the company (known as 'calls') and also for cancellation of shares in the event of non-payment (known as 'forefeiture'). Such articles tend to be long and detailed and an example can be seen in the model articles for public limited companies.

Cash and non-cash consideration

Section 583 of the Companies Act states that a share in a company is deemed to be paid in cash if the consideration received for it is a 'cash consideration'. A cash consideration means:

- cash received by the company;
- a cheque received by the company (that the directors have no reason for suspecting will not be paid);
- a release of a liability of the company for a liquidated sum;
- an undertaking to pay cash to the company at a future date; or
- payment by any other means giving rise to a present or future entitlement (of the company or a person acting on the company's behalf) to a payment, or credit equivalent to payment, in cash.

Any other kind of consideration will be non-cash consideration. This is significant for private companies because pre-emption rights do not apply to allotments of shares where the whole or part of the consideration is non-cash consideration. In addition, in some cases, stamp duty may be payable on any property transferred to the company as non-cash consideration. Remember that if your company has the Model Articles then the consideration – cash or otherwise – must be received by the company in full before the shares can be issued.

Bonus shares

Bonus shares are shares that are issued by a company to its shareholders fully paid, in proportion to their existing shareholdings. The shares are paid for by the company out of its reserves. This is sometimes known as a 'capitalisation' because the retained profits of the company are effectively turned into share capital. Although a shareholder's overall shareholding will increase, the value of each share will decrease due to there being a greater number of shares in issue.

Financial assistance

'Financial assistance' is a legal term used to describe an arrangement where a company provides assistance or help of a financial nature for the purpose of enabling someone to acquire its shares. Historically, financial assistance was outlawed for all companies because of certain perceived wrongdoings, among them the practice whereby a company manipulates the price of its shares by giving others the finance to buy them. Private companies are not prohibited from giving financial assistance (except in certain limited circumstances) but there are still issues to consider such as the directors' duty to promote the success of the company and the company's financial position. Although it is not required by the Companies Act, obtaining shareholder approval is generally recommended as a matter of good practice and to reduce the risk of the transaction being challenged by shareholders at a later date. As such, and despite the general absence of any statutory restrictions, professional advice is essential.

■ Returning funds to shareholders

Once shareholders have paid for their shares, the monies that they have paid belong to the company and form part of its share capital. Although shareholders may receive dividends, they have no right to a return of the money paid for their shares, except if the shares are redeemable (in which case the rights to redemption will have been determined at the point that the shares were issued) or in the event of a winding up (where any payments to shareholders can only be made after all other creditors have been satisfied). There are, however, two exceptions to this general rule which enable a company to return funds to its shareholders. These are:

- a purchase by a company of its own shares; and
- a reduction of capital.

Purchase by a company of its own shares

Although it may have a variety of applications, a share buy-back is commonly used by small private companies as a way to return excess funds to shareholders or to buy the shares of a shareholder who otherwise has no means of exit from a company. Section 690 of the Companies Act says that a limited company can purchase its own shares provided that there are no restrictions in the articles preventing it from doing so – there are no such restrictions in the Model Articles.

Shares can only be bought back if they are fully paid and there must be at least one non-redeemable share left in issue after the buy-back (otherwise the company could potentially be left with no shares and no shareholders), not including any shares held in treasury (see below).

The procedure for share buy-backs is set out in Part 18 of the Companies Act as amended by the Companies Act 2006 (Amendment of Part 18) Regulations 2013 (SI 2013/999). The rules and procedures differ depending on whether the company is a private company or a public company, whether the shares are being purchased 'off market' (i.e. in a private arrangement) or 'on market' (through a recognised investment exchange – unlikely for a private company), what source of funds the company is using to make the purchase and whether the shares are being purchased for the purposes of or pursuant to an employee share scheme. Shareholders must give their approval to the purchase and (in the case of an off-market purchase) the terms of the buy-back agreement, by way of an ordinary resolution. It is very important that the right procedure is followed. Not only is it an offence on the part of the company and every officer in default, but failure to properly observe the relevant provisions of Part 18 can also mean that the purchase will be void. As well as the procedural aspects there are also important (and complicated) tax issues to consider, both for the company and for the shareholder whose shares are being purchased. Needless to say, this is an area where professional advice is essential.

From an administrative point of view a buy back should be recorded in a company's statutory registers by making an entry in the account of the relevant shareholder to note the purchase and the cancellation of the shares by the company (or their purchase into treasury) and to reduce their shareholding by the appropriate amount. The shareholder's share certificate(s) should be cancelled and a balance certificate be issued if applicable. Notice of a buy-back must be given to the Registrar of Companies on form SH03, which must be filed within 28 days of the date on which the shares are delivered to the company. Stamp duty is payable on the sum paid by the company for the shares (unless it does not exceed £1,000) and form SH03 must be sent to HMRC for stamping before it is submitted to the Registrar. If the shares that have been bought back are cancelled, notice of the cancellation must be given on form SH06 (within 28 days, as above) with a statement of capital showing the up-to-date position regarding the company's issued share capital.

Helpful hints – Treasury shares

When a company purchases its own shares and does not cancel them, the shares are held by the company in 'treasury'. Until the changes made by the Amendment of Part 18 Regulations it was only possible for a public company to hold shares as treasury shares. Following the amendments to

Part 18 of the Companies Act both public and private companies are now permitted to hold their own shares in treasury subject to the source of funds used for the buy-back and subject to any restrictions in their articles. When shares are held in treasury the company must be entered in its own register of members as the holder of the shares but the company cannot exercise any rights attaching to them (the purported exercise of any such rights is void). Furthermore, treasury shares do not rank for dividends or any other distributions. Once in treasury the shares can be held indefinitely, be sold for cash consideration, be transferred for the purposes of or pursuant to an employee share scheme (e.g. in connection with the exercise of a share option) or be cancelled. These and the other rules concerning treasury shares are set out in Chapter 6 of Part 18.

Reduction of capital

A reduction of capital creates a reserve that is treated as a 'realised profit' for the purposes of the Companies Act. It can therefore be used, among other things, to create funds that can be distributed to shareholders as dividends, to finance a buy-back or redemption of shares or to reduce any realised losses of the company. Companies limited by shares have the power to reduce their share capital provided that there are no provisions in the company's articles that would prevent them from doing so (there are no provisions in the Model Articles to restrict this power).

Both public and private companies can reduce their capital by court approval, but private companies have a second option which is to reduce their capital by way of a special resolution of the shareholders supported by a 'solvency statement'. The solvency statement is a statement made by the company's directors that each director has formed the opinion that, as at the date of the statement:

- there is no ground on which the company could be found to be unable to pay (or otherwise discharge) its debts;
- if it is intended to wind up the company within 12 months of the date of the statement, the company will be able to pay (or otherwise discharge) its debts in full within 12 months of the commencement of the winding up; and
- that in any other case, the company will be able to pay (or otherwise discharge) its debts as they fall due during the year following the date of the statement.

The special resolution of the members must be passed within a maximum of 15 days after the solvency statement is made. The members have a right to see the solvency statement before they vote to approve the reduction of capital. On a reduction of capital by solvency statement, the company must still have at least one non-redeemable share in issue once the reduction has taken effect.

It goes without saying that the solvency statement should not be made lightly and that full and careful consideration needs to be given to the company's financial position before the directors sign it. Directors need to bear in mind their duties under the Companies Act, be sure that they are not acting contrary to the company's best interests and demonstrate the requisite skill, care and diligence that would be expected of them. If the directors deliver a solvency statement to the Registrar of Companies without having reasonable grounds for the opinions expressed in it then this is an offence on the part of every officer who is in default. Punishment is by fine or imprisonment. As with a share buy-back, professional advice in relation to a reduction of capital is essential.

■ Consolidation and subdivision of shares

Consolidations and subdivisions usually form part of the process whereby a company re-organises its share capital. A consolidation of shares occurs when shares of a certain nominal value are combined together so as to form a smaller number of new shares with a higher nominal value. For example, if a company carries out a consolidation of its ordinary shares of £0.10 so as to become ordinary shares of £1.00 then every ten £0.10 shares become one £1.00 share. A shareholder with 1,000 ordinary shares of £0.10 before the consolidation would have 100 ordinary shares of £1.00 afterwards.

A subdivision of shares is the opposite. Shares of a higher nominal value are divided so as to become a larger number of shares with a lower nominal value. Taking the shareholder in the above example, if each new £1.00 share was subdivided into ten shares of £0.10 each then that would reverse the consolidation and put the shareholder back into the position he was in to begin with.

The power of a company to subdivide or consolidate its shares is stated in s. 618 of the Companies Act. Section 618(3) says that this power can only be exercised by a resolution of the company's members. As the type of resolution is not specified, an ordinary resolution is sufficient unless the company's articles say otherwise. The power to consolidate and subdivide shares under s. 618 can be specifically excluded by a company's articles so that it cannot carry out either of these actions. The Model Articles contain no such exclusion. When a company consolidates or subdivides its shares the company must send notification to Companies House on form SH02 which must include a statement of capital showing the position of the company's issued share capital following the consolidation or subdivision. Appropriate entries need to be made in the register of members to record the consolidation or subdivision and new share certificates need to be issued to each shareholder whose shareholding has been affected. Previous share certificates should be recalled and cancelled but in any event will cease to be valid.

Re-designation

At its most straightforward a re-designation occurs when a company decides to rename a particular class of shares (e.g. this might involve re-naming a class of A ordinary shares as A1 ordinary shares in connection with a re-organisation of the company's share capital). However, if the re-designation also involves a variation of the rights attaching to the shares in question (or another class), the procedure for variation of class rights will need to be followed either in accordance with the company's articles or the Companies Act, as the case may be. Similarly if the re-designation involves creating a new class of shares, the articles of association will need amending to set out the rights attaching to the new class. Professional advice is essential.

▦ Checklist – allotting shares

✓ If the directors do not have authority to allot the shares, or an existing authority is not sufficient, a new authority must be obtained from the company's shareholders by way of an ordinary resolution. Any authority under s. 551 must comply with the requirements of that section.

✓ If the rights of pre-emption in s. 561 of the Companies Act will apply to the allotment then the pre-emption procedure under s. 562 must be followed or else the provisions of s. 561 must be disapplied by special resolution of the company's shareholders.

✓ It is normal practice for the persons applying for shares to provide the company with signed letters confirming the number of shares applied for and monies to be paid.

✓ Consider any issues concerning the capacity of the applicants to own shares (see Chapter 10).

✓ The directors must approve the allotments either at a board meeting or, subject to the articles, by a resolution in writing.

✓ Article 21 of the Model Articles requires all shares to be allotted as fully paid. If this or a similar article applies then the required subscription monies must be received by the company in full before the allotments can proceed.

✓ Once approved, details of the allotments must be notified to the Registrar of Companies on form SH01 within one month of the date of allotment.

✓ Details of the allotments must be entered in the register of members within two months of the date of allotment. Although not a legal requirement it is good practice to record the same or similar details in the register of allotments.

✓ Each allottee must be issued with a properly executed share certificate within two months of the date of allotment.

✓ At all stages professional advice should be taken.

Summary

- Shares confer rights on the person who holds them in relation to the company that issued them.
- The first shares in a company are issued on incorporation to the subscribers to the company's memorandum of association. Thereafter the power to allot new shares resides with the directors but they can only exercise that power if authorised by the shareholders or the articles.
- Ordinary shares are the basic building block of a company's share capital, conferring the right to vote and the right to participate in dividends and capital distributions. Ordinary shares rank last for payment in the event of a winding up.
- Other types of shares include preference shares, redeemable shares and convertible shares. These types of shares generally confer preferential rights or rights not normally ascribed to ordinary shares.
- The rights attaching to a class of shares will either be set out in the articles of association, or in the ordinary resolution by which the shareholders gave the directors the authority to allot them.
- There are various reasons why a company might issue shares with different rights. Investment or financing arrangements are a common example, as is issuing shares to family members or employees.
- Where the rights attaching to a particular class of shares are altered, the procedure set out in the Companies Act must be followed, unless there is a procedure set out in the articles.
- There are many issues to consider in relation to an allotment of new shares. Proper tax and legal advice should be taken in all cases.
- Directors can only allot shares if they have the authority to do so. In a private company authority can either come from s. 550 of the Companies Act or s. 551. Authorities under s. 551 must comply with the requirements of that section.
- The Companies Act gives existing holders of ordinary shares a right of first refusal in respect of the allotment of any new shares. These rights can be disapplied in different ways but all require shareholder approval.
- Shares can be paid for in cash or non-cash consideration, fully or partly paid. The Model Articles require all shares to be issued as fully paid.
- A company can return share capital to shareholders either by a reduction of capital or a buy-back of shares. The procedures are detailed and professional advice is essential.
- Consolidations, subdivisions and re-designations are generally used when a company re-organises its share capital. Again, professional advice is essential.

10 Register of members

▓ In this chapter

This chapter looks in detail at the register of members and explains:

- the information that must be included in the register and other rules in the Companies Act that are applicable;
- who can become a shareholder and how to deal with unincorporated associations;
- rules about the location and inspection of the register;
- the procedure for updating shareholders' details;
- the rules about share transfers and the procedure for dealing with them; and
- the procedure for dealing with the death of a shareholder.

▓ The register of members

The obligation to keep a register of members is enshrined in s. 113 of the Companies Act. It is referred to as a register of *members* as opposed to a register of *shareholders* because the obligation to keep one applies to all companies whether the company has a share capital or not. Section 112 states that:

> every person who agrees to become a member of a company, and whose name is entered in the register of members, is a member of the company.

Accordingly, a person does not become a member of a company (and is not able to exercise the rights of membership) until their name is entered in the company's register of members.

The register of members must contain the following information:

- the name and address of each member;
- the date on which each person was entered as a member; and
- the date on which each person ceased to be a member.

In a company limited by shares, the register must also show:

- the number of shares of each class held by each member;
- the distinguishing numbers of the shares (if the shares have distinguishing numbers); and
- the amount paid or agreed to be considered as paid on the shares held by each member.

It is not a legal requirement, but it is a good idea to include cross-references to the company's register of allotments and register of transfers so that each acquisition and disposal of shares can be easily matched with the relevant entry in the register of allotments or transfers. Each shareholder's details should be entered on a separate page. If a shareholder holds shares of different classes, these should also be entered on separate pages and treated as separate holdings (or 'accounts'). In the case of a company that does not have a share capital but has more than one class of members, the register must state the class to which each member belongs. An example of a register of members can be found in Appendix 4.

Rules about the register of members

As well as stipulating the information that must be kept in it, the Companies Act sets out some additional rules about the register of members as follows.

Joint holders

When shares are held jointly by more than one person, the names of all of the joint holders must be entered in the register of members in respect of the shares that are held jointly by them. However, for the purposes of the Companies Act, joint holders are regarded as a single member and only one address can be entered for them in the register (s. 113(5)). The address stated in the register is the address to which any communications from the company will be sent. If the shares held jointly confer the right to vote then the joint holders are not entitled to one vote each but to one vote between them. Note, however, that this is the case on a vote taken by way of a show of hands. On a vote by way of a poll, provided that there are sufficient shares to enable it, each joint holder could be appointed as proxy in respect of one or more of the shares held jointly and thereby vote individually, provided that ultimately no more than one vote is cast for each share (see Chapter 11).

Index

If a company has more than 50 members, then it must keep an index of the names of the members of the company and must keep it available for inspection at the same place as the register of members. The index must enable the account of any given member in the register of members to be readily found and must be updated on an ongoing basis in order to reflect any changes made to the register. Any updates to the index must be made within 14 days of the corresponding alteration in the register of members (s. 115). If the register is in such a form as to constitute an index in itself, then this rule does not apply, but otherwise failure to comply is an offence on the part of the company and every officer in default.

Single member companies

A limited company that is incorporated with only one member must include a statement in the account of the sole member saying that the company has only one member (s. 123). If a company becomes a single member company at any time during the life of the company a similar statement must be made in the account of the sole member including the date on which the membership fell to one. If the number of members increases to two or more at any time, then a statement must be entered in the register of members, in the account of the person who was formerly the sole member, that the company has ceased to have only one member and the date on which this occurred. Failure to comply is an offence on the part of the company and every officer in default.

Example wording: single member companies

Pursuant to section 123 of the Companies Act 2006, it is recorded that the company [was incorporated as] [became] a single member company on ………..………….. [date].

The company ceased to be a single member company on…………….. [date].

Former members

Entries in the register relating to people who have ceased to be members can be removed from the register after the expiration of 10 years from the date on which they ceased to be a member.

■ Can anyone become a shareholder?

With a few exceptions, the Companies Act does not place any restrictions on who can take shares in a company. However, shares are property and not all prospective shareholders will have the legal capacity to own them. Partnerships, clubs and associations are the kinds of organisations and bodies that should not be entered into a register of members. This is because they are all examples of 'unincorporated' bodies. These kinds of organisations do not have the legal personality of a natural person or an incorporated company and cannot own property in their own right. Such bodies can and do sometimes find their way into registers of members but this should be avoided if at all possible. The reason for this is that when shares are registered in the name of an unincorporated body, the directors can have no comfort or guarantee as to the authority of any person that purports to execute a transfer of shares on behalf of that body.

To explain this further, as far as a natural person is concerned, that person or their attorney (acting under a properly delegated power) has the authority to sign a stock transfer form to give effect to a transfer of their shares – there is therefore certainty about who has the right to execute a transfer of the shares. In the case of a limited company the directors also have certainty because the Companies Act provides rules that say when a document will be deemed in law to have been executed by that company (see Chapter 8). However, in the case of a club, partnership or other association, there are no rules that the directors can rely on that tell them who has the authority to execute a transfer of the shares. A club, partnership or association cannot sign anything in its own right because the law doesn't recognise it as a legal person.

Example

A company receives and accepts in error a stock transfer form to transfer shares to a partnership called ABC and Sons.

Some time later the company receives another stock transfer form to transfer all of the shares registered in the name of ABC and Sons into the name of Mr John Smith. The stock transfer form bears two signatures.

What should the company do? If the directors do not know who the partners are they will not know whether all of the partners have signed the stock transfer form. If that is the case, the directors cannot be sure that all of the partners are aware of and have consented to the transfer.

Accordingly, it would be advisable in this scenario for the directors to return the stock transfer form to the person who lodged it requesting that it be signed by all the partners and also requesting a declaration that the signatures on the form are those of all the partners in the partnership. The directors at least then have something to fall back on if the transfer is challenged at a later date.

Trusts

Trusts are explicitly prohibited from being entered in a company's register of members by the Companies Act. Section 126 states that:

> no notice of any trust, express, implied or constructive, shall be entered on the register of members.

There are many different types of trust and they can arise or be created in a number of different ways. Property that is subject to a trust is legally owned by the trustees but the trustees have no right to take any benefit from it. Rather, the trustees are under a duty to deal with and protect the property for those persons who are the beneficiaries of the trust (this is like the fiduciary relationship that directors have with their company).

Trusts present the same kind of problem as partnerships, clubs and associations. They often have names and this can give the impression that they are legal entities in their own right when in fact they aren't. Entering the name of a trust in a register of members gives no clue as to the identity of the true legal owners of the shares. Just as a company's directors may not know who the partners are in a particular partnership, they may also not know who the trustees are of a given trust. So, as with a partnership, the directors may not know who has the authority to execute a transfer of shares registered in the name of a trust.

Dealing with trusts and unincorporated bodies

Instead of registering shares in the name of an unincorporated body, shares should be registered in the names of one or more persons authorised (and trusted) to hold the shares on behalf of the body in question. For a partnership this could be one or more of the partners, for a club or association it could be the chairman or secretary. In the case of a trust, the shares should be registered in the names of all of the trustees.

Once shares have been registered in this way and provided that the articles contain an article similar to article 23 of the Model Articles, the directors do not need to be concerned with the rights of any underlying beneficiaries. This is because article 23 says that:

> except as required by law, no person is to be recognised by the company as holding any share upon any trust, and except as otherwise required by law or the articles, the company is not in any way to be bound by or recognise any interest in a share other than the holder's absolute ownership of it and all the rights attaching to it.

Essentially, this means that the legal owner of a share is the person whose name is entered in the register of members as the holder of that share. From the company's point of view, it is that person and that person alone, who can authorise a transfer or other disposal of the share and who can exercise any of the rights attaching to the share. The company does not have to take account of and is not liable for the claims of any underlying beneficiary. This applies whether shares are held by one person or are held jointly.

Minors

There is nothing to stop persons under the age of 18 from holding shares in a company however it can give rise to certain issues which are best avoided. That being the case it is normal practice for such shares to be registered in the name of an adult (usually a parent) who will then hold the shares on trust for the minor until they reach the age of 18.

Location and inspection

The register of members must be kept either at the company's registered office or at the company's single alternative inspection location (see Chapter 4). As noted above, if the company is obliged to keep an index of the names of its members, then this must be kept at the same place as the register of members.

Like most other company records, the register of members must be open to inspection by the company's members without charge and by any other person on payment of the prescribed fee (again, see Chapter 4). Unlike any other company records however, the right to inspect the register of members (or to be provided with a copy of it) is subject to certain important controls. These controls were introduced by the current Companies Act to prevent misuse of the information that must – by law – be entered in the register.

Section 116 request

Anyone wishing to inspect a company's register of members or wishing to be provided with a copy of it must make a request to the company in a form that complies with s. 116(4) of the Companies Act. The request must state:

- in the case of an individual, his name and address;
- in the case of an organisation, the name and address of an individual responsible for making the request on behalf of the organisation;
- the purpose for which the information is to be used;
- whether the information will be disclosed to any other person and if so:
  - where that person is an individual, his name and address;
  - where that person is an organisation, the name and address of an individual responsible for receiving the information on its behalf; and
  - the purpose for which the information is to be used by that person.

Receiving a section 116 request

If a company receives a request under s. 116 it should be reviewed carefully to ensure that it complies with the requirements of that section, as set out above. Particular attention should be paid to the stated purpose for which the information will be used because if the directors consider that the information will be used for an improper purpose, they can make an application to court for the court to rule on whether or not the purpose is proper. If satisfied that it is not, the court will direct the company not to comply with the request (and may direct the company not to comply other requests made for a similar purpose, whether made by the same person or not). Accordingly, having received a s. 116 request there are just two options as to what the company can do. The company must, within five days, either:

- grant the request; or
- if the directors are not satisfied that the request is made for a proper purpose,

make an application to court and notify the person who made the request that they are doing so.

It is very important that the company does not simply ignore the request and take no action on it as the failure or refusal to allow inspection of the register or to provide a copy of it is an offence on the part of the company and every officer in default, unless that refusal has been authorised by the court (s. 118).

What is a proper purpose?

Unfortunately the Companies Act does not define a proper purpose and this point has not, to date, been tested in court. However, the ICSA has produced a guidance note which sets out helpful examples of what may or may not be regarded as a proper purpose. Suggested proper purposes include matters such as:

- a shareholder checking that his details are accurately recorded in the register;
- checking the shareholdings of a deceased person by the executor (or a solicitor appointed by the executor) for probate purposes; and
- persons seeking shareholder information with a view to enforcing a judgment.

Suggested improper purposes include:

- any purpose that could be unlawful such as identity theft;
- communications to shareholders that the company considers would threaten, harass or intimidate members or would otherwise be an unwarranted misuse of shareholders' personal information; and
- marketing and commercial mailings.

The full content of the note is not repeated here but it is recommended reading as it also provides guidance on best practice for dealing with s. 116 requests. Given that the company only has five days to deal with these requests, they need to be identified and processed as soon as possible. It would be of great benefit if the company has already put a suitable procedure in place before any such requests are received.

It is important to remember that access to or copies of the register of members should not be given to anyone unless a formal request has been made under s. 116, even if the company is happy that it is for a proper purpose. All company officers and relevant employees need to be aware of this, as failure to observe the correct procedure could result in the directors being liable for breaches of data protection law.

The ICSA guidance note can be found on the ICSA website at www.icsa.org. uk.

Granting a request

When a request to inspect or to be provided with a copy of the register is granted, the company must comply with one final obligation. Section 120 requires the company to inform any person inspecting the register (or being provided with a copy) whether the information contained in the register is up to date and if not, the date to which it has been made up. As usual, failure to do this is an offence on the part of the company and every officer who is in default. As far as the actual mechanics of providing access to the register of members are concerned (whether by inspection or by copy), the same rules apply as to any other company records. These rules are set out in the Companies (Company Records) Regulations 2008 (SI 2008/3006) and are described in Chapter 4, along with details of the fees that the company can charge either for allowing an inspection or for providing copies.

Offences

It is also worth mentioning that s. 119 of the Companies Act sets out two offences in connection with requests under s. 116 that apply to persons making such requests, or the disclosure of information obtained as a result of such a request being granted. These are:

- knowingly or recklessly making a statement in a s. 116 request that is misleading, false or deceptive in a material particular; and
- disclosing information obtained by a s. 116 request to another person (as a result of something done or failed to be done) knowing that they might use the information for an improper purpose.

◼ Maintenance of the register of members

The register of members must be updated on an ongoing basis to reflect any changes. It is very important that this is done as not only is it a legal requirement, but from the company's point of view it is also essential to be able to identify clearly and easily who the company's shareholders are at any one time. Even in a small company with just a few shareholders, failing to properly keep track of any movements in the company's share capital or changes to the company's shareholders can give rise to problems at a later date – should a bank or other lender wish to inspect the register, for example, or in the due diligence process that precedes a sale of a company. It can also create doubts or uncertainty as to the extent of any given shareholder's shareholding, which in turn can lead to disputes. Engaging the services of a professional to try and unravel the history of a company's share capital can be an expensive exercise. It can be avoided by keeping on top of changes as they occur, following the correct procedures and ensuring that any necessary documentation is in place and kept for future reference. This part of this chapter describes how to deal with the most common events that must be reflected in the register of members, other than share allotments which are dealt with in Chapter 9.

Change of address

If a shareholder changes address then that shareholder's account needs to be updated to show the new address. As a security measure, any notice of a change of address should be in writing (not electronic form and not taken over the telephone), should be signed and dated by the shareholder and should state the shareholder's previous address as well as the new one. This notice should be kept safely for future reference. As an additional measure, a letter could be sent to the old and the new addresses to confirm that the company has received the notice. If a fraud is being attempted the shareholder should thereby be alerted.

Change of name

There are various circumstances in which a shareholder may change their name. These include marriage, divorce, an official change by deed poll or an unofficial change with no formality. Care needs to be taken before registering a change of name and the appropriate documentation should be requested and scrutinised before proceeding. The table below sets out the documentation that should be requested depending on the nature of the change.

Table 10.1: Required documentation

Nature of change	Documentation required
Marriage	The original marriage certificate or a certified copy
Divorce	The original decree absolute or a certified copy
Change of name by deed poll	The original deed poll or a certified copy
Unofficial change with no formality	A statutory declaration as to the change of name. Photo ID from before and after the name change – either originals or certified copies.
Change of name of a corporate shareholder	The original certificate on change of name issued by the Registrar of Companies or a certified copy

Once the appropriate documentation has been received it should be checked carefully against the details recorded in the register of members. Any queries or concerns should be addressed with the shareholder before making any changes. Copies of all relevant documents should be retained. The shareholder's account should be updated to reflect the change of name, preserving the previous name for future reference (e.g. by striking through it so that it remains visible) and stating the date on which the change was made. In all cases the shareholder's share certificate should be cancelled and a new certificate be issued in their new name.

Helpful hints: certified copies and statutory declarations

A 'certified copy' is a copy of a document that has been certified as a true and complete copy of the original by a solicitor, accountant, bank official or doctor. The person certifying the copy must examine the original, take a copy and then endorse the copy with a statement saying:

Certified as a true and complete copy of the original

Signed ....

Name ....

Occupation ....

Dated ....

A 'statutory declaration' is a formal and legal declaration by a person attesting the truth of certain stated facts. Statutory declarations are made pursuant to the Statutory Declarations Act 1835 and must be in the form prescribed by that act.

The declaration must be signed in the presence of a commissioner for oaths (a solicitor, barrister or notary public among others) who must also sign the declaration to confirm that they have witnessed the signature of the person making it. The declaration then becomes evidence of the matters that are stated in it.

Rectifying shareholder details

Minor errors in a shareholder's name or address can be corrected in the register of members under the supervision of an appropriate person such as a director or company secretary. No changes should be made that materially affect the identity of a shareholder. Substantive changes should generally not be made without a court order so, if in doubt, take professional advice.

Share transfers

A share transfer is the means by which one person can acquire some or all of the shares held by another person in a given company. Article 26(1) of the Model Articles states that shares can be transferred by 'an instrument of transfer in any usual form or any other form approved by the directors'. The usual form for an instrument of transfer is the 'stock transfer form'. They can be obtained from legal stationers, solicitors, accountants or other providers of legal documents. Once it has been properly completed and signed, a stock transfer form transfers the 'beneficial title' to the shares from the current owner to the new owner. The 'legal title' does not pass to the new owner until the transfer has been registered in the company's register of members (see article 26(4)). Until that time, the shares are held on trust by the former owner for the benefit of the new owner. This facet of English company law means that although a stock transfer form has been signed and completed, the new owner is not the legal owner and cannot exercise any of the rights attaching to the shares, until his name is entered in the register of members.

Completing a stock transfer form

It is important that stock transfer forms are completed correctly. If a company receives a stock transfer form that has not been completed properly then it should not be accepted and should be returned to the person who lodged it for the relevant deficiencies to be rectified. The stock transfer form must identify, among other things:

- the name of the company in which the shares are held;
- the number and class of shares being transferred;
- the person transferring the shares (the 'transferor'); and
- the person acquiring the shares (the 'transferee').

It must also state the consideration paid for the shares, the value of which will determine whether the transfer is subject to stamp duty or not (see further below). If a shareholder is transferring shares of more than one class, a separate stock transfer form needs to be completed for each class of shares. In the case of shares being transferred by joint shareholders, the names of each joint holder should be stated on the transfer form and each joint holder must sign it.

Some of the terminology used on the standard stock transfer form is fairly legalistic. This is because 'stock' doesn't necessarily mean 'shares' and the form has to cater for the transfer of all types of securities. Appendix 6 provides an example of a stock transfer form with notes as to what information needs to go where when the form is being used for a transfer of shares (as opposed to any other kind of security).

Stamp duty

A stock transfer form (or other instrument of transfer) is subject to stamp duty unless:

- the consideration for the transfer is nil;
- the transfer is exempt;
- the transfer qualifies for relief; or
- the consideration for the transfer is not chargeable consideration.

When stamp duty is not payable

If the consideration for the transfer does not exceed £1,000 then no stamp duty has to be paid. This means that if the consideration paid for the shares is

£1,000 or less then exemption from stamp duty can be claimed. This is done by completing certificate 1 on the reverse of the stock transfer form. The wording of the certificate should be noted because it requires a declaration that the consideration for the transfer does not exceed £1,000 *and* that the transfer does not form part of series of transfers where the overall or aggregate consideration *does* exceed £1,000. This is intended to prevent a single transfer from being split up into a number of smaller transfers to avoid paying stamp duty but could also apply where a number of apparently separate transfers are linked in some way.

Transfers are also exempt if no consideration is given for the transfer. Examples of when this might occur include:

- shares transferred as a gift;
- shares held in trust that are transferred from one trustee to another;
- shares transferred to a beneficiary under a trust when the trust is wound up; and
- shares transferred as security for a loan.

In this case, the word 'nil' should be clearly stated in the consideration box on the front side of the stock transfer form. If no consideration is given for the transfer then neither certificate on the reverse of the stock transfer form needs to be completed.

There are also certain types of transfer which are exempt from stamp duty in law such as transfers as part of a divorce settlement or when a civil partnership is dissolved. Where a transfer is for chargeable consideration, but is exempt from stamp duty by application of a statutory exemption, certificate 2 on the reverse of the stock transfer form must be completed. Certificate 2 also needs to be completed if the consideration for the transfer is not chargeable consideration. Chargeable consideration is:

- cash;
- other stocks and shares; or
- debt.

A stock transfer form does not need to be submitted to HMRC if either certificate 1 or certificate 2 has been completed, or the consideration for the transfer is nil. In any of these cases it should be sent directly to the company for approval and (subject to the same) registration.

Specific reliefs
There are certain circumstances in which specific reliefs from stamp duty can be claimed such as where shares are being transferred between companies in the same group or where a company acquires all of the shares in another company by allotting new shares to the selling shareholders as consideration for the transfer of their shares (known as a 'share for share exchange'). Various conditions apply to such reliefs and professional advice should be taken. Where a transfer qualifies for

stamp duty relief the stock transfer form must be sent to HMRC to be stamped as exempt.

If stamp duty is payable

If the consideration for the transfer is more than £1,000 then stamp duty will be payable and is normally paid by the person acquiring the shares (the transferee). The stock transfer form must be sent to the HMRC Stamp Office in Birmingham together with the correct amount of stamp duty (see the directory for the full address). The duty is calculated as 0.5% of the consideration, rounded up to the nearest £5.00 and must be paid within 30 days of the date of signature on the stock transfer form. If it is paid late, then penalties may be incurred. On receipt of the transfer form and payment, HMRC literally stamps the form to show that the duty has been paid.

Helpful hints: checking stamp duty

For a company receiving a stock transfer form, it is crucial to check that the form has either been stamped with the correct amount of stamp duty, has been certified as duty exempt under certificate 1 or certificate 2, or else that the consideration for the transfer is nil. This is because s. 17 of the Stamp Act 1891 makes it an offence to register a transfer of shares if the stock transfer form has not been properly stamped. In addition, an unstamped stock transfer form cannot be used in any legal proceedings until it has been stamped and penalties for late stamping have been paid. If the directors are not sure whether a stock transfer form has been stamped with the correct amount of duty it should be sent to HMRC for adjudication. This might be particularly relevant in cases where a series of transfers could appear to be linked.

Receiving a stock transfer form

Section 771 of the Act says that when a transfer of shares has been lodged with a company, the company must either:

- register the transfer, or
- give the transferee notice of refusal to register the transfer together with its reasons for the refusal.

In either case, this must be done 'as soon as practicable' or at the latest within two months after the date on which the transfer is received. Article 26(5) of the Model Articles gives the directors a general power to refuse any share transfer. Most standard articles include a provision of this sort and if so the decision to accept or reject a transfer rests with the directors. A meeting of the directors there-fore needs to be called so that they can make a decision to approve or reject the transfer, or to request such further information from the transferor or transferee as they need to make that decision. As mentioned in Chapter 3, a common addition to standard form articles are provisions to restrict share transfers by giving the other shareholders rights of pre-emption (a right of first refusal).

On receiving a stock transfer form, various basic checks need to be made before the directors formally resolve to approve or reject it.

- Check that the form has been completed correctly. For example, make sure that all required information has been provided and that the form does not purport to transfer shares of more than one class.
- If the company has more than one class of shares, check that the shares have been correctly identified by their class and nominal value.
- Check that there is a complete match between the transferor details stated in the form and the transferor's account in the company's register of members.
- The transfer must be accompanied by a valid, original share certificate (not a copy) in the name of the transferor representing at least the number of shares being transferred. If the share certificate has not been provided this must be surrendered to the company before the transfer can go any further.
- Check that the transferor details (as stated in the stock transfer form and in the register of members) also agree with the details shown on the share certificate accompanying the transfer.
- If the share certificate is a replacement for a certificate reported as lost or destroyed then check that the certificate provided is the duplicate issued by the company.
- Check the amount of the consideration for the transfer and make sure that the form has either been stamped correctly or certified as exempt. If an exemption has been claimed the consideration cannot exceed £1,000.
- If the transferor is not known to the directors and there is any doubt over the authenticity of the signature on the form, consider requesting an official document that bears the transferor's signature such as a passport or driving licence.

Processing a stock transfer form

The procedure for registering a transfer of shares is as follows.

- Record the transfer in the company's register of transfers showing the names of the transferor and transferee, the number and class of shares transferred and the date that the entry is made. The transfer should be given a reference number which should be stated in the register (share transfers, like share allotments, are usually just numbered consecutively).
- In the transferor's account in the register of members, an entry needs to be made to show the disposal of the shares and the new balance of the account. The reference number of the transfer from the register of transfers should be stated. It is also useful to add a note explaining the nature of the disposal (i.e. that this is a share transfer and who the shares have been transferred to).

- If the transferor no longer holds any shares in the company as a result of the transfer, the date on which he has ceased to be a member of the company must be stated in his account.

- In the transferee's account in the register of members, a corresponding entry needs to be made to show the acquisition of the shares and the new balance of the transferee's account. As above, the entry in the register of transfers should be referenced and a note made to indicate the nature of the acquisition and who the shares were transferred from.

- If the transferee is a new member of the company their full details must be entered in the register in accordance with the requirements of the Companies Act (see earlier).

- The date that is entered in the register of members for the disposal/acquisition should be the date on which the entries are made (not the date on the stock transfer form unless it is the same).

- The transferor's share certificate must be cancelled (usually done by striking it through and writing the word 'cancelled' in large letters across it) and stored safely with the company's statutory books and records. If the transferor's share certificate represented a greater number of shares than the number transferred then a 'balance certificate' should be issued by the company for the transferor's remaining holding.

- A new share certificate for the shares acquired by the transferee should be issued in the transferee's name. This must be done within two months of the date on which the transfer was received by the company (s. 776).

- The stock transfer form should be filed with the company's books and records and kept safely.

Rejecting a stock transfer form

Private companies can include provisions in their articles that place restrictions on who shares can be transferred to. For example, in a small family owned company, there may be a restriction in the articles that says that shares can only be transferred to immediate family members. The Model Articles do not contain any such restrictions other than the general power of directors to refuse a transfer in article 26(5). It should be noted, however, that this power must be exercised by the directors within the constraints of their general duties as directors – any decision to refuse a share transfer must be made in good faith and for the benefit of the company. Most standard articles (as used by solicitors and formation agents) are no different to the Model Articles in this respect.

There is nothing in the Act to give shareholders a right of first refusal on share transfers but provisions can be included in a company's articles that give other shareholders rights of pre-emption which entitle them to a right of first refusal on any shares that a fellow shareholder wishes to transfer. The rights of pre-emption will usually apply to all share transfers perhaps with certain specified types of transfer being permitted, such as transfers to family members or to the trustees of a family trust. Where a company's articles contain provisions of this sort they must be followed carefully unless all of the shareholders (other than the transferee) waive their pre-emption rights by notice in writing to the company. Professional advice is recommended.

If the directors do refuse a share transfer, the stock transfer form must be returned to the person who lodged it, together with the notice of refusal, unless the directors suspect that the transfer is fraudulent. As mentioned above, this must be done within two months of receiving the transfer form. The company must give its reasons for the refusal and must provide the transferee with such further information about the reasons for the refusal that the transferee may reasonably request (s. 771).

Reasons for rejecting a stock transfer form might include:

- missing or unclear information – such as the consideration paid for the shares, or the full name and address of the transferee;
- an inadequate or incomplete match between the transferor's details as stated on the form and the details recorded in the register of members;
- a query regarding stamp duty payable on the transfer;
- a query regarding the signature(s) of the transferor – missing signatures of one or more joint shareholders, for example;
- a suspicion that the transfer may be fraudulent; and
- a transfer to a person of whom the directors do not approve.

A note about joint shareholders

When joint shareholders wish to transfer some or all of their shares then all of the joint shareholders must sign the stock transfer form. When shares are registered in joint names on behalf of an unincorporated association or a trust, any change in the joint owners (other than as a result of a death) needs to be dealt with by way of a formal share transfer (e.g. if shares are registered in the name of four trustees and one of the trustees resigns his position, the name of the departing trustee cannot simply be removed from the register of members). All four trustees must sign a stock transfer form to transfer the shares held by them into the names of the three remaining trustees. The original share certificate bearing the names of the four joint holders must be surrendered to the company together with the stock transfer form. Once the transfer has been registered, a new share certificate must be issued in the names of the three remaining joint holders. The position is different if a joint shareholder dies, and this is explained further below.

Missing share certificates

It is not uncommon for a shareholder to lose his share certificate and this often comes to light when he wishes to transfer some or all of his shares. A share certificate is an important document as it is evidence of a shareholding and as noted above, a share transfer cannot be processed without the corresponding share certificate being surrendered to the company. There is a risk to a company in providing a shareholder with a replacement share certificate as the company can never be sure if the original certificate has genuinely been lost and two share certificates being in existence for the same shares could facilitate a fraud on the register. For this reason it is normal practice to ask the shareholder to sign a 'letter of indemnity' to confirm that the share certificate has been lost or destroyed and to indemnify the company against any claims that may be made against the company or its directors as a result of issuing the replacement certificate. When the shares are of high value, the company may also insist on the indemnity being joined in by a bank, insurance company or other financial institution so that it is in effect underwritten by the institution in question. A replacement share certificate should be clearly marked as a duplicate and the company should keep a note in its records that the original certificate has been lost and a duplicate certificate has been issued. The signed letter of indemnity should be kept safely.

Death of a shareholder

When receiving notice of the death of a shareholder the directors need to make sure that they have been provided with the correct documentation to enable them to register a change of ownership of the deceased shareholder's shares. The documentation required depends on whether the shareholder made a will or not and also depends on whether the shares were held jointly with another party. No requests to transfer a deceased shareholder's shares should be processed until the company has seen evidence to confirm the authority of certain specified persons to deal with the deceased shareholder's property.

Grant of probate

When a shareholder dies, any shares that they hold form part of the collection of property and assets that they leave behind them known as their 'estate'. If a shareholder has made a will then the will sets out how the property should be distributed and gives the names of the people who will be responsible for dealing with this. These people are known as 'executors'. The executors must apply to their local probate office for a document to prove their authority to deal with the deceased shareholder's estate and this is known as a 'grant of probate', or just 'probate' for short.

Letters of administration

If a shareholder dies without a will then they are said to have died 'intestate' and the distribution of their estate will be made in accordance with the rules of intestacy. In this case, the close relatives of the shareholder can apply for the right to deal with the shareholder's estate in the form of a 'grant of letters of administration'. Those people named in the grant of administration are known as 'administrators'.

Receiving notice of the death of a shareholder

Sometimes it will be the deceased shareholder's solicitors who contact a company to advise of the shareholder's death. Sometimes it may be the family of the deceased. In either case, evidence is required to prove who has authority to deal with the deceased shareholder's shares which must either be in the form of a grant of probate or letters of administration. An original copy of either document should be provided. Original copies can easily be identified as they will bear the impressed stamp of the probate office. Initially the solicitors or family may provide a copy of the death certificate. This can be accepted as proof of the shareholder's death but it does not establish who has authority to deal with the deceased shareholder's shares.

On receipt of a grant of probate or letters of administration, a careful check needs to be made between the name and address of the deceased as it appears in the document provided and the same details as they appear in the register of members. It is important to identify all shareholdings of the deceased including any joint shareholdings. If satisfied that there is a complete match, the shareholder's account(s) in the register of members should be noted with the fact of his death (by entering the word 'deceased' after his name) together with the names of the executors or administrators. The deceased shareholder's address should be amended to that of the executors or administrators. If there is not a clear or complete match between the information provided in the probate or letters of administration and the information in the register of members then further details should be requested to resolve this.

Sometimes the deceased shareholder's solicitors may send the company the deceased shareholders' share certificate(s) for endorsement. In this case, the fact of death should be stated on the certificate together with the names of the executors or administrators. The change should be initialled and dated by a company officer. A copy of the probate or letters of administration should be taken and kept securely before returning the original to the sender.

Rights of executors and administrators over a deceased shareholder's shares

When a shareholder dies, the legal title to his shares passes automatically to his executors. This is known as 'transmission'. A transmission of shares occurs where the legal ownership of shares is transferred from one person to another by operation of law. A stock transfer form is not required in these circumstances as the change of ownership takes place automatically.

Once they have become entitled to a deceased shareholder's shares, the articles of association will normally provide executors and administrators with two possible options as to what they can do with them. Under articles 27 and 28 of the Model Articles the executors or administrators can either:

- execute a stock transfer form to give effect to a transfer of the deceased shareholder's shares; or
- they can ask for their names to be entered in the register of members as the legal owners of the shares.

If the executors or administrators elect to become the holders of the shares then they must notify the company in writing of that wish. The written request is sometimes referred to as a 'letter of request'. If the executors or administrators elect to have the shares registered into their own names then for the purpose of making appropriate entries in the register of members a new account should be created in their names so as to preserve the original entries relating to the deceased shareholder. A note should be made in the account of the deceased shareholder to record what has happened to his shares. The letter of request itself should be kept safely for future reference. The original share certificates for the deceased shareholder's shares must be surrendered to the company for cancellation and a new share certificate issued in the names of the executors.

If the executors wish to have the shares transferred to another person then they must complete a stock transfer form (see article 28 of the Model Articles). A transfer of shares by executors or administrators should be dealt with in the same way as any other transfer. Under s. 773 of the Companies Act, executors or administrators can execute a stock transfer form as if they were themselves members of the company. Again, the original share certificate must be cancelled, and a new share certificate issued.

The executors may hold the legal title to the deceased shareholder's shares for some months before they are in a position to take any action. In this regard, article 27(3) of the Model Articles should be noted as this states that the executors or administrators will not have the right to attend or vote at a general meeting or to agree to a written resolution of the company unless their names are entered in the register of members as the owners of the shares to which they are entitled. Furthermore, until such time as the deceased shareholder's shares are transferred or registered in the name of the executors or administrators, any dividends paid to the deceased shareholder will form part of his or her estate along with any other property and assets.

If a company's articles include restrictions on share transfers then these provisions will still apply irrespective of the wishes of the deceased shareholder or the executors or administrators. For example, if a company's articles state that shares can only be transferred to family members then the executors are bound by this restriction regardless of any instructions left in the deceased shareholder's will. Similarly, if the articles contain provisions that give the other shareholders pre-emption rights on share transfers these articles may be drafted so that they take effect in the event of a transmission. In that case, the executors may be required by the articles to offer the shares to the other shareholders. If in doubt take professional advice.

Death of a joint shareholder

When two or more people hold shares jointly they each have complete ownership of all of the shares. This is the same as when people own a house jointly and rather than each person having a specified share in the house they each have a 100% stake in it. When property is owned jointly in this way and one of the joint owners dies, the 'rule of survivorship' comes in to effect and the property passes automatically to the remaining joint owners. So it is with joint shareholders. When a joint shareholder dies ownership of the shares passes automatically to the remaining joint shareholders. In order to record this in the company's register of members all the directors need to see is proof of death in the form of an original (or certified copy) death certificate. The fact of the joint shareholder's death should be noted and their name struck out from the relevant account in the register of members. A copy of the death certificate should be retained for the company's records. The joint shareholders' share certificate can either be endorsed with the fact of death of the relevant joint shareholder, or it can be cancelled and a new share certificate issued in its place.

■ Summary

- A company must keep and maintain a register of members which contains the details required by the Companies Act.
- There are various rules in the Act concerning the register of members such as those relating to joint shareholders, single member companies and the retention of the accounts of former members.
- Unincorporated bodies such as partnerships, clubs and trusts should not be entered in the register of members. Instead, shares owned by such bodies should be registered in the names of certain trusted individuals, all of the partners or all of the trustees, as the case may be.
- The register of members must be kept available for inspection by members and others but requests for inspection of the register must be made in accordance with the strict rules set out in the Companies Act.
- It is important that the register of members is kept up to date and that all changes are supported by the appropriate documentary evidence.
- Ownership of shares is transferred by way of a duly completed stock transfer form. A share transfer must not be registered unless the stock transfer form has been stamped as duty paid or is otherwise exempt from stamp duty.
- Although it is not a legal requirement it is normal practice for companies to maintain a register of share transfers which can help to keep track of changes of ownership.
- A company can place restrictions on share transfers by appropriate provisions in the articles of association. This might include giving existing shareholders a right of first refusal (pre-emption rights) on any share transfers except those that are permitted under the articles.

- When a shareholder dies, the right to his shares passes automatically to his personal representatives. This is known as transmission – a transfer of ownership that occurs by operation of law.
- Subject to the articles, the personal representatives can elect to have the shares registered in their names or can transfer them to someone else by completing a stock transfer form.
- In either case, the company will require proper evidence of the personal representatives' entitlement to the shares, either in the form of a grant of probate or letters of administration.
- When a joint shareholder dies, the rule of 'survivorship' applies and ownership of the shares resides with the remaining joint holders. No share transfer is necessary but the company must be provided with evidence of the death in the form of an original or certified copy death certificate.

11 Shareholders' decision-making: general meetings

■ In this chapter

This chapter introduces the decision-making powers of shareholders and explains the procedure for holding a general meeting, in particular with regard to:

- the decisions reserved to shareholders by the Companies Act;
- the difference between ordinary and special resolutions;
- calling a general meeting;
- the quorum for general meetings;
- the role and powers of the chairman;
- shareholder voting, voting by proxy and corporate representatives;
- the shareholders' right to circulate a statement in relation to a general meeting; and
- the shareholders' right to requisition a general meeting.

■ Shareholders' decision-making

Although shareholders have relatively little influence over the management of a company's affairs, the Companies Act gives them three main powers. These are:

- to vote on those matters that the Companies Act says can only be approved by a company's shareholders;
- to requisition a general meeting or the circulation of a written resolution; and
- to remove a director by ordinary resolution.

These are important rights for shareholders. They are governed by rules and procedures set out in the Companies Act and may be supplemented by additional provisions in the articles of association. The powers that the Companies Act reserves for shareholders generally concern matters that are of particular importance to them and to the company. They include (among others):

- authorising the directors to allot shares in the company;
- suspending the shareholders' rights of pre-emption in respect of an allotment

of shares (either a general suspension or suspension in respect of a particular allotment);

- altering the company's articles of association;
- changing the company's name;
- approving a purchase by the company of its own shares;
- approving a reduction of capital;
- approving a consolidation, sub-division or re-classification of shares in the company;
- removing and re-appointing the company's auditor; and
- removing a director by ordinary resolution.

As well as those matters stipulated by the Companies Act, a company's articles may also require shareholder approval to be given for additional matters (e.g. under article 30 of the Model Articles, a final dividend has to be declared by ordinary resolution of the company's shareholders). As mentioned in Chapter 3 there are some rules in the Companies Act that take effect subject to any provisions in a company's articles. For example, s. 618 allows a company to consolidate or subdivide its shares by ordinary resolution. However, s. 618(5) provides that this power can be restricted or excluded by the company's articles. As such, it is always essential to check both the Companies Act and the articles of association to ascertain the correct position on a particular matter and, if in doubt, to take professional advice. See Chapter 3.

Ordinary and special resolutions

Decisions of a company's shareholders are known as 'resolutions'. As well as setting out when shareholder approval is required for a particular decision or course of action, the Companies Act also states which type of shareholder resolution has to be passed in order to approve it. There are two different types of shareholder resolution – 'ordinary resolutions' and 'special resolutions'. An ordinary resolution is a resolution that is passed by a simple majority of the votes cast of shareholders voting in person or by duly appointed proxies (s. 282(1)). This means that over 50% of the votes cast must be in favour for the resolution to pass. A special resolution is a resolution that is passed by a majority of *not less* than 75% (s. 283(1)). Therefore a majority of 75% or over is required for a special resolution to pass.

When a special resolution is required, it is always specified in the Companies Act. As far as ordinary resolutions are concerned, s. 281(3) sets out a general rule that, where the Companies Act requires a resolution of the shareholders but does not say whether it should be an ordinary or a special resolution, an ordinary resolution is required unless the company's articles require a higher majority (or unanimity). In other words, if the Companies Act simply says 'resolution', then that means an ordinary resolution. Section 282(5) confirms that anything that can be done by ordinary resolution may also be done by special resolution, but it should be noted that the reverse is not the case – if the Companies Act requires a special resolution then an ordinary resolution will not have legal effect.

Once it is known that a particular decision needs to be put to the company's shareholders for approval there are two possible ways forward:

- to hold a 'general meeting' of the company's shareholders; or
- to circulate a shareholders' written resolution.

The rest of this chapter discusses the rules and procedures for calling and holding a general meeting. Written resolutions are dealt with in Chapter 12, along with other matters such as single member companies, annual general meetings, class meetings, record keeping and the important rules on company communications which always come into play one way or another in the course of putting decisions to a company's shareholders.

General meetings

Compared to the rules and procedures for directors' meetings, there is much more formality attached to the holding and running of a general meeting. In practice, most small private companies will need to hold a general meeting only very occasionally, if at all, as there is no longer a requirement in the Companies Act for such companies to hold an annual general meeting each calendar year (see Chapter 12). In companies with only a small number of shareholders it is usually easier and more practical for any shareholder decisions to be taken by way of a written resolution. There is far more administration involved in convening and holding a general meeting than there is in circulating a resolution in writing. As far as the Companies Act is concerned, there are only two decisions that cannot be dealt with by written resolution. These are:

- the removal of a director before the expiration of his term of office; and
- the removal of an auditor before the expiration of his term of office.

However, the more shareholders a company has, the less practical it becomes for decisions to be taken using this method. For companies with a large number of shareholders, holding general meetings may be a necessity and the directors will need to know and understand how to go about it. In addition, the Companies Act gives shareholders and, in certain circumstances the company's auditor, the right to require the directors to call a general meeting. As such, the need to hold a general meeting can arise unexpectedly, even in companies with just a few shareholders.

Rules and procedures

The rules about how to call and hold a general meeting are set out in the Companies Act but it doesn't cover everything and leaves out various procedural issues that need to be dealt with in the articles. It is in the interests of both shareholders and directors that general meetings run as smoothly as possible and as such most articles have detailed rules about general meetings. The Model Articles are no different. Accordingly, it is important to know what both the Companies Act and the Model Articles say in order to get the full picture.

The main issues to be aware of break down into the following:

- giving proper notice of the meeting – how to give it and who to give it to;
- how many shareholders must be present for the meeting to be quorate;
- who chairs the meeting, what is the chairman's role and what are his powers;
- who can attend a general meeting;
- voting at general meetings - voting on a show of hands and voting on a poll;
- voting by proxy and rules on appointing proxies;
- corporate representatives – how a shareholder which is a company can attend and vote at a general meeting;
- the right of shareholders to circulate a statement; and
- the right of shareholders to requisition a general meeting.

Each of these is considered below.

Notice

Calling a general meeting – also known as 'convening' a general meeting – is achieved by sending out a notice of the meeting to the company's shareholders. For the most part it is only a company's directors who have the power and authority to do this (s. 302). Although shareholders have the right to require the directors to call a general meeting, it is still the directors that must actually exercise that power. Only if the directors fail to call the requisitioned meeting within the time limits set out in the Companies Act can the shareholders take matters into their own hands. If the company has a secretary, then the directors may instruct the secretary to convene a general meeting on their behalf but this will always be a delegated power. The secretary cannot call a general meeting unless authorised and instructed to do so by the directors.

Contents of the notice

A notice of general meeting is a formal company document and so must clearly state the name of the company and the company number, as well as being headed up as a 'notice of general meeting'. There is no prescribed form for a notice of general meeting in either the Companies Act or the Model Articles but the Companies Act tells us what information a notice has to contain. Section 311 of the Act says that a notice of a general meeting must state:

- the time and date of the meeting;
- the place of the meeting; and
- the general nature of the business to be dealt with at the meeting.

Care needs to be taken to ensure that the notice is accurate in terms of the time, date and location of the meeting – an error of fact on any of these points will most likely render the notice ineffective. The statement about the 'general nature of the business to be dealt with' should be sufficient to enable a shareholder to understand the business that is to be transacted at the meeting. In practice it is usual to spell out the text of any resolutions that are to be put to the meeting which must be identified as either ordinary or special. In the case of a special resolution, it is essential that the notice contains the full text of the resolution. It will not be validly passed as a special resolution unless the notice specifies that it is a special resolution and sets out the text in full (s. 283(6)). It should also be noted that once a resolution has been specified as special it cannot then be passed as an ordinary resolution.

As well as the above, the notice must also include a statement to advise shareholders of:

- their right to appoint one or more proxies under s. 324 of the Companies Act; and
- any more extensive rights to appoint one or more proxies that may be contained in the company's articles.

The Model Articles do not contain any more extensive rights and this will be the same with most standard articles. If that is the case, only the first part of the above statement is required. Failure to include this statement in the notice will not affect the validity of the meeting or anything done at the meeting but it is an offence on the part of every officer of the company who is in default. Finally, the notice should state the authority by which it is issued (usually 'by order of the board'), the date of the notice and should be signed by either a director or the company secretary if the company has one.

What form does the notice have to take?

Under s. 308, notice of a general meeting must be given in one of the following ways:

- in hard copy form (e.g. sent by post);
- in electronic form (e.g. sent by e-mail); or
- by means of a website.

If the notice is given by means of a website, then the notification to the shareholder telling him that the notice is available to be viewed must state that it concerns a company meeting and specify the date, time and location of the meeting. The notice must remain on the website for the period beginning with the date of the notification and ending with the conclusion of the meeting (s. 309). (See Chapter 12 for an explanation of the overall procedure involved in sending company communications by website.)

How much notice has to be given?

Section 307 of the Companies Act states that a general meeting of a private company (not including an adjourned meeting), must be called by at least 14 days' notice. A company's articles can require a longer notice period but not a shorter one. Under s. 360, the 14-day notice period has to be 14 'clear days'. This means that it cannot include the day on which the notice is given (the day on which the shareholder receives it) and the day on which the meeting is held. In terms of determining when a shareholder has received the notice, s. 1147 sets out rules on deemed delivery that apply to all company communications. In the case of a notice of general meeting, the position is as follows.

- For a notice sent by post to an address in the UK where the company is able to show that it was properly addressed, prepaid and posted, the notice will be deemed to have been received 48 hours after it was posted.
- For a notice sent by electronic means where the company is able to show that it was properly addressed, the notice is deemed to have been received 48 hours after it was sent.
- Where the notice is given by means of publication on a website, it is deemed to have been received when it was first made available on the website or, if later, when the shareholder receives (or is deemed to have received) notification of the fact that the notice has been placed on the website.

In all cases, in calculating the 48-hour period, no account can be taken of any part of a day that is not a working day. These provisions on deemed delivery can be varied by a company's articles but the model articles do not alter them. For example, it is common for the articles to state that a communication sent by electronic means is deemed to be received at the time it was sent.

Helpful hints: calculating the right notice period

It is important to get the notice period right because if the correct notice is not given the meeting will generally be invalid. In calculating how much notice to give it is therefore advisable, if the circumstances allow, to err on the side of caution and to give more than just the minimum period of notice required by the Companies Act.

Example

If the directors of a company hold a directors' meeting on Monday 1 July and resolve to call a general meeting of the company, what is the earliest date on which the meeting can be held? If the notices are sent on Tuesday 2 July, they will be deemed to have been received by the shareholders 48 hours later on Thursday 4 July (in accordance with s. 1147) unless the articles say otherwise. This is the date on which the notice is given. From this point, 14 clear days are needed before the meeting can be held. The day of the meeting itself is not included in the period of clear days so the earliest that the meeting could be held would be Friday 19 July.

Failure to give proper notice

What if a company fails to give notice of a general meeting to one or more of its shareholders? Section 313 of the Companies Act says that any accidental failure to give notice to one or more of the company's shareholders is to be disregarded for the purposes of determining whether proper notice has been given. In other words, if the failure is accidental the notice will still be effective. If it is anything other than accidental the meeting may be invalid. However, a shareholder who does not personally receive notice of a general meeting but still attends and partic- ipates in the meeting is unlikely to be successful in challenging the validity of the notice (and thereby the validity of the meeting).

It needs to be noted that the relief provided by s. 313 does not apply to any notice given in respect of a general meeting that has been requisitioned by the shareholders themselves (whether the meeting is called by the directors, or called by the shareholders following the directors' failure to call the meeting – see later in this chapter). Failure to give notice of a requisitioned meeting to one or more shareholders will invalidate the meeting whether or not the failure was accidental.

Agreeing to shorter notice

In order to speed up the process of holding a general meeting, it is possible to hold the meeting on short notice (i.e. shorter than the 14 clear days required by the Companies Act) provided that a requisite majority of shareholders agree. The requisite majority is stipulated in s. 307 and is a majority in number of the shareholders having the right to attend and vote at the meeting who together hold shares that represent no less than 90% of the nominal value of the shares giving the right to attend and vote at the meeting.

What this translates as is that in order to hold a general meeting on short notice, the short notice must be agreed to by a majority of the shareholders who are entitled to attend and vote at the meeting (i.e. over 50% in number must agree); as long as that majority of shareholders (whether that be 60%, 70% or so on) hold between them 90% in nominal value of the shares giving the right to attend and vote at the general meeting.

So, in a company with 10 shareholders, at least six will have to agree to the short notice and even then, that agreement will only be effective if between them those six shareholders hold 90% or more (in nominal value) of the shares giving the right to attend and vote at the meeting. To extend this example, if each shareholder holds 10 shares, and each share has a nominal value of £1.00, then agreement will be needed from at least nine shareholders because only this will achieve the required percentage (90%) in nominal value.

The Companies Act allows the 90% threshold to be raised to 95% by a company's articles. This would make it slightly more difficult to obtain agreement, but the Model Articles do not do this. For companies with more than one class of shares, the position regarding the voting rights attaching to shares of each class should always be checked as the agreement to short notice can only be given by shareholders holding shares that confer the right to attend and vote at the general meeting. It is good practice for an agreement to short notice to be in writing. It should take the form of a statement, signed by the requisite majority of shareholders, confirming their consent to the meeting being held on less than the period of notice required by the Companies Act or by the company's articles, as the case may be.

Who does the notice have to be sent to?

Notice of a general meeting has to be sent to every member of the company and every director (s. 310). 'Member' includes any person who is entitled to a share as a result of the death or bankruptcy of a shareholder, provided that the company has been notified of their entitlement. Section 310 takes effect subject to the company's articles. So, for example, a company's articles may state that shares of a particular class do not confer the right to receive notice of (or to attend or vote at) general meetings of the company.

If the company has appointed an auditor, then s. 502(2) states that the auditor is also entitled to receive notice of all general meetings and any other communications relating to general meetings. The auditor may attend any general meeting of the company and is entitled to be heard on any business of the meeting that concerns him as auditor.

Resolutions that require 'special notice'

Some resolutions are considered to be of particular significance and these resolutions are not effective unless 'special notice' of the intention to propose them has been given to the company. This applies to a resolution to remove a director before the expiration of his term of office (and to appoint another director in his place, if applicable) and to a resolution to remove an auditor. Where special notice is required, this must be given by a member or members to the company at least 28 days before the meeting at which the resolution is going to be proposed. There are specific rules in the Companies Act about removing a director or auditor which must be observed and, as such, professional advice on the procedural aspects, including the giving of special notice, would generally be recommended.

Quorum

As with meetings of the directors, a general meeting of the shareholders must be 'quorate' in order to be valid. The meaning of quorum in the context of general meetings is the same as it is in the context of meetings of the directors – the quorum is the minimum number of shareholders that must be present in order for the meeting to proceed to business.

The quorum for a directors meeting is stipulated by the Model Articles, but the quorum for a general meeting is not. This is because the quorum requirement is set out in s. 318 of the Companies Act which states that a quorum is 'two qualifying persons'. A 'qualifying person' is:

- an individual who is a member of the company;
- a person who is authorised to represent a corporate member at the meeting; or
- a person appointed as a proxy of a member in relation to the meeting.

The rules relating to the appointment of proxies and corporate members are explained later in this chapter. What is important to note here is that two people who are authorised to represent the same corporate member will not form a quorum; neither will two people acting as proxy for the same member. If only two people were in attendance at the meeting, they would either have to be:

- members in their own right;
- representatives of two different corporate members; or
- appointed as proxy for two different members,

or any combination of the above as long as the two persons present are not representing the same shareholder. The common law rule that one person on his or her own does not constitute a quorum also applies here in the same way as it does to directors meetings. One member will not, by himself, constitute a quorum even though he has been appointed as proxy for another member or is a representative of a corporate member. The Companies Act requires two qualifying persons to be present, each one either representing themselves or a different member to the other.

When is a qualifying person 'in attendance' at a general meeting?

This is dealt with in article 37 of the Model Articles. A person attends a general meeting if that person has the right to both speak and vote at the meeting and is able to exercise those rights. Article 37(1) says that a person is able to exercise the right to speak when they are in a position to communicate to all persons attending the meeting any information or opinions which they have on the business of the meeting. Article 37(2) says that a person is able to exercise the right to vote at a general meeting when they are able to vote on resolutions put to the meeting and their vote can be taken into account at the same time as the votes of all the other persons attending the meeting. The reason for this somewhat complicated drafting lies in the fact that the article goes on to say that in determining attendance at a general meeting, it is immaterial whether any two or more members attending it are in the same place as each other. In other words, the Model Articles both anticipate and allow for, the fact that shareholders may participate in a general meeting without actually all being in the same place. It is for the directors to make appropriate arrangements to enable those persons attending a general meeting to exercise their rights to speak and vote (e.g. by way of suitable audio or audio-visual equipment).

Quorum for single member companies
For companies with only one member, whether a company limited by shares or a company limited by guarantee, the quorum is one qualifying person (s. 318(1): 'qualifying person' having the same meaning as set out above).

What if a quorum of members is not in attendance
If a general meeting is not quorate, Model Article 38 says that no business is to be transacted except the appointment of the chairman. The chairman must then take appropriate action, as explained below.

The chairman
As with meetings of the directors, general meetings need to be conducted in an orderly manner in accordance with the company's articles and any relevant provisions of the Companies Act. As such the chairman has an important role to play. He or she must ensure that the meeting runs smoothly and that all procedural legalities are properly observed. In general, the chairman must take the meeting through each item of business to be considered, allowing for questions or debate on each item (while keeping any such debate within appropriate limits) and then putting each item to a vote. To facilitate him doing this, the chairman is given certain powers and responsibilities by the Companies Act and by the Model Articles which can be summarised as follows.

Quorum
The chairman must determine whether a quorum is present and thereby whether the meeting can proceed to business. Article 41 of the Model Articles says that if a quorum is not present within half an hour of the time at which the meeting was due to start, the chairman must adjourn it. Similarly, the chairman must also adjourn the meeting if it ceases to be quorate at any point before it is finished.

Adjourning the meeting
Under Model Article 41, the chairman can adjourn the meeting if the meeting consents to an adjournment or if the chairman believes that an adjournment is necessary to ensure the safety of anyone attending the meeting or to ensure the business of the meeting is conducted in an orderly manner. The chairman must also adjourn the meeting if directed to do so by the meeting.

Allowing non shareholders to attend and speak at the meeting
Article 40 of the Model Articles allows the chairman to permit anyone who is not a shareholder, or who is otherwise not entitled to exercise the rights of

shareholders in relation to general meetings, to attend and speak at a general meeting. Implicitly, it is within the chairman's power to refuse entry to anyone who has no right to attend the meeting.

Conducting the business of the meeting

The chairman must take the meeting through each item of business to be considered and oversee any discussion and debate. This might include making sure that all shareholders who wish to speak are given the opportunity to do so, perhaps limiting the amount of time that each shareholder may have, or it may mean proposing to bring discussions to a close and putting the matter in question to a formal vote.

Voting

When the meeting is ready to take a vote on a resolution, it is the chairman's job to formally put the resolution to the meeting and to ask for votes in favour, votes against, and for any abstentions. Only shareholders with the right to vote may do so. Article 43 of the Model Articles states that any question concerning a person's right to vote at the meeting must be raised at the meeting (or the continuation of an adjourned meeting) and must be referred to the chairman, whose decision on the matter is final.

Poll votes

When a poll is demanded it is for the chairman to direct how it will be taken. The chairman himself has the right to demand a poll – another important power which is explained further below.

Declaring the outcome of a vote

By s. 320 of the Companies Act, when a vote is taken on a show of hands, the chairman's declaration as to whether the resolution has passed or has not been passed is conclusive evidence of that fact with no need for any proof of the number of votes for or against the resolution. It should be noted, however, that the chairman's declaration is not absolute and can be subject to the review or scrutiny of a court in the event of a dispute. This section does not have effect if the resolution is subsequently put to a poll vote.

Casting vote

Unlike the chairman of a directors' meeting, neither the Companies Act nor the Model Articles allow the chairman of a general meeting to have a casting vote. Where the result of a vote on an ordinary resolution is 50% in favour and 50% against, the resolution will simply fail.

Who should take the chair at a general meeting?

A member of a company can be elected to be the chairman of a general meeting by a resolution of the company passed at the meeting (s. 319). A person who has been appointed as a proxy for a member can also be elected to be chairman in the same way (s. 328). These rights are subject to any provisions of the company's articles stating who may or may not be chairman.

For companies with articles that follow the Model Articles on this point, it is the articles that apply rather than the Companies Act because article 39 of the Model Articles says that if the directors have appointed a chairman to chair their own meetings then that person must also chair general meetings if present and willing to do so. If the directors have not appointed a chairman or if the chairman is unwilling to chair the general meeting or is not present within ten minutes of the start time for the meeting, then:

- the directors present; or
- (if there are no directors present), the meeting,

must appoint a director or member to chair the meeting and this must be the first item of business that the meeting deals with.

Helpful hints: preparing to chair a meeting

Chairing a general meeting with even just a small number of shareholders can be a challenging and daunting task for the chairman. Preparation is key. The chairman and the other directors should prepare themselves for questions that may be asked, particularly if any resolutions to be proposed are likely to be controversial. On the day, it is common for the chairman to use a script to help him through the process. A solicitor or other professional advisor would be able to assist with this, as well as providing advice on any of the legal or procedural aspects of running the meeting.

Who can attend a general meeting?

General meetings are meetings of the company's shareholders but not all shareholders will necessarily have the right to attend. Whether a shareholder can attend a general meeting will depend on the rights that are attached to their shares. Different classes of shares may carry different rights concerning attendance and voting at general meetings. Some shareholders may have limited voting rights. Some shares may allow shareholders to attend but not to speak or to vote, others may carry no right to attend at all. The rights attaching to different classes of shares are generally set out in the articles.

Article 40 of the Model Articles states that a company's directors may attend and speak at general meetings whether or not they are shareholders. Under the same article, the chairman can permit other persons who are neither shareholders nor directors to attend and speak, as noted above. Under s. 502 of the Companies Act, a company's auditor has the right to attend general meetings of the company but may only speak on any business of the meeting that concerns him as auditor.

Voting at general meetings

Votes on resolutions put to a general meeting must be taken either on a show of hands or on a poll.

Voting on a show of hands

Under article 42 of the Model Articles, a resolution put to the vote of a general meeting must be decided on a show of hands unless a poll is demanded in accordance with the articles. When a vote is taken on a show of hands, the chairman of the meeting should ask for votes in favour of the resolution, for votes against it and for any abstentions. In each case, the shareholders present cast their vote by raising a hand at the appropriate time. The chairman counts the votes for and against and then declares whether the resolution is carried or not. Section 284 of the Companies Act states that, subject to a company's articles, on a vote on a show of hands, each member of the company present in person has one vote. Sometimes certain shareholders might be given enhanced voting rights with regard to certain matters, or even a power of veto (either by provisions set out in the articles or in a shareholders agreement) but there are no such provisions in the Model Articles. The position for proxies voting on a show of hands is different and is explained under 'voting rights of proxies' later in this section.

Voting on a poll

A vote on a poll is essentially a vote taken by way of a ballot. Rather than simply raising a hand, each shareholder completes a voting card on which they indicate their vote. Under s. 284 of the Companies Act, the default position regarding voting on a poll is that each shareholder has one vote in respect of each share that they hold. This is the key difference between a vote on a poll and a vote on a show of hands: a vote on a poll takes account of the size and extent of a shareholder's shareholding. To give an example, a shareholder (Shareholder A) holding 51 shares in a company that has five other shareholders will have just one vote on a show of hands but will have 51 votes on a poll. For an ordinary resolution to pass on a show of hands, assuming all shareholders were present in a general meeting, votes in favour would be needed from at least three of the other shareholders. On a poll, the vote of Shareholder A alone would be sufficient for the resolution to pass. Of course the reverse is also true and Shareholder A would be able to secure a negative result by voting against the resolution. As the result of a vote on a poll could be significantly different to a vote on a show of hands, it is important to be clear about who has the power to demand one.

Who can demand a poll?

So significant is the right to demand a poll that s. 321 of the Companies Act states that any provision of a company's articles that purports to exclude that right will be void except as it relates to a resolution to elect the chairman or to adjourn the meeting. That said, the Model Articles allow for a poll on any resolution. The right to demand a poll is normally set out in a company's articles but, if the articles are silent, then s. 321 of the Act will apply which allows a poll to be called by:

- at least five members having the right to vote on the resolution;
- a member or members representing not less than 10% of the total voting rights of all the members having the right to vote on the resolution; or
- a member or members holding shares in the company conferring a right to vote on the resolution, being shares on which an aggregate sum has been paid up equal to not less than 10% of the total sum paid up on all the shares conferring that right.

Any provision in a company's articles that sets out requirements more onerous than any of those in s. 321 is void. However, most standard articles will have provisions similar to those in article 44 of the Model Articles which allow a poll to be demanded by:

- the chairman of the meeting;
- the directors;
- two or more persons having the right to vote on the resolution; or
- a person or persons representing not less than one-tenth of the total voting rights of all the shareholders having the right to vote on the resolution.

'Voting rights' essentially means the number of votes that a person or persons would have when voting on a poll. The demand for a poll on a particular resolution must be made before the general meeting, or if made during the meeting, must be made either before the vote on a show of hands or immediately after the result of that vote has been declared. Any person who has made a valid demand for a poll can withdraw it provided that the poll has not yet been taken and the chairman consents to the withdrawal.

Article 44(2) of the Model Articles states that a poll must be taken immediately and in such manner as the chairman of the meeting directs. It is essential, therefore, for the smooth running of a meeting that voting cards be ready for use in case a poll is demanded. These should be drawn up as part of the preparations for the meeting. A copy of the company's register of members should also be available at the meeting so that the directors can confirm each shareholder's voting rights and deal with any queries about a person's eligibility to vote or to attend the meeting.

The chairman's right to call a poll

At common law it is the duty of the chairman to determine the true sense of the meeting – to find out whether the meeting, taken as a whole, is either in favour of, or against, each resolution. As such, the chairman should demand a poll where a vote on a show of hands produces a result that does not reflect the true sense of the meeting – ie the result does not reflect the view of the majority of shareholders or the shareholders holding a majority of the voting rights. Another important part of the preparation for a general meeting is to review the proxy appointment forms that the company receives, to note each shareholder's voting instructions and to count the votes for and against each resolution. Equipped with this information, the chairman should know if a vote on a poll would produce a different result to the result obtained from a show of hands.

Voting by proxy

The right to appoint a proxy is enshrined in s. 324 of the Companies Act which says that a member of a company is entitled to appoint another person as his proxy to exercise all or any of his rights to attend and to speak and vote at a meeting of the company. This is an inalienable right, which cannot be over-ridden by a company's articles. In the case of a company limited by shares, s. 324 provides that a shareholder can appoint more than one proxy as long as each proxy is appointed to exercise the rights attached to a different share or shares held by him. The voting rights of proxies are set out in s. 285 of the Act which states that:

- on a vote on a show of hands, every duly appointed proxy has one vote (s. 285(1)); and
- on a poll all or any of the voting rights of a member may be exercised by one or more duly appointed proxies (s. 285(3)).

The voting rights of proxies on a show of hands and on a poll are explained below.

Voting on a show of hands

The combined effect of ss. 285 and 324 is that a shareholder can appoint one proxy for each share that he holds; each proxy will have one vote on a show of hands. This means that a shareholder holding 10 shares in a company could appoint 10 proxies to represent him at a general meeting and each proxy would have one vote on a vote taken on a show of hands. Compare this to another shareholder who does not appoint any proxies, attends the meeting in person and therefore has just one vote on a show of hands.

The government had a practical purpose in taking this approach because it allows nominee shareholders to appoint the beneficial owners of their shares as proxies who can then each attend the general meeting and vote as they wish. However, the potential for unfairness – as illustrated by the above example – could tend to make voting on a poll a necessity in all cases. However, there are two points to make about this. First, the right of proxies to vote on a show of hands, as set out in s. 285(1), is subject to any provisions of a company's articles. Therefore, where a shareholder appoints more than one proxy, a company's articles could provide that those proxies will have one vote between them on a show of hands and not one vote each (but it is important to note that the Model Articles do not do this). Second, should a situation arise where the appointment of multiple proxies has produced a different result on a vote on a show of hands than would be expected on a poll, the chairman can (and probably should) call a poll. This would be in exercise of the right in article 44, in the case of a company with the Model Articles.

Section 285(2) deals with the situation where a person has been appointed as proxy by more than one shareholder and has been instructed by one or more of those shareholders to vote in favour of a particular resolution and by one or more of the other shareholders to vote against it. It says that if this happens, the proxy will have one vote for the resolution and one vote against it. This is also subject to any provisions in a company's articles, but again, the Model Articles do not contain anything to the contrary.

Voting on a poll

As noted above, s. 285(3) allows proxies to vote on a poll and enables shareholders to appoint more than one proxy to exercise their voting rights. The key point here is that however many proxies a shareholder appoints, those proxies cannot, between them, exercise more extensive voting rights than the shareholder who appointed them could exercise in person. Under s. 329, a person who has been appointed as a proxy to vote on a particular matter at a meeting automatically assumes the rights of his appointor (in respect of those shares or voting rights which he has been appointed to represent) to call or to join in a call for a poll on that matter. Whether voting on a show of hands or on a poll, a proxy must vote in accordance with any instructions given to him by the member who appointed him (s. 324A).

Appointing a proxy

The method for appointing and terminating the appointment of a proxy is normally dealt with by a company's articles but is supplemented by a few provisions in the Companies Act. Under article 45(1) of the Model Articles, a proxy can only be validly appointed by a notice in writing to the company known as a 'proxy notice'.

The proxy notice must:

■ state the name and address of the shareholder appointing the proxy;
■ identify the person appointed to be that shareholders' proxy and identify the general meeting in relation to which that person is appointed;
■ be signed by or on behalf of the shareholder appointing the proxy, or be authenticated in such other way as the directors may determine; and

■ be delivered to the company in accordance with the articles and any instructions contained in the notice of the general meeting to which they relate.

Article 45(2) allows the company to require proxy notices to be delivered in a particular form and to specify different forms for different purposes. It is normal and good practice for a company to send out a blank proxy notice together with the notice of the general meeting. This will then avoid any issues being raised as to whether a proxy notice is in an acceptable form. As well as the minimum information required by article 45(1), article 45(3) allows that the proxy notice may set out whether the proxy is to vote for or against each resolution to be proposed at the meeting (or is to abstain from voting). Although it is less likely to arise in small private companies, to cover the possibility that a shareholder may appoint multiple proxies, the proxy notice should be drafted to allow for this. It is important that proxy notices are suitable and properly drafted so professional advice may be needed.

To be effective, a proxy notice must be delivered to the company prior to the meeting and it is common for a company's articles to specify a cut-off time beyond which no further proxy notices will be accepted. Section 327 of the Companies Act states that the cut-off time for delivery of proxy notices cannot be more than 48 hours before the time for a general meeting, adjourned meeting or a poll not taken at the meeting at which it was demanded (e.g. this means that a cut off time of 72 hours prior to the meeting would be unacceptable and would be void). There are no provisions in the Model Articles that specify a cut-off time for delivery of proxy notices but, from an administrative point of view, it is sensible to have one. This could therefore be included in the notice of meeting, but it should not contravene s. 327.

Terminating a proxy appointment

Article 46(1) of the Model Articles states that a person who has validly appointed a proxy can still attend, speak and vote at a meeting in respect of which that proxy was appointed. The vote of the appointer overrides the vote of the proxy.

Failing this, a proxy appointment can only be revoked by a notice in writing to the company by or on behalf of the person who made the appointment (article 46(2)) and only takes effect if it is delivered before the start of the meeting or adjourned meeting that it relates to. Again, there is no cut-off time in the Model Articles for delivery of a notice of revocation. If a company were to specify a cut-off time in its articles then the provisions of s. 330 of the Companies Act would need to be observed as these place limits on how long before the meeting the cut off can be.

Administration of proxy notices

All proxy notices received by the company need to be reviewed and checked carefully. There should be a clear match between the name of the shareholder as it appears on the proxy notice and their name as it appears in the register of members. If there are any problems with any of the proxy notices, the company should try to resolve them as soon as possible. A count should be taken of each shareholder's voting instructions so that the chairman and the directors go into the meeting knowing the total proxy votes cast for and against each resolution. Not only does this assist the chairman in considering whether a poll should be called on a particular resolution, but it also speeds up the process of conducting a poll if a poll is demanded. Unless any proxies have been given discretion over which way to vote, only the votes of the shareholders who are present in person will need to be counted. Those votes added into the total from the proxy count give the overall result.

Corporate representatives

In the case of a company that holds shares in another company, a corporate representative is a person who has been authorised by the shareholder company to act as its representative at the general meeting and to exercise the rights attaching to the shares held by the company. The ability of a corporate shareholder to appoint a representative is enshrined in s. 323 of the Companies Act. As with proxies, a company can appoint more than one person to be its representative at the same meeting, but unlike proxies – where each proxy must be appointed to exercise the rights attaching to a different share or shares – there is no limit on the number of representatives that a company can appoint.

Section 323(3) states that on a vote on a show of hands, each representative has the same voting rights as the corporation would be entitled to if it were an individual member of the company. This means that where more than one representative has been appointed, each one is entitled to a vote on a show of hands. If a corporate shareholder appoints a number of representatives then this could potentially distort the result of a vote on a show of hands. If this were to happen, the chairman should call a poll.

On a vote on a poll the representatives can exercise their voting rights in different ways provided that they are exercising the rights attaching to different shares. Where the representatives purport to exercise voting rights attaching to the same shares and they purport to exercise the voting rights in the same way, then the votes cast in respect of those shares will stand. If the representatives purport to exercise the voting rights in different ways, the votes cast in respect of those shares will not be counted (s. 323(4)).

Appointing a corporate representative

A corporate shareholder should appoint a representative by a resolution of its own board of directors. The corporate representative should then take a certified copy of the relevant board minute to the meeting in question as evidence of their authority to attend the meeting as the company's representative.

Shareholders' right to circulate a statement

When a company has issued a notice of a general meeting, s. 314 of the Companies Act allows shareholders to require the company to circulate a written statement to the shareholders who were entitled to receive that notice. Such a statement must be in respect of either a specific resolution set out in the notice of meeting, or some other business to be dealt with at the meeting. It cannot be more than 1,000 words in length. This is an important right for shareholders as it provides a way for them to express a view on any proposed business to the company's other shareholders.

A request to circulate a statement must be made by either:

- shareholders representing at least 5% of the total voting rights of all the shareholders who have a right to vote; or
- by at least 100 shareholders who have a right to vote and hold shares in the company on which there has been paid up an average sum per member of at least £100 (s. 314(2)).

Shareholders in companies with less than 100 shareholders must rely on the former provision.

The request must be in hard copy or electronic form, it must identify the statement to be circulated, must be authenticated by the person or persons making it and must be received by the company at least one week before the meeting to which it relates. The costs of circulating the statement have to be borne by the shareholders who requested it unless the company resolves otherwise (s. 316(2)). If the company either receives the necessary funds less than one week before the meeting or does not receive them at all, there is no obligation to circulate the statement.

It is an offence for the officers of a company to fail to comply with a valid request to circulate a statement so if they are unsure what to do, they should take professional advice. If the company, or another person who claims to be aggrieved, believes that a request to circulate a statement amounts to an abuse of the right conferred by s. 314, the company can make an application to court for an order that the statement should not be circulated. Otherwise the statement must be circulated to each shareholder entitled to receive notice of the general meeting, at the same time as the notice (or as soon as reasonably practicable thereafter) and in the same manner.

Shareholders' right to requisition a general meeting

Another important power that shareholders have is the right to requisition a general meeting. Under s. 303 of the Companies Act, the directors of a company must call a general meeting once the company has received requests to do so from shareholders representing at least the required percentage of the paid-up capital of the company carrying the right to vote at general meetings. The required percentage is either 10% or 5% as follows:

- if it has been more than 12 months since the end of the last general meeting called and held in accordance with a shareholder requisition under s. 303, the required percentage is 5%;
- if it has been more than 12 months since the end of the last general meeting at which the shareholders had the right to circulate a resolution in the same way as they would have in the case of a requisitioned meeting (in law, under the company's articles of association or otherwise), the required percentage is also 5% (but note that the Companies Act does not give shareholders of a private company the right to add a resolution to the agenda of a general meeting – shareholders in a public company have the right to add a resolution to the agenda of an annual general meeting); and
- in all other cases it is 10%.

The request to call a meeting must state the general nature of the business to be dealt with at the meeting (in the same way that a notice of general meeting has to) and can also include the text of specific resolutions to be proposed at the meeting. If the shareholders of a company wish to remove a director and the company's articles provide no other way of doing so, then this is how the shareholders would need to go about it (of course, the resolution to remove the director would still have to be passed at the requisitioned meeting).

A shareholders' request to call a general meeting can be submitted in either hard copy or electronic form and be authenticated by the person or persons making it. If the directors of a company receive such a request, then professional advice may be needed. Section 304 sets out how the directors must respond and the time limits for doing so. The meeting must be called within 21 days of receiving the request and must be convened for a date not later than 28 days from the date of the notice of meeting. If the notice of requisition includes a resolution intended to be proposed at the requisitioned meeting, then that must be identified in the notice. However, if the resolution would be ineffective in law, ineffective under the company's constitution, is defamatory of any person or frivolous or vexatious then it cannot be moved at the requisitioned meeting.

Of course, from the shareholders' point of view, the efficacy of this procedure is lost if the directors take no action. Accordingly, s. 305 allows the shareholders who made the request to call the general meeting if the directors fail to do so within the time frame set out in s. 304. The meeting must be called for a date no more than three months after the date on which the directors became subject to the requirement to call a meeting; it must be called as nearly as possible in the same way as the directors are required to call general meetings and the notice of meeting must include the text of any resolution that was included in the original request. It would be advisable for shareholders who find themselves in this position to take advice about the relevant procedure. Directors should note that any reasonable expenses incurred by the shareholders in calling the meeting must be reimbursed by the company. The company must take any fees so reimbursed out of the fees or remuneration due or to become due to the directors in default.

■ Summary

- The power to authorise or approve certain key matters is reserved to a company's shareholders by the Companies Act.
- The approval of any such matters requires either an ordinary resolution or a special resolution. Ordinary resolutions are passed by a simple majority, special resolutions by a majority of 75%.
- Shareholder decisions must be taken either in a general meeting or by a written resolution. The written resolution procedure can be used for any decision other than a decision to remove an auditor or director.

Calling a general meeting

- General meetings must be called by the directors or someone acting on their authority, such as the company secretary. A general meeting can be requisitioned by shareholders under s. 303 of the Companies Act.
- Notice of the general meeting must be sent to all persons entitled to receive it, including the company's auditor, and must include the information required by the Companies Act.
- Subject to the articles, at least 14 clear days' notice must be given excluding the day of the meeting and the day on which the notice is deemed to be received.
- Where notice of a general meeting has been given, shareholders can require the circulation of a statement in connection with any business to be dealt with at the meeting.
- General meetings can be held on short notice provided that the required majority of shareholders agree.

At the start of the meeting

- The meeting cannot come to order unless a quorum is present. The quorum for a general meeting is two qualifying persons as set out in s. 318 of the Companies Act.
- Under the Model Articles, a person is treated as being in attendance at a general meeting if that person has the right to speak and vote at the meeting and is able to exercise those rights.
- Under article 39 of the Model Articles, the chairman of the meeting will be the chairman of the board of directors, if the directors have elected a chairman. If not or if the chairman is unwilling to take the chair or is not present, the meeting must elect a director or shareholder as chairman.

During the meeting

- The chairman has a key role in regulating the proceedings, taking the meeting through each item to be discussed and bringing the meeting to a vote. To this end the chairman has various powers.

- Votes are taken either on a show of hands or on a poll. The voting rights attaching to each class of shares will usually be set out in the articles of association.
- Subject to the articles each shareholder has one vote on a show of hands, and one vote per share on a poll.
- Shareholders can appoint a proxy to vote on their behalf. The default position under the Companies Act is that a shareholder can appoint more than one proxy provided each proxy is appointed to exercise the rights attaching to a different share or shares.
- Proxies can vote on a show of hands and on a poll. A company's articles could restrict the voting rights of proxies on a show of hands in the case of multiple appointments but the Model Articles do not do this.
- The appointment of multiple proxies could have the effect of distorting the outcome of a vote. If it appears to the chairman that this has happened he should exercise his power to call a poll.
- On each resolution the chairman should call for votes in favour, votes against and abstentions. The chairman's declaration of the outcome of a vote is conclusive evidence, but could be subject to review in the event of a dispute.

After the meeting

- Minutes of the meeting should be drawn up and signed by the chairman. These are conclusive evidence of the business conducted at the meeting unless proved otherwise.
- Any and all necessary filings and notices should be submitted to the Registrar of Companies as applicable. For more on minutes and Companies House filings, see Chapter 12.

12 Shareholders' decision-making: written resolutions and other matters

■ **In this chapter**

This chapter explains written resolutions and considers other matters relevant to shareholders' decision-making, in particular:

- the procedure for circulating a written resolution;
- the right of shareholders' to require the directors to circulate a written resolution;
- decision-making by a sole member, annual general meetings and class meetings;
- filing requirements when a resolution is passed;
- minutes and records of shareholders' decisions;
- hard copy and electronic communications;
- the rules on communications sent to a company;
- the rules on communications sent by a company; and
- other issues including rules on deemed delivery, authentication of documents and relevant provisions in the articles of association.

■ Written resolutions

As mentioned in the previous chapter, decisions of the shareholders of a private company do not have to be taken in a general meeting, but can be taken by way of a 'written resolution' (sometimes also referred to as a 'resolution in writing'). A written resolution is essentially a document that sets out the text of one or more resolutions that require shareholder approval. A copy of this is then sent to each shareholder entitled to vote on the resolutions who either indicates their agreement and sends it back to the company or simply ignores it and does nothing. For companies with a small number of shareholders this can be a far more efficient way of obtaining shareholder approval than holding a general meeting. The rules and procedures on written resolutions are set out entirely in the Companies Act and are not supplemented in any way by the Model Articles. The standard articles used by solicitors, formation agents and others usually adopt the same position.

Procedure

Just as the decision to call a general meeting will be made by a resolution of the directors, so is the decision to circulate a written resolution. Once the board has resolved to propose one or more resolutions to the company's shareholders by way of a written resolution and has approved the form and content of the written resolution document, s. 291 requires a copy of the written resolution to be sent to every 'eligible member'.

An eligible member is a person who would have been entitled to vote on the proposed resolution had a general meeting been held on the date on which the written resolution is sent out (s. 289). A person acquiring shares after that date, but before the written resolution has been passed, would not be an eligible member. Whether or not a person is 'entitled to vote' will depend on whether the shares that they hold confer the right to vote. Voting rights attaching to a particular class of shares are usually set out in the articles of association.

The date on which the written resolution is sent is known as the 'circulation date'. As far as it is reasonably practicable to do so the directors must send copies of the written resolution to all eligible members at the same time:

- in hard copy (e.g. sent by post);
- in electronic form (e.g. sent by e-mail); or
- by means of a website.

If it can be done without undue delay, it is also possible for the same copy of the written resolution to be submitted to each eligible member in turn, or for one copy to be sent to a certain number of shareholders, another copy to another number of shareholders and so on. The point being that the shareholders do not all have to indicate agreement to the same copy, or all indicate agreement to separate copies – a mixture of the two is perfectly acceptable. If the written resolution is not sent to each shareholder on the same date, then the circulation date is deemed to be the date on which it was first sent.

Section 291(4) requires that the written resolution be accompanied by a statement explaining to the member:

- how to signify their agreement to it; and
- the date on which the resolution will lapse if sufficient agreements have not been received.

If the directors fail to comply with any of the provisions of s. 291 this will be an offence (punishable by a fine) on the part of every officer in default, but it will not affect the validity of any resolutions that are duly passed.

It should be noted that under s. 502, a company's auditor (if the company has one) is also entitled to receive the same documents or communications as the eligible members of the company are entitled to. This would include the written resolution itself and any accompanying statement (see further below).

Voting on a written resolution

Section 284 of the Companies Act says that on a vote on a written resolution, each shareholder has one vote in respect of each share that they hold. This is subject to anything to the contrary in the company's articles but there is nothing in the Model Articles that varies it. As such, the voting rights that can be exercised on a written resolution are the same as they are on a poll (see Chapter 11). This is important to bear in mind because, unlike directors' written resolutions, shareholders' written resolutions do not have to be passed by unanimous agreement. The same majorities that are required to pass an ordinary and a special resolution in general meeting also apply to resolutions passed as written resolutions. A written resolution is passed when the required majority of eligible shareholders indicate their agreement to it (ss. 282 and 283).

Signifying agreement to a written resolution

Section 296 says that a member signifies his agreement to a written resolution when the company receives from him (or someone acting on his behalf) an authenticated document identifying the resolution to which it relates and indicating his agreement to the resolution (the meaning of 'authentication' is explained later in this chapter in relation to company communications). The authenticated document must be sent to the company in either hard copy or electronic form. In practice it is usual for the written resolution document itself to include a signature line for the shareholder to indicate their agreement so that there is no need to respond with a separate document – the shareholder signs (and dates) the written resolution where indicated and then returns it to the company. The only possible issue with this is that if there is more than one resolution proposed in the written resolution document, and it is not drafted to allow a shareholder to indicate his agreement to each individual resolution, then the result must be agreement to none of the resolutions or agreement to all. This approach may be appropriate in some cases but not in others – take advice. Once a shareholder has signified agreement to a written resolution, their agreement cannot be revoked (s. 296(3)).

When is a written resolution passed?

A written resolution is passed when the required majority of eligible members have signified their agreement to it. However, unless the articles say otherwise, the necessary agreements must be achieved within the period of 28 days beginning with the date on which the written resolution was circulated (s. 297). A written resolution that is not passed before the end of the 28-day period will fail. The directors need to monitor the agreements that are received, check each shareholder's voting entitlement and keep a running total of the aggregate votes cast. Remember that – subject to any variation by the articles of association – on a written resolution, each eligible shareholder has one vote for each share that he holds.

What form should a written resolution take?

A written resolution is a formal company document so should state the name of the company, the company number and the fact that it is a written resolution. Needless to say, it should also set out the exact wording of each resolution and should correctly identify them as ordinary or special resolutions whichever the case may be (a special resolution can only be passed as a special resolution if clearly identified as such in accordance with s. 283 and, once so specified, cannot then be passed as an ordinary resolution). As mentioned earlier, the Companies Act requires a written resolution to be accompanied by a statement informing the member how to signify agreement to it and the date by which it will lapse if sufficient agreements are not received. These statements can appear as a note at the end of the written resolution document, be attached as a separate document or could be dealt with in a covering letter. For clarity and transparency, it is also a good idea for the circulation date to be stated somewhere in the body of the written resolution document. In order to be effective, the text of each resolution needs to be drafted properly so professional advice may be needed.

Shareholders right to circulate a written resolution

Just as shareholders can requisition a general meeting, so can they also request the circulation of a written resolution. This right is set out in s. 292 of the Companies Act. A request is only effective if made by shareholders representing at least 5% of the total voting rights of all the shareholders entitled to vote on the proposed resolution. The required percentage of 5% can be reduced to a lower percentage by a company's articles, but the Model Articles make no change to it. Shareholders can also require the written resolution to be circulated together with a statement on the subject matter of the resolution of not more than 1,000 words in length (although the company, or another person who claims to be aggrieved, can apply for relief from circulating the statement on the basis that the shareholders are abusing their right). Section 292(2) states that any resolution may be properly moved as a written resolution unless it would be ineffective in law or under the company's articles (or for any other reason) is defamatory of any person, or is frivolous or vexatious. The request can be in hard copy or electronic form, must identify the resolution and any accompanying statement and must be authenticated by the person or persons making it.

Once in receipt of a valid request to circulate a written resolution, s. 293 requires that the company must circulate it to eligible members (together with any accompanying statement) within no more than 21 days, provided that the company has been provided with sufficient funds to enable it to do so or has otherwise resolved that the costs need not be paid by the requisitioning shareholders. The rules on circulation of a requisitioned written resolution (statements that must accompany it, rules on signifying agreement and so on) are the same as for a written resolution proposed by the directors. If the company fails to circulate the written resolution in accordance with s. 293 an offence is committed by every officer of the company who is in default, punishable by a fine. A contravention will not affect the validity of the resolution if passed. It should be noted that, unlike a requisitioned general meeting, there is no statutory right for the shareholders to circulate the written resolution themselves should the company not comply with their valid request. As such, if the directors failed to circulate a written resolution at the shareholders' request, they would then have to requisition a general meeting as described in Chapter 11.

For the best chance of a positive outcome, shareholders who are considering requisitioning the circulation of a written resolution should take advice. Directors in receipt of such a request will need to consider whether it is valid, whether the proposed resolutions can be properly moved as written resolutions and whether any accompanying statement is acceptable. They may wish to take advice on any of these points, as well as on the procedure for circulating the written resolution once any issues or concerns have been resolved.

Single member companies

In companies with only one member, one qualifying person present at a general meeting is a quorum (s. 318). In practice, however, it would be unlikely that a single member company would hold a general meeting unless the circumstances specifically required it – the written resolution option being the obvious alternative. In many small limited companies, the sole member may also be the sole director. Where this is the case, there is a risk that the separate roles of director and shareholder will merge. A person in this position needs to stay focused on which capacity they are acting in at any one time. Keeping proper records of all decisions made and being careful to ensure that the correct procedures have been followed at all times (however artificial it may seem) should help with this.

In the case of a sole member who is also a director of the same company, s. 231 of the Companies Act imposes an additional requirement where the company enters into a contract with the sole member which is not in the course of the company's ordinary business. Section 231 requires the terms of such contracts to be either:

■ set out in a written memorandum; or
■ recorded in the board minutes of the first meeting of the directors of the company following the making of the contract.

Failure to do this is an offence on the part of every officer of the company who is in default. As stated in the notes to the Companies Act, the aim of this section is to 'ensure that records are kept in those cases where there is a high risk of the lines becoming blurred between where a person acts in his personal capacity and when he acts on behalf of the company'.

Annual general meetings

Prior to the implementation of the Companies Act 2006, the law required all companies to hold an annual general meeting (AGM) in each calendar year. The business to be dealt with at an AGM might or might not be set out in a company's articles, but it would generally involve such things as receiving the annual report and accounts, appointing auditors for the coming year, re-appointing directors retiring by rotation and declaring a dividend. Now it is only public companies that have to hold AGMs by law. A private company only needs to hold an AGM if specifically required to by the company's articles. The Model Articles contain no such requirement and contain no provisions requiring directors to retire by rotation.

Class meetings

As explained in Chapter 9, in the case of a company that has issued more than one class of shares, a variation of the rights attached to one class of shares or another will require the consent of the shareholders of that class. If the procedure in the Companies Act applies, the required consent can be obtained either:

- by consent in writing from the holders of at least three-quarters in nominal value of the shares of the relevant class; or
- by a special resolution at a general meeting of the holders of that class.

If it is not practical or possible to gain the written consent of the relevant shareholders it will be necessary to use the general meeting route. Such meetings are known as 'class meetings'. Most of the rules in the Companies Act that apply to general meetings and any that are set out in the articles also apply to class meetings but there are some exceptions including the quorum requirements and the right to demand a poll. Take advice.

Resolutions – filing requirements

When a company passes a resolution, whether by way of a written resolution or in a general meeting, it can trigger an obligation to file a copy of the resolution with the Registrar of Companies.

Special resolutions

Under s. 29 of the Companies Act, when a company passes a special resolution, a notice that the resolution has been passed must be filed with the Registrar of Companies within 15 days from the date on which it was passed. All special resolutions must therefore be filed with the Registrar.

Ordinary resolutions

In contrast, when a company passes an ordinary resolution this will not, in the majority of cases, require a notice to be sent to the Registrar of Companies. There are exceptions to this however, the most common being a resolution to give, vary, revoke or renew the directors' authority to allot shares. When an ordinary resolution has to be filed it is subject to the same time limits as a special resolution.

What exactly needs to be filed?

For written resolutions, best practice is to file a print of the resolution signed by a director setting out the exact wording of the resolution and the date on which it was passed. It is not necessary to file the original signed copy or copies of the written resolution document or documents received back from all of the shareholders – these should be retained for the company's records. If a written resolution consists of a mixture of special and ordinary resolutions, the ordinary resolutions may be passed before the special resolutions. If that happens and the ordinary resolutions are among those required to be notified to the Registrar, the print should specify the different dates on which the resolutions were passed. The opposite also applies in that, where a written resolution consists of both ordinary and special resolutions and the ordinary resolutions are not required to be notified to the Registrar, they do not need to be included in the filing copy.

For resolutions passed at a general meeting the procedure is the same – the Registrar should be provided with a notice setting out details of the resolutions and the date on which they were passed, the notice being signed by a director of the company.

To avoid rejection by the Registrar, a notice must:

- correctly identify the company's name;
- correctly identify the company's registered number;
- state the date on which the resolution or resolutions were passed; and
- be signed by a director.

Example notices of shareholder resolutions for submission to the Registrar of Companies can be found in Appendix 7.

Other filings

Even if notice of a resolution does not need to be filed, the nature of the resolution may mean that information about the matters that have been resolved must be provided to the Registrar using one of the prescribed Companies House forms (e.g. if a company's shareholders resolve to consolidate or subdivide any of the company's shares, details of this must be submitted on form SH02). It is always important to check if any filings of this sort need to be made. Failure to file a particular form when there is an obligation to do so is an offence and also means that the company's filing record will not be up-to-date and accurate. A table setting out the more common decisions and events in the life of a company that trigger a requirement to file information with the Registrar of Companies (with a note on the filings that must be made in each case) can be found at Appendix 3. As well as the prescribed Companies House forms, sometimes other documents need to be filed as well. Probably the most common example of this is when a company makes an alteration to its articles. The Companies Act requires not only a copy of the special resolution to be filed, but also a copy of the amended or new articles in addition to the prescribed forms that must also be filed in certain circumstances (see Chapter 3 for more).

■ Minutes and records

Section 355 of the Companies Act requires all companies to keep records comprising:

- copies of all written resolutions;
- minutes of all proceedings of general meetings; and
- details of decisions of a sole member.

All of these records have to be kept for a minimum of 10 years from the date of the relevant resolution, meeting or decision and failure to do so is an offence on the part of every officer who is in default.

Records of written resolutions

All signed copies of written resolutions should be retained by the company. Where notice of a resolution has to be filed with the Registrar of Companies, this can be done by submitting a notice signed by a director, as mentioned above. There is no obligation to provide the original signed written resolution.

Minutes of general meetings

Section 356(4) states that the minutes of a general meeting, if purporting to be signed by the chairman of the meeting or by the chairman of the next general meeting, are evidence of the proceedings at that meeting. Under s. 356(5), where there is a record of the proceedings of a general meeting then:

- the meeting is deemed to have been duly held and convened;
- all proceedings at the meeting are deemed to have duly taken place; and
- all appointments at the meeting are deemed valid,

until anything is proved to the contrary. As such, minutes of general meetings are an important company document that provides proof – at least in the first instance – of the decisions that were made at the meeting.

As with minutes of board meetings there is no prescribed form for minutes of general meetings but the same general principles outlined in Chapter 8 apply here as well. As such, the minutes need to be as clear and accurate as possible without being excessively long and it is helpful in that respect if they take the form of numbered paragraphs (with appropriate sub-sections as required) with each paragraph dealing with a new item of business. As a guide, the minutes should include at least the following:

- the name of the company and its registered number;
- the date, time and location of the meeting;
- the names of the persons present;
- the name of the person chairing the meeting;
- confirmation that a quorum was present;
- a summary of each matter that was discussed;
- details of decisions/resolutions proposed to the meeting;
- whether such decisions/resolutions were passed; and
- details of any demands for a poll and their outcome.

Decisions of a sole member

Where a sole shareholder takes a decision otherwise than in a general meeting or by written resolution the sole member must provide the company with a record of the decision taken (s. 357). In so far as the Companies Act allows, it may be preferable for sole members to take decisions by written resolution so that there is always a clear and unambiguous record of the matters that have been resolved. It is an offence for a sole member not to provide the company with a record of any decisions they make, but it will not affect their validity.

Location and inspection of minutes and records

All of the records that a company has to maintain pursuant to s. 355 of the Companies Act must be kept either at the company's registered office or at its single alternative inspection location (if it has one). If the records are moved from one to the other then notice must be given to the Registrar either on form AD03 (if they are moved from the registered office to the SAIL) or on form AD04 (if they are moved from the SAIL to the registered office). It should be noted that the records must all be kept together wherever they (e.g. it would not be permissible to have records of general meetings at the registered office and records of written resolutions at the SAIL address).

Unlike minutes of board meetings or records of directors' unanimous decisions, records of general meetings, written resolutions and decisions of a sole member can inspected by shareholders. The company cannot charge a fee for this, but can charge for providing copies of any documents if it chooses to do so (see Chapter 4 for the applicable fees). Members of the public do not have any rights of inspection. All records should be kept securely and it may be advisable to keep electronic copies as a precaution against loss.

Company communications

As can be seen, the procedures relating to decision making by shareholders involve the exchange of communications between a company and its shareholders. There are rules in the Companies Act that deal with company communications and these are to be found in ss. 1143 to 1148 and Schedules 4 and 5. Together they are known as 'the company communications provisions'. Their purpose is to regulate the ways in which companies communicate with their shareholders, directors and others and vice versa. While the fax machine has been around for many years, the advent of the internet and other forms of electronic communication such as e-mail and text messaging means that there is now a wide variety of ways in which communications can be sent. The Companies Act allows for all methods of communication whether in hard copy or in electronic form and sets out rules for using each. The rules are divided into two separate parts comprising communications sent *to* a company on the one hand, and communications sent *by* a company on the other. These rules are explained in the remainder of this chapter.

Meaning of 'hard copy form' and 'electronic form'

The Companies Act defines when a document is in hard copy and when it is in electronic form. A hard copy document is one that is in a paper copy or similar form capable of being read. A document or information is sent in electronic form if it is sent or supplied by electronic means, such as e-mail or fax, or by any other means while in electronic form, such as sending a CD by post.

When a company or person sends a document or information in electronic form, it must be sent or supplied in a form that the company or person sending it reasonably considers will enable the recipient to read it and to retain a copy of it. A copy could be retained by printing the document for example, or by saving it to another location, such as the recipient's pc, laptop, or other data storage device. Anything sent in electronic form must therefore allow this basic functionality.

Communicatons sent to a company

The rules on communications sent to a company apply only to communications sent by a person. Communications sent to a company by another company (e.g. by a company that holds shares in another company) are governed by the rules on communications sent by a company. The effect of this is that, for a company communicating with another company in which it is a shareholder, there is no scope for deemed agreement to electronic communications, which there is in the case of person to company communications (explained below). In the case of company-to-company communications, electronic means can only be used if explicit consent or agreement has been given. Documents and information can be sent by a person to a company in either hard copy or electronic form as follows.

Sending in hard copy

Hard copy documents can be validly delivered to a company by hand or by post to:

- an address specified by the company;
- the company's registered office; or

- an address specified in a relevant provision of the Companies Act.

Sending a document to a company in hard copy is the default means of communication under the Companies Act as it requires no prior agreement from the company.

Sending in electronic form

The key difference between sending in hard copy and sending in electronic form is that documents or information can only be sent to a company in electronic form if the company has agreed to it (and has not revoked that agreement) or if the company is *deemed* to have agreed to it by a provision of the Companies Act.

If a company gives an electronic address in either:

- a notice of a general meeting;
- a proxy form sent out by the company in relation to a general meeting, or an invitation to appoint a proxy issued by the company in relation to a general meeting; or
- a document accompanying or containing a proposed written resolution,

then it is deemed to have agreed that the recipient can use that electronic address in sending any communications to the company in relation to the notice, proxy form or written resolution as the case may be. This is subject to any conditions or limitations specified in the notice so if the company does not wish to receive electronic communications it should make this clear by including a suitable statement to that effect. Even including standard contact details such as a fax number or e-mail address would give rise to a deemed agreement to using those methods of communication so care needs to be taken.

When sending an electronic communication to a company the sender must use the delivery address that has been specified by the company for the purpose, or, in the case of deemed agreement, must use the address that the company is deemed to have specified. If sending documents or information in the form of a disk or some other data storage device the same rules apply as to sending a document or information in hard copy, as set out above (i.e. it can be sent to the registered office, an address specified by the company, or an address specified in the Companies Act). It should be noted, however, that since information or a document in the form of a disk or other device is in an electronic format, this is still a form of electronic communication and can therefore only be used if the company has agreed.

Communications sent by a company

The rules on communications sent by a company apply to communications by a company to its members, directors or debenture holders. They cover hard copy communications as well as electronic communications and also deal specifically with communicating by means of a website.

Sending in hard copy

When a company sends a document or information in hard copy form it must either be handed to the recipient in person, or be sent or supplied by hand or by post:

- to an address specified for the purpose by the recipient;
- to a company at its registered office;
- to a member (in his capacity as a member) at the address recorded in the register of members;
- to a director (in his capacity as a director) at the address recorded in the register of directors; and
- to an address that is specified in any relevant provision of the Companies Act.

If the company is unable to obtain any of the addresses listed above, then the last known address of the recipient should be used.

Sending in electronic form

As with electronic communications sent by a shareholder to a company, a company can only send communications to a shareholder in electronic form if the recipient has agreed to it or is deemed to have agreed to it by a relevant provision of the Companies Act. In the case of communications sent by a company to its shareholders deemed agreement to electronic communication can only arise in connection with the use of a website (explained below). When sending a document or information in electronic form, the company must use the address that has been specified for the purpose by the intended recipient or in the case of a company, the address that is deemed to have been specified by a provision of the Act.

A shareholder can agree to receive all types of documents by e-mail or just certain specified documents. Companies need to keep and maintain a record of the addresses provided by shareholders and others for the purposes of electronic communications, as well as a record of the documents that each recipient wishes to receive in electronic form. Such records should be confidential and kept separate from the company's statutory records. They also need to be kept up to date – a shareholder can revoke or vary their agreement to electronic communications at any time.

If sending documents or information in the form of a disk or some other data storage device, the same rules apply as to any hard copy communications sent by a company that are set out above. Again, note that the communication itself is not in hard copy if the documents or information are in electronic form, so is only permitted if the intended recipient has agreed to it.

Communicating by means of a website

The idea behind the use of websites is that it enables companies to dramatically cut down on their use of paper in communicating with their shareholders. This is particularly relevant in the case of large listed companies where the annual reports and accounts can be very lengthy but the option to use a website is open to all companies and is not limited to one class of documents or another. A company can supply documents or information to a person using a website if that person has specifically agreed to it, or is deemed to have agreed to it and has not revoked that agreement. This is the only form of electronic communication by a company where deemed agreement by the intended recipient is possible.

Deemed agreement to use of a website

The first proviso for using a website is that the company's members must have passed an ordinary resolution authorising the company to use this form of communication or there must be an equivalent authority in the company's articles of association. In the Model Articles this is covered by article 48 (see further below). For companies that go down the resolution route, this is one of the ordinary resolutions that must be filed with the Registrar of Companies and must be filed within 15 days.

Next, two further conditions must be met which are:

- the person must have been asked individually by the company to agree that the company can send or supply documents or information to him by means of a website (this can be in general, or just relate to certain specified documents or information); and
- the company must not have received a response from the person (electing to continue to receive communications in hard copy) within the period of 28 days beginning with the date on which the company's request was sent.

Furthermore, in order for a deemed agreement to be valid, the company's request must make it clear what the effect will be if the recipient fails to respond and it cannot be sent less than 12 months since the company sent a previous request in respect of the same or a similar class of documents or information. This does not prevent the company from sending general invitations to its shareholders to confirm their agreement to electronic communications (e.g. to allow the company to use e-mail). It means that a request to communicate by a website (with the potential for deemed agreement) can only be sent once in a 12-month period.

Making the document or information available

Any documents made available on a website must be in a form that the company reasonably considers will enable the reader both to read it and to retain a copy. As such, consideration needs to be given to the kind of file that is used and whether a link to the software that is needed to open the file might need to be provided. Once the document or information is available, the company must notify the recipient by:

- advising them of the presence of the document or information on the website;
- providing them with the address of the website;

- providing instructions on where on the website the document or information is located; and
- explaining how to access it.

The notification can be sent in hard copy or, if the intended recipient has agreed to it, in electronic form to the e-mail address provided by the member. The document or information must be made available on the website throughout the whole of any period that is specified in any provision of the Companies Act, or if no period is specified, the period of 28 days starting on the date on which the notification of availability is sent to the recipient.

Any document or information that is provided by means of a website is treated as being sent (for the purposes of the Companies Act) either:

- on the date on which the notification of availability is sent to the intended recipient; or,
- if later, the date on which the document or information first appears on the website after the notification is sent.

◼ Deemed delivery

As mentioned in Chapter 11, s. 1147 of the Companies Act sets out rules that say when a document or information that has been sent by a company is deemed to have been received by the intended recipient.

Delivery by post

For documents and information sent by post to an address in the United Kingdom (whether in hard copy, or in electronic form such as a disk) where the company is able to show that they have been properly addressed, prepaid and posted, the documents and information will be deemed to have been received by the intended recipient 48 hours after they were posted.

Delivery by electronic means

For documents and information sent by electronic means, where the company is able to show that they have been properly addressed, the documents and information are deemed to have been received 48 hours after they were sent.

Delivery by means of a website

Where documents or information are supplied by means of publication on a website, they are deemed to have been received by the intended recipient when first made available on the website or, if later, when the recipient receives (or is deemed to have received) notification of the fact that the documents or information have been placed on the website.

In all cases, when calculating the period of hours, no account is to be taken of any part of a day that is not a working day. In relation to any documents or information sent by a company to its members, the rules on deemed delivery can be varied by a company's articles. There is nothing in the Model Articles that alters the position.

Why is deemed delivery relevant?

There are some provisions in the Companies Act that turn (at least in part) on the rules on deemed delivery. An example of this is the provisions relating to the notice period for general meetings. The notice period begins on the day that the notice is received by the shareholder, so it is essential to know when that is deemed to be. In a broader context, the rules also give certainty to the company about whether it has discharged its responsibilities in respect of sending documents and information to its shareholders and others. Provided a company can produce proof of delivery of a document, the intended recipient is deemed to have received it by operation of s. 1147 (subject to any relevant provisions in the articles). This is important because, for example, any business conducted at a general meeting can be invalidated if it can be shown that one or more shareholders were not given proper notice of the meeting.

Authentication of documents

Various provisions of the Companies Act refer to documents being or needing to be authenticated by the sender and the meaning of this term is explained in s. 1146. Essentially, authentication refers to the way in which a document (and its contents) sent by a person to a company is verified as being sent by that person.

Hard copy documents

Documents or information sent in hard copy are authenticated if signed by the person sending or supplying them. If there is any doubt about the authenticity of a person's signature then the company should request supporting evidence such as a certified copy of an official document bearing the person's usual signature (e.g. a driving licence or passport).

Documents in electronic form

Documents or information in electronic form are authenticated if the identity of the sender is confirmed in a manner that is specified by the company. If the company has made no specifications, the document or information is authenticated if the communication either contains, or is accompanied by, a statement of the identity of the sender and the company has no reason to doubt the truth of that statement.

Right to hard copy

Where a company supplies a document or information to a member in electronic form, the member is still entitled to be provided with a hard copy version on request. The company must send the member a hard copy version within 21 days of receiving the request and is not permitted to make any charge for doing so. Failure to comply is an offence on the part of the company and every officer who is in default.

Relevant provisions in the Model Articles

Article 48 of the Model Articles deals with the means of communication that a company can use. Article 48(1) permits anything sent or supplied by or to the company under the articles to be sent or supplied in any way in which the Companies Act provides for documents or information to be sent or supplied by or to the company. This means that companies with the Model Articles (or an article similar or identical to article 48(1)) are free to use any form of communication permitted by the Companies Act, subject always to the applicable rules and procedures in the Act.

Help and guidance

A company that wishes to benefit from the advantages inherent in using electronic communications with their shareholders has a number of issues to consider. Even in small companies there is a need for proper management and controls. The ICSA guidance note on electronic communications with shareholders ('Electronic Communications with Shareholders 2007' (reference number 160207)) is a valuable resource that gives help and advice on the many issues involved, from managing the process of inviting shareholders to agree to communications (by means of a website or otherwise) to the various technical points that can arise in complying with the requirements of the Companies Act. Retaining proof of sending of an electronic communication, keeping records of electronic addresses, dealing with IT failures, enabling shareholders to retain copies of documents sent to them and the problem of viruses are just some of the points that are covered. The guidance note is essential reading for any company wishing to use electronic communications and can be downloaded from the ICSA's website.

Summary

- Private companies are able to pass shareholder resolutions as written resolutions with the exception of a resolution to remove an auditor and a resolution to remove a director.

Written resolutions
- The directors must formally approve the written resolution in a board meeting (or by a unanimous decision) and resolve to circulate it.

- The written resolution document must set out the text of each resolution and clearly identify any special resolutions.
- A written resolution must be circulated to each eligible member. In the case of a company with more than one class of shares, the articles should be checked to ascertain voting entitlements and/or the entitlement to receive written resolutions.
- As far as possible, the written resolution must be circulated to all eligible members at the same time. It is not necessary to circulate a separate copy to each eligible member provided that the same copy can be circulated to each without undue delay. The date on which it is circulated is known as the circulation date.
- The written resolution must be accompanied by a statement informing the shareholder how to indicate agreement to it and the date on which it will lapse. A written resolution will lapse if the company has not received the required agreements within 28 days of the circulation date.
- The majorities required to pass an ordinary and special resolution as a written resolution are the same as if these resolutions were passed in a general meeting. A shareholder signifies agreement by 'authenticating' (usually signing) the document and returning it to the company.
- Shareholders representing at least 5% of the total voting rights of all the shareholders entitled to vote on a proposed resolution can request that the directors circulate a written resolution.
- On receipt of such a request, the directors must circulate the written resolution (together with any accompanying statement) within no more than 21 days, as long as the requisitioning shareholders have provided the funds to enable them to do so or the company has resolved that the costs need not be paid by them.

Other matters

- In the case of a company with one shareholder, the quorum for a general meeting is one but it would be unlikely for such a company to hold general meetings unless the written resolution option cannot be used.
- Private companies are not required to hold annual general meetings unless the articles include a provision that specifically requires them to.
- When a company proposes to vary the rights attaching to a particular class of shares the consent of the shareholders of that class is required. The proposal can be made at a meeting of the members of the class in question, which is known as a class meeting.
- Whenever a company passes a resolution as a special resolution it must notify the Registrar of Companies. This also applies to some ordinary resolutions. The passing of a resolution may also trigger a requirement to submit a prescribed Companies House form and other documents to the Registrar.

- Companies must keep copies of all written resolutions, minutes of all proceedings of general meetings and details of decisions of a sole member.
- The rules concerning company communications are set out in the Companies Act. The general position is that companies, directors and shareholders can each communicate with each other in hard copy, but agreement is required to electronic communications.
- In some circumstances, a company can be deemed to have agreed to receive electronic communications, such as when an address for electronic communications is included in a notice of general meeting or a written resolution.
- Deemed agreement by shareholders is only possible in relation to requests to supply information or documents by way of a website and is subject to the rules set out in the Companies Act.
- The Companies Act contains provisions that stipulate when a document or information is deemed to have been received by the intended recipient which is important, for example, when calculating the correct period of notice that has to be given for a general meeting.
- The ICSA guidance note on electronic communications with shareholders is an excellent source of advice on company communications.

13 Sources of finance

David Frederick

> ### ■ In this chapter
>
> This chapter explains the main sources of long and short-term finance for a company and the advantages and disadvantages of each, in particular:
>
> - equity finance including Venture Capitalists and Business Angels;
> - debt finance including debentures and bank loans;
> - bank overdrafts;
> - trade credit;
> - debt factoring and invoice discounting; and
> - government grants and the enterprise finance guarantee.

All companies need finance in order to meet the costs of their day-to-day operational activities and their long-term business growth or development plans. A company's initial financing requirements are likely to be met by the founders and will need to cover set-up costs, the costs of any assets as well as working capital to pay for stock and/or materials and the costs involved in the process of producing a product that can be sold or in providing a service for a fee. The advantage for the founders of using their own funds is that it enables them to maintain complete control and ownership of the business. However, it may be some time before revenues are sufficient to meet outgoings so it is crucial to ensure that the company has enough funds to enable it to survive until it does. If the founders are unable to finance the company themselves, they will need to look to other sources.

By contrast, a more established company may be able to meet its financing needs out of its retained profits but where these are insufficient, perhaps where a significant project or plan of expansion is being contemplated, the directors will also need to consider other means of finance. Whether a new start up or an established company, the level of finance and the most appropriate source or sources will depend on a number of factors including the nature of the company and its business, the reasons why it is needed and the risks and costs involved. In this respect, the possible sources of finance can be grouped into two broad categories – long term and short term, which can also be seen as permanent or temporary.

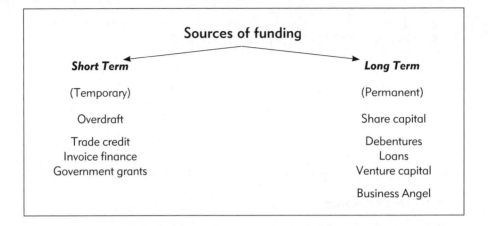

Long-term finance

The long-term sources of funding for a company can be separated into debt finance and equity finance. Debt finance refers to loans and debentures and essentially involves the acquisition by a company of fixed-term repayable borrowings from parties external to the company. Debt financiers usually provide their funds at a fixed rate of interest over an agreed term. Equity finance refers to funds obtained from investors who in return receive shares in the company. Such investment might be provided by people close to the founders such as friends and family (particularly at an early stage in the company's development) or more formally and where larger sums of money are required, from Venture Capitalists or Business Angels. Accordingly, when looking at long-term finance, the choice that a company faces is essentially between debt and equity.

Debt vs equity

Whether a company's needs are best met by debt or equity will depend on a number of factors. One issue to consider is cost. Debt finance is often cheaper than equity because it is seen as being safer from the point of view of the lender. This is because the company must make interest payments in accordance with the terms of the loan agreement (whether it has any profits or not) and the holder of a secured debt ranks above shareholders for payment out of the assets of an insolvent company. However, the reverse side is that interest payments impose a recurring financial liability upon the company, so the directors must be confident that the company will be able to meet its liabilities (e.g. in a business where revenues are not regular or are higher at certain times of the year than at others, debt finance may not be the best option). Another issue is whether the company has suitable assets on which a lender can secure their loan. As such, new companies, companies with existing long-term debt or companies that lack tangible assets may not be able to raise debt finance.

Equity finance does not impose the same financial burden upon the company because dividend payments can only be made if the company has sufficient distributable profits to make them. Since this represents a risk to investors, they will generally expect a higher return on their investment compared to a debt financier. In addition, equity finance reduces the founder shareholders' stake in the company. If the investor receives voting shares, a degree of control is also lost.

There are many other issues to think about and there is no one right answer. It is not uncommon, for example, for a company to meet its financing needs from a combination of debt and equity and other sources. When considering long-term finance it is essential to take professional advice from an accountant, solicitor or independent financial adviser.

Preparing a business plan

Whatever type of finance a company is seeking, it is essential to prepare a business plan to market the company to prospective financiers and demonstrate the investment opportunity that the company will provide to them. Preparing a business plan is also a valuable exercise in itself as it forces the directors to focus on where they want the company to go and how it is going to get there. A business plan should include, among others:

- an executive summary – a short introductory section highlighting the main points of the company's offering;
- details of the company's management team including their roles, background and experience;
- information about the company's products or services;
- an analysis of the target market for the company's products or services and the company's competitors;
- the company's strategy and plans (showing how the loan or investment will be used) together with supporting research and data;
- the company's key selling points and competitive advantages;
- the amount of funding needed and when it is needed;
- forecasts showing how the loan or investment will facilitate growth and revenues sufficient to enable repayment of the loan or a return on investment; and
- the company's accounts and financial information for the last three years.

While there is a good deal of information and guidance about writing a business plan freely available, it may also be advisable to seek help from a professional such as an accountant, particularly in relation to financial forecasts and projections. The stronger a business plan is, the better it will stand up to the scrutiny of potential financiers. Once the initial version has been finalised, the business plan should be reviewed regularly and updated as necessary. Since a business plan forms a key part of a company's pitch, it should be tailored to appeal to its target audience, whichever type of financier that may be.

■ Equity finance

A company's initial capital comes from the founder shareholders (the subscribers to the company's memorandum of association) on incorporation. As explained in Chapter 1, shareholders are the owners of a company and take their shares in exchange for their investment into the company. The total nominal value of the shares issued by a company makes up the company's issued share capital and the monies paid for the shares are the company's initial source of finance.

A company may seek to raise additional funds after its formation by issuing further, new shares to prospective buyers. Private companies, unlike public companies, cannot make their shares openly available to the public. Shares in private companies can only be sold to individuals who have been invited to purchase shares by the company and in the first instance this is likely to be friends and family or people who are in some way close to the company, the founder shareholders and/or the directors. As a company grows it may choose to raise funds through the issue of shares to other private investors, such as a Venture Capitalist or a Business Angel, because (among other reasons) the funds that can be raised from such investors will generally exceed the level that can be provided from friends and family.

As mentioned earlier, issuing shares in return for investment does not impose a fixed recurring financial burden upon the company in the way that a loan does but the issue of shares to new investors reduces the initial subscribers' overall percentage of ownership which can result in a loss of control (if voting shares are issued), reduced dividends and a reduced equity stake in the company. As explained in Chapter 9, a company can issue different classes of shares each with different rights and the type of shares taken by an investor will determine the rights that he or she has in relation to the company. Agreeing what these rights will be is likely to form a significant part of the negotiation of terms with an investor, particularly in the case of a Venture Capitalist or a Business Angel.

Ordinary shares and preference shares

Where a debt financier will receive regular interest payments, an investor will be looking for returns in the form of dividends and a growth in value of his shares. The most basic shares that a company can issue – ordinary shares – confer only the right to vote and to participate in dividends and capital distributions. While dividends cannot be guaranteed in any given year, an investor will want to make sure that, when there are distributable profits, he will receive a fixed and enhanced share of them. This could be achieved by issuing a separate class of ordinary shares with specific rights (such as say, A ordinary shares) but is usually done by issuing shares with preferential rights known as preference shares. Preference shares provide the right to a fixed dividend and also to participate in any general dividends declared by a company, usually with the right to receive them ahead of ordinary shareholders. Preference shares are also likely to rank ahead of ordinary shareholders for payment if a company fails and has to be wound up. However, preference shares usually have no or limited voting rights, meaning that the founder shareholders maintain voting control over the company.

Cumulative preference shares

Holders of cumulative preference shares have the right to have their fixed dividend payment met in subsequent years if it cannot be paid in a given year. The dividend 'rolls over' to the following year and so on in each year until it can be paid. In the event of a winding up, the cumulative preference shares may entitle the holders to be paid any cumulative dividends owing to them ahead of any distribution to any other shareholders.

Redeemable shares

Redeemable shares are sold with the condition that, at some future date, the company can buy the shares back, the terms of the redemption being defined at the outset. Redemption might be triggered by a specified date or event or can be at the request of the shareholder or the company. Redeemable shares can therefore provide an investor with a way to recoup some or all of his investment.

In reality, an investor may require shares of more than one class giving him a range of rights, controls and entitlements that provide the best security for his investment and the best return. Advice from a professional with expertise in corporate finance is essential.

Advantages of equity finance

The main advantages of equity finance can be summarised as follows.

- Capital is raised by the company without any recurring costs such as those involved in servicing debt finance.
- It can be a suitable form of finance for companies that lack assets on which debt can be secured or that have insufficient funds to make regular interest payments.
- There is no concern over the funding being withdrawn as in the case of debt finance or some forms of short-term finance as investors invariably take a long term view and often do not expect to gain returns overnight.
- Some investors will provide the company with more than just capital finance. Business Angels and Venture Capitalists (see below) often bring additional expertise to the company to assist its growth and development.
- Investors are often able or willing to provide additional funding if the company should require it. This avoids the company incurring the further costs of raising additional finance.

Disadvantages of equity finance

The main disadvantages of equity financing include the following.

- If the external investors acquire shares with voting rights attached to them this results in a reduction in the control and decision-making power vested with the owner-directors. However, this may yield greater returns in the future.
- Sourcing and securing equity finance is a timely and costly process. The directors will have to collate and prepare information about the company for the investors (in terms of both historical and future projections). During the period of information gathering and approaching potential investors the directors may not be focusing on the company's principal activities.
- External investors (Venture Capitalists and Business Angels in particular) will usually undertake a due diligence review of the company and seek an historical profile of the company's performance to date. They will also seek to ascertain and scrutinise the projections for the future to help determine how their investment might perform.
- Potential investors will seek comprehensive background information on the founders and the business. They will look carefully at past results and forecasts and will probe the management team. However many businesses find this process useful for business planning and strategic purposes, regardless of whether or not any fundraising is successful.
- Investors will monitor the company's activities post investment and will require the company to provide them with regular and timely financial and non-financial information.

Venture Capitalists

Venture Capitalists, also known as private equity financiers, are private firms that provide finance to companies in return for a share in the company. Venture Capitalists are less risk averse than banks, meaning that they are prepared to invest in riskier enterprises and tend to look for investment opportunities where there is the chance of a high rate of return. Traditionally, venture capital finance was only available to companies seeking over £250,000; however, there are some providers of venture capital who will consider small investment needs of under £250,000.

Before a company embarks on a search for venture capital finance, there are various issues that the directors should consider to determine whether they and the company are fit and ready for it. For example, does the company have high growth prospects and does the management team have an ambition for rapid growth? Does the product or service have a distinct competitive edge or unique selling point? Does the management team have relevant industrial sector experience and knowledge, with clear leadership and complementary team members? Are the owner-director(s) willing and prepared to sell some of their shares/issue new shares to an unknown private equity investor?

Venture capital may be suitable for a company that requires the following types of finance:

- seed capital – the development of a business concept prior to start-up;

- start-up – the company incorporation and product development phase;
- early stage – the initial production and selling phase; and
- expansion – the growth of an established business to its next phase.

A company seeking venture capital finance can search the BVCA (British Private Equity and Venture Capital Association) directory of members or else consult their professional advisers. Contact details for the BVCA can be found on its website at www.bvca.co.uk.

Advantages of venture capital
The main advantages of venture capital finance can be summarised as follows.

- Venture Capitalists are able to provide finance for riskier propositions which banks are more inclined to avoid or reject.
- It may be possible to raise higher amounts of funding from a Venture Capitalist than from other sources of finance.
- Venture capital often comes with business advice and expertise to assist the development and growth of the company.
- If the company experiences difficulties the Venture Capitalist will seek to work with the company to turn the business around, unlike debt finance and other forms of outside finance.
- Venture Capitalists are committed to the company through to exit stage.
- Companies financed by venture capitalists have historically had faster growth rates because of the provision of finance and non-financial business support.
- Venture capital finance is not secured on assets.
- Venture Capitalists are not preferential investors. If the company fails they will lose their investment just like any other shareholder.

Disadvantages of venture capital
The main disadvantages of venture capital finance can be summarised as follows.

- Venture Capitalists often impose conditions and constraints in the financial package that they put together for the company (e.g. they may put a cap on the directors' remuneration).
- A Venture Capitalist will often require the right to appoint a non-executive director to the board.
- Venture Capitalists will require regular financial reports such as monthly management accounts and business progress reports to monitor the company's performance.
- The search for and securing of a suitable Venture Capitalist can be relatively time consuming and costly. The process may span three to six months and cost in the region of 5% of the finance raised. For smaller amounts, the costs may reach 10%.
- During the search for a suitable Venture Capitalist, the company's trading

performance may be adversely affected as management time and attention is diverted to the search process.

■ It is not uncommon for a venture capital finance investment deal to fail at the eleventh hour because of an inability to reach agreeable terms.

Business Angels

A Business Angel is a high net worth individual who invests their own money, or as a member of a syndicate, in high growth companies. Similar to Venture Capitalists, Business Angels provide the company with access to their expertise, experience and business contacts to facilitate the growth of the company. Business Angels have a high degree of commitment and seek the same commitment levels from companies approaching them for finance. An individual investment in a company may range from £10,000 to £250,000. However, companies seeking larger sums of finance can obtain this from a Business Angel syndicate.

Most Business Angels use a combination of the following factors to assess a company's proposition:

■ the expertise and track record of the company's founders and management;
■ the company's competitive edge or unique selling point;
■ the characteristics and growth potential of the market;
■ compatibility between the management, the company's proposal and the business angel's skills and investment preferences; and
■ the financial commitment of the company's founders.

Business Angels are individuals who don't seek publicity therefore there is no directory that can be freely searched. A suitable Business Angel can be identified via the Business Angel introduction agencies, details of which can be found on the UK Business Angels Association website (www.ukbusinessangelsassociation. org.uk) via angel networks, business incubators or via Business Angel syndicates.

Advantages of Business Angel finance

The main advantages of Business Angel finance can be summarised as follows.

■ Business Angels have a tendency to favour start-ups seeking smaller amounts of finance.
■ Business Angels invest across all sectors, therefore all sectors have an opportunity to attract the right angel investor. This is especially the case with technology companies. Although such companies often come with a higher degree of risk, this does not deter angel investors.
■ Business Angels are widely dispersed across the country whereas Venture Capitalists are often located in close proximity to the main financial centres.
■ Business Angels may be flexible in their approach to investment in the right company providing the base criteria are satisfied. Business Angels may have

a longer investment horizon (sometimes referred to as 'patient money') and lower targeted rates of return.

■   The cost of raising finance is relatively low compared to institutional finance.

■   Business Angels are value-added investors. They bring their personal business skills to the company thus facilitating the growth of younger enterprises.

Disadvantages of Business Angel finance

The main disadvantages of Business Angel finance can be summarised as follows.

■   Business Angels will require a share in the company and this may be a larger stake than a company may ideally wish to relinquish. However, the size of the stake requested by the Business Angel is designed to safeguard and secure their investment. The larger share required by Business Angels may also reflect the degree of risk in the investment.

■   The time required to search and attract the right Business Angel for a company may be lengthy.

■   Business Angels endeavour to work closely with a company therefore they will not invest in any company if they believe there will be a clash of personalities with the company owners.

■   Business Angels may not be suitable to companies seeking under £10,000 or over £250,000.

Debt finance

In meeting a company's long-term financing needs, the other possible source of funding is debt. Debt finance can either be in the form of debentures or bank loans.

Debentures

The term 'debenture' is used to describe the contract or written agreement that arises in relation to a bank or other lender making a loan of money to a company. The terms will be determined at the outset but usually a loan is repayable on a fixed date with a fixed rate of interest payable to the debenture holder. Interest due and payable to debenture holders must be paid before the payment of dividends to shareholders. Debentures are normally (but are not required to be) secured on the assets of the company which may be by way of a 'fixed' or a 'floating' charge. A fixed charge is secured over a specific asset with the consequence that the company cannot then sell or take any other action in relation to that asset without the permission of the lender. In contrast, a floating charge attaches to various assets of a business without encumbering the company's ability to make use of them. A floating charge only becomes fixed on the occurrence of certain events which cause the charge to crystallise.

If a debenture is secured by a charge, then the provisions of Part 25 of the Companies Act concerning the registration of charges at Companies House come into effect. The majority of Part 25 was repealed on 6 April 2013 and replaced by new provisions setting out a revised registration regime. Charges created on or before 5 April 2013 are subject to the old Part 25 and charges created on or after 6 April 2013 are subject to the new one.

Under the new Part 25, where a company creates a charge – subject to certain specified exceptions – the company or any person interested in the charge must submit prescribed details and documentation relating to the charge to Companies House (together with a registration fee), or else be exposed to the consequences of non-registration. The information and documentation can be delivered in hard copy or electronically. If the required details of a registerable charge are not delivered to Companies House, the charge is void against a liquidator, administrator and any creditor of the company. In this respect it is the security on the company's assets that is void, not the contract or obligation for repayment. This means that the charge holder will be treated as an unsecured creditor for the purposes of the distribution of assets in a winding up (see Chapter 17). At the same time, when a charge becomes void in this way the money secured by it immediately becomes payable. Although the failure to register a charge presents risks to both the company and the charge holder it is usually the latter or the latter's professional advisers that will deal with registration. All charges must be registered within 21 days starting with the day following the day on which they are created unless an extension is granted by the court.

As well as registering its charges at Companies House, a company must also keep its own records of any charges that it creates. The old Part 25 required a company to keep a register of its charges (containing specified details about each charge) as well as copies of any instruments creating them and this still applies to any charges created on or before 5 April 2013. The new Part 25 (in respect of charges created on or after 6 April 2013) requires a company to keep copies of every instrument creating a charge capable of registration, and every instrument effecting any variation or amendment of such a charge. In a change from the previous law, details of charges created after 6 April 2013 need not be entered into a company's register of charges. This means that a company that has no charges created on or before 5 April 2013 does not need to have such a register. The register of charges (where a company has one) and any instruments creating or amending charges must be available for inspection by shareholders and creditors of the company free of charge and by others on payment of the prescribed fee (see Chapter 4). An example of a register of charges can be found in Appendix 4.

Advantages of debentures
The main advantages of debentures can be summarised as follows.

■ Debenture holders receive a fixed rate of interest for their investment in a company and rank ahead of shareholders for payment when a company becomes insolvent. As such, they perceive their investment to be less risky than shareholders, which may make it easier to raise this type of finance. In addition, the rate of interest paid on debentures is often less than the returns to debt financiers (see later in this chapter).

- Debentures are a tax-efficient source of finance in comparison to equity finance. Debenture interest is a tax-deductible expense, which results in a company being charged a lower level of corporation tax. Dividends paid to shareholders are paid from post-tax profits.
- Debenture holders do not have any voting rights, consequently the ownership of a company is not diluted.
- Debenture holders do not participate in any growth in profits enjoyed by shareholders.

Disadvantages of debentures

The main disadvantages of debentures can be summarised as follows.

- Debentures result in a legal obligation to pay interest and to repay the principal. If these obligations are not met, the debenture holder can require sale of the assets against which they are secured or force the company into insolvency proceedings.
- Debentures increase the financial gearing of a company and, as a result, might reduce its capacity to raise additional external debt in the future.
- The repayment of debentures on their maturity might represent a material cash outflow from the company and, as such, it requires effective cash management and budgeting.
- Some debentures have restrictive covenants attached, which may hinder the operational flexibility of the company in the future.
- The repayment of debentures and interest payments can become difficult for a company during periods of economic austerity. Fixed payments of debenture interest during a period of declining sales and profits may put a company's cashflow under pressure.

Bank loan

A bank loan is finance obtained from a bank for a fixed period of over one year. Banks often require a guarantee from the company's directors or some form of security for the sum of the loan. As mentioned in Chapter 1, if a director is required to personally guarantee a loan the benefit of separate financial liability (one of the key attractions of a limited company) is lost. The costs associated with a loan are the agreed rate of interest and an arrangement fee. The rate of interest is usually the bank's base rate plus a premium. The premium levied by the bank is determined by the bank's perceived risk attached to the lending. Factors that may influence the bank's decision to approve or refuse a loan include the age of the company, its past financial performance, its business sector and the purpose for which the loan is required.

Advantages of a bank loan

The main advantages of a bank loan include the following.

- Once the loan has been agreed, the finance is available for the agreed term and there is no risk of it being withdrawn by the bank, unless there is a breach of any of the terms of the loan agreement.
- The interest charge can be fixed. This enables the company to budget for a known fixed repayment charge over the duration of the loan.
- Where a loan is required to purchase a fixed asset, the loan can be matched against the expected life span of the asset.
- The loan interest is a tax deductible business expense for the company.

Disadvantages of a bank loan

The main disadvantages of a bank loan include the following.

- Banks often request a director's loan guarantee or some form of security as part of the loan agreement. This provides the bank with protection and a guarantee of repayment in the event that the company fails. A guarantee from a director exposes him or her to personal financial liability in the event of a default.
- The loan arrangement fee is usually set as a sliding scale percentage of the loan. The arrangement fee will decrease as the size of the loan increases.
- A company will be charged an early redemption fee for the early repayment of a loan. This is a compensation for disrupting the bank's cash flow and its loss of future interest payments.
- Some banks may request that 'key man' insurance is taken out if they feel the business is reliant upon a key person. This represents an additional charge for the company.
- The bank may impose set terms concerning a company's borrowing ratio as part of the loan agreement, to avoid the company taking on too much debt.

Short-term funding

Once a company can finance its day-to-day operational needs internally it may also be able to fund small-scale projects in the same way. In either case, the directors should use cash-flow forecasts both to monitor the company's position and to ensure that it is able to meet its liabilities as they fall due. If a company is unable to meet its short-term obligations and commitments through revenue and profits generated by its operational activities, it will no longer be able to continue trading and will need to consider liquidation or disposal. However, this would not necessarily mean that the company was not profitable. It is quite possible for a company that is profitable from an accounting perspective to not have the liquid funds that it needs to meet its outgoings. In this scenario a lack of available cash may be an indicator of poor financial management and it would be strongly recommended that the company look at, or take advice on, the means by which its cash flow (and cash-flow management) can be improved. Even for companies which actively manage their finances, situations may still arise where resources are insufficient to cover their costs. A key responsibility of the company's management team is to identify such shortfalls or potential shortfalls and then to consider sources of short-term funding to cover the deficit.

Overdraft

Probably the most flexible form of short-term funding is an overdraft. An overdraft is an agreed borrowing facility granted by a company's bank to help a company meet its daily operational costs. The facility essentially provides companies with a cash buffer to help them manage their short-term cash flow position. Overdrafts have two separate charges. First, there is an arrangement fee for the service and this is a recurring annual charge. Second, there is the cost of using the overdraft, which is usually set at several percentage points above the bank base rate. The interest charged for an overdraft will often be determined by a set of commercial factors about the company. These factors will include the nature of the business, the risk exposure, the management team and the age of the company.

Advantages of an overdraft

The main advantages of an overdraft can be summarised as follows.

- An overdraft is a flexible source of finance that is available for use when required by the company.
- Apart from the arrangement fee, the majority of the cost of usage is only incurred and paid when the overdraft facility is used.
- There is no charge incurred for early repayment.
- It is usually easy to arrange.

Disadvantages of an overdraft

The main disadvantages of an overdraft can be summarised as follows.

- An overdraft may be recalled or reduced by the bank at any time.
- Overdrafts may be secured against business assets or require a personal guarantee from the company's directors.
- Interest rates are always variable. This makes planning for these charges more difficult than the use of fixed interest rate borrowings.
- Extending the overdraft facility or exceeding the agreed overdraft facility will incur additional charges.
- Overdrafts are only available from a company's business bank.

Trade credit

Trade credit refers to the payment terms that a supplier of goods and services stipulates in their dealings with a purchaser – it is the period within which the supplier requires payment for the goods or services that they have provided. In some sectors, the standard terms of credit are 30 days but it may be greater or less than 30 days subject to the terms and conditions of any given supplier. Despite imposing specified payment terms it is not uncommon for suppliers to receive payment beyond their required payment date. In some cases, suppliers experience payment at double or triple their specified payment period. Deferring payment to a supplier beyond the credit term is akin to the supplier granting the buyer a free overdraft. Trade credit may be an attractive proposition for buyers in the short term, but repeated use may have long-term commercial consequences. Every buying company using trade credit should recognise that they may also be a supplier in another business transaction and they may also experience delays in receiving their payment. Small companies should note that, in practice, some large companies often ignore their credit terms. It is not uncommon for 30 days' credit to move into 70 or 90 days' credit.

Advantages of trade credit

- Goods can be purchased and payment made to the supplier once the goods are sold and cash received.
- There is no interest incurred if payment is made within the agreed terms of credit.
- Cash flow burden is reduced for the duration of the term of credit.

Disadvantages of trade credit

- Any discount given by the supplier for early payment is lost.
- Payment beyond the specified credit term may result in the company developing a poor credit history and might damage the relationship with the supplier.
- Late payments may result in future purchases being restricted to cash payment only.

Invoice finance

Invoice finance is a means of improving a company's cash flow and maintaining working capital on the basis of the company's invoices. Customers can take a long time to pay, which means that cash owed to a company may not be received for some time after the delivery of the product or service to which it relates. Invoice finance essentially amounts to using a company's invoices as an asset against which money is borrowed from a third party under the terms of an invoice finance agreement. There are two types of invoice finance: factoring (or 'debt factoring' as it is also known) and invoice discounting.

Factoring

Factoring is the process whereby a company sells its outstanding invoices (its debtors – also known as its 'debtors book') to a third-party factor provider.

Invariably, factor providers are subsidiaries of banks or financial institutions. The factor provider gives the company access to about 75–80% of the debtor's balance, either immediately or if not immediately, then within a shorter time period than the company's standard credit terms. For example, company ZYX with a debtors balance of £100,000 may be able to realise £80,000 of the cash owed to it within a week or 10 days of setting up a factor arrangement.

Once a factor has been instructed he then takes responsibility for collecting the payment from the company's debtors subject to the terms of the factor agreement.

There are two types of factoring agreements: recourse and non-recourse. In a recourse agreement, the company is responsible for any debtors that cannot be collected by the factor provider. However, in the case of a non-recourse agreement, the factor provider takes on the responsibility for any uncollected monies and bad debts himself.

Factoring has two associated costs:

- an agreed fee incurred at the commencement of the agreement; and
- a percentage fee against the funds withdrawn, which is usually levied on a monthly basis.

Factoring is generally suitable for companies that fulfil the following conditions:

- sales occur via business-to-business activities;
- the aged debtors profile does not exceed three months;
- there is an absence of staged payment arrangements;
- the contractual arrangements between the company and its debtors are simple and do not involve any warranty arrangements; and
- a single debtor is not responsible for a significant percentage of the total debtors balance outstanding.

In addition, some factor providers set a minimum turnover threshold for instructing companies. The turnover threshold may be set at £50,000 or the prevailing VAT registration threshold. However, some factor providers will consider small to medium-sized enterprises subject to a 12–18-month track record.

Invoice discounting

Invoice discounting is similar to factoring in that it allows a company to raise money against its debtors but, unlike in a factoring agreement, the company maintains control of its debtors' book and credit control/debt collection remains in-house. Similar criteria apply to a company seeking to use invoice discounting as a means of short-term finance as to a company seeking to use debt factoring. Invoice discounting is not an option for companies who are not engaged in the selling of products or services on credit to other businesses.

Prior to engaging with a company, an invoice discounter will visit the company to ascertain an understanding of the business and to assess the scope for a possible invoice discounting relationship. Invoice discounting fees comprise two elements:

- the discount fee which is generally usually several percentage points above the UK bank base lending rate; and
- a credit management fee which is based upon turnover, with a ceiling of 2–3% of a company's turnover.

The invoice discounter releases agreed cash percentages to a company based upon the company's debtors balance. As part of the terms of the invoice discounting agreement, the invoice discounter will require daily downloads of a company's sales daybooks so they can have an up-to-date picture of the company's position. This allows the discounter to release appropriate funds to the company and monitor sales receipts to ensure that they are paid as soon as the company receives payment from its debtors.

Advantages and disadvantages of factoring and invoice discounting

The main advantages and disadvantages of factoring and invoice discounting are summarised in the table below.

Table 13.1: Advantages and disadvantages of factoring and invoice discounting

	Advantages	Disadvantages
Factoring	A company can save time from the use of factoring because the factor provider chases the debtors on the company's behalf. Directors are not required to provide personal guarantees or use their home as collateral as the sales are the security for the factor provider. Factoring is available to businesses irrespective of size.	The use of a factor provider to collect outstanding debts may damage a company's client relationship. A company's client relationship may be damaged further if a factor provider is aggressive in their debt collection policy. Poor quality debts will reduce the amount of debts that are collectable by the factor provider.
Invoice discounting	Allows a company to access finance much faster than the standard 30 or 40 days' credit payment period. The costs of invoice discounting are known in advance and are based upon the value of the sales invoices. This enables the company to know in advance and plan for the factoring fees.	Invoice discounting charges reduces the margins and profitability of the sales that are recovered by the factor provider. Any advance receipts received from debtors must be repaid to the invoice finance provider before a company can leave an invoice financing relationship.

Government grants

Central and local government over the years have provided a variety of grants to aid business development. A grant is usually a single one-off payment to a company. Qualifying for a grant is usually subject to meeting one or more specific requirements. The most common requirements have been in relation to geographic location, employment generation (or unemployment reduction) innovation and technology or specific sectors. Government grants are often linked to or associated with central government economic policies, therefore they should not be regarded as a staple source of business finance, but a bonus which will not necessarily be repeated. A professional such as an accountant, solicitor or independent financial advisor can give advice on the government grants and incentives that are available. The main advantages and disadvantages of government grants are summarised below.

Advantages of government grants

- Government grants serve as a useful source of additional cash flow for a company.
- Grants are non-repayable and there is often no penalty clause if any objectives attached to the funding is not met.
- A grant is never attached to government having access to, or a stake in, the company or a voice in its management.
- General grants do not have any restrictions upon their application within the business.

Disadvantages of government grants

- Government grants are based upon specific qualification requirements, therefore not every company will be eligible to submit an application for a grant.
- Government grants applications are often a relatively bureaucratic and time-consuming process. This is compounded by the periodic reporting of specific requirements if a grant application is successful.
- The success rate of obtaining a government grant may be low due to the existence of high demand and strong competition.
- The availability of government grants has a finite life span. The grant will be available until the total funds assigned by the government have been exhausted or there is a change in funding criteria or government policy.

Enterprise finance guarantee

Over the past three decades successive UK governments have recognised the challenges facing viable small companies seeking to raise bank finance with a lack of security and have provided support for this purpose. The current programme to address this problem is the Enterprise Finance Guarantee Scheme (EFGS).

The EFGS is designed to assist bank lending to viable small businesses that do not have sufficient security of their own to obtain bank finance. The EFGS seeks to enable these businesses to secure the working capital and investment they require. The government provides the banks with a guarantee for 75% of the loan value made to these companies.

The EFGS is available across most sectors for companies seeking loans of £1,000 through to £1 million with a maximum turnover of £41 million. Loans are repayable over a period of between three months and 10 years. The government charges the borrower a premium equivalent to 2% per annum on the outstanding balance of the loan, which is assessed and collected quarterly throughout the life of the loan.

There is no automatic entitlement to receive a guaranteed loan and a pre-qualification process does not exist. Participating banks have delegated authority to determine who qualifies on commercial terms. Further details can be obtained from the Department of Business, Innovation and Skills (BIS).

Summary

- Company finance can be classified as either long term or short term.
- Long-term sources of finance can be grouped into debt finance and equity finance.
- Equity finance refers to funds secured by way of the allotment of shares in a company. Initial capital may come from the founders or those close to them. Over time, a company may seek investment from private individuals, a Venture Capitalist or a Business Angel.
- The allotment of shares to a private investor results in the dilution of the founder shareholders' stake in the company and a loss of control, to one degree or another. Investors will look to protect their position by taking shares that give them preferential rights.
- The main forms of debt finance are loans and debentures. A debenture is the name given to a contract or agreement that evidences a loan. Debenture holders receive a fixed rate of interest on their investment and rank ahead of unsecured creditors in the event of a liquidation.
- Debentures are normally secured on a company's assets either by way of a fixed charge, a floating charge or both. Most company charges are registerable at Companies House. Failure to register a registerable charge renders it void against a liquidator, administrator and any creditor of a company.
- Interest on a bank loan is set at the bank's base rate plus a premium which reflects the bank's view of the risk involved. Directors may be required to personally guarantee a bank loan, making them personally liable in the event of a default by the company.
- Short-term sources of funding include bank overdrafts, trade credit and invoice finance.

- There are two forms of invoice finance – debt factoring and invoice discounting. A debt factor purchases a company's debts at an agreed percentage of their full value. An invoice discounter advances cash to a company on the basis of a company's debtors' balance.
- The nature and availability of government grants tends to depend on the government of the day and its economic and other policies. A grant is usually a single one-off payment.
- The Enterprise Finance Guarantee scheme is intended to encourage lending by banks to small businesses that lack significant assets on which a loan can be secured.

14 Accounting and tax
David Frederick

In this chapter

This chapter considers the areas of company accounting, preparation of accounts and taxation with regard to:

- the component parts of an effective accounting system;
- the retention of accounting records;
- the difference between statutory accounts and management accounts;
- an overview of statutory accounts including the profit and loss account, balance sheet and distribution;
- an overview of management accounts and their importance in monitoring a company's financial position; and
- taxation including VAT, corporation tax, PAYE and income tax.

The accounting system

Every company has an accounting system underpinning its operation. The accounting system enables and facilitates the production of periodic financial and management accounting reports for statutory purposes and internal decision making. An effective accounting system requires a reliable bookkeeping system because all business transactions enter the periodic accounting reports via the bookkeeping system. The essential records that a company needs to allow the effective functioning of its bookkeeping system and subsequent accounting reporting system are as follows: bank statements and paying-in slips; purchases and sales invoices/receipts; and details of assets, liabilities, income and expenditure.

These records should be entered into a company's books of prime entry. These books are set out below and Figure 14.1 shows their integration with the company's business transactions.

Figure 14.1: Business transactions and books of prime entry integration

Business transactions				
Sales	Purchases	Cash receipts or payments	Sales returns	Purchase returns

⇩ ⇩ ⇩ ⇩ ⇩

Book of prime entry				
Sales day book	Purchase day book	Cash book	Sales returns day book	Purchase returns day book

Sales day book
This book records the sales invoices that a company has sent out to its customers. Every sale, whether cash or credit, should result in the company raising an invoice. These invoices should be recorded in the sales day book by goods value, VAT and total invoice value.

Sales returns day book
It is not unusual for goods sold to customers to be returned either because they were faulty or they were the wrong goods. These returns are recorded in the sales returns day book. The sales returns day book should be completed in exactly the same way as the sales day book in respect of goods returned from customers. When the individual entries are made in the sales ledger they will reduce the amount owed by the customer. The sales returns will also reduce the actual sales made by the company. This will initiate the issue of a credit note.

Purchases day book
This book is for the recording of the company's purchases with a list of the invoices from its suppliers. It is completed in exactly the same way as the sales day book.

Purchase returns day book
Purchases returns are goods a company returns to the supplier. In effect, they are negative purchases in that they reduce the amount owed to the supplier who

should send a credit note to the company. This will be completed in exactly the same manner as the purchase day book. When the entries are made to the purchase ledger they will reduce the amounts owing to the suppliers and will reduce the company's purchases.

Cash books

For accounting purposes 'cash' includes, for example, cash, cheques and bank transactions. The 'cash book' records all 'cash' transactions including coins, banknotes, cheques, direct debits, credit transfers and banker's drafts. The cash book is split into columns for cash and bank transactions. The left hand side (debit) of the cash book is for recording the money received by the company in the form of cash, cheques etc, whereas the right hand side (credit) of the cash book is for recording the payment of expenses out of the company in the form of cash, cheques, direct debits or credit card payments.

In addition to these five books of prime entry a company should also have a sales and purchase ledger.

Sales ledger

The sales ledger contains an account for each customer and shows the company how much is owed by each of its customers. At the end of each day or periodically, each invoice from the sales day book should be entered against the individual customer's account in the sales ledger to ensure the company has an up-to-date balance of the outstanding money owed by its customers.

Purchase ledger

The purchase ledger contains an account for each supplier and shows the company how much money it owes to each of its suppliers. At the end of each day or periodically, each invoice from the purchase day book should be entered against the individual suppliers' account in the sales ledger to ensure the company has an up-to-date balance of its outstanding debts to its suppliers.

A company registered for VAT will be required to keep the following additional records and documents:

- a VAT account;
- VAT sales invoices; and
- VAT purchase invoices.

If a company employs staff, including the owner or director(s), it must maintain a payroll system either in-house or outsourced. Irrespective of the location of the payroll system it must be capable of generating the following information:

- payments made to employees;
- statutory deductions from employee's salaries and wages;
- details of employee benefits and expenses; and
- records of statutory payments such as sick pay and maternity pay.

Accounting systems

It would be unusual today if a new company chose to set up a manual accounting system. The choice of accounting system facing today's new company is often between the use of a spreadsheet or a specific accountancy program.

A company choosing the latter is faced with deciding to use a desktop-based or a cloud-based (remote storage access) accountancy program. Given the increasing range and complexity of accountancy programs available, it is essential that company directors discuss their company's requirements with a firm of accountants or their tax adviser before choosing which system would be most appropriate for their company.

Retention of accounting records

HM Revenue & Customs (HMRC) requires companies to retain their accounting records for at least six years from the end of the corporation tax accounting period. For example, if the accounting period ends on 31 December 2013, the company will need to keep their records for that period until at least 31 December 2019. However, the records do not have to be kept in their original format. The records may be held in the following formats:

- scanned PDF;
- files saved on a CD-ROM; and
- files saved on an optical imaging system.

The only exceptions to this rule apply to the following accounting records:

- dividend vouchers;
- bank interest certificates; and
- Construction Industry Scheme (CIS) vouchers.

Where an alternative storage format is used the accounting records must be legible and available in a readable format if required at a later date by HMRC or for any statutory purpose.

Although HMRC requires companies to retain their accounting records for six years, the Registrar of Companies only requires private limited companies to retain their records for three years.

Accounts

Accounts is the generic name given to the periodic reports produced by a company on its financial performance for internal or external users to make economic and management decisions about the company. Two types of accounts are produced by a company for its users; financial and management accounts. Despite the two types of accounts being different in name and format they are produced from the same accounting transactions and books of prime entry outlined earlier.

The main difference between financial accounts and management accounts

Figure 14.2: The requirements for keeping company records

Business records	Records	Minimum period for keeping records
Essential company accounting records	■ Bank statements ■ Bank paying-in books ■ Purchase receipts ■ Sales invoices ■ Assets ■ Liabilities ■ Income and expenditure	Six years from the end of the corporation tax accounting period
Payroll	■ Payments made to employees ■ Statutory deductions from employee's salaries and wages ■ Details of employee benefits and expenses ■ Records of statutory sick pay and ■ Records of statutory maternity pay	Three years (in addition to your current year)
VAT	■ VAT account ■ VAT sales invoices ■ VAT purchase invoices ■ Import and export records	Generally you must keep all your business records that are relevant for VAT for at least six years

is a company has a statutory duty to produce financial accounts at least annually whereas a company does not have any statutory duty to produce management accounts. The purpose, presentation and users of the two types of accounts are different.

Figure 14.3: Financial v management accounts

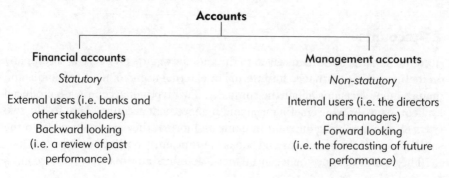

Accounts

Financial accounts

Statutory

External users (i.e. banks and other stakeholders)
Backward looking
(i.e. a review of past performance)

Management accounts

Non-statutory

Internal users (i.e. the directors and managers)
Forward looking
(i.e. the forecasting of future performance)

▓ Financial accounts

A company is required to prepare and file its annual financial accounts each year with the Registrar of Companies and with HMRC. It is the statutory duty of directors that a company prepares accounts for each financial year. The statutory financial accounts must include the following:

- a profit and loss account for the accounting year end;
- balance sheet as at the year end;
- explanatory notes to accompany these two accounting statements;
- a directors' report including a business review; and
- an auditor's report, where appropriate.

However, there are certain filing exemptions for small and dormant companies, which will be examined later. The accounting year-end date is known as the accounting reference date by the Registrar of Companies (see Chapter 4 for more on this).

The filing of annual accounts to the two statutory agencies has different submission deadline dates. Annual accounts for private limited companies must be filed with the Registrar of Companies within nine months of the accounting year-end. HMRC requires annual accounts to be filed within 12 months of the year-end and, in addition, HMRC requires the filing of company tax returns with the annual accounts. However, if any corporation tax is due and payable, this must be paid within nine months and one day of the accounting year-end.

An exception to the above standard filing requirements applies to any private limited company filing their first annual accounts for a period greater than 12 months.

If a private limited company is filing its first annual accounts for such a period then it must submit its annual accounts to the Registrar of Companies within 21 months of the date of incorporation.

Statutory accounts approval

A company's director or board of directors must approve the annual accounts before their distribution and submission to the statutory agencies (the Registrar of Companies and HMRC). The board of directors and the auditors are required to approve and sign various reports before the accounts are distributed.

A director or the company secretary must sign the directors' report on behalf of the board of directors and print their name under the report. If the report has been prepared under the small companies provisions a statement to that effect should be included above the signature.

If the company is subject to an audit, the auditor must sign the auditor's report and print their name under it before the report is attached to the accounts.

A director or the company secretary must sign the balance sheet on behalf of the board of directors and print their name under the balance sheet. If the company is claiming any small company exemptions the appropriate statements must be included above the signature.

Distribution of statutory accounts

At the end of each financial year, a company must distribute its annual accounts to the following:

- every shareholder;
- every company debenture holder;
- every person who is entitled to receive notice of general meetings;
- the Registrar of Companies; and
- HMRC.

Profit and loss account

A profit and loss account is a statement of the annual sales less the annual expenses incurred by the organisation. The residue of the sales less the expenses incurred is the operating profit for the year. The operating profit provides the basis for the charging of corporation tax before any distribution of dividends to shareholders. A sample profit and loss account is shown in Figure 14.4. If a company is registered for VAT, the sales and the expenses in the profit and loss account are always recorded net of VAT. This practice occurs because VAT is accounted for separately to HMRC since it is money held in a company's custody on behalf of the government and is paid to HMRC periodically.

Turnover

Turnover is the net value of the sales a company made during the year. Cost of sales is the cost incurred in generating those sales. Gross profit is the difference between turnover and cost of sales before the deduction of any other operating expenses.

Sales and distribution costs

Sales and distribution costs are the costs associated with the selling and delivery of the company's output to its customers. The administration expenses are all of the general expenses incurred in the daily operation of the company. These will include, for example, staff costs, office expenses, professional fees, printing, postage and stationery. The administration expenses may be regarded as the company's overheads.

Operating profit

Operating profit is the income a company generates from its trading activities before the deduction for any cost of borrowing. Interest charges incurred on external borrowing are deducted from the operating profit to produce the profit before taxation or pre-tax profit.

After the deduction of corporation tax a company is left with its post-tax profit. This is the amount of profit a company can use at its discretion. The post-tax profit may be applied in four general ways:

- to re-invest for the future;
- to distribute to shareholders;
- to set aside provisions for known or unknown contingent liabilities; or
- to transfer to general reserves until a later date.

The residue after the appropriation is the profit retained for the year. This is the residual profit a company has at the end of the accounting period after it has set aside the payment to each stakeholder.

Figure 14.4: Sample profit and loss account

A Company
Profit and Loss Account
For the year ending 31 December 201X

	£
Turnover	105,000
Cost of sales	30,000
Gross profit	75,000
Sales and distribution costs	10,000
Administrative expenses	20,000
Operating profit	45,000
Net interest	5,000
Profit before tax	40,000
Tax on profit on ordinary activities	8,000
Post-tax profit	32,000
Dividends	12,000
Retained profit for the year	20,000

Balance sheet

A balance sheet provides a statement of a company's assets owned, liabilities owed and its net worth as at the year end. A sample balance sheet is shown in Figure 14.5.

Fixed assets

Fixed assets are the long-term assets of a company, such as plant, machinery and equipment shown at net book value. Net book value is the cost of the asset less the accumulated depreciation.

Current assets

Current assets are short-term assets owned by a company (e.g. stock, debtors and cash at bank). The current assets are always recorded in order of illiquidity.

Stock
Stock is the valuation at the date of the balance sheet of items held by the company for resale in future periods.

Debtors
Debtors are the sales to customers where payment is still outstanding at the year end and should be collectable by the company within the next 12 months.

Cash at bank
Cash at bank should be the balance shown in the cash book as at the date of the balance sheet subject to adjustment for unpresented cheques and other known items not yet credited or debited to the bank statement.

Creditors due within 12 months
Creditors due within 12 months represent any outstanding bills that remain unpaid at the year-end, which should be discharged in the next 12 months. An example of such a creditor is the corporation tax liability which will be payable within nine months plus one day of the balance sheet date. These creditors will often be separated into trade creditors and sundry creditors.

Net current assets
Net current assets or 'working capital' is the difference between current assets and current liabilities. This represents the short-term solvency of a company.

Creditors due over 12 months
Creditors due over 12 months are the providers of long-term finance to a company.

Net assets
Net assets is a measure of the difference between the total assets and total liabilities of a company.

The lower section of a balance sheet represents the internal financing of a company. The main elements are the share capital, revenue reserves and capital reserves as shown in Figure 14.5.

The share capital is the monetary value of the shares purchased and fully paid for by the shareholders. Revenue reserves are the accumulation of retained trading profits which a company may keep for internal use or for distribution to its shareholders in the future. Capital reserves are reserves which a company has accumulated from non trading activities. They may be used by the company, but are non-distributable to the shareholders. The shareholder's funds represent the capital owned by the shareholders which equals the net assets.

Figure 14.5: Sample balance sheet

A Company
Balance sheet
As at the year ended 31 December 201X

	£	£	£
Fixed assets			15,000
Current assets			
Stock	1,000		
Debtors	2,500		
Cash at bank	17,500	21,000	
Creditors due within 12 months			
Trade creditors	5,000		
Net current assets			16,000
Creditors due over 12 months			10,000
Net assets			21,000
Capital and reserves			
Share capital	1,000		
Revenue reserves	20,000		
Shareholder's funds			21,000

Auditor

An auditor is a qualified accountant from a recognised supervisory body who provides an independent report on the preparation of a company's financial statements with regard to its compliance with current company law and the prevailing accounting and auditing standards. The auditor also gives an opinion upon whether the financial statements provide a true and fair view of the company's financial position at the year-end.

The recognised supervisory bodies are as follows:

- Institute of Chartered Accountants in England & Wales;
- Institute of Chartered Accountants in Scotland;
- Institute of Chartered Accountants in Ireland; and
- Chartered Association of Certified Accountants.

Membership of one of the recognised supervisory bodies by itself does not qualify a member to be an auditor. The accountant or the firm of accountants must be approved and hold a current audit practising certificate.

Dormant company

A dormant company is any company that has no significant accounting transactions during the accounting period. A significant transaction is a transaction that is required to be recorded in the company's accounting records. Dormant companies are granted certain filing exemptions by the Companies Act.

Small and medium-sized companies

Companies are classified as small, medium or large by reference to the following factors:

- turnover;
- balance sheet total (current and fixed assets); and
- employees.

To qualify as either a small or medium company, any two of the criteria in Figure 14.6 must be met.

Small companies can file abbreviated accounts with the Registrar of Companies and are exempt from filing any of the following:

- a profit and loss account;
- a directors' report including a business review; and
- an auditor's report.

All small companies with year ending on or after 1 October 2012 are exempt from the audit requirements. However, the shareholders can demand an audit if they deem it necessary.

Figure 14.6: Determinants of company size

	Small Less than	Medium Less than	Large Above
Annual turnover	£6.5m	£25.9m	£25.9m
Balance sheet total	£3.26m	£12.9m	£12.9m
Employees	50	250	250

Management accounts

Unlike financial accounts, management accounts are not a statutory requirement. This fact may explain why so many companies do not prepare them for their business. Management accounts are internally prepared accounts primarily for the benefit of the management. Management accounts serve the twin purposes of planning and control of the company.

The most important management accounts that a company should prepare are:

- an annual operating budget;
- periodic budget performance reports; and
- a cash budget, also known as a cash flow forecast.

Annual budget

An annual budget is a financial statement of the annual plan of a company. The budget may be separated into months (as shown in Figure 14.7) or quarters.

The budget should be prepared prior to the start of the financial year as it will be the basis of monitoring the progress of the company throughout the year.

Figure 14.7: An example of a six month's budget

Annual operating budget for the period 1 April–30 September

	Total Apr–Sep £	Apr £	May £	Jun £	Jul £	Aug £	Sep £
Sales							
Product A	412,800	64,000	67,200	70,400	57,600	73,600	80,000
Product B	590,400	91,200	96,000	100,800	105,600	86,400	110,400
Total	1,003,200	155,200	163,200	171,200	163,200	160,000	190,400
Expenditure							
Purchases	751,000	112,000	123,000	129,000	120,000	123,000	144,000
Salaries	132,000	22,000	22,000	22,000	22,000	22,000	22,000
Administration	32,500	5,000	5,000	5,000	5,000	5,000	7,500
Premises	18,000	0	0	9,000	0	0	9,000
Marketing	14,000	7,000	0	0	7,000	0	0
Professional fees	6,000	0	0	0	0	0	6,000
Bank charges	7,200	1,200	1,200	1,200	1,200	1,200	1,200
Plant & machinery	20,000	0	0	0	0	20,000	0
Total	980,700	147,200	151,200	166,200	155,200	171,200	189,700
Surplus	22,500	8,000	12,000	5,000	8,000	(11,200)	700

The annual operating budget or its periodic breakdown will not reveal the monthly profit or loss, but will show a surplus or deficit because the budget is not prepared using the same basis as the statutory financial accounts. An accountant can assist a company to produce budgeted statutory financial statements. Periodic budget performance reports may be used to monitor the progress of the company throughout the accounting year and are important for identifying where cash flow problems may arise – as can be seen for the month of August in the above example. This enables the directors to plan for any difficulties that may lie ahead.

Periodic budget performance reports

At the end of each reporting period, monthly or quarterly, a company can monitor its actual performance against its original budget estimates. This helps to establish how accurate the forecasting process is. It is important that the forecasting process is as accurate as possible given the reliance placed upon it for long-term planning purposes.

The example in Figure 14.8 reveals that in April, a company made £4,800 more sales than they had budgeted. However the favourable (F) position is the result of selling £11,000 more than the budget for product X and sold £6,200 less than budgeted for product Y. The latter gave rise to product Y producing an adverse (A) result for the month.

Expenditure for April was £1,700 less than budgeted, hence a favourable (F) position. However, an examination of the total expenditure highlights £1,000 adverse spending on marketing with favourable or no variances in all other areas.

Adverse and favourable variances should never be interpreted as good or bad. Variances provide areas that require investigation to ascertain the reason for them.

An alternative to examining the absolute variances may be to focus on variances within a set plus or minus range, for example, plus or minus 5%.

Figure 14.8: An example of a periodic budget monitoring report

	Budget Apr £	Actual Apr £	Variance Apr £		
Sales					
Product X	64,000	75,000	(11,000)	F	–17.19%
Product Y	91,200	85,000	6,200	A	6.80%
Total	155,200	160,000	(4,800)	F	–3.09%
Expenditure					
Purchases	112,000	110,000	2,000	F	1.79%
Salaries	22,000	22,000	0		
Administration	5,000	4,500	500	F	10.00%
Premises	0		0		
Marketing	7,000	8,000	(1,000)	A	–14.29%
Professional fees	0		0		
Bank charges	1,200	1,000	200	F	16.67%
Plant & machinery	0	0	0		
Total	147,200	145,500	1,700	F	1.15%
Surplus	8,000	14,500	(6,500)	F	–81.25%

Cash budgets

A cash budget is exactly the same in concept as an annual budget except it is based on when the cash is expected to be received or paid out by a company. An example is shown in Figure 14.9.

Figure 14.9: An example of a six-month cash flow forecast

	Apr £	May £	Jun £	Jul £	Aug £	Sep £	Total £
Receipts							
Product A	38,400	65,920	69,120	62,720	67,200	77,440	380,800
Product B	63,840	94,560	99,360	104,160	92,160	103,200	557,280
Total	102,240	160,480	168,480	166,880	159,360	180,640	938,080
Payments							
Purchases	89,600	98,400	103,200	96,000	98,400	115,200	600,800
Salaries	22,000	22,000	22,000	22,000	22,000	22,000	132,000
Administration		5,000	5,000	5,000	5,000	5,000	25,000
Premises	0	0	0	9,000	0	0	9,000
Marketing	3,500	3,500	0	3,500	3,500	0	14,000
Professional fees	0	0	0	0	0	6,000	6,000
Bank charges	0	0	3,600	0	0	3,600	7,200
Plant & machinery	0	0	0	0	20,000	0	20,000
Total	115,100	128,900	133,800	135,500	148,900	151,800	814,000
Net cash	(12,860)	31,580	34,680	31,380	10,460	28,840	124,080
Opening cash	25,000	12,140	43,720	78,400	109,780	120,240	25,000
Closing cash	12,140	43,720	78,400	109,780	120,240	149,080	149,080

The only difference between Figures 14.7 and 14.9 is the timing of the sales and expenditure. Hence the titles in Figure 14.9 are 'receipts' and 'payments'. Sales and expenditure are not always received or paid out when incurred therefore the cash flow forecast reflects the timing of the transactions.

The cash flow forecast is the most important management accounting tool for any company, especially a newly established one, because cash is sacrosanct in any business. It is often said that, 'sales is vanity, profit is sanity, but cash is king'.

The absence of cash flowing through a company will be its death knell as it is the life-blood of any business. In a similar manner to the periodic budget monitoring reports, periodic cash flow reports are used by company directors to monitor the cash flow position of the company. In simple terms, if the directors are aware of a position of excess cash inflows, the cash can be put to work for the company. Conversely, if the company has a cash shortfall, the directors can seek a cash injection.

Management accounts can be supported by several key management accounting performance measures:

$$\text{Break-even sales revenue} = \frac{\text{Overheads}}{\text{Gross profit/Unit selling price}}$$

This performance measure informs the management of the value of sales that must be generated before a company can realise a profit.

$$\text{Break-even output} = \frac{\text{Overheads}}{\text{Gross profit}}$$

The break-even output is an indicator of how many units must be sold before a company can realise a profit.

$$\text{Inventory holding days} = \frac{\text{Average stock held x 365}}{\text{Cost of sales}}$$

Inventory holding days informs a company about how long its inventories are being held within the company before being converted into cash. The inventory holding days will vary between industry and sector, therefore a company can benchmark its performance against others in its sector and against itself over time.

$$\text{Debtors collection period} = \frac{\text{Debtors}}{\text{Sales}} \times 365$$

$$\text{Creditors payment period} = \frac{\text{Trade creditors}}{\text{Cost of sales}} \times 365$$

■ Taxation

A company will encounter the following three forms of taxation during its business life:

- Value Added Tax (VAT), which concerns the sales and purchases of a company;
- PAYE/NIC, which concerns the payment of employees; and
- corporation tax, which concerns a company's earnings.

VAT

VAT is a tax charged on goods and services by UK registered businesses. It also applies to some imports to the UK. A company must charge VAT on its sales if it is registered for VAT and supplies VAT taxable goods and services either to a VAT registered or non-VAT registered buyer. A company has to register for VAT if its turnover of VAT taxable goods and services supplied within the UK for the previous 12 months is more than the current registration threshold or it expects to reach the threshold in the next 30 days. Failing to register on time will render a company liable to penalties. The threshold for VAT is amended annually by the government at the time of the budget.

For the purposes of charging VAT, goods and services are classified as being either inside or outside the scope of VAT. Items which are outside the scope of VAT are known as exempt services. Those which are inside and therefore subject to VAT are charged at standard rate, (currently 20%), reduced rate (currently 5%) and zero rate. A company that is selling exempt goods and services cannot register for VAT as their output is outside the VAT tax system.

VAT registered companies will receive their own unique nine-digit VAT number from HMRC. This number must be included on every company invoice as this provides evidence to clients and customers that a company is VAT registered and entitled to charge VAT.

VAT is money a company collects and holds in its custody on behalf of the Treasury. Every quarter, a VAT-registered company has to submit a VAT return to HMRC and pay over the net VAT that they have collected. The net VAT is the difference between the VAT which a company has charged its customers on its own sales, less the VAT which has been charged to it on its own purchases. HMRC allows VAT registered companies one month from the end of each quarter to submit their VAT return and make the appropriate payment.

From 1 April 2012 it has been mandatory to submit all VAT returns online. There has been an exemption for a small number of businesses. Online filing currently has an extension of an additional seven days for filing and making payments. It must be emphasised that the payment must be with HMRC by the month end plus the seventh day following the end of the VAT quarter. In addition, payments can be made to HMRC by direct debit. HMRC currently gives those paying their VAT by direct debit an extra 10 calendar days.

There are three VAT schemes in place designed to help small companies: flat-rate VAT, annual accounting and the cash accounting scheme. Each scheme has its own entry and exit conditions. Although the schemes are designed to help small companies, it is always best practice for a company to seek professional advice before joining any of them.

Flat-rate scheme
Under the flat-rate scheme, a company is no longer required to record the VAT on every transaction. The quarterly VAT liability is based upon the company's gross turnover for the quarter multiplied by a set VAT percentage based upon its trading activity determined by HMRC.

Cash accounting scheme
The cash accounting scheme allows members to pay VAT after they have received payment from their customers. Similarly, VAT is only reclaimable once suppliers have been paid.

Annual accounting scheme
The annual accounting scheme allows members to make nine monthly, or three

quarterly, interim payments during the year and make a balancing payment or receive a balancing refund at the end of the year. A VAT return is only completed once at the end of the year.

PAYE

PAYE (Pay As You Earn) is the system used by HMRC to collect income tax and National Insurance contributions from employees and company directors each pay date throughout the year. A company is responsible for the deduction of income tax and national insurance from the gross salary of all employees each time they are paid and for making payment to HMRC. In addition, the company will be subject to making an employers' National Insurance contribution to HMRC each time staff are paid.

A company operating a PAYE system must ensure it is in compliance with the Minimum Wage Act 1998. The minimum wage is increased annually on 1 October.

A company can apply to register for PAYE via the HMRC website (www.hmrc. gov.uk). On registration, a company may choose to operate its PAYE scheme internally or outsource it. Whichever option a company chooses, it has a responsibility to make statutory deductions of income tax and an employee's National Insurance contributions from its employees at each pay run, subject to the employee's tax code. Each UK tax payer is given a tax code by HMRC each year. The tax code denotes the amount of income the tax payer may earn before being subject to income tax.

Under the PAYE system, the annual allowance is spread over the year. A tax payer who is paid monthly will be allowed one-twelfth of their tax code on an accumulated basis to be deducted from their gross salary to date before their income is subject to income tax. Employee's National Insurance is deducted from their gross salary subject to it exceeding the annual lower earnings threshold. As an employer, a company will pay employer's National Insurance contributions based upon the monthly gross income of each employee.

The total of the employees' deductions plus the employers' National Insurance contributions is payable to HMRC by the nineteenth of the month following the payroll run. The current deadline for the receipt electronically by HMRC is the twenty-second of the month. To assist small businesses, companies with a payroll liability under £1,500 per month may elect to make quarterly PAYE payments to HMRC. Failure to pay on time will render a company liable to penalties and late interest charges.

From April 2013, every time a company pays an employee they will have to submit the payroll deductions, such as income tax and national insurance contributions to HMRC. This will render the traditional end-of-year reports redundant. The additional change to the PAYE system is that at the end of each payroll run, a company will have to submit to HMRC details of the dates of any starters and leavers.

Under the PAYE system there are two special schemes, SSP (Statutory Sick

Pay) and SMP (Statutory Maternity Pay). These are special rules appertaining to employees who fall sick or become pregnant. The rules regarding these two conditions require particular attention as they do not remain static; companies are advised to seek specialist advice if they have employees who fall under either.

Corporation tax

A limited company pays corporation tax based on its annual taxable profit. However, corporation tax has three particular features for every company. A company is required to:

- inform HMRC that it is liable for corporation tax;
- pay the correct amount of corporation tax on time; and
- file a company tax return and annual accounts in the prescribed formats.

On incorporation, a new company will receive from HMRC a form CT41G (Corporation Tax – Information for New Companies). The company directors are responsible for completing and returning this form to HMRC within three months of starting business activity. This notifies HMRC that a corporation tax liability may arise from the activity.

Large companies are required to pay their corporation tax in quarterly instalments throughout the year. All other companies are required to pay their corporation tax within nine months plus one day of the accounting year end.

Company tax returns must be filed within 12 months of the accounting year-end. Since 1 April 2011, all companies are required to file their company tax returns electronically in the computer language, iXBRL. This will make it necessary for a company to seek the assistance of an accountant or tax adviser.

The UK has two corporation tax rates: the main rate and the small profits rate. The main rate is payable when a company's taxable profit exceeds £1.5 million. The small profits rate is payable when a company's taxable profit is £300,000. Sandwiched between the main and small profits rate is a hybrid or marginal rates of corporation tax applicable to a company with taxable profit between £300,000 and £1.5 million. The prevailing corporation tax rates are shown in Figure 14.10.

The Chancellor of the Exchequer sets corporation tax rates annually in the Spring Budget and also in the preceding autumn statement.

A company pays corporation tax based upon its taxable profit and not the accounting profit. As shown in Figure 14.4, the accounting profit of a company is the annual turnover less the annual business expenses. However some expenses, which are included in the financial accounts when preparing the accounting profit, are not allowable for corporation tax purposes. Examples of disallowable expenses include depreciation, fines or client entertaining. The computation of a company's corporation tax liability is a three-stage process.

Figure 14.10: Corporation tax rates 2011/12–2014/15

	Taxable profit	1 April 2011	1 April 2012	1 April 2013	1 April 2014
	£	%	%	%	%
Small company rate	0-300,000	20%	20%	TBC	TBC
Marginal rate	300,001–1,500,000	27.5%	25%	TBC	TBC
Main rate	Over 1,500,000	26%	24%	23%	22%

Stage 1
The accounting profit is calculated by deducting the annual business expenses from the annual turnover.

Stage 2
The accounting profit is adjusted for any non-allowable business expenses included in stage one. The accounting profit is adjusted adding back to the accounting profit the items of disallowable expenditure.

Stage 3
The taxable profit is computed after deducting any capital allowances from the adjusted accounting profit.

Capital allowances
Capital allowances is the method by which HMRC allow the value of a company's fixed assets (i.e. those assets which have a useful life of more than 12 months) to be written-off against profits. These assets cannot be charged to the accounts in the year of acquisition, but instead have their cost deducted from the annual profits over their life span. Capital allowances are the taxation equivalent of depreciation accounting. The nature of fixed assets means their full value cannot be charged to the annual accounts on acquisition. However, when calculating the accounting profits, an annual depreciation charge is made in the accounts for these assets to reflect their annual consumption. Despite their similarity, it is essential to recognise that depreciation is not allowable for the computation of corporation tax and depreciation charges are always added back to the computed accounting profit. Capital allowances are allowable for corporation tax, therefore the capital allowances for fixed assets are deducted from the adjusted accounting profit to derive the taxable profit.

However, capital allowances are a technical area of taxation and should always be discussed with a suitably qualified accountant or tax adviser.

Case study: DLFK Limited

DLFK Limited annual accounts for the period had an accounting profit of £48,000. The accounts included a charge for the following expenses; client entertainment, £3,500 and a depreciation charge of £25,000 for a new machine that cost £100,000 during the period. The machine is expected to last four years. DLFK taxable profit for the period is as follows:

	£	£
Accounting profit		48,000
Add Back		
Client entertainment	3,500	
Depreciation	25,000	28,500
Adjusted profit		76,500
Less		
Capital allowance		
100,000 @ 18%		18,000
Taxable profit		58,500
Corporation tax @20%		11,700

The capital allowance was based upon the prevailing rate of 18%. At various times in the UK tax system there have been modifications to capital allowances through the introduction of one-off allowances for capital expenditure. From April 2012, any business investing £25,000 per annum or more in plant or machinery qualifies for a 100% first-year annual investment allowance (AIA). The total cost of the investment in plant and machinery up to £25,000 is written off against the adjusted profit. Any excess capital investment is applied against the prevailing capital allowance rate for the item.

Applying the AIA to the case of DLFK Limited produces a revised corporation tax position.

	£	£
Accounting profit		48,000
Add Back		
Client entertainment	3,500	
Depreciation	25,000	28,500
Adjusted profit		76,500

Continued overleaf

	£	£
Less		
AIA	25,000	
Capital allowance		
75,000 @ 18%	13,500	38,500
Taxable profit		38,000
Corporation tax @20%		7,600

The AIA is a variable feature within the UK tax system therefore a company should always seek advice to find out whether it is still in existence and the prevailing rate.

Corporation tax year

The financial year for the charging of corporation tax is 1 April–31 March. A company may choose any 12-month period for its accounting year. Popular accounting year-end dates are 31 March, 30 June, 30 September and 31 December. The choice of a company's year-end is an independent decision for them and their professional advisers. If a company's financial year does not end on 31 March, they will always straddle two fiscal years for corporation tax computation. The straddling of two fiscal years is not a problem, but when corporation tax differs between the two fiscal years, a company should engage an accountant or tax adviser to apportion their profits (or losses) into the respective financial years before computation of any corporation tax liability.

Income Tax

A company does not pay income tax, but a company director in receipt of a salary and dividends from a company will be subject to the payment of income tax. A company director will also be required to complete and electronically file a Self-assessment Tax Return (SATR) to HMRC. Under self-assessment regulations, a company director has a statutory responsibility to notify HMRC of his or her annual total worldwide earnings.

It is imperative that it is recto recognised that earnings are the summation of all income streams. A SATR must be submitted electronically to HMRC annually by 31 January and all payments due for the year ended the previous 5 April are paid. If a company director has not received an HMRC notification to file a SATR by 5 October and they received taxable earnings during the previous fiscal year ended 5 April, the director must notify HMRC. The fiscal tax year for income tax is different from the corporation tax year. The income tax fiscal year is 6 April–5 April.

Summary

- All companies must have an effective accounting system which enables the production of statutory accounts (for external users) and management accounts (for internal monitoring and decision making).
- Business transactions must be entered into the appropriate books of prime entry, namely the sales day book, purchase day book, cash book, sales returns day book and purchase returns day book.
- In addition to these books of prime entry, the accounting system should also include a sales ledger and a purchase ledger. Companies that are registered for VAT must keep additional VAT records.
- HMRC requires companies to keep their accounting records for at least six years from the end of the corporation tax accounting period. They do not have to be kept in their original format but can be kept as scanned PDF, files saved on a CD-ROM or files saved on an optical imaging system.
- Financial accounts are produced to comply with legal requirements while management accounts are used for internal management purposes. Both are prepared from the same accounting records made in the company's books of prime entry.
- Private companies must file statutory accounts with the Registrar of Companies within nine months of the end of the company's accounting period, and with HMRC within 12 months as well as a company tax return.
- Subject to certain exemptions statutory accounts must consist of a profit and loss account, a balance sheet, explanatory notes, a directors' report including a business review, and an auditor's report, where appropriate.
- Management accounts are forward looking and are used for the planning and control of a company's finances. The most important management accounts that a company should prepare are an annual operating budget, periodic budget performance reports and a cash budget, also known as a cash flow forecast.
- The management accounts can be used to generate various key performance measures that can assist in analysis of the company's financial performance and can be used for benchmarking purposes.
- Company taxation encompasses VAT which concerns the sales and purchases of a company, PAYE/NIC which concerns the payment of employees, and corporation tax which concerns a company's earnings.
- Directors in receipt of a salary and dividends are subject to the payment of income tax.

15 Health and safety

Health and safety is concerned with the responsibility that employers have for the safety and wellbeing of the people that they employ. The common law has for a long time recognised that employers have a duty to provide safe premises for their employees, safe tools, safe plant and machinery and a safe system of work – meaning proper training, sufficient workers to carry out the task and working conditions that are generally suitable. These considerations are all encompassed within the duty of care that an employer owes to his employees. A breach of this duty that results in injury or loss to an employee could give rise to a claim for compensation such as a personal injury claim. Claims of this sort are known as 'civil' actions because they can be brought by one individual against another – they do not need to be instigated by the state or a regulatory authority.

Health and safety law stands alongside the common law but with a different purpose. The liability of an employer under the enacted law is not civil but criminal. As such, actions for breaches of the statutes are brought by the appropriate regulatory authorities and the statutory law is not there to procure compensation for injured employees but to set and enforce minimum standards for health and safety. The consequences of a breach of health and safety law can be serious

– large financial penalties for a company, and for directors found personally liable, fines, imprisonment and disqualification. As such, health and safety is something that has to be taken seriously.

The legal framework

Health and safety law is built on the general duties and principles set out in the Health and Safety at Work etc. Act 1974 (HASWA).

HASWA places a general duty on employers to ensure, as far as is reasonably practicable, the health, safety and welfare at work of all of their employees (s. 2(1)). Under s. 2(2) this includes but is not limited to:

- the provision and maintenance of safe plant and systems of work;
- arrangements for the safe use, handling, storage and transport of articles and substances;
- the provision of necessary information, instruction, training and supervision;
- maintaining the place of work in a safe condition with safe means of access in and out; and
- provision and maintenance of a safe working environment with adequate welfare facilities and arrangements,

in each case 'so far as is reasonably practicable'.

The inclusion of the words 'so far as is reasonably practicable' is deliberate and key because it means that the duties under HASWA are not absolute. What an employer has to do is to take reasonable precautions to eliminate risks to his employees, but any action that the employer takes should be proportionate to the risk in question in terms of the time and cost involved in reducing or eliminating it. Where the benefit obtained from implementing a preventative measure is grossly disproportionate to the cost, the employer need not take that action. Ultimately, what is or is not disproportionate will be a matter for a court to decide but, in general, the standard is that of a reasonable employer (i.e. what would a reasonable employer do in the same circumstances?).

HASWA is not just concerned with the safety of employees but also with the safety of any other persons who may be affected by the employer's workplace be they agency workers, employees of another employer occupying the same premises, visitors to the workplace and so on. At the same time, employees themselves are under a duty to:

- take reasonable care for their own health and safety and for others who may be affected by their actions or inaction; and
- to cooperate with their employer in the exercise of his legal duties under health and safety law.

Accordingly, employees can be liable for a breach of health and safety law, just as employers can.

Regulations and Approved Codes of Practice

The body of regulation that has followed since the implementation of HASWA is dense and sets out many specific requirements telling employers exactly what they are expected to do in order to safeguard the health and safety of their employees and others. Some of the regulatory requirements apply in all cases, some only apply to employers with a certain number of employees and some apply only to employers whose business activities involve certain specific risks and hazards. In some cases the regulations are accompanied by a counterpart document known as an Approved Code of Practice (or ACOP for short). These ACOPs help to explain what the relevant regulations say and give guidance to employers about what they have to do to comply with them. The ACOPs are important because they can be taken into account in the event of a breach of the law in evaluating the extent to which an employer has complied with his legal obligations.

The Health and Safety Executive

The independent regulator for health and safety is the Health and Safety Executive (HSE). The HSE has a dual role both in enforcing health and safety law and in assisting employers in meeting their obligations by the provision of information and advice. A visit to the HSE's website (www.hse.gov.uk) will reveal the huge range of information that is available to employers on all aspects of health and safety law. Specific regulations, ACOPs and general guidance can all be obtained from here.

Health and safety is a huge (and hugely important) area and cannot be covered in a single chapter. However, in the sections that follow, we consider the main requirements of the law that apply to most employers before highlighting some of the specific rules that apply only in certain circumstances. We then look at how the law is enforced.

■ Requirements affecting the workplace

There are a wide range of basic health, safety and welfare requirements that apply to most workplaces. These are set out in the Workplace (Health, Safety and Welfare) Regulations 1992 which are accompanied by an Approved Code of Practice. The requirements break down into issues concerning:

- the working environment;
- safety;
- facilities; and
- housekeeping and maintenance.

What follows is a non-exhaustive summary of the main requirements.

The working environment

The law sets out rules that set basic standards for temperature, ventilation, lighting, room dimensions and work stations:

Temperature	During working hours the workplace temperature must be 'reasonable'. What will be 'reasonable' may differ from one workplace to another and the nature of the work being carried out there. In workplaces where there are sources of heat, cold or humidity, then risk assessments need to take account of the effect of these factors on employees' health. All workplaces must be adequately thermally insulated where necessary, and the excessive effects of sunlight on temperature must be avoided.
Ventilation	Workplaces must be ventilated by a sufficient quantity of fresh or purified air. In environments where the air quality is affected by the work carried out this issue may need particular attention and require the implementation of a ventilation system.
Lighting	Lighting must be suitable and sufficient to enable employees to do their work safely and without eye strain; so far as is reasonably practical, light sources should be natural rather than artificial. In any room or area where a sudden loss of light (e.g. in the event of a power cut) would expose the employees working there to danger, suitable and sufficient artificial light must be installed. Stairs and corridors must be well lit.
Room dimensions	All rooms where employees work must have sufficient floor area, height and unoccupied space to ensure the employees' health, safety and welfare.
Work stations	Work stations must be suitable for the people using them and for the work being carried out. Where work is done sitting down, seating that is appropriate to the person and the work they are doing must be provided, including foot rests where necessary.

Safety

Basic standards of safety in the workplace are concerned with safe passage of pedestrians and vehicles, safe opening and closing of skylights and windows, safe doors and gates and safe escalators.

Safe passage	All traffic routes for pedestrians and vehicles must be suitable and sufficient to allow pedestrians and vehicles to circulate safely, must be free from obstructions (so far as possible) and must not be uneven, slippery or sloping so as to create a risk to those who use them. Handrails should be provided where appropriate, and must be provided on staircases. Traffic routes should not cause danger to the persons working near them. Traffic routes for vehicles must be sufficiently separated from any doors or gates and from any pedestrian traffic route that leads on to them. Where vehicles and pedestrians use the same traffic route, they must be sufficiently separated.

Falls into dangerous substances	Fencing must be used to prevent falls into structures containing dangerous substances.
Translucent doors and walls	Any translucent door, wall, partition or gate (or any translucent part of a door, wall, partition or gate) must be made of suitable safety material or otherwise protected against breakage and should incorporate signage or markings to make it visible.
Skylights and windows	Windows and skylights must be capable of being opened and closed without presenting any risk or hazard, and when open must not expose any person to a risk or hazard. They must also be of a design that allows for safe cleaning.
Doors and gates	Doors and gates must be safely constructed and incorporate any appropriate safety devices. Sliding doors or gates must be fitted with devices to prevent them from coming off their track during use. Doors or gates that open upwards must be fitted with a device to prevent them from falling back down. Powered doors and gates must incorporate suitable safety features. Doors and gates that open both ways must enable a person using them to see who or what is on the other side.
Escalators and moving walkways	These must function safely, incorporate any necessary safety devices and be fitted with one or more emergency stop controls which are easily identifiable and readily accessible.

Facilities

Workplaces must provide facilities to meet the basic welfare needs of employees including toilets and washing facilities, drinking water, changing facilities (and facilities for storing clothing), areas for resting and eating.

Toilets	Toilets must be provided that are adequately ventilated and lit. They must be kept in a clean and orderly condition.
Washing facilities	Washing facilities must be provided in the immediate vicinity of the toilet facilities providing running hot and cold or warm water, soap and towels (or other means of washing and drying). They must be sufficiently ventilated and lit and kept in a clean and orderly condition. If the nature of the work requires it (or there are other health reasons) the washing facilities should include showers. Separate toilet and washing facilities must be provided for men and women except where they are provided in a room with a lockable door which is intended for use by one person at a time.

Drinking water	An adequate supply of wholesome drinking water must be provided. Drinking water must be marked as such and employees must be provided with cups unless the water is supplied by way of a water fountain.
Clothing storage and changing facilities	Where the work requires special clothing to be worn, and employees cannot be expected to change in another room, designated changing facilities must be provided. Secure storage for an employee's clothing that is not worn at work, and for any special clothing that is worn at work but is not taken home, must be provided. If necessary for health reasons, work and non-work clothes must be capable of being stored separately and as far as is reasonably practicable, facilities for drying clothing must also be provided.
Facilities for rest and to eat meals	Employees must be provided with somewhere to rest and to eat meals. Suitable seats must be provided in an area where protective equipment does not have to be worn. In offices, employees can eat and rest in work areas provided they will not be subject to excessive disturbance. Where food could be contaminated, suitable and sufficient eating facilities should be provided. Rest facilities for pregnant women and nursing mothers must be provided.

Housekeeping and maintenance

In satisfying the requirements to provide a safe workplace, employers must ensure that the workplace equipment and facilities are properly maintained and that the workplace is kept clean. Required standards of cleanliness may vary from one workplace to another. Maintenance applies to all equipment and facilities which, if they became faulty, would result in the employer being in breach of his obligations under the law, including equipment and devices intended to prevent or reduce hazards. This would include implementing a system for regular inspection, testing and adjustment for such equipment and devices as emergency lighting, fences and guard rails, powered doors and escalators, to name just a few.

■ Requirements for managing workplace risks

Central to the fulfilment of an employer's duties under HASWA is the obligation to identify and manage the risks in his workplace. Again, the law here is prescriptive, telling employers what they have to do and the majority of these requirements are set out in The Management of Health and Safety at Work Regulations 1999.

Risk assessments

Employers must carry out risk assessments to identify the risks and hazards in their workplace and the measures that the employer needs to take to deal with them and thereby secure compliance with the law. The scope of the assessment covers both employees and any non-employees who might also be affected such as visitors and contractors and members of the public. It also includes employees of another business that operates from the same premises.

In carrying out a risk assessment, an employer must:

- identify all the hazards posed in a particular situation;
- identify the persons who are at risk paying particular attention to the young or inexperienced and any persons with special needs or disabilities;
- evaluate each risk in terms of the likelihood of it occurring, the number of people exposed to it, the severity of the injuries that could result, and the existing control measures;
- assess the existing control measures and decide whether new control measures may be required to reduce or eliminate the risk; and
- implement the new control measures as appropriate.

A risk assessment is not just a one-off exercise. Where there is any reason to think that the original or previous assessment is no longer valid, or the risks or circumstances have changed the assessment needs to be reviewed or repeated. An employer might wish, therefore, to set a time-scale for reassessing each situation to ensure that the control measures are still effective or whether anything needs to be changed or new measures brought in. The requirement is not to remove all risks but to take reasonable steps to reduce them to their lowest level, or to remove them where possible. Where risks cannot be removed or reduced they must still be identified and brought to the attention of those affected or likely to be affected with suitable advice being provided. It is also important to consider the competency of all persons exposed to a particular risk where factors such as skills, experience, age, disability and so on might have an impact on a person's ability to deal with it, and make any additional suitable arrangements to protect them. Where an employer employs five or more employees the significant findings of all risk assessments must be recorded in writing but it is good practice for all employers to keep a written record, regardless of the number of employees.

System of risk management

Based on the findings of the risk assessments, employers must put in place appropriate arrangements for the planning, organisation, control, monitoring and review of the preventative and protective measures. In short, the management and control of risks must be made a significant part of how the employer's business is run. This is not a small task and the law recognises that many employers will need assistance and advice to ensure that they are taking the right actions. As such, all employers are required to appoint a 'competent person' to help them.

Competent person

All employers must appoint someone (known as a 'competent person') to assist them in complying with health and safety law. Competency is judged on training, experience and knowledge of the employer's workplace or industry so does not necessarily mean that the services of someone outside the business have to be retained. In fact, the regulations require that where there is a competent person employed in the employer's organisation, that person must be appointed to the role in preference to an outsider. It will generally be the responsibility of the competent person to carry out risk assessments and to advise the employer on the specific rules and regulations that apply to his business. As such it is important that the competent person has the skills and knowledge to do this. If a competent person cannot be appointed from within an organisation, then external help and advice will be needed.

Consulting employees

Consultation with employees facilitates a two-way communication process whereby employers can bring matters concerning health and safety to the attention of their employees, and employees can have a say in the policies, procedures and other measures that affect their health and wellbeing at work. The way in which employers must consult with employees is different depending on whether or not the employees are represented by a trade union. Whichever is the case, employers are legally required to consult with their employees on all matters relating to their health and safety at work and in particular with regard to:

- the introduction of health and safety measures which may substantially affect them;
- arrangements for appointing competent persons to help in complying with health and safety law;
- any information the employer must give to his employees about workplace risks and hazards, the measures in place to remove or reduce them and emergency procedures;
- the planning and organisation of health and safety training; and
- the health and safety consequences of introducing new technologies into the workplace.

More information can be found on the HSE website and in the applicable regulations: the Health and Safety (Consultation with Employees) Regulations 1996 (SI 1996/1513) and the Safety Representatives and Safety Committees Regulations 1977 (SI 1977/500).

Serious and imminent dangers

All employers must decide upon and put in place suitable procedures to be followed in the event of an emergency. The types of emergency situation that might arise will vary from one business to the next, but might include fire, gas leak, chemical or other contamination, flooding or a bomb threat. The point of this requirement is to identify the worst-case scenarios before they happen and to produce a plan for dealing with them. The employer must nominate competent persons who will be responsible for implementing the procedures in the event of an emergency which should be focused on evacuating the premises and preventing re-entry or the resumption of work until it is safe. See also the requirements on fire risks, below.

Health and safety policy

Employers who employ five or more employees must have a written health and safety policy. The policy should explain how the company will comply with its legal obligations setting out the arrangements for risk management and stating who within the company has responsibility for doing what. The health and safety policy is an important document. Not only does it demonstrate a commitment to health and safety, but it is also a way of engaging with employees about health and safety issues. The health and safety policy should be regularly reviewed and updated in accordance with any changes in the company's procedures or arrangements. Example and template health and safety policies can be found on the HSE website.

Providing information and training

In addition to making the health and safety policy available to employees, employers must also display the Health and Safety Executive's health and safety law poster in a place where employees can easily read it. The poster provides a breakdown of the main legal obligations on employers and employees. As an alternative to the poster, employees can be provided with a pocket card version which contains the same information. Both can be obtained from the HSE website.

It is also a legal requirement that employees be notified of the name of the company's first aiders (and their whereabouts), and the location of the first aid box and accident book.

All employees have to be made aware of the risks that they are exposed to in their particular role or the particular parts of the workplace in which they work as well as the control measures that are in place to deal with those risks. In addition, they must be appraised of the kinds of emergency situation that could arise and the procedures to be followed in those situations. The identity of the employer's competent persons must be provided, as well as information about any risks notified to the employer by another employer operating out of the same building or premises.

All of the above information should be provided to an employee as part of their compulsory health and safety training. The law says that all employees have to be provided with adequate health and safety training on commencement of their employment and at any time thereafter when they are exposed to new or increased risks as a result of:

- being transferred to a new role or being given new responsibilities;
- the introduction of new work equipment or a change respecting work equipment already in use;
- the introduction of new technology; or
- the introduction of a new system of work or a change to a system of work already in use.

The training must be repeated periodically where it is appropriate to do so and must be adapted to take account of any new or changed risks. In addition, health and safety training must take place during an employee's normal working hours and be free of charge to the employee. It is important to keep training records so that you know what training each employee has had and when it was provided. If any of the company's procedures change, such as a change to the emergency procedures (even if only on a temporary basis), it must be brought to the attention of all employees affected.

New or expectant mothers

The law places specific obligations on employers in terms of assessing the risks to pregnant women or new mothers. The working environment must be assessed for risks, not just to the mother but to the new or unborn child. Not only is failure to do this a breach of the relevant regulations but it also amounts to discrimination on the grounds of sex. The HSE provides examples of the sorts of issues that could be of particular concern to new or expectant mothers including:

- movements and postures;
- manual handling;
- shocks and vibrations;
- noise;
- working with chemical or biological agents;
- stressful working conditions; and
- workstation suitability.

It should be pointed out that the consideration of risks to a new or expectant mother has to form part of every risk assessment whether or not there are any new or expectant mothers in an employer's workforce. Once notified by an employee that she is pregnant, the employer must implement the risk control measures formulated as part of the risk assessment. There is no legal obligation to perform another separate risk assessment but there is nothing to stop an employer from doing that if they so wish. The employer must consider whether the risks can be removed or, if this is not possible, whether the risks can be avoided by altering the working conditions or hours of work. If this is not possible, an employer must offer the employee alternative work (with no detriment as to hours, pay, benefits etc). If that is not possible, an expectant mother has the right to be suspended on full pay until such time as her maternity leave commences.

First aid and accidents

First aid is the administration of essential aid to preserve a person's life until the arrival of trained medical practitioners. The Health and Safety (First Aid) Regulations 1981 (SI 1981/917)(which are accompanied by an ACOP) set out detailed requirements for the provision of first aid in the workplace. First aid must be provided in the event of any injury or illness, whether or not the cause of the injury or illness is work-related.

The ACOP that accompanies the Regulations states that the aim of first aid is to:

- give immediate assistance to casualties with both common illness and injuries, and those likely to arise from specific hazards at work; and
- to summon an ambulance or other professional help.

Under reg. 1, an employer must provide:

- adequate equipment and facilities for administering first aid; and
- such number of suitable persons as is adequate and appropriate for rendering first aid to injured persons.

There are no fixed rules in the Regulations to determine what level of equipment and 'suitable persons' must be provided. The ACOP requires employers to carry out an assessment of first aid needs and come to their own conclusions, although there is guidance in the ACOP about the appropriate level of cover that should be provided in different circumstances and scenarios.

In making an assessment of their company's first aid needs, employers should consider (among others):

- the nature of the work and workplace hazards and risks;
- the size of the organisation;
- the nature of the workforce;
- the organisation's history of accidents;
- the needs of travelling and remote workers;
- work patterns; and
- the remoteness of the site from emergency medical services.

Equipment and facilities

The ACOP states that the minimum level of first-aid equipment is a suitably stocked and properly identified first aid container. At least one first aid box should be kept at each work site or each part of the work premises containing a sufficient quantity of first aid materials suitable for the circumstances of the work carried out there and the related hazards. All first aid boxes should be identified by a white cross on a green background.

As to contents there are no mandatory requirements but the ACOP gives guidance on the items that should be included. The contents should be examined regularly to check that they are in order and to consider whether they are still adequate and suitable. Any items or materials that are used should be replenished quickly.

The assessment of first aid needs might indicate that additional and/or specialised equipment is needed. Any such equipment should be maintained and checked regularly with further assessments as to suitability and whether any different or further equipment is needed.

First-aid rooms should also be provided if the assessment of needs identifies this as necessary. This will generally be in workplaces where there are significant risks as a result of work processes, equipment and machinery or dangerous substances; a large number of employees; or where the workplace is in a remote location. First-aid rooms should contain the essential and appropriate facilities and equipment to be able to deal with the likely injuries or illness that might occur and should be easily accessible to stretchers and be clearly signposted and identified.

Appointed persons and first aiders

Based on the assessment of first-aid needs, employers must decide whether the nature and size of their business necessitates the provision of qualified first aiders or whether one or more appointed persons is sufficient.

Appointed persons

Having at least one appointed person is the bare minimum requirement for all employers whose assessment of first aid needs leads them to conclude that qualified first aiders are not necessary. Appointed persons are responsible for looking after the first-aid equipment and facilities and calling the emergency services when they are needed. Appointed persons are not required to administer first aid; indeed they should not do so unless they have appropriate training.

First aiders

First aiders must have formal training and hold a certificate in providing first aid at work. There are two possible qualifications for first aiders:

- first aid at work (FAW); and
- emergency first aid at work (EFAW).

The difference between the two is that the EFAW training is tailored to providing first aid in emergency situations only, whereas the FAW training is broader and more detailed enabling the provision of first aid in a wider range of situations. The certificates in either qualification are valid for three years and are renewed by undertaking a refresher training course before they expire. Training courses must be approved by the HSE and a list of approved training providers can be found on the HSE website.

The ACOP requires that where an employer's needs assessment indicates that qualified first-aiders are required, the employer must provide a sufficient number of such persons at all locations where it is appropriate to provide them. It is important to bear in mind that whether an employer provides appointed persons or qualified first-aiders, there must be an appropriate number of people in those roles available at all times. As such, the number provided must be sufficient to allow for absences due to holidays, illness and for any other reason. Where a workplace presents hazards from chemicals or dangerous machinery, it may be necessary for first aiders to have such additional training as is required to enable them to deal with injuries arising from those hazards.

It should be noted that the above is a summary only and that the ACOP provides thorough guidance on the various factors that should be considered in determining the level of first-aid equipment and personnel to provide. The HSE website also features an interactive first-aid assessment tool that provides appropriate advice based on the employer's responses to various questions.

Information and training

Under reg. 4 of the Regulations, employers have a duty to inform their employees of the arrangements made in connection with providing first aid in the workplace. This includes the location of equipment, facilities (such as first-aid rooms) and personnel. This can be achieved by displaying posters or notices giving the appropriate information.

Accident records and reporting

Obligations to keep records of accidents are imposed on employers by the Social Security (Claims and Payments) Regulations 1979 (SI 1979/6238) and the Reporting of Injuries, Diseases and Dangerous Occurrences Regulations 1995 (SI 1995/3163) (as amended by the 2012 Amendment Regulations (SI 2012/199) – the latter also requiring notification of deaths, certain injuries and dangerous occurrences to the appropriate regulatory authority.

The Social Security (Claims and Payments) Regulations 1979

These Regulations (which relate to the payment of state benefits) require all employers who have or who normally have 10 or more employees to keep an accident book (reg. 25). Under reg. 24, employees who suffer a work-related injury must inform their employer either in writing or orally as soon as practicable after an accident occurs, giving the required details which are:

- the full name, address and occupation of the injured person;
- the date and time of the accident;
- the place where the accident happened;
- the cause and nature of the injury; and
- the name, address and occupation of the person notifying the above details, if not the injured person.

The employee's obligation to report an injury is also satisfied if the details are entered into the accident book either by the injured employee or someone acting on their behalf. The accident book must be kept readily available for this purpose. Records of accidents recorded pursuant to the regulations must be retained for at least three years from the date of entry.

The Reporting of Injuries, Diseases and Dangerous Occurrences Regulations 1995 (as amended by The Reporting of Injuries, Diseases and Dangerous Occurrences (Amendment) Regulations 2012) (RIDDOR)

Under RIDDOR, employers are required to notify the appropriate regulatory authority of certain specified events arising out of or in connection with work, namely:

- deaths;
- major injuries;
- dangerous occurrences;
- accidents which result in an injured person being incapacitated for more than seven consecutive days; and
- occupational diseases.

The major injuries that must be reported are stipulated in the regulations and include any fractures, other than to the fingers, thumbs or toes; any amputation; dislocation of the shoulder, hip, knee or spine; loss of sight (whether temporary or permanent); and loss of consciousness caused by asphyxia or by exposure to a harmful substance or biological agent. Similarly, the dangerous occurrences and occupational diseases that must be reported are also set out in the regulations.

Employers are required to keep records of:

- any of the reportable events; and
- any injuries arising out of or in connection with work where the injured person is incapacitated for more than three consecutive days.

These records can be made in the company's accident book provided that it is able to capture the required information. The HSE publish their own standard form accident book which can be used for the purposes of recording events and accidents under RIDDOR and the Social Security (Claims and Payments) Regulations 1979. The pages in the book can be removed so as to be stored separately once they have been completed so that all personal data is kept secure, in compliance with data protection laws. Records made pursuant to RIDDOR must be kept for at least three years from the date on which the relevant record was made.

An accident book forms an important part of an effective risk management system and all employers should keep one whether they are specifically required to do so or not. Reviewing details of the injuries sustained by employees may reveal trends suggesting that current preventative measures are not working. In the same way, a minor injury may be the result of a near-miss such that it highlights the risk of something much more serious occurring. All accidents should be investigated to establish their cause and to re-assess whether the risk controls in place are adequate.

Fire risk

Under the Regulatory Reform (Fire Safety) Order 2005 (SI 2005/1541) any person in control of non-domestic premises must put in place appropriate measures to deal with the risk of fire. Such a person is referred to in the Order as the 'responsible person' and, in the case of a workplace this will be the employer if the workplace is to any extent under the employer's control.

The principle duty on the responsible person is enshrined in article 8 which requires the responsible person to take such general fire precautions as will ensure, so far as is reasonably practicable, the safety of his employees. The general fire precautions that should be put in place relate to:

- measures to reduce the risk of fire and the risk of the spread of fire on the premises;
- measures relating to escape from the premises in the event of a fire, including ensuring that the number, distribution and dimensions of emergency routes are adequate; that they are clearly indicated, kept clear at all times and equipped with emergency lighting; that they lead to a place of safety and that emergency doors open in the direction of escape;
- measures relating to fire fighting including provision of appropriate automatic and non-automatic equipment ensuring that the latter is easily accessible, simple to use and indicated by signs; nominating competent persons to implement the fire fighting measures and providing appropriate training; and arranging necessary contacts with emergency services;
- measures relating to appropriate systems for detecting fires and raising the alarm;
- measures relating to action to be taken in the event of a fire including establishing appropriate emergency procedures; regular fire drills; instruction and training of employees; and nominating competent persons to take control in an evacuation situation.

As well as general fire precautions, if the nature of the work gives rise to any particular fire risks the responsible person must also put in place the appropriate technical or organisational measures to prevent or reduce those risks.

In order to identify the general fire precautions that need to be taken, the responsible person must make an assessment of the risks. The assessment must consider all those persons that are exposed to the risks (including all employees and all other people who could be affected) paying particular attention to young persons and persons with special needs such as those with a disability. If any dangerous substances are present or may be present on the premises from time to time, the assessment must also include consideration of the specific matters set out in the regulations including the hazardous properties of the substance; how it is used in the work process; the arrangements for safe handling, storage and transport; the risk of ignition (if flammable); the scale of the anticipated effects; and the effect of safety measures that have been or will be taken in accordance with the requirements of the Order. If the responsible person has five or more employees, then details of the risk assessment must be recorded in writing as to:

- the significant findings, including the measures which have been or will be taken by the responsible person in accordance with the requirements of the Order; and
- any group of persons identified by the assessment as being particularly at risk.

As with other areas of risk management, the responsible person must appoint one or more competent persons to assist in identifying and implementing the appropriate preventative and protective measures. Once the risk assessment has been completed and appropriate preventative and protective measures put in place, the responsible person is then under a duty to operate a system for the effective planning, organisation, control, monitoring and review of those measures. As with other risk assessments, employees must be provided with information about:

- the risks identified;
- the preventative and protective measures put in place;
- the procedures to be followed in the event of an emergency; and
- the identity of those persons appointed to deal with fire fighting and with the evacuation procedures.

Enforcement of the requirements of the Order is by local fire and rescue services whose inspectors have the power to enter and inspect premises without warning. Failure to comply is a criminal offence punishable by a fine and/or imprisonment.

Specific workplace risks and hazards

There are a number of sets of regulations that deal with specific risks and hazards and examples of these are given below. Some of the risks and hazards that are covered by these regulations are not uncommon and as such they will apply to many employers. Note that more than one set of regulations can apply in any particular case and the information in the table overleaf should not be treated as definitive or exhaustive.

It can be a daunting task for an employer to try and find out what regulations exist that might apply to his business and this is another reason why the law requires all employers to take health and safety advice from a competent person. At the same time, as mentioned earlier, the website of the Health and Safety Executive offers a wide range of detailed information to help employers identify their obligations and work out what they need to do to comply with them.

Risk or hazard	Applicable regulations
Working at height	The Work at Height Regulations 2005
Noise	The Control of Noise at Work Regulations 2005
Manual handling	The Manual Handling Operations Regulations 1992
Screens and workstations	The Health and Safety (Display Screen Equipment) Regulations 1992
Asbestos	Control of Asbestos Regulations 2012
Dangerous substances	The Control of Substances Hazardous to Health Regulations 2002 The Dangerous Substances and Explosive Atmospheres Regulations 2002
Vibration	Control of Vibration at Work Regulations 2005

Work-related stress

As well as considering risks to the physical wellbeing of their employees (and other non-employees) employers must also take account of their employees' psychological health and any workplace issues that could negatively affect this. This is underpinned by both the common law duty of care that an employer has for the wellbeing of his employees at work and the general duties in HASWA and the Management of Health and Safety at Work Regulations 1999.

The HSE defines stress as 'the adverse reaction a person has to excessive pressure or other types of demand placed upon them'. In carrying out their risk assessments, employers must consider any hazards or issues that could be a cause of work-related stress and formulate measures to control those risks. To assist employers in doing this, the HSE has published a set of Management Standards identifying the six main causes of workplace stress and the actions that employers should take to minimise the risks to their employees arising from those specific areas. The six main areas identified and the standards to be achieved in each area are summarised below.

Demands	This is concerned with issues concerning workload, work patterns and the work environment. Employees should be given adequate and achievable demands related to hours worked. Demands should be matched to skills and abilities.
Control	Control is about the degree of choice and flexibility an employee has in how they do their job. Where possible employees should determine their own pace of work and should be encouraged to use their skills and develop new ones. They should be consulted about working patterns, and have some say about when they take breaks.

Support	This relates to issues about the encouragement and resources given to or available to employees. A culture of support should exist to ensure that employees are adequately supported by their managers and are supportive of their colleagues. Policies and procedures should be in place for dealing with and encouraging the reporting of unacceptable behaviour.
Relationships	Relationships are about promoting positive behaviour and dealing with unacceptable behaviour. Employers should engender a culture of fairness and mutual respect and ensure systems are in place to deal with unacceptable behaviours such as bullying.
Role	This is concerned with whether employees understand their role and with avoiding giving employees conflicting roles. Employees should have a clearly defined role which is explained to them and the constituent requirements of an employee's role should be compatible.
Change	Change is about how organisational changes are managed. Employers should provide information to and consult with employees concerning all change likely to affect them. Timetables for change should be published and support and training should be provided where appropriate

Just as with other workplace hazards, risks of stress-related ill health must be removed where possible and, where that is not possible, reduced to their lowest possible level. Of course, the HSE Management Standards are recommendations only and do not have the force of law, but they do set a benchmark for practices that should reduce work-related stress to a minimum. A company's policies and procedures for dealing with stress at work should be incorporated into the health and safety policy.

As with other forms of workplace injury, health issues arising as a result of stress can result in a civil claim for compensation. Employers need to watch for signs of stress in their employees and then take appropriate action to address it. To be able to hold an employer liable in a civil action for stress-related injury an employee must be able to establish that:

- there was a breach of the employer's common law duty to provide a safe working environment; and
- the harm suffered by the employee was a result of stress linked to the working environment; and
- the employer was negligent in that the condition was foreseeable and the employer failed to take action to prevent it.

More useful information about stress at work and managing work-related stress issues can be found on the HSE and ACAS websites, the website of the Stress Management Society and the website of the Chartered Institute of Personnel and Development. Full contact details are provided in the Directory.

■ Enforcement of health and safety law

The main regulatory body for the enforcement of health and safety law in England and Wales is the Health and Safety Executive (HSE), although some aspects are dealt with by local authorities and others by the local fire authority and such other authorities as may be specified by particular regulations. Enforcement action is generally dealt with by health and safety inspectors.

Inspectors

On a ground level, it is the role of health and safety inspectors to deal with breaches or suspected breaches of health and safety law. Inspectors have the right to:

- enter premises (accompanied by any person he thinks necessary) where he has reason to believe activities are being carried out which could endanger public safety;
- enquire into the causes of any safety issues;
- examine and search any premises, plant, materials, equipment, records or any other documents and take samples, measurements, recordings, copies and conduct tests;
- demand assistance from any person he considers necessary; and
- if the inspector is a medical practitioner, to carry out any medical examinations he considers necessary.

In the event that a breach of health and safety law is discovered, if the breach is minor, an inspector may just give appropriate advice to the employer about what they need to do to rectify the situation. Beyond that, an inspector has the power to issue an improvement notice or a prohibition notice. An improvement notice will be issued when the inspector considers that there is no immediate danger but that some remedial action should be taken within a specified period of time. A prohibition notice can be issued on a person who is in control of activities which, in the opinion of the inspector, involves serious risk of personal injury. An employer can appeal against either form of notice. An improvement notice is automatically suspended on appeal (pending the outcome) but a prohibition notice can only be suspended by order of a court. In addition, inspectors can charge the company a fee for the time spent in dealing with any material breaches including inspection, investigation and enforcement action – this is known as a 'fee for intervention'.

Prosecutions

Under s. 33 of HASWA it is a criminal offence to breach any of the obligations imposed by the Act and any health and safety regulations. The decision to prosecute is taken by the relevant enforcing authority. The HSE's official Enforcement Policy Statement sets out the general principles and approach that the enforcing authorities are expected to follow. According to this statement, the purpose of enforcement is to:

- ensure that dutyholders [persons under a legal duty for complying with health and safety law] take action to deal immediately with serious risks;
- promote and achieve sustained compliance with the law; and
- ensure that dutyholders who breach health and safety requirements and directors or managers who fail in their responsibilities, may be held to account.

The Enforcement Policy Statement also sets out the factors that should lead to a prosecution including, among others, where:

- death was a result of a breach of the legislation;
- the gravity of an alleged offence, taken together with the seriousness of any actual or potential harm, or the general record and approach of the offender warrants it;
- there has been reckless disregard of health and safety requirements;
- there have been repeated breaches which give rise to significant risk, or persistent and significant poor compliance; and
- there has been a failure to comply with an improvement or prohibition notice, or there has been a repetition of a breach that was subject to a simple caution.

Some cases may be clear cut because the regulations place an absolute duty on the employer to do one thing or another. Where the law applies 'so far as is reasonably practicable' the enforcing authority will need to show that there was a risk or a hazard and that the employer had not taken any action or sufficient action to control or remove it. A breach does not have to have resulted in an injury in order for a prosecution to be brought. Penalties are in the form of fines and imprisonment, depending on the severity of the breach and of any injury which occurred as a result of it. In the case of a company (where obviously imprisonment is not possible) the penalty will be in the form of a fine, and such fines can be substantial. There can be other consequences that follow for a company such as the stigma of a criminal conviction, the effect on a company's reputation and the effect on its ability to obtain compulsory employer's liability insurance.

Directors and managers

Although the law at present does not place any duties on individual directors and managers they are not immune from prosecution. Under s. 37 of HASWA, if an offence is committed by a company then a director, manager, secretary or other similar officer of the company will also be guilty of that offence if it can be proved that it was committed:

- with their consent;
- with their connivance; or
- as a result of neglect on their part.

The HSE Enforcement Policy Statement requires enforcing authorities to give consideration to the management chain and the role of individual directors and managers with a view to bringing a prosecution if any of the above criteria apply. If convicted, an individual director or manager can face an unlimited fine and a prison sentence of up to two years. Furthermore, under s. 2(1) of the Company Directors' Disqualification Act 1986, conviction for a breach of a health and safety offence is grounds for disqualification for a period of up to five years in the magistrates' court and up to 15 years in the crown court. It goes without saying then that the implications of a health and safety breach for an individual director can be very serious indeed.

Gross negligence manslaughter

Where a death occurs as a result of a breach of health and safety law the enforcing authorities may liaise with the police with regard to a potential prosecution for the common law offence of gross negligence manslaughter. A trial for this offence must be heard in the crown court so is tried by jury. To prove the offence it must be established that:

- the director, secretary, manager or other owed a duty of care to the deceased (such as the duty to provide a safe place and system of work);
- that the director, secretary, manager or other breached that duty of care;
- that the breach caused or was a substantial cause of the death; and
- that the breach was so grossly negligent that it should be treated as criminal.

Whether or not the breach was so grossly negligent that it amounts to a criminal behaviour is a matter for the jury. Convictions for gross negligence manslaughter are relatively uncommon but if proven, are punishable by a maximum of life imprisonment.

Corporate manslaughter

A company can be prosecuted for the offence of manslaughter under the Corporate Manslaughter and Corporate Homicide Act 2007. This Act has been introduced to replace the common law offence of gross negligence manslaughter as it applied to companies as the requirements of the common law made it notoriously difficult to achieve a conviction.

An organisation will be guilty of the offence of corporate manslaughter if the way in which its activities are managed or organised by senior management causes a person's death and amounts to a gross breach of a relevant duty of care owed by the organisation to the deceased person.

'Senior management' is defined as the persons who play significant roles in:

- the making of decisions about how the whole or a substantial part of the organisation's activities are to be managed or organised; or
- the actual managing or organising of the whole, or a substantial part, of those activities.

This means that those responsible for direct management are caught as well as those responsible for making the high-level decisions about strategy, policy and compliance.

A 'relevant duty of care' is any of the following duties owed by an organisation:

- to its employees or to other persons working for the organisation (such as the duty to provide a safe system of work);
- to any person as the occupier of premises (such as the duty to ensure that buildings and premises are kept in a safe condition);
- in connection with the supply of goods and services (including duties owed by an organisation to customers for the safety of its products);
- in connection with any construction or maintenance operations;
- in connection with the carrying on of any other activity on a commercial basis; and
- in connection with the use or keeping by the organisation of any plant, vehicle or other thing.

It is a matter for the judge to determine whether a relevant duty of care exists. It is for the jury to decide whether the breach of the relevant duty was a gross breach. The Act states that a breach will be a gross breach if the alleged conduct falls far below what can reasonably be expected of the organisation in the circumstances. In making their decision, the jury must consider whether the evidence shows that the organisation failed to comply with any health and safety legislation and, if so, how serious that failure was and how much of a risk of death it posed. The jury can also consider:

- the extent to which the evidence shows that there were attitudes, policies, systems or accepted practices within the organisation that were likely to have encouraged or resulted in tolerance of the failure to comply with health and safety law; and
- any health and safety guidance relating to the alleged breach (meaning any code, guidance, manual or similar publication concerned with health and safety made or issued by an authority responsible for the enforcement of health and safety legislation).

The Act applies to organisations only and places no liability on individuals. However, directors, secretaries and senior managers continue to be liable under HASWA and the common law offence of gross negligence manslaughter, as explained above. Furthermore, a company can be charged with the offence of corporate manslaughter and a health and safety offence at the same time. The consequences of a conviction for corporate manslaughter can be very serious and include:

- large fines (which the Sentencing Guidelines Council suggest will seldom be less than £500,000 and may be millions of pounds);
- a court order to remedy the breach of the duty of care and any matter resulting

from the breach that was a cause of the death; as well as any deficiency in the company's health and safety policies, systems and practices; and

■ a court order requiring the company to publicise the conviction, the amount of any fine imposed on it and the terms of any remedial order.

Advice for directors

Directors and senior management need to take health and safety matters seriously. Besides the obvious moral imperative, the ability to demonstrate a responsible and committed approach to workplace health and safety can be a strong mitigating factor in any enforcement action. The HSE has issued a guidance note for directors in partnership with the Institute of Directors called 'Leading Health and Safety at Work'. Aimed at directors of companies of all sizes, the guidance stresses the importance of health and safety matters being given regular board-level attention and being made the responsibility of a director, senior manager or a committee of the board. It sets out core actions and suggested good practice in the four key areas of:

■ planning the direction for health and safety and formulating a health and safety policy;

■ implementing an effective system to manage health and safety risks in a sensible, responsible and proportionate manner;

■ establishing procedures for monitoring health and safety matters and for receiving reports and information; and

■ reviewing health and safety performance.

The guidance can be found on the HSE website.

Summary

■ Health and safety law is built on the principles enshrined in the Health and Safety at Work etc. Act 1974. The law is vast and places a wide range of duties and responsibilities on employers.

■ Employers have a general duty to ensure, as far as is reasonably practicable, the health, safety and wellbeing at work of their employees.

■ The Workplace (Health, Safety and Welfare) Regulations 1992 set out a wide range of duties and requirements in relation to such basic workplace issues as the working environment, safety, facilities and housekeeping and maintenance.

■ A key duty of employers is to manage workplace risks. This is set out in the Management of Health and Safety at Work Regulations 1999.

■ Fundamental to the process of managing risks is the requirement to carry out risk assessments in each part of the workplace paying particular attention to the young or inexperienced, persons with special needs and new and expectant mothers.

- All employers must make an assessment of their company's first aid needs and then make suitable arrangements for the provision of fist aid.
- The Reporting of Injuries, Diseases and Dangerous Occurrences Regulations 1995 requires certain workplace incidents to be reported to the appropriate regulatory authority.
- All employers must make an assessment of fire risk in the workplace and identify the fire precautions that need to be taken.
- Various specific workplace risks and hazards are addressed by their own specific regulations.
- Wellbeing at work includes psychological wellbeing and employers must take account of the risks to their employees in respect of work-related stress.
- The main regulatory body for the enforcement of health and safety law is the Health and Safety Executive. Health and safety inspectors have various powers to enter premises and investigate breaches of health and safety law.
- Companies and directors (as well as company secretaries, managers and other similar officers) can all be prosecuted for breaches of health and safety law.
- Where a death occurs, a company can be prosecuted for the offence of corporate manslaughter under the Corporate Manslaughter and Corporate Homicide Act 2007. Individual directors and others can be prosecuted for the common law offence of gross negligence manslaughter.
- It is essential that directors and senior managers are aware of their health and safety responsibilities and seek to embed health and safety issues and considerations in the company's procedures, processes and day-to-day operations.

16 Corporate governance

In this chapter

This chapter provides an introduction to corporate governance principles and practices, with particular regard to:

- what corporate governance is and how it is defined;
- the aims of corporate governance;
- corporate governance in the UK;
- the main concerns of corporate governance as reflected in the UK Corporate Governance Code 2012;
- how corporate governance is relevant to private limited companies;
- the ecoDa guidance and principles for unlisted companies; and
- the related areas of corporate social responsibility, ethics and bribery.

What is corporate governance?

The term 'corporate governance' is used more and more frequently these days. It has been used a good deal in the wake of the UK financial crisis and in relation to the problems in the UK banking sector, as well as other scandals and corporate failures in recent years. Indeed, when large corporations collapse, corporate governance failings are often cited as being the root cause.

But what exactly is corporate governance? Throughout this book we have explained the laws, both the common law and statute law that determine how limited companies should be run. However corporate governance is not law – it is something else. It stands alongside the law supplementing it with a set of principles and ideas that should – it is hoped – prevent the kind of abuse of power or mismanagement that could lead to a company's failure. It is about establishing and implementing accepted norms and standards for the way in which companies are run.

Definitions of corporate governance
Unfortunately it is not possible to give one all-encompassing definition of

corporate governance. Ideas about what corporate governance is tend to differ from one source to another. The first corporate governance code in the UK (the Cadbury Code – see below) defined corporate governance fairly simply as 'the system by which companies are directed and controlled'. In contrast, the definition offered by the Organisation for Economic Co-Operation and Development (the OECD) in its Principles of Corporate Governance is more detailed:

> Corporate governance involves a set of relationships between a company's management, its board, its shareholders and other stakeholders. Corporate governance also provides the structure through which the objectives of the company are set, and the means of attaining those objectives and monitoring performance are determined. Good corporate governance should provide proper incentives for the board and management to pursue objectives that are in the interests of the company and its shareholders and should facilitate effective monitoring.

Different views of corporate governance

On one view, corporate governance is just about the relationship between directors and shareholders and this is arguably the view expressed in the Cadbury definition. This view is a product of the separation of ownership and control in a limited company. Those persons with ownership of the company (the shareholders) are not in day-to-day control of how the company is run or of those people who are running the company on their behalf (the directors). This is sometimes referred to as the 'agency problem'. In this context, a company's system of governance should ensure that directors engage with their shareholders; that they provide them with quality information about the company's activities and how it is being run; and that measures are put in place to prevent abuses of power and to try and align the directors' interests with those of the shareholders.

However some people advocate a much broader view of corporate governance. They might agree that companies should be run principally to benefit the company's shareholders but believe that companies and their directors should take account of the other individuals or groups of individuals who have an interest in the company or are affected by what the company does. Such people or groups of people are known as 'stakeholders'. This is more in line with the OECD definition. If we consider the different groups of people who may be affected when a company fails it is not difficult to see why this view has its supporters.

What happens when a company fails?

Here are some of the possible consequences that might result from the failure of a company:

- The company's directors might be made personally liable for the debts of the company under insolvency law; they may face fines or imprisonment for a variety of offences and, in addition may be disqualified from acting as directors.

- The shareholders may lose their investment in the company, as may banks, lenders and other creditors. For some creditors, the loss of the sums owed to them could have consequences for their own financial stability.
- In the largest companies, a high proportion of the shares will usually be held by 'institutional investors' – pension funds, investment trusts and insurance companies. The failure of such companies can wipe out huge sums from these investments.
- The company's employees lose their jobs and possibly some, if not all, of their pension. If any employees received shares in the company (e.g. by way of an employee incentive scheme) these are now worthless.
- Large companies may play a vital role in the economy of a particular area. Small local companies and businesses may depend on the larger company for the bulk of their trade. When the large company collapses, they too become vulnerable.
- The broad range of individuals affected may find themselves in severe financial difficulties suffering distress and uncertainty, particularly if they are unable to find new work.

In the broader view, corporate governance is not just concerned with the relationship between a company's directors and shareholders, but also with the company's relationship with its employees, banks, investors, creditors, suppliers, local community, the wider world, the environment and even future generations. Even if a lack of good governance does not result in disaster, irresponsible or unethical business practices can impact negatively in any number of ways on the company and its various stakeholders.

Is corporate governance important?

Despite having its critics, the importance of good governance has gained in recognition in the last few decades and this does not seem set to change. Its cause is strengthened by each new scandal and corporate failure. One thing is for sure: the corporate world has come under increasing scrutiny. Now more than ever companies are expected to adhere to certain standards in the way that they conduct themselves, in how they manage their activities and in how those activities impact on the world at large. The reach of corporate governance goes beyond the commercial world of limited companies extending to charities, public bodies and other organisations. Some commentators believe that corporate governance is still in its infancy and that it is a developing area which still has some way to go. Nevertheless the wealth of information about corporate governance that is now in the public domain, as well as the various codes, principles and reports can seem overwhelming so it is useful to go back to the beginning to see where corporate governance started in the UK.

Corporate governance in the UK

The development of corporate governance in the UK was both triggered and continues to be influenced by real events. A succession of corporate failures in the late 1980s and early 1990s led to the first formal report on corporate governance. This was known as the Cadbury Report. The report, put together by a committee under the guidance of Sir Adrian Cadbury, made a number of recommendations about how companies should structure and conduct their internal business. In essence, the committee looked at the best, most successful and most respected companies in the UK and drew conclusions about what those companies were doing that made them that way. From this, the committee made their recommendations which took the form of a code (the Cadbury Code). The committee did not want their code to result in mere box-ticking by companies and their directors, so it did not contain rules but rather a series of principles. Companies could decide how best to apply the principles in their own individual circumstances, but a new requirement was added to the Listing Rules (the rules that apply to companies with a listing on the London Stock Exchange) requiring all listed companies to report each year on whether they had complied with the code and, if they had not, to explain why.

In the years since the Cadbury Report, there have been a number of other reports on specific aspects of corporate governance (such as non-executive directors, risk management and director's remuneration, among others) which have resulted in a number of revisions to the Cadbury Code that ultimately lead to the code that exists today – the UK Corporate Governance Code 2012.

Main concerns of the UK Corporate Governance Code

Many countries around the world have adopted their own codes of corporate governance. There are various themes that recur in these codes and various concerns that they have in common even if the way in which each code deals with them may differ. So what are some of the main concerns of corporate governance, as they appear in the UK Corporate Governance Code?

The Code is made up of five separate sections that deal with:

- leadership of a company and the role of the board of directors;
- the effectiveness of the board of directors;
- accountability, risk management and narrative reporting;
- directors' remuneration; and
- relations with shareholders.

Each section is made up of a number of 'main principles' (each being a statement of a general principle in no more than one or two sentences) which may or may not be expanded in more detail by 'supporting principles' and then backed up by 'code provisions' setting out specific actions that a company should take in the context of the main and supporting principles. The Code itself is supported by three other guidance notes issued by the Financial Reporting Council that are intended to assist companies in applying the principles of the Code in relation to board effectiveness, audit committees and internal controls.

The UK Code is not law but the requirement for companies with a listing on the London Stock Exchange to set out in their annual reports whether they have complied with it and explain any deviations still remains. This is referred to as 'comply or explain'. No other companies are required to do this, although any company can use the UK Code as a basis for its own system of governance if it wants to do so. That said, the UK Code is formulated to address the governance issues faced by large listed companies and, as such, many of the code provisions go beyond what will be appropriate for a small private company (more about this later). The concerns of corporate governance that are dealt with in the Code are described below.

The board of directors

As pointed out earlier in this book, the authority to run a company is delegated to a company's directors by its shareholders. Although they are restrained by rules in the Companies Act and a company's articles of association, the directors occupy a position of considerable power. As a principle of good governance measures should be put in place to ensure that the directors lead the company effectively and do not abuse or misuse the power that they have been given. To this end the Code requires that:

- the board of directors should understand that their role in the company is to set the company's strategic aims and objectives. The board should understand that in this respect it has a role that is separate from the day-to-day running of the company; and
- the directors should all participate fully in decision-making, and should challenge the views of other directors where appropriate. No one individual director should be allowed to dominate the board's decision-making processes and there should be a schedule of matters reserved for the board's decision.

The composition of the board of directors is also important:

- the board should be made up of directors who between them have the skills and experience necessary to enable it to fulfil its responsibilities;
- the procedure for appointing new directors to the board should be formal and transparent – directors should be appointed purely on their suitability and merit and cronyism should always be avoided (the nominations committee has a key role in this – see below);
- the balance of skills and experience on the board should be reviewed periodically and appropriate changes should be made when necessary;
- all directors should be able to give whatever time to the company is necessary to enable them to carry out their role and duties effectively; and

- directors should receive an induction on joining the board and should regularly update and refresh their skills and knowledge.

In Chapter 8 it was noted that there is no regulatory requirement that stipulates how often a company's directors should meet in a formal board meeting. However, the Code states that:

- the board should meet sufficiently regularly to discharge its duties effectively; and
- all directors should be provided with the information that they need to enable them to discharge their duties. Someone (in the Code the company secretary and the chairman) should be responsible for ensuring the flow of information between senior management and the board. This is particularly important for non-executive directors who do not have a management or executive role.

Case study: Mirror Group Newspapers

Robert Maxwell is perhaps the classic example of the domineering executive chairman. Maxwell acquired Mirror Group Newspapers in 1984. At the time the company was struggling but he brought it back to profitability. In the years that followed, he sought to expand his group of companies, floating Mirror Group Newspapers on the LSE in 1990. However after his death in 1991 the dire financial position of Mirror Group Newspapers became apparent and the then Department for Trade and Industry commenced an investigation into the company's affairs. The inspectors found that, among other things, Maxwell:

- dominated the management of all of his companies;
- personally controlled the movement of cash within and between his companies, running them and the pension funds as if they were one;
- had sole signatory authority for an unlimited amount over the bank accounts of each group company;
- took money from the pension funds of the companies on a regular and unsecured basis to finance the expansion of the group (ultimately resulting in significant losses);
- carefully managed the presentation of the financial position of the companies and the pension funds so that any disclosures were minimised; and
- used the cash and pension funds of Mirror Group Newspapers for the benefit of his other businesses.

Non-executive directors

Non-executive directors are directors who do not also have an executive role in the running of the company's business (see Chapter 6). In corporate governance terms they have an important part to play and this is recognised in the Code which states that non-executive directors should (among others):

- constructively challenge and help develop proposals on strategy;
- scrutinise the performance of management in meeting agreed goals and objectives;
- satisfy themselves on the integrity of the financial information; and
- satisfy themselves that financial controls and systems of risk management are robust and defensible.

The effectiveness of a non-executive director in providing this sort of balance and scrutiny can be compromised if they lack independence. As far as the Code is concerned, there are various factors that can undermine the independence of a non-executive director such as if he has been an employee of the company within the last five years; has close family ties with any of the company's advisors, directors or senior employees; or has significant links with other directors through involvement in other companies.

Committees of the board

A common feature of corporate governance codes is the requirement to establish separate board committees which have specific functions within the company's governance framework, independent from the main board. The UK Code requires companies to have three committees, namely:

- a nominations committee;
- an audit committee; and
- a remuneration committee.

Nominations committee

The role of the nominations committee is to lead the process for the appointment of new directors. In doing this, the committee must assess the balance of skills and experience on the board and then draw up a specification for a particular appointment. A majority of the members of this committee should be independent non-executive directors. Essentially the purpose of the nominations committee is to ensure that the appointment of new directors is transparent and determined against objective, rather than subjective, criteria.

Audit committee

The audit committee (which should be made up of independent non-executive directors) is perhaps the most important of the three board committees. It is tasked with, among others, monitoring the company's financial statements, reviewing internal financial controls, reviewing the internal control and risk management systems, making recommendations to the board about the appointment, re-appointment and removal of the company's auditor, monitoring the auditor's independence and objectivity and the effectiveness of the audit process. The audit committee is also responsible for ensuring that proper procedures are in place to enable irregularities or concerns to be reported by staff and investigated.

Remuneration committee

The remuneration committee, which must also be made up of non-executive directors, is responsible for setting the remuneration package of each executive director including benefits such as pension rights and compensation payments for loss of office.

Financial reporting

Some of the notable corporate failures in recent years came about as a result of financial irregularities and malpractice, including questionable accounting practices. For example, manipulation of financial data can make a company appear outwardly successful when, in fact, it is heading for disaster. As such, ensuring the integrity of a company's financial information, accounting methods and audit process is another key concern of corporate governance. The Code requires that all information and reports produced by directors are fair, balanced and understandable and that internal control measures should be employed to ensure the accuracy and reliability of the company's financial statements.

Non-financial reporting

As well as ensuring that the company's financial information is accurate, the board is responsible for ensuring the integrity of the non-financial information that it releases. The majority of this will be included in the company's annual report and accounts. All companies have to include information of this sort to one degree or another (as determined by the Companies Act and other regulations) but the UK Code requires additional disclosures about specific matters such as:

- the identity of the chairman and the chief executive;
- the identity of the members of each board committee;
- specific details about the work carried out by each committee;
- the non-executive directors that the board considers to be independent; and
- the board's review of the risk management and internal control systems.

Directors' remuneration

Directors' remuneration is a sensitive issue. Reports appear fairly regularly in the media of shareholders expressing anger at directors receiving pay increases or bonuses despite the poor performance of the company, particularly if this is in the context of pay freezes for employees and even redundancies. In addition, when large compensation payments are paid to a director for loss of office it can often appear as a reward for failure. Linked to that is the problem of lengthy notice or contract periods which may effectively enable a director to embed themselves on their board. The obvious principles here are that:

- the procedure for determining directors' remuneration should be formal and transparent;
- no director should be involved in deciding his or her own remuneration;

- a significant part of a directors' remuneration should be linked to performance; and
- notice or contract periods should not be excessive (the Code stipulates one year or less).

As mentioned above, the UK Code charges the remuneration committee with the task of fixing each director's remuneration package and designing the performance related elements.

Risk management

It is generally acknowledged that in order to succeed companies need to take risks. As a principle of good governance, the board should take a considered and responsible approach to risk and decide what risks they are willing to take to achieve the objectives that they have set for the company. At the same time, the board should implement and maintain sound risk management and internal control systems. These systems should be reviewed periodically to check their effectiveness.

Case study: Barings Bank

In Chapter 7, a reference was made to the collapse of Barings Bank, at one time a long-established and well-respected financial institution. This bank was brought down by the activities of a single trader (Nick Leeson) who accumulated huge trading losses on the Singapore stock exchange that he managed to conceal from his superiors. When eventually they were discovered, the debts were so large that the bank had no chance of surviving them. In the aftermath of the bank's collapse, the management were heavily criticised. How was it that Nick Leeson was able to carry on for so long undetected? One particular fact that came to light was that he had been in charge of two key functions that would normally be kept separate. Nick Leeson both placed trades on the Singapore stock exchange and dealt with the back-room function of maintaining the trading accounts. That, together with other issues that were uncovered, led to the conclusion that the bank's internal control systems were simply not adequate. Had the roles been separated, had Nick Leeson been more closely supervised, had his activities been subject to internal audit (audits were never carried out fully) and had the management ensured that they had a proper understanding of what he was doing (and the risks involved) the disaster could have been avoided. The blame for all of this was laid at the feet of the bank's directors.

As a result of the Barings scandal and other corporate failures, implementing a sound system of internal control is now a firmly established principle of corporate governance. The recent failings in the UK banking system have served to highlight further the need for adequate risk management and controls.

The relationship between directors and shareholders

This issue recalls the 'agency problem' that was mentioned at the beginning of this chapter. In the words of the UK Code, the directors should have a 'dialogue with shareholders based on the mutual understanding of objectives'. This is essentially about open and transparent communication between the company and its shareholders. As mentioned earlier, directors are entrusted with the running of the company and in comparison to shareholders are in a position of considerable power. This is particularly so in large listed companies where it can be difficult for the many disparate shareholders to exert any influence over the board. Good governance requires that shareholders are not put in this position in the first place and that the directors listen to the concerns of all shareholders and not favour one group over another. This can be achieved by disclosure of information, constructive use of general meetings (and in the case of public companies the annual general meeting in particular) but also by informal discussion and engagement. In this context, large institutional investors have a key role in using their voting power effectively so as to challenge the board of directors when appropriate and to express concern at poor governance practices. Representative bodies such as the Association of British Insurers (ABI) and the National Association of Pension Funds (NAPF) have their own corporate governance and voting policies which their members are encouraged to follow and apply. This is bolstered by the UK Stewardship Code which aims to promote greater engagement by institutional shareholders with the companies in which they invest. The Stewardship Code sets out principles and guidance that UK authorised asset managers are required to follow on a 'comply or explain' basis.

▦ Is corporate governance relevant to a small private company?

The problem for small private companies is that the UK Corporate Governance Code was not written with them in mind. The Code reflects many of the issues that are relevant to all companies, but is primarily concerned with companies with a listing on the London Stock Exchange. Governance issues in smaller unlisted companies tend to be different. In recognition of this the European Confederation of Directors' Associations (ecoDa) have issued a guidance document for unlisted companies entitled 'Corporate Governance Guidance and Principles for Unlisted Companies in Europe'. The Guidance was written in collaboration with, among others, the UK Institute of Directors (IoD) and the IoD has adapted it for the UK market.

The ecoDa Guidance

The Guidance takes as its starting point the fact that unlisted companies of all sizes (including start-ups, single owner-managed companies, family businesses, private equity-owned companies, joint ventures and subsidiary companies) make up the vast majority of companies in the UK and yet these companies have, to date, been largely ignored by policy makers for corporate governance purposes. It suggests various reasons why a separate set of principles and guidance for such companies is appropriate. Principal among these is that the corporate governance challenges of unlisted companies are different from those of listed companies. Listed companies often have large numbers of minority shareholders who have no say in or influence over the management or stewardship of the company, which is itself run by professional managers who do not have significant ownership stakes. As such the governance framework for listed companies usually focuses on ensuring that shareholders can exercise effective control over the management of the board, as can be seen with the UK Corporate Governance Code. This contrasts starkly with the majority of unlisted companies (and small companies in particular) which are often owned and controlled by a small number of individuals and sometimes by just one person. In this context, the Guidance proposes that corporate governance is not concerned with protecting the rights of shareholders who have no involvement in the management of a company but with:

> establishing a framework of company processes and attitudes that add value to the business and help ensure its long-term continuity and success.

The Guidance acknowledges that the particular size and circumstances of each individual company will determine what kind of corporate governance framework will be appropriate, and in particular it emphasises that this will change as a company grows. One of the issues for a small private company is that as it expands, the current owner-managers may need to consider bringing in outsiders (directors and/or investors) to help the company achieve its objectives. At this point the corporate governance framework needs to become more formal, detailed and wider in scope. Relinquishing control can be difficult for the founders and as such a gradual 'phased' approach is recommended.

The benefits of corporate governance for unlisted companies

According to the Guidance, the main benefits of implementing a corporate governance framework are as follows.

Defining roles

An effective corporate governance framework defines roles, responsibilities and an agreed distribution of power amongst shareholders, the board, management and other stakeholders. For small companies it is especially important for the owner-manager to recognise and understand that the company is not an extension of his or her private property.

Supporting growth

At some point in a company's life it will no longer be feasible for the founder to run the company on his or her own. A sound corporate governance framework can help to facilitate the transition from an owner-manager set up, to bringing in outsiders to help to take the company forward. An important part of this is establishing an organised and efficient means of delegation coupled with appropriate reporting lines and controls. The corporate governance framework should also play a key part in monitoring and managing risks as the company grows in size and complexity.

Obtaining finance
Lenders and investors may prefer to deal with a company if they see that its affairs are managed in accordance with accepted principles of good governance.

Societal expectations
Large listed companies are not the only ones that can come under scrutiny by the media and the public for the way that they conduct themselves. The demands of society for greater accountability and transparency in the corporate world apply to unlisted companies just as they do to those companies who are more obviously in the public eye.

Building reputation
Good corporate governance practices can strengthen a company's reputation and standing in the eyes of key stakeholders such as lenders, investors, employees, customers and the local community. Poor corporate governance practices may have the opposite effect.

Main concerns of the ecoDa Guidance

The Guidance lists seven key concepts which it regards as being the foundations of an effective corporate governance framework These are:

- delegation of authority;
- checks and balances;
- professional decision-making;
- accountability;
- transparency;
- conflicts of interest; and
- aligning incentives.

These themes and concepts echo some of the concerns of the UK Corporate Governance Code however the ecoDa Guidance addresses their relevance and application in the context of an unlisted company.

Delegation of authority
In a small owner-managed company, the owner-manager may well have sole responsibility for the running of the company. When the company reaches a point when

the owner-manager can no longer run the company on his or her own, he or she must delegate authority to others. The Guidance advises that at this point the roles, powers and authorities of directors and management should be formally defined. In terms of the directors and managers, each person should know the extent of their authority. A schedule of matters that are reserved for the decision of the board and a schedule of matters that are delegated to executive management should be drawn up and then be reviewed regularly to ensure that each remains appropriate and provides the right balance between control and flexibility. In terms of the company's shareholders, the balance of power between shareholders and directors can be clearly established by way of the articles of association and perhaps even more effectively by a shareholders' agreement. However the Guidance suggests that as a company grows, it should move away from the use of shareholders agreements in the interests of transparency and openness.

Checks and balances

A key principle of corporate governance for all companies (see the example of Robert Maxwell earlier) is that no one person should have unfettered power over the company's decision making. The purpose of a system of checks and balances is to ensure that the actions or proposed actions of each person are subject to review and an appropriate degree of scrutiny. Major decisions should be taken collectively (and should be first among the matters reserved for the board as a whole). The system of checks and balances doesn't just apply to the board of directors, but to the company as a whole and forms an important part of a company's risk management system. Role profiles for each individual can bring clarity and ensure that each is aware of their responsibilities and the limits on their authority. This can also focus attention on whether all relevant activities and functions have been allocated. In addition, the use of such profiles also makes it easier to hold individuals to account for any failure to fulfil their duties and responsibilities. Internal audits should be carried out to check whether key tasks have been performed, whether processes are being followed and to uncover wrongful acts, such as theft.

Professional decision making

Bringing in outsider directors will change the way in which decisions are made. The shift from a sole owner-manager set up to a board of two or more directors means that decision-making needs to become more formal. As such the Guidance recommends that a more professional approach to decision-making should be taken at this point. The rules and procedures for directors' decision-making are explained in Chapter 8.

Accountability

A company should have a hierarchy of accountability. At the top is the board of directors which is accountable to the company's shareholders and other stakeholders. Moving downwards, each level of management should monitor and supervise the level below. This should be facilitated by formal and effective reporting lines. Each level of management should understand the nature and scope of their responsibilities and, as the company grows, the rules on business conduct (including ethical principles) should be formalised.

Transparency

The Guidance integrates another common notion in corporate governance which is that directors, managers and employees are likely to give more thought to their conduct and actions if they perceive that they are being observed. This is to do with transparency and disclosure. It was noted earlier that listed companies are subject to certain disclosure requirements which are supplemented by additional requirements in the UK Corporate Governance Code. Unlisted companies are not subject to the same level of disclosure as listed companies but the Guidance suggests that such companies may decide to disclose more information than they are legally obliged to as a means of gaining the confidence of external stakeholders.

Non-executive directors

Linked to the concepts of transparency and of checks and balances is the role of non-executive directors. As noted earlier, non-executive directors have an important function in an effective corporate governance framework in terms of monitoring and, if appropriate, challenging the decisions and actions of the executive directors. The Guidance proposes that the appointment of a non-executive director is a key stage in the development of an unlisted company – it signals the company's willingness to become more open and accountable in respect of its decision-making and performance assessment.

Conflicts of interest

Directors must be aware of their duty to promote the success of the company and have a clear understanding that the company is not merely an extension of their own property. Accordingly, decision making should be objective and not self-interested. As explained in Chapter 7, the Companies Act requires all directors to declare any interest that they have in transactions with the company (s. 177) and requires directors to avoid situations in which they have or may have a conflict of interest (s. 175). Companies must establish rules and procedures on how conflicts of interest are dealt with by appropriate provisions in the articles of association. The Guidance suggests that directors should abstain from decision making when appropriate and ultimately should be prepared to leave the board if their conflict of interest could be detrimental to the success of the company.

Aligning incentives

As with the UK Corporate Governance Code, the Guidance also highlights the issue of remuneration. It states the need to ensure that a company's remuneration policy incentivises behaviour from directors, managers and employees in a way that is consistent with the long-term interests of the company. In this respect the issues for unlisted companies are very similar to those of listed companies namely:

- What are the benchmarks and criteria for measuring performance?
- Who within the company makes the decisions about each person's remuneration package?
- How much information about remuneration should the company disclose?

■ The ecoDa Principles

Like the UK Corporate Governance Code, the ecoDa Guidance includes a number of headline principles of best practice for establishing a sound system of governance. The first nine of these are stated as being applicable to all unlisted companies and the next five as being applicable only to large and more complex unlisted companies. The principles are set out below.

Principles applicable to all unlisted companies

1 Shareholders should establish an appropriate constitutional and governance framework for the company.
2 Every company should strive to establish an effective board which is collectively responsible for the long-term success of the company, including the definition of the corporate strategy. However, an interim step on the road to an effective (and independent) board may be the creation of an advisory board.
3 The size and composition of the board should reflect the scale and complexity of the company's activities.
4 The board should meet sufficiently regularly to discharge its duties, and be supplied in a timely manner with appropriate information.
5 Levels of remuneration should be sufficient to attract, retain and motivate executives and non-executives of the quality required to run the company successfully.
6 The board is responsible for risk oversight and should maintain a sound system of internal control to safeguard shareholders' investment and the company's assets.
7 There should be a dialogue between the board and shareholders based on the mutual understanding of objectives. The board as a whole has responsibility for ensuring that a satisfactory dialogue with shareholders takes place. The board should not forget that all shareholders have to be treated equally.
8 All directors should receive induction on joining the board and should regularly update their skills and knowledge.
9 Family-controlled companies should establish family governance mechanisms

that promote coordination and mutual understanding amongst family members as well as organise the relationship between family governance and corporate governance.

Principles applicable to large and/or more complex unlisted companies

10 There should be a clear division of responsibilities at the head of the company between the running of the board and the running of the company's business. No one individual should have unfettered powers of decision.

11 Board structures vary according to national regulatory requirements and business norms. However, all boards should contain directors with a sufficient mix of competencies and experiences. No single person (or small group of individuals) should dominate the board's decision-making.

12 The board should establish board committees in order to allow a more effective discharge of its duties.

13 The board should undertake a periodic appraisal of its own performance and that of each individual director.

14 The board should present a balanced and understandable assessment of the company's position and prospects for external stakeholders, and establish a suitable programme of stakeholder engagement.

Each principle is supported by key points which expand on the general principle. This is followed by further considerations about how to implement the general principle in practice. Many of the key points and considerations reflect certain of the corresponding supporting principles and code provisions of the UK Corporate Governance Code. As such, basing a system of governance on the Guidance should set a company on the road towards building a system that is comparable to that of a UK listed company. A copy of the Guidance can be obtained from the ecoDa website (www.ecoda.org) and the version adapted for the UK can be obtained from the Institute of Directors website (www.iod.com).

▣ Corporate social responsibility

Corporate social responsibility (or CSR for short) is a concept born of the broader stakeholder view of corporate governance. Like corporate governance itself, there is no one accepted definition of what CSR is. In general though, CSR is about the responsibility that companies should take for the way that they conduct themselves within society and the effect that they can have (positive and negative) on any number of stakeholder groups. As such, CSR is concerned with – among others – issues such as ethics, sustainability, the environment, local communities, human rights, human wellbeing, current and former employees, suppliers and customers. In its 'Renewed EU Strategy 2011–14 for Corporate Social

Responsibility' the European Commission provides a helpful definition of CSR as 'the responsibility of enterprises for their impacts on society'. It says that:

> To fully meet their corporate social responsibility, enterprises should have in place a process to integrate social, environmental, ethical, human rights and consumer concerns into their business operations and core strategy in close collaboration with their stakeholders, with the aim of:
>
> - maximising the creation of shared value for their owners/stakeholders and for their other stakeholders and society at large; and
> - identifying, preventing and mitigating their possible adverse impacts.

The UK Corporate Governance Code does not make any direct reference to CSR issues but in drafting the current Companies Act, the UK government has attempted to embed CSR-type considerations into the process of company decision making. This can be seen in s. 172 of the Act which enshrines the duty of directors to promote the success of the company. As explained in Chapter 7, in fulfilling this duty, directors are to have regard to (amongst others):

- the likely consequences of any decision in the long term;
- the interests of the company's employees;
- the need to foster the company's business relationships with suppliers, customers and others;
- the impact of the company's operations on the community and the environment;
- the desirability of the company maintaining a reputation for high standards of business conduct; and
- the need to act fairly as between the members of the company.

The business argument for CSR is similar to that for corporate governance in that it will tend to enhance a company's reputation and credibility in the eyes of its stakeholders and as such may help the company win business, obtain finance and generally improve its long term sustainability. Suppliers and consumers are increasingly sensitive to CSR issues and this can influence their decisions about the companies that they deal with. At the same time, being seen to be acting in a socially responsible way can avoid the unwanted attention of pressure groups and the media. There can also be practical benefits (e.g. addressing environmental issues may mean that a company achieves greater efficiencies in its operations resulting in costs savings).

The range of issues relevant to CSR is without limit. Companies should give thought to the effects of all aspects of their activities at all points in the company's supply chain – the labour they use, the prices paid to their suppliers, the countries and political regimes that they deal with and any way in which their activities impact on the environment being just some among others. Closer to home there is a growing expectation that companies should invest in their local communities and support and develop the people who work for them.

Ethics

Closely linked to corporate social responsibility are the issues of ethics and ethical behaviour. Like most concepts in corporate governance ethics is difficult to pin down, but in a business context it is essentially concerned with the values by which companies (and those who run and work for them) conduct themselves within the wider legal and moral framework of the society in which they operate. The well-known economist Milton Friedman argued that the purpose of corporations and the value of their contribution to society is in the creation of wealth. In his view, to stray from this would ultimately be harmful to the corporation and the society in which it operates. This view has its supporters but it ignores the fact that companies often have to make choices that balance the company's commercial needs and objectives against a course of action that may be ethically or morally questionable. The range of behaviour that might advance a company's commercial aims, but which may be ethically questionable, could include:

- paying or giving a substantial gift to someone involved in a tender process in order to gain a competitive advantage over other companies involved in the same process;
- advertising products in a way that misrepresents them;
- using suppliers in developing countries where working conditions and pay are poor, or where child labour is common; and
- implementing work processes which are harmful to the environment.

The code of ethics

The purpose of a code of ethics is to enable a company to set out its vision for the kind of company that it wants to be and the values that it intends to adhere to in achieving its commercial objectives. It is an accepted principle of good governance that a company should decide what its approach to ethics and corporate social responsibility will be, to set its vision and values accordingly and then to be transparent about this with its stakeholders – the idea being that customers, suppliers, lenders and others can all make informed decisions (based on their own values and beliefs) about the companies with which they wish to do business.

Of course, once it has set its values a company must stand by them. Commentators tend to agree that, to be effective, a code of ethics needs to be a 'living' document that should be formulated and endorsed by the board of directors and embedded in the company's business operations. As such, it needs to be communicated to all employees, supported by appropriate training and guidance and be reviewed and updated on an ongoing basis. A code of ethics will usually set out rules and guidelines on employees' conduct as well as the broader values which determine how the company as a whole will conduct itself. As such, a code of ethics could cover such employee-related matters as:

- conflicts of interest;
- equality and diversity;

- confidentiality;
- legal and regulatory compliance;
- exploitation of company property or of an employee's position, for personal gain;
- procedures for reporting unethical or illegal behaviour; and
- conduct in relation to customers, suppliers and others.

It could then encompass wider issues concerning:

- supporting local communities and social enterprise;
- dealings and relations with suppliers and manufacturers in developing countries;
- human rights issues; and
- environmental impacts and sustainability.

Needless to say, this list is not exhaustive and issues relevant to one company may not be relevant to another. Nevertheless the aim of a code of ethics is to at least identify the issues that are relevant and to then formulate a policy to guide the company's officers and employees in their decision-making as it relates to those issues.

The Bribery Act 2010

One particular concern of business ethics is the need to prevent the giving and receiving of bribes. Ethical values can and do differ from one society to the next and as such, there are some countries where bribes are a part of normal business life. Sometimes these are in the form of 'facilitation payments' which are payments made to government or other officials in order to expedite (or at least to enable) the execution of particular processes that are merely within the normal course of business. Some companies may not have cause to deal with officials in countries where such payments are the norm, however bribery can be a domestic issue as well as a foreign one. All companies incorporated in the UK or conducting business in the UK need to be mindful of the provisions of the Bribery Act 2010.

The Bribery Act creates offences in relation to:

- offering, promising or receiving a bribe;
- requesting, agreeing to receive or accepting a bribe;
- bribing a foreign public official; and
- failing to prevent bribery.

The scope of these offences means that both a company (in respect of failing to prevent bribery) and those who work for it (in terms of offering or accepting a bribe) can be liable under the Act. There is a defence available to a company if it can prove that it had adequate procedures in place designed to prevent bribery and, as such, it is important that all companies explicitly prohibit all forms of bribery and implement appropriate controls to prevent it, including implementing a formal anti-bribery policy which might set out (among others):

- the company's commitment to ethical business practices;
- the prohibition on making or accepting bribes;
- rules and limits on accepting gifts and hospitality;
- procedures for reporting conduct that might amount to a bribe (and identifying what such conduct might be); and
- procedures for reporting corporate hospitality and gifts.

A company's anti-bribery measures should form part of its overall internal risk management system. As with other internal policies, appropriate training and guidance should be given to all persons within a company with a record of such training being kept. For help and guidance in relation to implementing appropriate controls on bribery speak to a professional with experience in this area, such as a solicitor.

Summary

- There is no one all-encompassing definition but corporate governance is generally concerned with the way in which companies are run and managed and their relationships with all those who have a stake or interest in them.
- A number of notable company failures in the last two decades have been attributed to corporate governance failings as have many of the problems and crises that have beset the UK banking sector in more recent years.
- As a result of such failings the importance of good governance has gained hugely in recognition alongside increasing public demand for transparency and accountability in both the public and private sectors.
- Corporate governance first gained momentum in the UK with the publication of the Cadbury Report in the early 1990s. More reports and guidance followed which are now encapsulated in the UK Corporate Governance Code 2012 and the supporting guidance on board effectiveness, audit committees and internal controls.
- The UK Corporate Governance Code reflects many of the concerns of corporate governance including the role and effectiveness of the board of directors, the need for checks and balances, internal controls, directors' remuneration and the relationship between directors and shareholders.
- Companies with a listing on the London Stock Exchange must state in their annual report whether they have complied with the Code and if they have not, explain why. This is known as 'comply or explain'.
- Corporate governance issues in private and unlisted companies manifest themselves in a different way. The ecoDa guidance is the first set of principles and guidance to be written specifically for unlisted companies.
- The ecoDa guidance addresses the corporate governance issues facing small private companies taking particular note of the transition from an owner-manager set up to a more formal company structure.

- Although it is not addressed in any detail in most corporate governance codes, corporate social responsibility has become a significant concern of good governance, gaining in importance due to societal expectations of responsible business behaviour.
- CSR issues are embedded in the Companies Act in relation to the matters that directors are required to consider in pursuing a company's commercial objectives.
- Closely linked to CSR, ethics is concerned with the conflict between actions and activities that may further a company's business but which could be at odds with accepted moral values.
- A code of ethics can be used to set a company's vision and values and to embed these in its culture and day-to-day operations.
- The Bribery Act addresses the specific issue of corruption and creates offences in relation to bribing, being bribed and failing to prevent bribery.

17 Insolvency
David Frederick

In this chapter

This chapter provides an overview of insolvency procedures with particular regard to:

- when a company is deemed to be insolvent;
- the procedures for winding up an insolvent company;
- the procedures that can be used to try and save an insolvent company;
- the liability of directors in insolvency and the liquidator's power to reverse company transactions;
- staying aware of a company's financial position and the signs that could indicate a company is approaching insolvency; and
- the order of distribution of assets in a liquidation.

What is insolvency?

Insolvency describes the situation where a company is unable to continue operating at a profit and does not have the liquid funds (the cash) to pay its debts as they fall due. There are many reasons why a company may become insolvent and insolvency does not necessarily mean that the business itself is a failure or is not viable. Insolvency can be the result of poor cash-flow management, poor stock management, or expanding too quickly without sufficient working capital, to give just a few examples.

There are two general tests for insolvency under English law which are known as the cash-flow test and the balance sheet test.

The cash-flow test

A company is deemed to be insolvent if it is currently unable or will in the future, be unable to pay its debts as and when they fall due for payment.

The balance sheet test

A company is deemed insolvent if the values of its liabilities are greater than its assets after making provisions for uncertain and future liabilities.

In addition to these two general tests, in practice a company is insolvent if either of the following two conditions are satisfied:

- a creditor who is owed more than £750 has served a formal demand for an undisputed sum at the company's registered office and the debt has not been paid for three weeks; or
- a judgement or other court order made against the company has not been satisfied.

Insolvency does not have to mean the end of a company's life. The recent experience of English football clubs and high street names are testimony to this fact. When a company becomes insolvent the path to the end result – survival or dissolution – is dependent upon the strength or viability of the underlying business. The first question to be asked of the company is what is the strength of the underlying business? If the underlying business is strong it may be possible to save it. For a company with a weak business the only possible option may be a winding up ('winding up' refers to the liquidation or legal closure of a company). The figure below summarises the possible courses of action for an insolvent company, depending on whether there is a possibility of saving the business or not.

Figure 17.1: Possible courses of action for an insolvent company

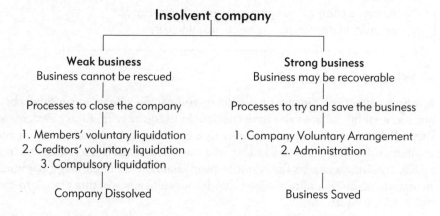

In the following two sections each of the different insolvency procedures and each of the different business recovery procedures are considered in turn.

Insolvency procedures

An insolvent company without a business that can be rescued only has one available option and that is to be liquidated (wound up). Liquidation is the process of putting a company to sleep once all its assets have been identified, realised and distributed as appropriate. When all that is left of the company is an empty shell, it can be dissolved by application to the Registrar of Companies. Liquidations can either be voluntary or compulsory. Voluntary procedures are instigated by the company itself and fall into two categories – members' voluntary liquidations and creditors' voluntary liquidations. In a compulsory liquidation a winding up is forced on a company whether the directors and shareholders want to take this course of action or not.

Members' voluntary liquidation

A members' voluntary liquidation (or MVL for short) is the procedure used to wind up a company that is solvent. Winding up a solvent company may seem a strange notion, but if a company has served its purpose and has nowhere left to go, the directors may propose to close the company down so that the assets of the company remaining after the payment of its debts can be distributed among the company's shareholders. In order to take the MVL route, not only must the company be solvent, but it must also be able to pay its creditors in full. The procedure requires the majority of the directors of the company to make a statutory declaration of solvency. This is a declaration that, having conducted a full inquiry into the affairs of the company, the directors are satisfied that it will be able to discharge its debts in full within 12 months from the commencement of the winding-up process. Included within the declaration will be a statement of the company's assets and liabilities at the latest date preceding the declaration.

To commence the MVL, the company's shareholders must pass a special resolution within five weeks of the date of the directors' declaration of solvency, and then appoint one or more liquidators to conduct the winding up. The liquidator (as in all insolvency procedures) must be a licensed insolvency practitioner.

A notice of the special resolution must be published in the London *Gazette* within 14 days of the general meeting at which it was passed. In addition, the company must submit a copy of the declaration and the special resolution to the Registrar of Companies within 15 days.

If at any time during the winding-up process it appears to the liquidator that the company cannot in fact discharge its debts in full, the process must change to that of a creditors' voluntary liquidation. This changes the situation significantly, particularly for the company's directors, as it means that the company is actually insolvent.

Creditors' voluntary liquidation

A creditors' voluntary liquidation (or CVL for short) is the procedure used to wind up a company that is insolvent and there is no part of the business that can be saved. Once a decision to enter a CVL has been made trading has to cease.

As with a MVL a CVL requires the shareholders of a company to pass a special resolution to commence a winding up and then nominate a liquidator to conduct the proceedings. A meeting of the company's creditors must be held within 14 days of the date on which the special resolution was passed. All known creditors must be given at least seven days' notice of the meeting and a notice of the meeting must also be placed in the London *Gazette* and in two local newspapers. Despite these requirements creditors' attendance is usually low.

In advance of the creditors' meeting the directors of the company are required to prepare a statement of affairs which is a summary (sworn under oath) of the company's financial position. This is made available to creditors at the meeting where they will also be able to ask questions of the directors. The creditors are entitled to vote on the nomination of their own liquidator and if the outcome of this is to nominate a different liquidator to the shareholders, the creditors' vote takes precedence.

Once appointed the liquidator must be provided with a copy of the statement of affairs. This must also be filed with the Registrar of Companies within five business days of the creditors' meeting. The powers of the directors with regard to the company cease and they no longer have any active involvement in the company or the winding up. The liquidator seeks to identify and realise all the assets of the company to enable them to be distributed to the creditors in the order prescribed by the Insolvency Act. If there is any surplus it will be distributed to the company's shareholders (in accordance with any rights set out in the company's articles of association) however this is often a rare occurrence in the case of a CVL.

Compulsory liquidation

A compulsory liquidation is the process of winding up a company as a result of a court order granted following a successful petition. The petition is often made by creditors but can be made by others including the company (following a special resolution of the shareholders) and the Secretary of State on the grounds of public interest (such as following an investigation by the Insolvency Service). The circumstances in which a petition for compulsory liquidation can be made are set out in s. 122 of the Insolvency Act 1986, the most common reason being the inability of the company to pay its debts. The petition must be advertised in the London *Gazette* in advance of the court hearing. If the court grants a winding-up order, a copy must be filed with the Registrar of Companies immediately.

The Official Receiver (an officer from the Insolvency Service) is usually appointed by the liquidator as a result of the court granting the winding-up order. A private practice insolvency practitioner can be appointed as a liquidator at the request of the Official Receiver or the company's creditors. Part of the Official Receiver's role in all compulsory liquidations is to investigate the company's affairs and reasons for its failure.

Business recovery procedures

For an insolvent company with a business that can be rescued there are three possible options for trying to bring the company back to life. These are:

- administration;
- a company voluntary arrangement; or
- pre-pack administration.

Administration

When a company is put into administration, an insolvency practitioner is appointed as the administrator of the company to take control of its affairs in order to achieve the best possible outcome for the company's creditors as a whole. The administrator must determine what the purpose of the administration will be. There are three possible purposes which are stated in Schedule B1 of the Insolvency Act 1986 as follows:

- to rescue the company as a going concern; or if this is not possible
- to achieve a better result for the company's creditors as a whole than would be likely if the company were wound up (without first being in administration); or if that is also not possible
- to realise property in order to make a distribution to one or more secured or preferential creditors.

One of the key features of an administration is that once it is in effect, the company has the benefit of a 'moratorium' on action by creditors. This essentially means that creditors are not permitted to take action against the company for recovery of their debts without the consent of the administrator or the court. This gives the administrator the time and space to try and re-organise the company's affairs.

An administrator may be appointed by court order following a hearing or can be appointed by way of an out of court procedure (subject to certain conditions and restrictions) by:

- the directors; or
- any holder of a 'qualifying floating charge' (QFC – a floating charge that meets the requirements of the Enterprise Act 2002 in that it consists of a charge over the whole or substantially whole of the company's property and purports to give the holder the power to appoint an administrator or an administrative receiver).

The out-of-court appointment of an administrator is only possible if the company or directors have not previously appointed an administrator or had the benefit of a moratorium or a company voluntary arrangement (CVA – see below) in the last 12 months. In addition, the directors cannot use the out-of-court procedure if a winding-up petition is outstanding (although the holder of a QFC can). In this case the company must apply for an administration order by the court route. If there is an outstanding winding-up petition then the grant of an administration order will automatically dismiss it. The out-of-court appointment of an administrator by the holder of a QFC will not dismiss it, but will only suspend it.

Duties and powers of the administrator

Once appointed, the administrator is an officer of the court and must act in the interests of the company's creditors as a whole. The administrator is required to prepare proposals for how he will proceed with the administration (including the purpose that he proposes to achieve) which must be sent to all creditors and members of the company, as well as to the Registrar of Companies.

The administrator has various powers including:

- to do anything necessary or expedient for the management of the affairs, business and property of the company;
- to sell or otherwise dispose of the company's property;
- to carry on the company's business;
- to remove or appoint directors of the company;
- to call a meeting of members or creditors of the company; and
- to apply to court for directions in connection with his functions.

The end of administration

The Enterprise Act 2002 introduced a time limit of 12 months for an administration. As such, an administration will automatically come to an end 12 months after it began unless an extension is agreed by the company's creditors or granted by court order.

Apart from this automatic termination, there are several other ways in which the administration process can be brought to an end as follows:

- an administrator must apply to court to bring the administration to an end if the administrator believes that the purpose of the administration is not achievable; that administration was not the correct course of action; or following a resolution by a meeting of the company's creditors;
- an administrator appointed out of court may apply to court to bring the administration to an end if the administrator believes the purpose of administration has been achieved;
- a creditor may apply to court to terminate an administration on the grounds that the appointment of the administrator was made with an improper motive;
- where there are insufficient assets to pay secured creditors in full, the administrator may terminate the administration and commence a creditors' voluntary liquidation; and
- if the administrator believes the company has no realisable assets to make distributions to its creditors he must notify the Registrar of Companies and the company will then be dissolved.

Administrative receivership

Administrative receivership is becoming increasingly uncommon. An administrative receiver is a person appointed under the terms of a debenture secured by a floating charge over the assets of a company to realise the secured assets for the benefit of the debenture holder. To be able to appoint an administrative receiver the appointor (debenture holder) must have a charge that pre-dates 15 September 2003, when the Enterprise Act 2002 came into effect. This is because the Enterprise Act shifted the emphasis of insolvency procedures towards business recovery and introduced the new regime for administrations. There are some 'old' charges in existence, but they are falling in number as are the opportunities to appoint insolvency practitioners as administrative receivers.

Company Voluntary Arrangement (CVA)

A Company Voluntary Arrangement (CVA) is a legally binding agreement between a company and its creditors for the payment of a company's debts. It enables an insolvent company to continue trading whilst paying off its debts at an agreed percentage of their full value. A CVA is generally only appropriate or possible if the company has already or is likely to return to profitability in the near future and its debts can be paid off over a period of time, usually three years.

A CVA will require the agreement of a minimum of 75% of the company's creditors in value terms to accept the company's proposal to pay them a reduced amount in satisfaction of the sums owed to them. As a formal arrangement, a CVA requires approval by the court and once approved is binding on all creditors. An insolvency practitioner must be appointed, initially to oversee the proposals for the CVA, thereafter to manage it.

A CVA prevents the creditors from taking action against a company to recover any money owing to them unless the company is in breach of the terms of the CVA. A CVA will be deemed to have ended when the arrangement has been completed or in the event of a breach of the CVA terms.

Under the Insolvency Act 2000 small companies can seek a moratorium of 28 days during which to put a CVA proposal to the company's creditors. The moratorium prevents creditors from taking action against the company during this period. For these purposes a company is classified as small if it satisfies any two of the following three conditions:

- turnover of less than £5.6 million;
- a balance sheet total of less than £2.8 million; and
- less than 50 employees.

The moratorium does not require a court hearing but does require the filing of certain documents at court. The moratorium commences from the date the documents are filed and it ends on the day of the creditors' meeting to consider the company's proposals for the CVA.

Although a CVA can be an effective way of saving a company from liquidation it is essential that the root source of the company's financial problems is identified and addressed to avoid a repetition in the future. Some common contributory factors are:

- poor sales;
- relatively high fixed costs;
- bad debt; and
- poor financial management.

If the cause of the insolvency is not diagnosed and remedied, a company may find itself back in the same situation, post CVA. If an insolvent company has non-transferable contractual agreements such as licenses it may be particularly advantageous for the company to trade through a CVA.

Pre-pack administration

A pre-pack administration is a business recovery procedure where all or part of the business is sold by way of an administration. The distinguishing feature of a pre-pack is that a purchaser for the company and the terms of the sale are agreed before the administrator is appointed. The purchaser may be one of the following:

- a new company;
- a competitor; or
- the existing management.

The identification of a prospective buyer in advance of the appointment (which is done without the involvement of unsecured creditors) and the fact that the business or assets are often sold to the existing management has led to some criticism of the use of pre-packs as a company rescue package. However, new rules governing pre-pack administration were introduced on 1 January 2009 by way of the Insolvency Service's Statement of Insolvency Practice 16. Under the new rules, the administrator is required to explain to creditors the full background to their appointment and why a 'pre-pack' sale would be the most advantageous outcome for the creditors. The administrator is also required to disclose a range of key information to creditors with their notice of appointment including:

- the name of the purchaser of the business;
- the price paid;
- details of any connection between the purchaser and the former directors or members;
- details of valuations received; and
- details of the company's assets.

The aim of the new rules is to introduce greater transparency in the pre-pack administration process. In effect, creditors of the insolvent company will have better access to information about the new owners of a troubled business.

Directors' liabilities in insolvency

The financial failure of a company is something that the regulatory authorities take seriously and company directors may be exposed to personal liability and disqualification as a result.

Disqualification

Once appointed, administrators, administrative receivers and liquidators have a statutory duty to report to the Secretary of State for Business, Innovation & Skills on the conduct of all directors who have held office at any time during the last three years of a company's trading. This report serves as the basis to determine whether there are grounds for disqualification of any of the directors under the Company Directors' Disqualification Act 1986 (see Chapter 7). As well as the possibility of disqualification, the Insolvency Act creates specific offences and liabilities for directors of insolvent companies and also gives a liquidator the power to reverse various company transactions.

Liabilities under the Insolvency Act

There are numerous offences and liabilities in the Insolvency Act that apply to directors of an insolvent company. Among the potential problem areas that directors need to be aware of are:

- wrongful trading;
- fraudulent trading;
- misfeasance; and
- re-use of an insolvent company's name.

Wrongful trading (s. 214)

A director is deemed to have engaged in wrongful trading under s. 214 of the Insolvency Act 1986 if at some time before the commencement of the winding up of the company, the director knew or ought to have concluded that there was no reasonable prospect that the company would avoid going into insolvent liquidation and did not take every step with a view to minimising the potential loss to the company's creditors as they ought to have taken.

A director found liable under s. 214 can be made to contribute such sum to the assets of the company as a court may determine. A court also has the power to make an order for disqualification under the Company Directors' Disqualification Act 1986.

Fraudulent trading (s. 213)

Fraudulent trading is trading with the intent to defraud creditors. As with wrongful trading, the court can require a director found liable under s. 213 to make such contributions to the company's assets as the court thinks proper. Fraudulent trading is also a criminal offence under s. 993 of the Companies Act which attracts a maximum prison sentence of 10 years, although it should be noted that this offence applies to a company whether or not it has been or is in the course of being wound up. A director held liable for fraudulent trading (either under the Companies Act or the Insolvency Act) can also be disqualified under the Company Directors' Disqualification Act 1986.

Misfeasance (s. 212)

A director (or other officer of a company) will have committed an act of misfeasance if they have misapplied or retained, or become accountable for any money or other property of the company, or been guilty of any breach of any fiduciary or other duty in relation to the company. The broad terms of this section give scope to the liquidator to ask the court (on application) to examine the behaviour of the person or persons in question and, if the court finds fit, to require such person or persons to repay, restore or account for the money or property (with interest) or to contribute a sum to the company's assets in compensation for their breach of duty.

Re-use of an insolvent company's name (s. 216)

The liquidation of a company can give rise to what has become known as 'phoenix company syndrome'. This is the practice whereby directors of a liquidated company start up a new company with the same business as the liquidated company, usually at the same premises and with a similar name. To deter this practice, a director or shadow director of a liquidated company is prohibited from being appointed as a director or participating in the management of a company with the same or a similar name for a period of five years unless they have been given the express permission of the court. This is applicable whether or not there was a director disqualification order and contravention can result in a fine or imprisonment.

Reversing transactions

Whether acting in good or bad faith, directors may decide to take certain actions with regard to the company's assets in a way that disadvantages creditors, or favours one creditor or group of creditors over another. The Insolvency Act 1986 gives liquidators powers to challenge certain transactions entered into in the period leading up to a company's insolvency so as to put the company into the position it would have been in had the transaction in question not gone ahead. Some of these are explained below.

Preferences (s. 239)

At the onset of liquidation, it may appear reasonable to a director to set a priority or preference for repaying the company creditors, such as repaying unsecured creditors. However, the repayment of creditors is the responsibility of the liquidator in accordance with the prescribed hierarchy set out in the Insolvency Act 1986 and the Enterprise Act 2002. If as a result of the actions of the company there are insufficient assets for the liquidator to make payment to the higher-ranking creditors in accordance with the law, the liquidator can apply to the court for an order that the company is restored to its state prior to the preferential discharge of creditors.

Undervalue transactions (s. 238)

With an insolvency situation approaching, a director may choose to sell off assets of the company at less than market value to either realise cash quickly or put them outside the liquidation process. However, acting with such expediency is not necessarily in the interest of the company's creditors. As such, if a company disposes of assets at below market value prior to the onset of insolvency (the exact time frames are defined in the Insolvency Act) the liquidator can apply to court for an order to restore the company to its pre disposal state.

Floating charge avoidance (s. 245)

If a director has personally obtained a floating charge over the assets of the company this would result in the director having a higher priority over unsecured creditors in the event of a liquidation. This situation is not permitted by the Insolvency Act. A floating charge granted to a person connected with the company in the period of two years before the onset of insolvency is nullified by s. 245. Where the floating charge is granted to a person who is not connected with the company the relevant time period is 12 months.

Extortionate credit transactions (s. 244)

A liquidator may seek redress from the court if it is found that the company entered into an extortionate credit transaction within three years of the date on which the company entered liquidation or administration. An extortionate credit transaction is defined as a transaction for provision of credit to the company where the terms of the transaction require grossly exorbitant payments on the part of the company or otherwise grossly contravene the ordinary principles of fair dealing. Where the court upholds a claim under s. 244 it may vary the terms of the transaction or have the whole transaction set aside.

▨ Advice for directors

The above liabilities and the powers of liquidators may seem alarming and indeed they must be taken seriously. However, it is a commercial reality that insolvencies do happen and if the company's directors have used skill and judgement, have conducted themselves with honesty and in accordance with their legal duties and obligations and taken the right advice when it was needed, the risks to directors are greatly reduced.

Taking responsibility

As explained in Chapter 6, directors are in a position of trust with regard to the resources and assets of their company therefore it is essential that they keep abreast of the company's financial position and its wider implications, such as the potential risk of insolvency. Directors must have sufficient knowledge and understanding of the company's business to enable them to fulfil their fiduciary duties. Awareness is crucial – ignorance of these matters or delegating them to someone else will not relieve a director of liability.

Understanding the business

The directors' understanding of the business must be full and holistic. Some of the key elements that constitute a holistic understanding of the business are:

- an awareness and understanding of the break-even sales revenue and volume of the business;
- an understanding of the difference between cash and profit – cash is the operational medium that enables the business to meet its ongoing obligations, whereas profit is what is reported at the end of the year or trading period;
- knowledge of the working capital requirements of the business – knowing the time period between the purchase of business inputs on credit through to conversion into a sale, to the receipt of the sale proceeds, and then to the payment of the creditor;
- an understanding of the profitability of the business and/or each product/ service; and
- knowledge of the monthly cash position and the future cash commitments.

Monitoring financial data

The directors' need to be aware of the up-to-date financial position of their company is not best served by a company's annual accounts but by the management accounts (see Chapter 14). In addition a monthly or quarterly cash-flow forecast will show the directors the company's current financial position and where it is heading for the forthcoming periods (months or quarters). Moreover, the cash flow forecast provides an indication of the cash position at the end of each month. This enables the directors to know whether they have sufficient cash to meet future obligations. Similarly, the cash-flow forecast provides a guide to where the company will be in cash terms in one or three months' time.

Monthly or quarterly management accounting information may be supplemented by accounting ratios based upon the statutory financial statements. The key areas that can be examined using the financial statements are profitability, solvency, working capital management and financial gearing. Despite the usefulness of accounting ratios, they are based upon the past performance of the company and should not necessarily be relied upon as indicators of the future or of whether insolvency is looming. This is because the company's position may have changed since the production of the financial statements from which the ratios are calculated.

Nevertheless, directors should understand the objectives of the following four key ratios.

- Profitability – these ratios seek to assess how productive the company has been in generating a profit from its resources.

- Solvency – this group of ratios provide an assessment of a company's ability to meet its short-term debts.
- Working capital management – this group of ratios provide an assessment of how effectively a company manages its working capital. The focus is on the rate at which money is collected from debtors, paid to creditors, and stock converted into sales revenue.
- Financial gearing – this group of ratios provide an assessment of a company's ability to meet its external debt obligations and its dependence upon external debt.

Directors can obtain information regarding sector specific ratios from the company's accountant. Alternatively, Dunn & Bradstreet's industry and asset-specific benchmarking tools 'Industry Norms and Key Business Ratios', provides a comprehensive coverage of ratios classified by industry and asset size.

Recognise the warning signs

Some of the warning signs which could indicate that a company is heading towards insolvency include:

- declining or stagnant sales and profits;
- the company constantly residing in its overdraft zone;
- repeated late payment to suppliers and creditors;
- client orders not being fulfilled;
- inventory shortages or run outs;
- deteriorating cash flows; and
- escalating costs.

It is important to recognise that individually these and any other indicators do not guarantee a company will become insolvent. However, collectively they offer a high likelihood of a company entering insolvency if no counteractive or corrective action is taken by the company's directors.

The decision to cease or continue trading

When a company gets into a situation where it may be approaching insolvency the directors are under a duty to minimise losses to the company's creditors. From this point onwards, the directors can face difficult decisions. Putting the company into an insolvent liquidation too soon may not be in the creditors' best interests. Continuing to trade when it should be clear that the company cannot avoid an insolvent liquidation (running up more debts and increasing the losses of the company's creditors) could result in the directors being liable under s. 214 of the Insolvency Act 1986 for wrongful trading.

In this situation the directors should be meeting regularly to review and consider the company's financial position. Whatever decisions are made, a full and complete record should be kept in the minutes. In addition, sufficient and appropriate background to such decisions should be provided for future reference.

It may be important later for the directors to evidence the decisions that they made as well as their reasons for making them. A third party, as in the case of *Commissioners of Customs & Excise v Elm Milk Limited* (2006) may be entitled to have access to the minutes. This case illustrates the importance of keeping proper records.

> ### Case example: *Commissioners of Customs & Excise v Elm Milk Limited* (2006)
>
> Customs & Excise were appealing against a Tribunal decision to prevent Elm Milk Ltd from recovering input tax incurred in the purchase of a motor car, which Elm Milk said was used solely in the course of Elm Milk's business. The Tribunal had allowed Elm Milk's appeal, despite the fact that there were no physical restraints preventing private use of the car, (which was used by a Mr Phillips, the director and sole employee of the company). VAT recovery on the purchase of cars is permitted only where there is 100% business use.
>
> Customs cited the case of *Customs v Upton* (2002), where a sole trader had bought a Lamborghini for use in his business and used it for no other purpose. In that case the Court of Appeal found that nothing had been done to prevent private use by the person and so ruled in favour of HMRC, despite concluding that the taxpayer had no intention of actually using the motor car otherwise than for business. By contrast, the key factor in Elm Milk's success was a board minute noting the company's intention to limit the use of the vehicle to business purposes. If Mr Philips had used the car for non-business related purposes, then it would have been a breach of his terms of employment.

Professional advice

Company directors should always consider the appointment of an external team of professional advisors for support at the start of the life of a company and then refer to additional advisors as and when required – more information about this is given in chapter 18. Whether the company has an existing support framework or not, it is essential that professional help and advice is sought at the earliest signs of insolvency. This should be from an insolvency practitioner and not from the local Citizens' Advice Bureau or Debt Management Bodies as only insolvency practitioners are licensed to offer independent professional advice on business recovery and insolvency. If the company has an accountant or solicitor they should be able to refer the directors to an insolvency practitioner or alternatively, an insolvency practitioner can be found by contacting either:

- the Insolvency Service; or
- R3, the Association of Business Recovery Professionals.

The Insolvency Service is an executive agency of the Department for Business, Innovation and Skills (BIS) that provides a framework and means for dealing with financial failure and dealing with misconduct in the UK economy. R3 (The Association of Business Recovery Professionals) provides information and signposting to insolvency practitioners who are able to advise and work with underperforming and financially distressed businesses and individuals.

An insolvency practitioner will advise the directors on the possible courses of action and navigate the company through the correct path to dissolution or safety. Such intervention often saves directors and the company from disaster further along the line. The majority of insolvency practitioners will not charge a fee for their initial meeting.

■ Order of distribution of assets in a liquidation

The law prescribes set rules that govern the order of distribution of a company's assets in a winding up. These are set out in the Insolvency Act 1986 and the Enterprise Act 2002. The effect of the rules is to place creditors into defined groups and to stipulate the order of priority in which each of the different groups is paid. Each group of creditors must be paid in full before the liquidator or administrator moves on to the next.

The order of distribution

Although there are exceptions, the general position on the order of distribution is as follows.

1 Fixed charge holders who have provided finance secured on a particular asset of the company (such as a mortgage) have priority over all other creditors.
2 The fees of the liquidator must be discharged before all other creditors other than fixed charge holders.
3 Preferential creditors have the first call on the assets after the liquidator fees have been discharged. Preferential creditors are unsecured creditors who are given preferential status under Schedule 6 of the Insolvency Act 1986. This formerly caught taxes owing to HMRC but the Enterprise Act 2002 has relegated HMRC from the list. Debts that fall into this category now include pension contributions, unpaid wages (subject to certain restrictions) and holiday pay.
4 Once all preferential creditors have been paid, any creditors with a floating charge rank next. However before any distribution is made, the Enterprise Act 2002 will usually require a certain proportion of the floating charge assets to be set aside for payment to unsecured creditors.
5 Unsecured creditors are then paid out of any remaining assets and the proportion set aside of any floating charge assets. Unsecured creditors are those who have not secured their debt by way of a fixed or floating charge. Normal

trade debts such as monies owed to the company's suppliers will fall into this category.

6   If there are any residual assets after payment to unsecured creditors they are distributed to the company's shareholders, in accordance with any class rights set out in the articles of association.

Summary

- In general terms, a company is insolvent if it is unable to pay its debts when they fall due or if the value of its liabilities is greater than the value of its assets.

- There are various different insolvency procedures, some are concerned purely with the winding up and closure of a company while others are concerned with business rescue.

- The procedures for winding up a company are a members' voluntary liquidation or a creditors' voluntary liquidation. A members' voluntary liquidation is only possible where a company is solvent. An insolvent company can also be wound up by order of the court and this is known as a compulsory liquidation.

- Business recovery procedures include administration, company voluntary arrangements and pre-pack administrations. Business recovery procedures are not always successful and may ultimately result in a liquidation.

- In an insolvency situation the directors have a duty to minimise losses to creditors. If directors fail to do this, they can be ordered by a court to contribute to the assets of their company in respect of the offence of wrongful trading set out in the Insolvency Act.

- Other liabilities in the Insolvency Act include fraudulent trading and misfeasance. Liquidators also have the power to reverse certain company transactions.

- The insolvency practitioner appointed to a company in any insolvency process is under a duty to report to the Secretary of State on the conduct of the company's directors.

- The insolvency practitioner's report forms the basis for any applications for disqualification of a company's directors under the Company Directors' Disqualification Act 1986.

- Directors must be aware of their responsibilities to their company and ensure that they have a full understanding of its business and have access to regular and timely financial data.

- At the first signs of insolvency, the directors must seek advice from a licensed insolvency practitioner. Any decisions and discussions concerning the continuation or cessation of trading should be recorded.

- The order of distribution of assets in a liquidation is prescribed by the Insolvency Act 1986 and the Enterprise Act 2002. The holders of fixed charges rank first for payment and shareholders rank last.

18 Support frameworks

David Frederick

■ In this chapter

This chapter sets out the main sources of support that a company may need during its lifetime and considers:

- when to seek professional advice and how to choose a professional adviser;
- the services and support that can be provided by a company's two main external advisers – accountants and solicitors;
- other sources of support including a company's bank, chartered secretaries, human resources advisers, insolvency practitioners, public relations advisers, independent financial advisers, tax advisers, patent attorneys, trade mark attorneys and health and safety advisers; and
- resolving conflicts within a company.

References are made throughout this book to the occasions in the life of a company where professional advice is advisable or essential. In the majority of cases, company directors will not be able to establish a business and resolve all the problems they encounter as the business progresses without recourse to some outside help or advice. Indeed, the changing business environment is so dynamic that it is inadvisable for a small company to attempt to start-up and grow without professional support. The primary sources of help for a new company are an accountant, a solicitor and a chartered secretary. However the range of advice that a company might need as it grows extends beyond legal, accounting and financing matters. The commercial environment in the twenty-first century is such that a new company may need a team of professionals at its disposal as it develops to maturity.

■ Seeking professional advice

At a minimum, company directors will need to obtain professional advice at three stages during the life cycle of a company: pre-start-up, start up, and growth. The professional advice and advisers required at each stage will depend upon the company, sector and business needs. Regrettably, too many start-up companies often overlook professional advice at the pre-start-up stage and do not seek advice until after the company has been incorporated. Although this decision may be perfectly fine for some new companies there are many others for whom this may prove to be costly and where an earlier injection of professional advice may have resulted in an alternative course of action being taken, saving money and/or time. Creating different share classes, placing restrictions on share transfers, defining rights to appoint or remove directors and implementing effective tax planning measures are just a few examples of matters that it is often preferable to consider at an early stage. Accordingly, it is advisable that professional advice be sought right at the outset.

Although professional advice can seem expensive, the effective use of professional advisers can generally be measured in terms of:

- the time and costs saved compared to directors carrying out the work (or attempting to carry out the work) themselves;
- access to experience and expertise in the area in question;
- the identification of alternative options that the directors may not have considered or been aware of; and
- the certainty that the right (or most appropriate) course of action is being taken and that the work is being carried out properly.

All of the above applies even more so in relation to situations or procedures that the directors are not familiar with. A technique that new company owners may use to identify their needs is to undertake a self-assessment of their own skills portfolio and match these against the requirements of the company. The resultant skills (and knowledge) gap identified will readily pinpoint the areas where professional advice is required. Alternatively, an assessment of where the company currently stands and where the company wants to go will suggest the type of advice and support that will be needed to facilitate the transition.

Although the needs of one business will differ from those of another, the professional advisers that a company may need at some stage during its life might include:

- accountant
- business relationship manager
- chartered secretary
- human resource adviser
- independent financial adviser
- insolvency practitioner
- public relations adviser
- solicitor
- tax adviser
- patent attorney and/or trade mark attorney
- health and safety adviser/assessor.

Choosing a professional adviser

Selecting a professional adviser should involve the same level of due diligence as any major purchase. As in all areas of life, directors should be mindful of the fact that buying cheap may be expensive in the long term; equally, a high price doesn't necessarily mean better quality. Obtaining a recommendation from a trusted business associate or another professional is a good starting point. An alternative is to identify and approach the professional body of the particular kind of adviser that is being sought. Details of the professional bodies for the categories of advisers identified in this chapter can be found in the directory at the end of the book. All professional bodies will provide access to advisers within a given locality or based upon specified criteria.

Stage two of the search process is to meet the adviser and in this respect many professional advisers offer a free introductory session or meeting. These sessions provide an opportunity to gain some useful advice and also to assess whether the professional adviser is right for the business. As far as possible, it is a good idea to go into these meetings with a clear specification of requirements. Too many disputes or failed relationships between advisers and their clients arise from misunderstandings over what the client is trying to achieve and what the adviser can deliver. Over time, a professional adviser can (and hopefully should) become an integral part of a company's support network therefore it is also important to reflect upon the personality fit with the company and the directors.

■ Accountants

An accountant can assist a company with an understanding of its finances at different stages of the business. At the commencement of the company's business an accountant will be able to help structure the cash-flow forecast and identify any potential financial or cash-flow problems that may be on the horizon. He or she can also provide important practical advice and tips about how to set up effective accounting record, controls and reporting systems. An important question to ask at this stage is whether or not – putting aside the commitment and enthusiasm of the founders – the business is a viable proposition. An accountant will be able to take a rational view and examine the short- and long-term financial prospects of the venture based upon the information presented and an examination of the business projection and environment. The areas an accountant may highlight include:

- the profitability of the venture;
- the sustainability of the profit; and
- benchmarks against which the projected profit can be measured.

In addition, an accountant will be able to provide advice on the accounting and tax-compliance matters for the book-keeping and financial accounts. However, the most effective use (and main role) of an accountant is in relation to ongoing strategic tax planning. This may range from:

- when to convert from a sole trader to a company;
- how to structure the employee-directors' remuneration;
- the acquisition of fixed assets; and
- planning company disposal and valuation.

An accountant is a key adviser in the development of a growth-orientated business and should be engaged in any strategic decision of the company. Such decisions invariably impact upon the company's short- and long-term finances.

It is important to note that unlike 'solicitor' the term 'accountant' is generic and has no legal protection in the UK. This means that anyone can call themselves an accountant whether or not they possess any recognised qualifications. As such, it is advisable to find an accountant who is qualified with one of the UK regulatory bodies. The two most common qualifications found in the UK are with the Institute of Chartered Accountants in England & Wales (ICAEW) and the Association of Chartered Certified Accountants (ACCA). The members of the ICAEW have the letters ACA or FCA after their name to denote member or fellow member. Similarly the members and fellow members of the ACCA have the letters ACCA or FCCA after their name, with the same meanings. These professional bodies can assist in locating a qualified accountant but, as mentioned earlier, it is also worth seeking a recommendation from a business associate or another professional adviser, such as a solicitor.

Solicitors

Just as it is important to take advice from an accountant at the start of a new business venture, so it is also a good idea to involve a solicitor. Companies and their directors are subject to a wide array of laws and regulations and a solicitor can help not only to ensure that they stay within the law but can also advise on how to operate within the legal restraints to the company's best advantage. In terms of a new start up, a solicitor can provide help and advice with regard to:

- choosing a company name;
- incorporating a new company;
- deciding the appropriate capital structure;
- drafting the articles of association;
- negotiating and drafting a shareholders' agreement;
- writing up the company's statutory books and other records;
- preparing directors' service contracts; and
- advising on any industry-specific, sector-specific and other regulations applicable to the new business.

A chartered secretary with the right experience and knowledge can also help with most, if not all, of these matters as well. As a company grows and develops the services of a solicitor might be required in relation to (among others) any of the following:

- advising on intellectual property matters;
- providing advice and assistance on equity or debt financing;
- strategy and tax-planning;
- allotting new shares and/or creating new classes of shares;
- drafting standard terms and conditions;
- negotiating contract terms for one-off transactions or arrangements;
- disputes between directors and/or shareholders;
- insolvency matters, either in relation to the company or other companies of which the company is a creditor;
- the acquisition of another business or part of a business;
- preparing the company for a sale;
- streamlining a group structure and closing down un-needed dormant subsidiary companies;
- administrative and company secretarial type services such as writing up statutory books and other records, changes of company name, preparation of documentation for directors' and shareholders' decision-making, preparation and filing of documents with the Registrar of Companies;
- advising on share buy backs, reductions of capital and other reorganisations of share capital;
- employment and human-resources related matters;
- property related matters; and
- health and safety, data protection, consumer credit, environmental law and any other regulatory issues.

As with an accountant, a solicitor can become a key support to a company so it is time well spent for the directors to find someone with whom they have a rapport and are happy to work. The value of a good and long-standing relationship is that the solicitor will come to know the business and the directors and understand their personalities and objectives. Having such an adviser on hand to give advice when it is needed, even if it just requires a ten-minute phone call, can be a great benefit.

It is unlikely that a single solicitor will have expertise in all of the areas listed above and indeed a solicitor who claimed to do so should be approached with caution. Firms of solicitors range from small one or two partner 'high street' set-ups to large national and multinational organisations. Individual solicitors specialise in particular areas of the law, so for example a 'corporate finance' solicitor will have expertise in (among others) company financing, acquisitions and disposals, company formations, capital structures, management buy-outs (and buy-ins), shareholders agreements and articles of association. For matters relating to contracts and other agreements, a solicitor with expertise in commercial law would be recommended, for intellectual property matters an intellectual property lawyer, and so on.

As a general rule, the larger law firms tend to cater more for commercial clients than non-commercial and have teams made up of solicitors with expertise in the many distinct but related areas that come under the umbrella of 'business law'. Dealing with any given transaction, issue or project may require input from a number of different solicitors within the same firm, each with their own areas of expertise. Smaller firms tend to focus more on the domestic areas of law such as wills and probate, family law, personal injury and so on but may also undertake corporate work. It is likely that the fees charged by a high street firm in a small town will be lower than those charged by a national law firm with offices in a city centre. While costs are an important consideration it is also important to make sure that the firm or solicitor in question has the necessary skills, knowledge and experience in the relevant areas of the law.

Solicitors are subject to regulation by the Solicitors' Regulation Authority and a directory of regulated firms can be searched on the Law Society website. However, just as it is with choosing an accountant, a recommendation from a trusted source is a good place to start.

Other forms of help and advice

In addition to accountants and solicitors, other sources of help, support and advice for a company include the following.

Business relationship manager

As banks have developed their services over the past several decades the business relationship manager has replaced the traditional bank manager. A business relationship manager will be responsible for monitoring the business transactions flowing into and out of a company's bank account on a daily basis. In addition to being custodian of the company's funds a business relationship manager can provide the company with access to a range of additional resources and tools to support its credit management. These services can range from card processing machines to a range of credit management software. Providing periodic reviews of the company's cash flow and management accounts will give the business relationship manager a broader understanding of the business and its short- and long-term credit requirements. Furthermore, this will enable him or her to sign-post the company to the bank's network of other business support personnel.

Chartered secretary

Although private companies are no longer required to appoint a company secretary, the tasks and responsibilities that would normally come within the remit of a company secretary still remain. These tasks and responsibilities are described in Chapter 6 which also highlights the importance of ensuring that, should a company decide not to appoint a secretary (which will be the case for many small start-ups), they are allocated to someone else. This could be a director, someone within senior management or an employee with relevant experience and knowledge. Alternatively, it is not unusual for smaller companies to outsource the company secretarial function to a firm of solicitors, chartered secretaries or accountants, a formation agent or other service provider. The term 'chartered secretary' refers to someone who is qualified under the qualifying scheme of the Institute of Company Secretaries and Administrators (ICSA), is admitted as an associate or fellow of the Institute and who has a wealth of practical experience on how to address the complexities of corporate law and governance requirements. Many chartered secretaries work independently or within the larger company secretarial practices, law firms, accountancy practices and other independent corporate services providers.

Human resources adviser

The expansion of employment legislation and its increasing complexity and rate of change warrants any company with employees having direct access to a human resource adviser (HR). A HR adviser will be responsible for ensuring the company directors are kept abreast of the correct methods of conduct in relation to employment matters from recruitment to retirement. A HR adviser would seek to ensure that the company has all the necessary operational policies regarding employees and that these are kept up to date. In addition, a HR adviser would continually keep directors aware of changes in employment law and address such issues as employment contracts, family-friendly policies, statutory maternity pay, statutory sick pay, recruitment and retirement policies.

Insolvency practitioner

As mentioned in Chapter 17, any company encountering financial difficulties should take advice from a licensed Insolvency Practitioner (IP) without delay. Early intervention by an IP may enable a company to overcome the difficulties it is experiencing or otherwise ease the transition into company closure without the risk of the directors breaching the laws of insolvency.

Public relations adviser

A company will always need to safeguard and manage its reputation in the marketplace, especially in the age of social media and this is where a public relations (PR) adviser can add value to a company. A PR adviser will be able to optimise a company's use of all forms of media and communication in order to build, maintain and manage the company's reputation. Areas of activity that a PR adviser may undertake for a company include:

- planning, developing and implementing PR strategies;
- liaising with the media, individuals and other organisations; and
- collating and analysing media coverage.

Overall, a PR adviser would seek to develop and maintain effective relationships with a company's stakeholders.

Independent financial adviser

A company will usually engage the services of an independent financial adviser (IFA) to gain specialist knowledge on how to use any cash resources that the company may have and to obtain advice on particular financial products or services such as pensions. An IFA would undertake research into the market then advise the company on the products and services available to address their requirements. Some IFAs may specialise in particular areas such as pensions or commercial mortgages. An IFA will work alongside and often in collaboration with a company's accountant to ensure the company's financial well-being is fully addressed.

Tax advisers

Although a company might typically look to an accountant to provide tax advice, the directors might choose to appoint a chartered tax adviser (CTA) as well. A CTA can provide a company with advice on all aspects of its tax affairs from incorporation to acquisition and merger, and closure. Along with an accountant, a CTA will be able to help a company to develop and implement the most tax-efficient strategies. Furthermore, a CTA is an effective ally for any company that encounters taxation disputes with HMRC.

Patent and trade mark attorneys

In recent years, intellectual property has become a growth resource within companies and so it is important for companies to protect and make the most of their intellectual property. A patent attorney is a qualified professional who can provide specialist advice in relation to drafting patents and who is also trained in the other areas of intellectual property law namely design rights, copyright and trade marks.

A patent attorney can assist a company in protecting its intellectual property by the appropriate means of registration. They can also provide advice on seeking redress from third parties who infringe a company's intellectual property rights. 'Patent attorney' is a protected term and it is an offence for a person to call themselves a patent attorney unless their name is entered on the official Register of Patent Attorneys. The register can be searched on the website of the Chartered Institute of Patent Attorneys.

Trade mark attorneys are specialists in the area of trade marks. Among others, trade mark attorneys provide advice and assistance in relation to:

- the registration of trademarks;
- licensing agreements for the use of trademarks by others; and
- actions to prevent unauthorised use of a trademark.

It should be noted that use of the term 'trademark attorney' is not protected in law. Protection is only given to the term 'Registered Trade Mark Attorney' as this denotes a qualified trademark attorney whose name is entered on the official

Register of Trade Mark Attorneys. This register can be searched on the website of the Institute of Trade Mark Attorneys.

Health and safety adviser/assessor
As explained in Chapter 16, all employers are required to appoint a 'competent person' to assist them in complying with their duties and obligations under health and safety law. If this role cannot be fulfilled by someone inside the employer's organisation it must be outsourced to an external health and safety adviser.

Conflict resolution

A particular situation where a company may need help and advice is in relation to internal disputes. Disputes between owner-managers (and owners and managers) are not uncommon. They can arise for any number of reasons but could be as a result of issues relating to:

- financial policy and the level of dividends;
- remuneration;
- disagreements over strategy and objectives;
- exclusion from management or decision-making; and
- diversion of business opportunities away from the company.

Whatever the cause, such disputes hinder the operation of a company, adversely affect its value and damage its relationship with its lenders, investors and others. It is important therefore to try and resolve them as soon as they become apparent.

Resolving conflict situations
The last resort in a situation where a conflict cannot be resolved is either court action (where the outcome will be uncertain for all involved) or for the company to be wound up (where the value of the company as a going concern is lost). Therefore, before any drastic action is taken, mediation should be considered as the first option. A solicitor or other professional can help with this and put the parties in contact with an independent mediator who will help them to try to come to a compromise and a resolution. If successful, a settlement agreement will be drawn up which, once it has been signed, forms a contract binding on the parties.

Preventing conflicts
Rather than waiting for a dispute to arise before taking action to resolve it, it may be preferable to try and minimise the chance of it occurring in the first place. Like any relationship, a business relationship requires clear and open communication between the parties. In an ideal scenario, owner-managers should establish at the outset of a new venture what their aims and objectives for the business are and then try to iron out any differences. If owner-managers do not do this and are

not aware of each-other's expectations, it is more likely that conflicts will arise at some point in the future. As mentioned in Chapter 3, a solicitor will always recommend a shareholders' agreement as an effective means of both preventing and resolving conflicts on a wide range of issues. Engaging the services of a solicitor or other professional to help in identifying areas which have the potential to cause conflict, negotiating a way forward and then regulating these areas in a shareholders agreement can help to prevent problems and difficulties later on.

Summary

- In most cases directors will not be able to establish a new business without professional help and advice. This should be sought at the outset.
- The benefits of using external advisers can be measured in terms of time and costs savings. The experience and knowledge of a professional adviser will often enable them to cut through a problem quickly or suggest a more appropriate or suitable course of action.
- Choosing an adviser should be approached with the same degree of care and due diligence as any other procurement process. Most professionals have their own representative bodies which can help in locating their members. Recommendations from others are another good starting point.
- Costs are a significant factor but engaging the services of a professional should (ideally) be the start of a long-standing relationship so personality fit is also important.
- The three main sources of advice in starting a new venture are an accountant, a solicitor and a chartered secretary.
- Other professionals that a company may need to refer to during its lifetime include trademark attorneys, patent attorneys, insolvency practitioners and independent financial advisers.
- Conflicts within a company can occur for any number of reasons. Before more drastic action is taken, mediation should always be considered as a first option.
- A shareholders' agreement can help both in preventing and dealing with conflicts. However, it is crucial that such an agreement is entered into at the beginning of a new venture.

Appendix 1: Summary of the main differences between private companies and public companies

Private limited company	Public limited company
Must have a name ending in the word 'limited' or 'ltd' (or the Welsh equivalents)	Must have a name ending in 'public limited company' or 'plc' (or the Welsh equivalents)
Cannot offer its shares for sale to the public	Can, subject to detailed requirements, make general invitations to the public to buy its shares
Can be incorporated with one director	Must have at least two directors
Does not have to appoint a company secretary (unless required to do so by the articles)	Must have a company secretary who is qualified in one of the ways set out in the Companies Act and who appears to the directors to have the requisite knowledge and experience to fulfil that role
Has no minimum share capital requirement and can begin trading as soon as the company has been incorporated	Cannot start trading until the company has issued shares with an aggregate nominal value of £50,000 (or the equivalent in euros) of which 25% has been paid up in full together with the whole of any premium, and has obtained a trading certificate from Companies House
Has nine months from the end of the financial year in which to file accounts at Companies House	Must file accounts within six months of the end of the financial year
Is not subject to any obligation to hold an annual general meeting (unless required to do so by the company's articles)	Must hold an annual general meeting within six months of the financial year end
Directors can resolve not to appoint an auditor if they reasonably believe that audited accounts will not be required	Must appoint an eligible auditor (as defined by the Companies Act)
Can file abbreviated accounts at Companies House if certain criteria are met	May not file abbreviated accounts
Do not need to lay their accounts before members in a general meeting	Must present their accounts to members in a general meeting
Can propose shareholder resolutions by way of a resolution in writing	Can only propose shareholder resolutions in a general meeting

Appendix 2: Matters dealt with by the articles and matters dealt with by the Companies Act (a non-exhaustive list)

Description	Articles or Companies Act	Reference
A company's objects	The Companies Act provides that unless restricted by the articles, a company's objects are unrestricted.	Section 31(1).
Appointing a director	There are no provisions in the Companies Act that set out a procedure for the appointment of a director so this must be dealt with in the articles.	Article 17 of the Model Articles.
Authorisation of a director's situational conflict of interest	Directors of companies formed under the current Companies Act are able to authorise their situational conflicts of interest unless such an authorisation would be invalidated by the company's constitution.	Section 175(5)(a).
Directors' authority to allot shares	An authority for the directors to allot shares can be included in the articles. Otherwise authority is given by ordinary resolution of the shareholders. In either case the authority must comply with the requirements of s. 551 of the Companies Act. The directors of a company with one class of shares have unlimited authority to allot shares of that class under s.550 of the Act except to the extent that they are prohibited from doing so by the articles.	Section 550 and section 551.
Notice required of a general meeting	The Act requires 14 clear days' notice of a general meeting unless the articles specify a longer period.	Section 307(3).
Power of a company to allot redeemable shares	This is set out in the Act and will apply unless excluded or restricted by the articles.	Section 684(1) and 684(2).
Power of a company to subdivide or consolidate its shares	These powers are also set out in the Act and will apply unless excluded or restricted by the articles.	Section 618.

Description	Articles or Companies Act	Reference
Quorum for a general meeting	The Act states that two qualifying persons are a quorum provided that they are not a proxy for the same member or are not corporate representatives of the same corporate member. This number can be increased by the articles. If the articles are silent the Act will apply.	Section 318(2).
Quorum for a general meeting: single member company	The Act states that one qualifying person is a quorum. This is not subject to the articles.	Section 318(1).
Removing a director.	The Companies Act sets out a procedure for the removal of a director by ordinary resolution of a company's shareholders. This cannot be excluded or varied by the articles.	Section 168.
	The articles may include provisions for automatic termination (e.g. on bankruptcy) and additional provisions for removal (e.g. by notice in writing from a majority shareholder).	Article 18 of the Model Articles.
Rules on directors' decision-making	There are no procedural rules for directors' decision-making in the Companies Act, so these must be set out in the articles (although articles generally only specify minimum requirements while allowing directors to formulate their own rules and procedures). There are, however, rules in the Act that apply in relation to the disclosure of interests in transactions and the exercise by the directors of the power to authorise another director's conflict of interest.	Sections 175, 177 and 182. Articles 7–16 of the Model Articles.
Shareholders rights of pre-emption on share transfers	There are no rights of this kind in the Companies Act. Any pre-emption rights on share transfers must be set out in the articles. There are no such provisions in the Model Articles.	Not applicable.
Shareholders' written resolutions	The rules on shareholders' written resolutions are set out in the Companies Act. Two aspects can be altered by a company's articles which are the percentage of shareholders who can requisition the circulation of a written resolution (s. 292) and the period of time after which a written resolution will lapse if not passed (s. 297).	Sections 288–300.
Variation of class rights	The Companies Act sets out a procedure for variation of class rights which will apply in the absence of any provisions in the articles.	Section 630.
Voting rights attaching to shares	The default position under the Companies Act is that shareholders have one vote on a show of hands and one vote per share on a poll and on a written resolution. This is subject to any contrary provisions in the articles.	Section 284.

Appendix 3: Events that trigger an obligation to file information with the Registrar and corresponding filing requirement (non-exhaustive)

Event	What has to be filed	Time limit
Changes to company officers		
Appointment of a director	Form AP01	14 days
Appointment of a corporate director	Form AP02	14 days
Appointment of a secretary	Form AP03	14 days
Appointment of a corporate secretary	Form AP04	14 days
Change of details of a director	Form CH01	14 days
Change of details of a corporate director	Form CH02	14 days
Change of details of a secretary	Form CH03	14 days
Change of details of a corporate secretary	Form CH04	14 days
Termination of appointment of a director	Form TM01	14 days
Termination of appointment of a secretary	Form TM02	14 days
Accounts		
Change of accounting reference date	Form AA01	An accounting period cannot be altered once the accounts for that period are overdue.
Registered office and SAIL		
Change of registered office address	Form AD01	Does not have legal effect until registered.
Notification of a single alternative inspection location	Form AD02	14 days
Relocation of company records from the registered office to the SAIL	Form AD03	14 days
Relocation of company records from the SAIL to the registered office	Form AD04	14 days

Event	What has to be filed	Time limit
Change of company name		
Change of name by shareholder resolution	Form NM01 Special resolution Fee	Does not have legal effect until registered
Change of name by shareholder resolution where approval of a government department or other body is required	Forms NM01 and NM06 Special resolution Fee	Does not have legal effect until registered
Shares and share capital		
Grant of authority to directors to allot shares	Ordinary resolution	15 days
Renewal, variation or revocation of directors' authority to allot shares	Ordinary resolution	15 days
Allotment of new shares	Form SH01	1 month from the date of allotment
Consolidation of shares **or** redemption of shares **or** subdivision of shares **or** reconversion of shares into stock	Form SH02	1 month
Purchase by a company of its own shares	Form SH03 (stamped by HMRC) Form SH06 (notice of cancellation of shares)	Within 28 days of the shares being delivered to the company
Constitutional changes		
Alteration to the articles of association	Special resolution Copy of the new or amended articles	15 days
Addition to, removal of or alteration to a company's objects	Form CC04	Not legally effective until registered
Correcting information on the public record		
Application for removal of information from the public record by the Registrar of Companies	RP02A	Can only be used in respect of information filed on or after 1 October 2009

continued overleaf

Event	What has to be filed	Time limit
Second filing of a form previously filed which contained inaccuracies	RP04 Amended form	Can only be used in respect of information filed on or after 1 October 2009
PROOF		
Filing information using a paper form where the information is subject to PROOF	Applicable form Form PR03	As per form type being filed
Annual filing requirements		
Accounts	Report and accounts meeting the requirements of the Companies Act, as determined by the size of the company	Within nine months of the accounting year end
Standard form dormant accounts (only suitable for companies which have never traded and where the only transaction entered into the company's accounting records is the issue of subscriber shares)	Form AA02	Within nine months of the accounting year end
Annual return	Form AR01 Fee	Within the period of 28 days after the made-up date

Appendix 4: Statutory registers

Register of directors

Name _____   Nationality _____
Former names_____   Date of birth _____
Service address _____   Business occupation _____
_____   Country/state of residence _____
_____
_____

Appointment   Termination
Dated _____   Dated _____
Filed _____   Filed _____
Minute _____   Minute _____

Register of directors' residential addresses

Name _____
Former names_____
Residential address_____
_____
_____
_____

Appointment   Termination
Dated _____   Dated _____

Register of secretaries

Name _____
Former names_____
Service address _____
_____
_____
_____

Appointment   Termination
Dated _____   Dated _____
Filed _____   Filed _____
Minute _____   Minute _____

Register of members

Name _____

Address _____

Class of shares _____

Date of entry as member _____

Date of cessation of membership _____

Date of entry	Entry number		Certificate number	Number of shares			Price per share	Total amount paid or agreed to be considered as paid	Notes
	Allotment	Transfer		Acquired	Disposed	Balance			

Register of charges

Mortgage or charge number	Date of mortgage or charge	Date of registration	Date of release	Description of mortgage or charge	Person(s) entitled to charge	Amount secured	Interest rate	Property charged

Appendix 5: Non-statutory registers

Register of allotments

Class of shares:

Name and address	Allotment number	Date		Number of shares		Certificate number	Price per share	Amount paid	Folio no.	Notes
		Application	Allotment	Applied for	Allotted					

Register of transfers

Class of shares:

Transfer number	Transfer date	Transferor		Transferee		Shares Transferred	Price per share	Total amount paid
		Name and address	Certificate	Name and address	Certificate			

Appendix 6: Completing a stock transfer form

(Above this line for registrars only)	
The consideration for the transfer. Consideration money £.............................	Certificate lodged with the Registrar (For completion by the Registrar/Stock Exchange)

Name of undertaking	*The name of the company in which the shares are held.*
Description of security	*The class and nominal value of the shares.*

Number or amount of shares, stock or other security and, in figures column only, number and denomination of units, if any	Words *The number of shares being transferred in words.*	Figures *The number and the nominal value of the shares being transferred in figures.*

Name(s) of registered holder(s) should be given in full: the address should be given where there is only one holder. If the transfer is not made by the registered holder(s) insert also the name(s) and capacity (e.g. Executor(s)) of the person(s) making the transfer.	In the name(s) of *The name and address of the current holder of the shares being transferred (the transferor). In the case of a joint holding, the names of all joint holders must be given.*

I/We hereby transfer the above security out of the name(s) aforesaid to the person(s) named below Signature(s) of transferor(s) *The person transferring the shares (transferor) signs in this box. If the shares are held jointly, each joint holder must sign.*	Stamp of selling Broker(s) or, for transactions which are not stock exchange transactions, of Agent(s), if any, acting for the Transferor(s) *The date on which the transferor signs the form* Date_____

Full name(s), full postal address(es) (including county or, if applicable, Postal District number) of the person(s) to whom the security is transferred. Please state title, if any, or whether Mr,. Mrs or, Miss. Please complete in type or in Block Capitals.	*The name and address of the person(s) that the shares are being transferred to (the transferee(s)).*

I/We request that such entries be made in the register as are necessary to give effect to this transfer	
Stamp of buying broker(s) (if any)	Stamp or name and address of person lodging this form (if other than the buying broker(s))
For use by brokers.	*Name and address of person lodging form with the company.*

Appendix 7: Example notices to the Registrar of Companies in respect of the passing of a shareholder resolution (i) as a written resolution and (ii) at a general meeting

---

Company number: ....

THE COMPANIES ACT 2006

PRIVATE COMPANY LIMITED BY SHARES

WRITTEN RESOLUTION

– of –

.... LIMITED

Pursuant to Chapter 2 of Part 13 of the Companies Act 2006, the following resolution was passed by the members of the company as an ordinary/special resolution on............................ .

ORDINARY/SPECIAL RESOLUTION

THAT...

....

Director

Company number: ....

THE COMPANIES ACT 2006

PRIVATE COMPANY LIMITED BY SHARES

ORDINARY/SPECIAL RESOLUTION

– of –

.... LIMITED

At a general meeting of the company duly convened and held at .... on..........................
the following resolution was passed by the members of the company as an ordinary/special resolution.

ORDINARY/SPECIAL RESOLUTION

THAT...

....

Director

Appendix 8: Model articles for private companies limited by shares

PART 1 INTERPRETATION AND LIMITATION OF LIABILITY

Defined terms

1. In the articles, unless the context requires otherwise—

'articles' means the company's articles of association;

'bankruptcy' includes individual insolvency proceedings in a jurisdiction other than England and Wales or Northern Ireland which have an effect similar to that of bankruptcy;

'chairman' has the meaning given in article 12;

'chairman of the meeting' has the meaning given in article 39;

'Companies Acts' means the Companies Acts (as defined in section 2 of the Companies Act 2006), in so far as they apply to the company;

'director' means a director of the company, and includes any person occupying the position of director, by whatever name called;

'distribution recipient' has the meaning given in article 31;

'document' includes, unless otherwise specified, any document sent or supplied in electronic form;

'electronic form' has the meaning given in section 1168 of the Companies Act 2006;

'fully paid' in relation to a share, means that the nominal value and any premium to be paid to the company in respect of that share have been paid to the company;

'hard copy form' has the meaning given in section 1168 of the Companies Act 2006;

'holder' in relation to shares means the person whose name is entered in the register of members as the holder of the shares;

'instrument' means a document in hard copy form;

'ordinary resolution' has the meaning given in section 282 of the Companies Act 2006;

'paid' means paid or credited as paid;

'participate', in relation to a directors' meeting, has the meaning given in article 10;

'proxy notice' has the meaning given in article 45;

'shareholder' means a person who is the holder of a share;

'shares' means shares in the company;

'special resolution' has the meaning given in section 283 of the Companies Act 2006;

'subsidiary' has the meaning given in section 1159 of the Companies Act 2006;

'transmittee' means a person entitled to a share by reason of the death or bankruptcy of a shareholder or otherwise by operation of law; and

'writing' means the representation or reproduction of words, symbols or other information in a visible form by any method or combination of methods, whether sent or supplied in electronic form or otherwise.

Unless the context otherwise requires, other words or expressions contained in these articles bear the same meaning as in the Companies Act 2006 as in force on the date when these articles become binding on the company.

Liability of members

2. The liability of the members is limited to the amount, if any, unpaid on the shares held by them.

PART 2 DIRECTORS
DIRECTORS' POWERS AND RESPONSIBILITIES

Directors' general authority

3. Subject to the articles, the directors are responsible for the management of the company's business, for which purpose they may exercise all the powers of the company.

Shareholders' reserve power

4.—(1) The shareholders may, by special resolution, direct the directors to take, or refrain from taking, specified action.

(2) No such special resolution invalidates anything which the directors have done before the passing of the resolution.

Directors may delegate

5.—(1) Subject to the articles, the directors may delegate any of the powers which are conferred on them under the articles—

(a) to such person or committee;

(b) by such means (including by power of attorney);

(c) to such an extent;

(d) in relation to such matters or territories; and

(e) on such terms and conditions

as they think fit.

(2) If the directors so specify, any such delegation may authorise further delegation of the directors' powers by any person to whom they are delegated.

(3) The directors may revoke any delegation in whole or part, or alter its terms and conditions.

Committees

6.—(1) Committees to which the directors delegate any of their powers must follow procedures which are based as far as they are applicable on those provisions of the articles which govern the taking of decisions by directors.

(2) The directors may make rules of procedure for all or any committees, which prevail over rules derived from the articles if they are not consistent with them.

DECISION-MAKING BY DIRECTORS

Directors to take decisions collectively

7.—(1) The general rule about decision-making by directors is that any decision of the directors must be either a majority decision at a meeting or a decision taken in accordance with article 8.

(2) If—

(a) the company only has one director, and

(b) no provision of the articles requires it to have more than one director,

the general rule does not apply, and the director may take decisions without regard to any of the provisions of the articles relating to directors' decision-making.

Unanimous decisions

8.—(1) A decision of the directors is taken in accordance with this article when all eligible directors indicate to each other by any means that they share a common view on a matter.

(2) Such a decision may take the form of a resolution in writing, copies of which have been signed by each eligible director or to which each eligible director has otherwise indicated agreement in writing.

(3) References in this article to eligible directors are to directors who would have been entitled to vote on the matter had it been proposed as a resolution at a directors' meeting.

(4) A decision may not be taken in accordance with this article if the eligible directors would not have formed a quorum at such a meeting.

Calling a directors' meeting

9.—(1) Any director may call a directors' meeting by giving notice of the meeting to the directors or by authorising the company secretary (if any) to give such notice.

(2) Notice of any directors' meeting must indicate—

(a) its proposed date and time;

(b) where it is to take place; and

(c) if it is anticipated that directors participating in the meeting will not be in the same place, how it is proposed that they should communicate with each other during the meeting.

(3) Notice of a directors' meeting must be given to each director, but need not be in writing.

(4) Notice of a directors' meeting need not be given to directors who waive their entitlement to notice of that meeting, by giving notice to that effect to the company not more than 7 days after the date on which the meeting is held. Where such notice is given after the meeting has been held, that does not affect the validity of the meeting, or of any business conducted at it.

Participation in directors' meetings

10.—(1) Subject to the articles, directors participate in a directors' meeting, or part of a directors' meeting, when—

(a) the meeting has been called and takes place in accordance with the articles, and

(b) they can each communicate to the others any information or opinions they have on any particular item of the business of the meeting.

(2) In determining whether directors are participating in a directors' meeting, it is irrelevant where any director is or how they communicate with each other.

(3) If all the directors participating in a meeting are not in the same place, they may decide that the meeting is to be treated as taking place wherever any of them is.

Quorum for directors' meetings

11.—(1) At a directors' meeting, unless a quorum is participating, no proposal is to be voted on, except a proposal to call another meeting.

(2) The quorum for directors' meetings may be fixed from time to time by a decision of the directors, but it must never be less than two, and unless otherwise fixed it is two.

(3) If the total number of directors for the time being is less than the quorum required, the directors must not take any decision other than a decision—

(a) to appoint further directors, or

(b) to call a general meeting so as to enable the shareholders to appoint further directors.

Chairing of directors' meetings

12.—(1) The directors may appoint a director to chair their meetings.

(2) The person so appointed for the time being is known as the chairman.

(3) The directors may terminate the chairman's appointment at any time.

(4) If the chairman is not participating in a directors' meeting within ten minutes of the time at which it was to start, the participating directors must appoint one of themselves to chair it.

Casting vote

13.—(1) If the numbers of votes for and against a proposal are equal, the chairman or other director chairing the meeting has a casting vote.

(2) But this does not apply if, in accordance with the articles, the chairman or other director is not to be counted as participating in the decision-making process for quorum or voting purposes.

Conflicts of interest

14.—(1) If a proposed decision of the directors is concerned with an actual or proposed transaction or arrangement with the company in which a director is interested, that director is not to be counted as participating in the decision-making process for quorum or voting purposes.

(2) But if paragraph (3) applies, a director who is interested in an actual or proposed transaction or arrangement with the company is to be counted as participating in the decision-making process for quorum and voting purposes.

(3) This paragraph applies when—

(a) the company by ordinary resolution disapplies the provision of the articles which would otherwise prevent a director from being counted as participating in the decision-making process;

(b) the director's interest cannot reasonably be regarded as likely to give rise to a conflict of interest; or

(c) the director's conflict of interest arises from a permitted cause.

(4) For the purposes of this article, the following are permitted causes—

(a) a guarantee given, or to be given, by or to a director in respect of an obligation incurred by or on behalf of the company or any of its subsidiaries;

(b) subscription, or an agreement to subscribe, for shares or other securities of the company or any of its subsidiaries, or to underwrite, sub-underwrite, or guarantee subscription for any such shares or securities; and

(c) arrangements pursuant to which benefits are made available to employees and directors or former employees and directors of the company or any of its subsidiaries which do not provide special benefits for directors or former directors.

(5) For the purposes of this article, references to proposed decisions and decision-making processes include any directors' meeting or part of a directors' meeting.

(6) Subject to paragraph (7), if a question arises at a meeting of directors or of a committee of directors as to the right of a director to participate in the meeting (or part of the meeting) for voting or quorum purposes, the question may, before the conclusion of the meeting, be referred to the chairman whose ruling in relation to any director other than the chairman is to be final and conclusive.

(7) If any question as to the right to participate in the meeting (or part of the meeting) should arise in respect of the chairman, the question is to be decided by a decision of the directors at that meeting, for which purpose the chairman is not to be counted as participating in the meeting (or that part of the meeting) for voting or quorum purposes.

Records of decisions to be kept

15. The directors must ensure that the company keeps a record, in writing, for at least 10 years from the date of the decision recorded, of every unanimous or majority decision taken by the directors.

Directors' discretion to make further rules

16. Subject to the articles, the directors may make any rule which they think fit about how they take decisions, and about how such rules are to be recorded or communicated to directors.

APPOINTMENT OF DIRECTORS

Methods of appointing directors

17.—(1) Any person who is willing to act as a director, and is permitted by law to do so, may be appointed to be a director—

(a) by ordinary resolution, or

(b) by a decision of the directors.

(2) In any case where, as a result of death, the company has no shareholders and no directors, the personal representatives of the last shareholder to have died have the right, by notice in writing, to appoint a person to be a director.

(3) For the purposes of paragraph (2), where 2 or more shareholders die in circumstances rendering it uncertain who was the last to die, a younger shareholder is deemed to have survived an older shareholder.

Termination of director's appointment

18. A person ceases to be a director as soon as—

(a) that person ceases to be a director by virtue of any provision of the Companies Act 2006 or is prohibited from being a director by law;

(b) a bankruptcy order is made against that person;

(c) a composition is made with that person's creditors generally in satisfaction of that person's debts;

(d) a registered medical practitioner who is treating that person gives a written opinion to the company stating that that person has become physically or mentally incapable of acting as a director and may remain so for more than three months;

(e) by reason of that person's mental health, a court makes an order which wholly or partly prevents that person from personally exercising any powers or rights which that person would otherwise have;[1]

(f) notification is received by the company from the director that the director is resigning from office, and such resignation has taken effect in accordance with its terms.

Directors' remuneration

19.—(1) Directors may undertake any services for the company that the directors decide.

(2) Directors are entitled to such remuneration as the directors determine—

for their services to the company as directors, and

for any other service which they undertake for the company.

(3) Subject to the articles, a director's remuneration may—

(a) take any form, and

(b) include any arrangements in connection with the payment of a pension, allowance or gratuity, or any death, sickness or disability benefits, to or in respect of that director.

(4) Unless the directors decide otherwise, directors' remuneration accrues from day to day.

(5) Unless the directors decide otherwise, directors are not accountable to the company for any remuneration which they receive as directors or other officers or employees of the company's subsidiaries or of any other body corporate in which the company is interested.

Directors' expenses

20. The company may pay any reasonable expenses which the directors properly incur in connection with their attendance at—

(a) meetings of directors or committees of directors,

(b) general meetings, or

(c) separate meetings of the holders of any class of shares or of debentures of the company, or otherwise in connection with the exercise of their powers and the discharge of their responsibilities in relation to the company.

---

[1] Removed by the Mental Health (Discrimination) Act 2013 – see Chapters 3 and 6.

PART 3 SHARES AND DISTRIBUTIONS
SHARES
All shares to be fully paid up
21.—(1) No share is to be issued for less than the aggregate of its nominal value and any premium to be paid to the company in consideration for its issue.

(2) This does not apply to shares taken on the formation of the company by the subscribers to the company's memorandum.

Powers to issue different classes of share
22.—(1) Subject to the articles, but without prejudice to the rights attached to any existing share, the company may issue shares with such rights or restrictions as may be determined by ordinary resolution.

(2) The company may issue shares which are to be redeemed, or are liable to be redeemed at the option of the company or the holder, and the directors may determine the terms, conditions and manner of redemption of any such shares.

Company not bound by less than absolute interests
23. Except as required by law, no person is to be recognised by the company as holding any share upon any trust, and except as otherwise required by law or the articles, the company is not in any way to be bound by or recognise any interest in a share other than the holder's absolute ownership of it and all the rights attaching to it.

Share certificates
24.—(1) The company must issue each shareholder, free of charge, with one or more certificates in respect of the shares which that shareholder holds.

(2) Every certificate must specify—

(a) in respect of how many shares, of what class, it is issued;

(b) the nominal value of those shares;

(c) that the shares are fully paid; and

(d) any distinguishing numbers assigned to them.

(3) No certificate may be issued in respect of shares of more than one class.

(4) If more than one person holds a share, only one certificate may be issued in respect of it.

(5) Certificates must—

have affixed to them the company's common seal, or

be otherwise executed in accordance with the Companies Acts.

Replacement share certificates
25.—(1) If a certificate issued in respect of a shareholder's shares is—

(a) damaged or defaced, or

(b) said to be lost, stolen or destroyed,

(c) that shareholder is entitled to be issued with a replacement certificate in respect of the same shares.

(2) A shareholder exercising the right to be issued with such a replacement certificate—

(a) may at the same time exercise the right to be issued with a single certificate or separate certificates;

(b) must return the certificate which is to be replaced to the company if it is damaged or defaced; and

(c) must comply with such conditions as to evidence, indemnity and the payment of a reasonable fee as the directors decide.

Share transfers

26.—(1) Shares may be transferred by means of an instrument of transfer in any usual form or any other form approved by the directors, which is executed by or on behalf of the transferor.

(2) No fee may be charged for registering any instrument of transfer or other document relating to or affecting the title to any share.

(3) The company may retain any instrument of transfer which is registered.

(4) The transferor remains the holder of a share until the transferee's name is entered in the register of members as holder of it.

(5) The directors may refuse to register the transfer of a share, and if they do so, the instrument of transfer must be returned to the transferee with the notice of refusal unless they suspect that the proposed transfer may be fraudulent.

Transmission of shares

27.—(1) If title to a share passes to a transmittee, the company may only recognise the transmittee as having any title to that share.

(2) A transmittee who produces such evidence of entitlement to shares as the directors may properly require—

(a) may, subject to the articles, choose either to become the holder of those shares or to have them transferred to another person, and

(b) subject to the articles, and pending any transfer of the shares to another person, has the same rights as the holder had.

(3) But transmittees do not have the right to attend or vote at a general meeting, or agree to a proposed written resolution, in respect of shares to which they are entitled, by reason of the holder's death or bankruptcy or otherwise, unless they become the holders of those shares.

Exercise of transmittees' rights

28.—(1) Transmittees who wish to become the holders of shares to which they have become entitled must notify the company in writing of that wish.

(2) If the transmittee wishes to have a share transferred to another person, the transmittee must execute an instrument of transfer in respect of it.

(3) Any transfer made or executed under this article is to be treated as if it were made or executed by the person from whom the transmittee has derived rights in respect of the share, and as if the event which gave rise to the transmission had not occurred.

Transmittees bound by prior notices

29. If a notice is given to a shareholder in respect of shares and a transmittee is entitled to those shares, the transmittee is bound by the notice if it was given to the shareholder before the transmittee's name has been entered in the register of members.

DIVIDENDS AND OTHER DISTRIBUTIONS

Procedure for declaring dividends

30.—(1) The company may by ordinary resolution declare dividends, and the directors may decide to pay interim dividends.

(2) A dividend must not be declared unless the directors have made a recommendation as to its amount. Such a dividend must not exceed the amount recommended by the directors.

(3) No dividend may be declared or paid unless it is in accordance with shareholders' respective rights.

(4) Unless the shareholders' resolution to declare or directors' decision to pay a dividend, or the terms on which shares are issued, specify otherwise, it must be paid by reference to each

shareholder's holding of shares on the date of the resolution or decision to declare or pay it.
(5) If the company's share capital is divided into different classes, no interim dividend may be paid on shares carrying deferred or non-preferred rights if, at the time of payment, any preferential dividend is in arrear.
(6) The directors may pay at intervals any dividend payable at a fixed rate if it appears to them that the profits available for distribution justify the payment.
(7) If the directors act in good faith, they do not incur any liability to the holders of shares conferring preferred rights for any loss they may suffer by the lawful payment of an interim dividend on shares with deferred or non-preferred rights.

Payment of dividends and other distributions

31.—(1) Where a dividend or other sum which is a distribution is payable in respect of a share, it must be paid by one or more of the following means—
(a) transfer to a bank or building society account specified by the distribution recipient either in writing or as the directors may otherwise decide;
(b) sending a cheque made payable to the distribution recipient by post to the distribution recipient at the distribution recipient's registered address (if the distribution recipient is a holder of the share), or (in any other case) to an address specified by the distribution recipient either in writing or as the directors may otherwise decide;
(c) sending a cheque made payable to such person by post to such person at such address as the distribution recipient has specified either in writing or as the directors may otherwise decide; or
(d) any other means of payment as the directors agree with the distribution recipient either in writing or by such other means as the directors decide.
(2) In the articles, 'the distribution recipient' means, in respect of a share in respect of which a dividend or other sum is payable—
(a) the holder of the share; or
(b) if the share has two or more joint holders, whichever of them is named first in the register of members; or
(c) if the holder is no longer entitled to the share by reason of death or bankruptcy, or otherwise by operation of law, the transmittee.

No interest on distributions

32. The company may not pay interest on any dividend or other sum payable in respect of a share unless otherwise provided by—
(a) the terms on which the share was issued, or
(b) the provisions of another agreement between the holder of that share and the company.

Unclaimed distributions

33.—(1) All dividends or other sums which are—
payable in respect of shares, and
(a) unclaimed after having been declared or become payable,
(b) may be invested or otherwise made use of by the directors for the benefit of the company until claimed.
(2) The payment of any such dividend or other sum into a separate account does not make the company a trustee in respect of it.
(3) If—
(a) twelve years have passed from the date on which a dividend or other sum became due for payment, and
(b) the distribution recipient has not claimed it,

(c) the distribution recipient is no longer entitled to that dividend or other sum and it ceases to remain owing by the company.

Non-cash distributions

34.—(1) Subject to the terms of issue of the share in question, the company may, by ordinary resolution on the recommendation of the directors, decide to pay all or part of a dividend or other distribution payable in respect of a share by transferring non-cash assets of equivalent value (including, without limitation, shares or other securities in any company).

(2) For the purposes of paying a non-cash distribution, the directors may make whatever arrangements they think fit, including, where any difficulty arises regarding the distribution—

(a) fixing the value of any assets;

(b) paying cash to any distribution recipient on the basis of that value in order to adjust the rights of recipients; and

(c) vesting any assets in trustees.

Waiver of distributions

35. Distribution recipients may waive their entitlement to a dividend or other distribution payable in respect of a share by giving the company notice in writing to that effect, but if—

(a) the share has more than one holder, or

(b) more than one person is entitled to the share, whether by reason of the death or bankruptcy of one or more joint holders, or otherwise,

(c) the notice is not effective unless it is expressed to be given, and signed, by all the holders or persons otherwise entitled to the share.

CAPITALISATION OF PROFITS

Authority to capitalise and appropriation of capitalised sums

36.—(1) Subject to the articles, the directors may, if they are so authorised by an ordinary resolution—

(a) decide to capitalise any profits of the company (whether or not they are available for distribution) which are not required for paying a preferential dividend, or any sum standing to the credit of the company's share premium account or capital redemption reserve; and

(b) appropriate any sum which they so decide to capitalise (a 'capitalised sum') to the persons who would have been entitled to it if it were distributed by way of dividend (the 'persons entitled') and in the same proportions.

(2) Capitalised sums must be applied—

(a) on behalf of the persons entitled, and

(b) in the same proportions as a dividend would have been distributed to them.

(3) Any capitalised sum may be applied in paying up new shares of a nominal amount equal to the capitalised sum which are then allotted credited as fully paid to the persons entitled or as they may direct.

(4) A capitalised sum which was appropriated from profits available for distribution may be applied in paying up new debentures of the company which are then allotted credited as fully paid to the persons entitled or as they may direct.

(5) Subject to the articles the directors may—

(a) apply capitalised sums in accordance with paragraphs (3) and (4) partly in one way and partly in another;

(b) make such arrangements as they think fit to deal with shares or debentures becoming distributable in fractions under this article (including the issuing of fractional certificates or the making of cash payments); and

(c) authorise any person to enter into an agreement with the company on behalf of all the persons entitled which is binding on them in respect of the allotment of shares and debentures to them under this article.

PART 4 DECISION-MAKING BY SHAREHOLDERS
ORGANISATION OF GENERAL MEETINGS
Attendance and speaking at general meetings

37.—(1) A person is able to exercise the right to speak at a general meeting when that person is in a position to communicate to all those attending the meeting, during the meeting, any information or opinions which that person has on the business of the meeting.

(2) A person is able to exercise the right to vote at a general meeting when—

(a) that person is able to vote, during the meeting, on resolutions put to the vote at the meeting, and

(b) that person's vote can be taken into account in determining whether or not such resolutions are passed at the same time as the votes of all the other persons attending the meeting.

(3) The directors may make whatever arrangements they consider appropriate to enable those attending a general meeting to exercise their rights to speak or vote at it.

(4) In determining attendance at a general meeting, it is immaterial whether any two or more members attending it are in the same place as each other.

(5) Two or more persons who are not in the same place as each other attend a general meeting if their circumstances are such that if they have (or were to have) rights to speak and vote at that meeting, they are (or would be) able to exercise them.

Quorum for general meetings

38. No business other than the appointment of the chairman of the meeting is to be transacted at a general meeting if the persons attending it do not constitute a quorum.

Chairing general meetings

39.—(1) If the directors have appointed a chairman, the chairman shall chair general meetings if present and willing to do so.

(2) If the directors have not appointed a chairman, or if the chairman is unwilling to chair the meeting or is not present within ten minutes of the time at which a meeting was due to start—

(a) the directors present, or

(b) (if no directors are present), the meeting,

must appoint a director or shareholder to chair the meeting, and the appointment of the chairman of the meeting must be the first business of the meeting.

(3) The person chairing a meeting in accordance with this article is referred to as 'the chairman of the meeting'.

Attendance and speaking by directors and non-shareholders

40.—(1) Directors may attend and speak at general meetings, whether or not they are shareholders.

(2) The chairman of the meeting may permit other persons who are not—

(a) shareholders of the company, or

(b) otherwise entitled to exercise the rights of shareholders in relation to general meetings, to attend and speak at a general meeting.

Adjournment

41.—(1) If the persons attending a general meeting within half an hour of the time at which the meeting was due to start do not constitute a quorum, or if during a meeting a quorum ceases to be present, the chairman of the meeting must adjourn it.

(2) The chairman of the meeting may adjourn a general meeting at which a quorum is present if—

(a) the meeting consents to an adjournment, or

(b) it appears to the chairman of the meeting that an adjournment is necessary to protect the safety of any person attending the meeting or ensure that the business of the meeting is conducted in an orderly manner.

(3) The chairman of the meeting must adjourn a general meeting if directed to do so by the meeting.

(4) When adjourning a general meeting, the chairman of the meeting must—

(a) either specify the time and place to which it is adjourned or state that it is to continue at a time and place to be fixed by the directors, and

(b) have regard to any directions as to the time and place of any adjournment which have been given by the meeting.

(5) If the continuation of an adjourned meeting is to take place more than 14 days after it was adjourned, the company must give at least 7 clear days' notice of it (that is, excluding the day of the adjourned meeting and the day on which the notice is given)—

(a) to the same persons to whom notice of the company's general meetings is required to be given, and

(b) containing the same information which such notice is required to contain.

(6) No business may be transacted at an adjourned general meeting which could not properly have been transacted at the meeting if the adjournment had not taken place.

VOTING AT GENERAL MEETINGS
Voting: general
42. A resolution put to the vote of a general meeting must be decided on a show of hands unless a poll is duly demanded in accordance with the articles.

Errors and disputes
43.—(1) No objection may be raised to the qualification of any person voting at a general meeting except at the meeting or adjourned meeting at which the vote objected to is tendered, and every vote not disallowed at the meeting is valid.

(2) Any such objection must be referred to the chairman of the meeting, whose decision is final.

Poll votes
44.—(1) A poll on a resolution may be demanded—

(a) in advance of the general meeting where it is to be put to the vote, or

(b) at a general meeting, either before a show of hands on that resolution or immediately after the result of a show of hands on that resolution is declared.

(2) A poll may be demanded by—

(a) the chairman of the meeting;

(b) the directors;

(c) two or more persons having the right to vote on the resolution; or

(d) a person or persons representing not less than one tenth of the total voting rights of all the shareholders having the right to vote on the resolution.

(3) A demand for a poll may be withdrawn if—

(a) the poll has not yet been taken, and

(b) the chairman of the meeting consents to the withdrawal.

(4) Polls must be taken immediately and in such manner as the chairman of the meeting directs.

Content of proxy notices

45.—(1) Proxies may only validly be appointed by a notice in writing (a 'proxy notice') which—

(a) states the name and address of the shareholder appointing the proxy;

(b) identifies the person appointed to be that shareholder's proxy and the general meeting in relation to which that person is appointed;

(c) is signed by or on behalf of the shareholder appointing the proxy, or is authenticated in such manner as the directors may determine; and

(d) is delivered to the company in accordance with the articles and any instructions contained in the notice of the general meeting to which they relate.

(2) The company may require proxy notices to be delivered in a particular form, and may specify different forms for different purposes.

(3) Proxy notices may specify how the proxy appointed under them is to vote (or that the proxy is to abstain from voting) on one or more resolutions.

(4) Unless a proxy notice indicates otherwise, it must be treated as—

(a) allowing the person appointed under it as a proxy discretion as to how to vote on any ancillary or procedural resolutions put to the meeting, and

(b) appointing that person as a proxy in relation to any adjournment of the general meeting to which it relates as well as the meeting itself.

Delivery of proxy notices

46.—(1) A person who is entitled to attend, speak or vote (either on a show of hands or on a poll) at a general meeting remains so entitled in respect of that meeting or any adjournment of it, even though a valid proxy notice has been delivered to the company by or on behalf of that person.

(2) An appointment under a proxy notice may be revoked by delivering to the company a notice in writing given by or on behalf of the person by whom or on whose behalf the proxy notice was given.

(3) A notice revoking a proxy appointment only takes effect if it is delivered before the start of the meeting or adjourned meeting to which it relates.

(4) If a proxy notice is not executed by the person appointing the proxy, it must be accompanied by written evidence of the authority of the person who executed it to execute it on the appointor's behalf.

Amendments to resolutions

47.—(1) An ordinary resolution to be proposed at a general meeting may be amended by ordinary resolution if—

(a) notice of the proposed amendment is given to the company in writing by a person entitled to vote at the general meeting at which it is to be proposed not less than 48 hours before the meeting is to take place (or such later time as the chairman of the meeting may determine), and

(b) the proposed amendment does not, in the reasonable opinion of the chairman of the meeting, materially alter the scope of the resolution.

(2) A special resolution to be proposed at a general meeting may be amended by ordinary resolution, if—

(a) the chairman of the meeting proposes the amendment at the general meeting at which the resolution is to be proposed, and

(b) the amendment does not go beyond what is necessary to correct a grammatical or other non-substantive error in the resolution.

(3) If the chairman of the meeting, acting in good faith, wrongly decides that an amendment to a resolution is out of order, the chairman's error does not invalidate the vote on that resolution.

PART 5 ADMINISTRATIVE ARRANGEMENTS
Means of communication to be used
48.—(1) Subject to the articles, anything sent or supplied by or to the company under the articles may be sent or supplied in any way in which the Companies Act 2006 provides for documents or information which are authorised or required by any provision of that Act to be sent or supplied by or to the company.

(2) Subject to the articles, any notice or document to be sent or supplied to a director in connection with the taking of decisions by directors may also be sent or supplied by the means by which that director has asked to be sent or supplied with such notices or documents for the time being.

(3) A director may agree with the company that notices or documents sent to that director in a particular way are to be deemed to have been received within a specified time of their being sent, and for the specified time to be less than 48 hours.

Company seals
49.—(1) Any common seal may only be used by the authority of the directors.

(2) The directors may decide by what means and in what form any common seal is to be used.

(3) Unless otherwise decided by the directors, if the company has a common seal and it is affixed to a document, the document must also be signed by at least one authorised person in the presence of a witness who attests the signature.

(4) For the purposes of this article, an authorised person is—

(a) any director of the company;

(b) the company secretary (if any); or

(c) any person authorised by the directors for the purpose of signing documents to which the common seal is applied.

No right to inspect accounts and other records
50. Except as provided by law or authorised by the directors or an ordinary resolution of the company, no person is entitled to inspect any of the company's accounting or other records or documents merely by virtue of being a shareholder.

Provision for employees on cessation of business
51. The directors may decide to make provision for the benefit of persons employed or formerly employed by the company or any of its subsidiaries (other than a director or former director or shadow director) in connection with the cessation or transfer to any person of the whole or part of the undertaking of the company or that subsidiary.

DIRECTORS' INDEMNITY AND INSURANCE
Indemnity
52.—(1) Subject to paragraph (2), a relevant director of the company or an associated company may be indemnified out of the company's assets against—

(a) any liability incurred by that director in connection with any negligence, default, breach of duty or breach of trust in relation to the company or an associated company,

(b) any liability incurred by that director in connection with the activities of the company or an associated company in its capacity as a trustee of an occupational pension scheme (as defined in section 235(6) of the Companies Act 2006),

(c) any other liability incurred by that director as an officer of the company or an associated company.

(2) This article does not authorise any indemnity which would be prohibited or rendered void by any provision of the Companies Acts or by any other provision of law.

(3) In this article—

(a) companies are associated if one is a subsidiary of the other or both are subsidiaries of the same body corporate, and

(b) a 'relevant director' means any director or former director of the company or an associated company.

Insurance

53.—(1) The directors may decide to purchase and maintain insurance, at the expense of the company, for the benefit of any relevant director in respect of any relevant loss.

(2) In this article—

(a) a 'relevant director' means any director or former director of the company or an associated company,

(b) a 'relevant loss' means any loss or liability which has been or may be incurred by a relevant director in connection with that director's duties or powers in relation to the company, any associated company or any pension fund or employees' share scheme of the company or associated company, and

(c) companies are associated if one is a subsidiary of the other or both are subsidiaries of the same body corporate.

Glossary

accounts: a broad term which can refer to a company's published accounts or its internal management accounts.

accounting ratios: ratios that are calculated from a company's financial records which can be used to interpret the financial information and measure performance.

accounting reference date: the date that marks the end of a company's accounting year end for the purposes of preparation and filing of statutory accounts.

actual authority: in agency terms the authority that an agent has been given by his principal – his true authority.

administration: an insolvency procedure enabling the reorganisation and/or restructuring of a company with the protection of a moratorium against creditor action.

agency problem: in the context of corporate governance this refers to the separation of ownership and control between the directors and shareholders of a company, the 'problem' being the potential misalignment of their respective interests.

agent: a person who is authorised by another person (the agent's 'principal') to act on the principal's behalf and to bind the principal in contracts and arrangements with third parties.

allotment: shares are allotted to a person when that person acquires the unconditional right to be included in the company's register of members in respect of the shares; see also 'issue' which has a different meaning, however the terms 'allotment' and 'issue' are often used interchangeably.

annual return: a return of information that all companies must make to the Registrar of Companies within every 12-month period providing a snapshot of the company as to (among others) its directors, shareholders, issued share capital and registered office.

apparent authority: in agency terms, the authority that a person has as a result of the way in which they have been held out by the principal.

articles of association: often referred to as a company's internal rule book the articles are a company's main constitutional document which governs the relationship between the company and its directors and shareholders and sets out their respective powers, rights and obligations.

BIS: the Department for Business Innovation and Skills.

board of directors: the collective term for a company's directors acting together as the governing body of the company, having the powers and authorities that are bestowed upon it by the company's constitution.

board meeting: a formal meeting of the board of directors.

board resolution: a formal resolution or decision of the board of directors.

business name: a trading name which in the case of a company is different to the company's registered name; in the case of a sole trader is a name other than his or her surname; and in the case of a partnership is a name other than the names of the partners.

buy-back: see 'share buy-back'.

certified copy: a copy of a document which is certified as a true and complete copy of the original by a person of good standing such as a solicitor, accountant, bank manager or doctor.

certificate of incorporation: a legal document evidencing the creation of a company.

certificate on change of name: a legal document evidencing the change of name of a company.

charge: a legal form of security for a loan or debt that attaches to particular assets either by way of a fixed charge or a floating charge.

class rights: the rights attaching to a particular class of shares.

code of ethics: a formal document setting out a company's vision and values and code of ethical conduct.

common law: legal rules and principles not enshrined in statute but accepted as the common law of the land based on custom and as declared and developed by the courts through decisions made in various cases over time.

Companies House: an executive agency of BIS, Companies House is the registry for companies incorporated in the UK.

Companies House form: a form prescribed by Companies House for the purposes of submitting information required to be provided under the Companies Act.

company: an association formed by its first members through the legal process of incorporation and which is a separate legal person.

company limited by guarantee: a company that is not permitted to issue shares and where the liability of the members is limited to a fixed amount that each member agrees to contribute to the assets of the company in the event of a winding up.

company name: the name of a company as registered on Companies House records (see also 'business name').

company names adjudicator: sitting within the UK Intellectual Property Office, the company names adjudicators deal with objections concerning the use of company names, in accordance with provisions set out in the Companies Act.

company secretary: an officer of a company with no legally defined role but who generally has responsibilities with regard to the administrative, governance and compliance aspects of a company's affairs.

company voluntary arrangement: a compromise agreement or arrangement between a company and its creditors for the payment of the company's debts, supervised by a licensed insolvency practitioner.

compulsory liquidation: a liquidation that is commenced following a successful petition to the court, usually by a creditor.

connected person: persons who are considered to be connected with a director such as a spouse or civil partner, any other person whom the director lives with in an enduring family relationship, the director's children and step-children, the director's parents and a body corporate in which the director has an interest in at least 20 per cent of the share capital.

consolidation: the process whereby two or more shares are combined to create one share having a nominal value equal to the total nominal value of the consolidated shares (see also 'subdivision').

corporate director: a company which acts as a director of another company.

corporate governance: principles and best practice concerning the way in which companies are run and directed. There is no one definition of what corporate governance is, in the broader view it also encompasses issues relating to corporate social responsibility and business ethics.

corporate manslaughter: an offence created by the Corporate Manslaughter and Corporate Homicide Act 2007 by which a company can be found liable for a person's death.

corporate social responsibility: an area of corporate governance which proposes that, in relation to their stakeholders, companies should conduct themselves in accordance with accepted standards of responsible business practice. In this context 'stakeholders' is often defined in the widest possible terms.

creditor: a person or company that a company owes money to.

creditors' voluntary liquidation: the process for winding up an insolvent company.

date of incorporation: the date on which a company was formed. The date of incorporation is stated on a company's certificate of incorporation.

debenture: a document evidencing or acknowledging a debt owed by a company and (usually) granting security over the company's assets by way of a fixed and/ or floating charge.

debtor: a person or company that owes money to a company.

de facto **director**: a person acting as a director who has not been formally or validly appointed.

derivative claim: a claim brought by a member of a company against a director in accordance with the procedure set out in the Companies Act. The claim is brought by the member on the company's behalf.

directors' general duties: refers to the seven general duties of directors which are codified and set out in the Companies Act. Prior to the Companies Act, directors' duties existed only in the common law.

disqualification order: a court order preventing a person from (among others) acting as a director of a company without the consent of the court for the period of time specified in the order. Breach of a disqualification order is a criminal offence.

disqualification undertaking: an alternative to a disqualification order, an out-of-court undertaking by a director not to act as a director without the consent of the court for a specified period of time. Disqualification undertakings may only be accepted in certain circumstances. Breach of a disqualification undertaking is a criminal offence.

dissolution: the legal closure of a company by application to the Registrar of Companies. The Registrar can also dissolve companies himself in certain circumstances in exercise of powers granted to him under the Companies Act. All property and assets of a dissolved company (if any) pass automatically to the crown. A dissolved company can be brought back to life by a procedure known as 'restoration'.

dividend: a payment made to a company's shareholders out of the company's distributable profits. In a company with more than one class of shares, dividends are paid in accordance with the rights attaching to each class.

dormant company: a company with no 'significant accounting transactions' – transactions that are required to be entered in the company's accounting records in accordance with s. 386 of the Companies Act. For this purpose certain transactions such as payment for shares taken by the subscribers to the company's memorandum can be disregarded.

duty of skill and care: refers to the duty of directors to exercise reasonable care, skill and diligence – one of the seven codified general duties of directors set out in the Companies Act.

electronic communication: a communication sent in electronic form such as by email, text or on a disk.

electronic filing: a form or document filed with the Registrar of Companies in electronic format using either approved software or the Companies House WebFiling service.

electronic incorporation: the process of incorporating a company electronically using either approved software or the incorporation facility available on the Companies House website.

enlightened shareholder value: refers to the view that it is in the long-term financial interests of shareholders that their company is run in a socially and environmentally responsible manner.

ethics: moral principles, codes and values.

executive director: a director with a full-time employment role within a company's executive management.

filing: the process of submitting or presenting documents or information to the Registrar of Companies.

fiduciary duties: duties owed by one person to another in respect of property or powers entrusted to the former by the latter.

fixed charge: a charge which is fixed on a particular asset or assets, this is an encumbrance which prevents the owner of the asset from taking any action on it without the prior consent of the charge holder.

floating charge: a charge which hovers over the assets that are subject to it and which crystallises and becomes fixed on the occurrence of specified events.

formation agent: a provider of company formation services and other company-related services.

fraudulent trading: a criminal offence set out in s. 993 of the Companies Act of carrying on any business of a company with the intent to defraud creditors. Also, under s. 213 of the Insolvency Act, if in the course of a winding up it appears that any business of a company has been carried on with the intent to defraud creditors the court can require any persons who were knowingly a party to the fraud to contribute such sums to the company's assets as the court thinks proper.

Gazette: the newspaper of the British government used to publicise and record official and legal information. Three separate editions of the *Gazette* are published each working day: the London *Gazette*, the Edinburgh *Gazette* and the Belfast *Gazette*. Each edition carries notices relevant to the whole of the UK as well as notices specific to England and Wales, Scotland and Northern Ireland, respectively.

general meeting: a formal meeting of a company's shareholders.

grant of probate: an official document that is evidence of the appointment of the executors of a deceased person's estate.

hard copy form: information or documents sent in paper format.

holding company: defined by s. 1159 of the Companies Act, generally a company is the holding company of another company (its subsidiary) if it holds a majority of the voting rights in that company.

incorporation: the process by which a company is created, also referred to as 'formation' and 'registration'.

Insolvency Service: an executive agency of the Department for Business, Innovation and Skills. From its website: 'The Insolvency Service exists to provide the framework and the means for dealing with financial failure in the economy and with the misconduct that is often associated with it.'

insolvent/insolvency: a situation in which a company is unable to pay its debts as they fall due or where the company's liabilities exceed its assets.

institutional investor: companies and organisations who invest their funds as part of their business (such as insurance companies) or invest the funds of others (such as pension funds).

instrument of transfer: a document used to give effect to the transfer of ownership of shares – the usual form of document used for this purpose is the stock transfer form.

intellectual property: intangible property such as inventions, designs and trade marks which can be protected by intellectual property rights.

internal controls: a system for identifying and managing the risks within a business.

issue: in relation to shares a share is issued when the name of the person entitled to the share is entered in the company's register of members as the holder of that share; see also 'allotment' which has a different meaning although the two terms are often used interchangeably.

issued capital: refers to the shares that a company has issued.

joint shareholder: a shareholder who holds shares jointly with one or more other persons

letters of representation: a grant to the personal representatives of a person who has died without leaving a will which confers on them the authority to administer the deceased person's estate.

limited liability: the limit on a shareholders liability for the debts of a company or a member's liability for the debts of a limited liability partnership.

limited liability partnership: a particular kind of partnership formed by registration with Companies House and which, unlike a normal partnership, is a separate legal person.

liquidation: the process of winding up or closing down a company whether solvent or insolvent.

listed company: a company whose shares are admitted to trading on a recognised investment exchange.

majority shareholder: in general a person holding over 50% of the voting rights in a company.

management accounts: accounts produced by a company for internal decision-making and monitoring purposes.

mediation: a form of dispute resolution in which an independent third party helps the parties in dispute come to a settlement.

member: in relation to a company, a person whose name is entered in the company's register of members.

members' voluntary liquidation: the process for winding up a solvent company.

memorandum of association: under previous Companies Acts an important part of a company's constitution, now a greatly simplified document confirming the first shareholders' wish to form a company and to take shares in it. The memorandum has no ongoing significance once a company has been incorporated.

minority shareholder: in general a person holding less than 50% of the voting rights in a company.

minutes: a formal record of the proceedings of a meeting and the decisions made.

misfeasance: a cause of action under s. 212 of the Insolvency Act 1986 involving the misapplication or retention by a director of any money or other property of the company or any breach of any fiduciary or other duty in relation to the company.

model articles: the standard form articles for private companies limited by shares, private companies limited by guarantee and public limited companies prescribed by the Secretary of State under powers granted by the Companies Act.

moratorium: in relation to insolvency proceedings, a period of time during which a company's creditors are prohibited from taking any action for the recovery of the sums owed to them.

natural director: a director who is a real (as opposed to artificial) person.

negligence: the breach of a legal duty of care.

nominal value: the fixed value of a share which a company ascribes to it in accordance with s. 542 of the Companies Act. The nominal value of a share is distinct from its fair value or market value. Also known as the 'par value'.

non-executive director: a director who does not have a full-time executive role in the management of a company.

non-statutory registers: registers which are not a legal requirement under the Companies Act but which most companies keep and maintain as a matter of good practice; two common examples being the register of allotments and register of transfers.

objects: a statement of the business and activities that a company proposes to carry on together with the powers needed to pursue them.

officer: as per s. 1173 of the Companies Act, a director, manager or secretary of a company. In the case of an 'officer in default' this is broadened to also include any person who is to be treated as an officer of the company for the purposes of the provision of the Companies Act in question.

official receiver: an officer of the court who, in relation to a company, may be appointed as provisional liquidator after presentation of a petition for a winding-up order or who is appointed as the first liquidator following the grant of such an order.

ordinary resolution: a resolution requiring approval by a majority of a company's shareholders having the right to vote on it.

ordinary share: the basic building block of a company's share capital carrying the right to vote and to participate in dividends and capital distributions.

ostensible authority: see 'apparent authority'.

paid-up: refers to shares which have been paid for in full as to both the nominal value and any premium.

partly paid: refers to shares which have not been paid for in full.

partnership: as per the definition set out in the Partnership Act 1890, a partnership is 'the relation which subsists between persons carrying on a business in common with a view to profit'. Unlike a company, a partnership is not a legal person.

par value: see 'nominal value'

passing off: a common law tort which can be used to protect an unregistered trademark.

personal representatives: persons having the authority to deal with the administration of a deceased person's estate either by way of a grant of probate or letters of administration.

poll vote: a vote by way of a ballot in which (subject to a company's articles) shareholders are entitled to one vote for each share that they hold.

pre-emption rights: rights of first refusal. The Companies Act gives existing ordinary shareholders (as defined in the Act) pre-emption rights in relation to the allotment of new shares. A company's articles of association may include provisions that give shareholders rights of pre-emption in relation to share transfers.

preference share: shares which carry preferential rights in relation to ordinary shares, usually in respects of dividends and order of payment on a winding up.

presenter: a term used to refer to a person submitting or 'presenting' information or documents to the Registrar of Companies.

principal: in agency terms, the person from whom an agent's powers and authority are derived.

probate: see 'grant of probate'.

proxy: a person appointed by a shareholder to attend a general meeting and to vote in his place.

PROOF: 'protected online filing' – an agreement between a company and Companies House that the company will always file certain information electronically.

qualifying floating charge: a floating charge that meets the requirements of the Enterprise Act 2002 in that it consists of a charge over the whole or substantially whole of a company's property and purports to give the holder the power to appoint an administrator or an administrative receiver.

quasi loan: an arrangement whereby a company agrees to pay a director's creditor on the basis that the director will repay the company at a later date.

quorum: either in relation to a directors' meeting or a shareholders' meeting, the minimum number of directors or shareholders who must be present in order for the meeting to be validly constituted.

ratification: validating an otherwise invalid act by retrospectively confirming or approving it.

redeemable share: a share which can be re-purchased by the company either at the option of the company and/or the shareholder depending on the terms agreed at the time when the share was issued.

remuneration: payments and benefits that an employee is entitled to in respect of services provided by the employee to a company.

registered office: a company's official address at which legal and other documents can be validly served and at which certain company records must be kept if not kept at a single alternative inspection location.

resolution: a formal decision of directors or shareholders.

risk assessment: in health and safety terms the process of identifying risks, the persons affected by them, the severity of the likely injuries that might result from them, whether the control measures in place are adequate and any further measures needed to control them.

secretary: see 'company secretary'

service address: an address for correspondence that directors must provide to the Registrar of Companies which can (and ideally should) be different from their residential address.

service contract: an agreement setting out the terms of an executive director's employment with a company.

shadow director: a person who has not been appointed as a director but who directs or gives instructions to a company's true directors.

share buy-back: the purchase by a company of its own shares. The procedure for a share buy-back is set out in the Companies Act.

share capital: see 'issued share capital'.

share certificate: a certificate evidencing a shareholder's holding of shares in a company.

share premium: the part of the price paid for a share over and above its nominal value.

shareholder: a person holding shares in a company.

shareholders' agreement: an agreement made between shareholders regarding any number of issues concerning the company's internal management which may but usually does not form part of a company's constitution.

shelf company: a ready-made company incorporated with nominee directors and shareholders which can be bought 'off the shelf' and then transferred to the purchaser.

single alternative inspection location: a location in the same part of the UK in which a company is incorporated at which certain company records can be kept as an alternative to keeping them at the registered office.

special resolution: a shareholder resolution requiring a majority in favour of 75% or over.

stakeholder: a person or group of persons with an interest in a company or who are in some way affected by a company's activities.

stamp duty: in relation to a share transfer the duty payable on a stock transfer form.

statement of affairs: a summary of a company's financial position sworn under oath in relation to insolvency proceedings.

statute law: laws and regulations which come into being as a result of being enacted by parliament.

statutory books: see 'statutory registers'.

statutory declaration: a written declaration signed in the presence of a commissioner for oaths attesting the truth of the facts stated in it.

statutory registers: registers containing information relating to a company's directors, shareholders and any charges over the company's assets which companies must maintain in accordance with the Companies Act. See also 'non-statutory registers'.

stock transfer form: a standard form of instrument of transfer set out in Schedule 1 to the Stock Transfer Act 1963 (as amended).

subdivision: the process whereby shares of a certain nominal value are divided into shares of a smaller nominal value, the total nominal value of the shares remaining the same (see also 'consolidation').

subscriber(s): the person or persons whose names are stated in and who sign or otherwise authenticate a proposed company's memorandum of association. In doing so they confirm their wish to form a company and to take at least one share in it. The shares taken are referred to as 'subscriber shares'.

subsidiary: see 'holding company'.

tort: a wrongful act which in law gives rise to a civil liability, such as the tort of negligence or the tort of passing off.

trademark: a sign that distinguishes the goods and services of one trader from those of another. A form of intellectual property, a trademark can either be registered or unregistered.

transfer: the change of ownership of shares in a company that is effected by way of a stock transfer form or other instrument of transfer.

transferee: in relation to a transfer of shares, the person to whom the shares are transferred.

transferor: in relation to a transfer of shares, the person who transfers their shares.

transmission: a change of ownership of shares which occurs by operation of law and does not require a stock transfer form or other instrument of transfer.

winding up: a generic term that refers to the closure or liquidation of a company either solvent or insolvent.

written resolution: an alternative to holding a general meeting. A written resolution is a document setting out one or more proposed resolutions that is circulated to a company's shareholders for approval. The written resolution is passed when the required agreements are received by the company.

wrongful trading: as set out in s. 214 of the Insolvency Act 1986, in relation to an insolvent company the act of continuing to trade at a time when the directors knew or ought to have concluded that there was no reasonable prospect that the company would avoid going into an insolvent liquidation. The court can order any directors found liable to contribute such sums to the company's assets as the court thinks proper.

Directory

ACAS
www.acas.org.uk

Association of British Insurers
www.abi.org.uk

Association of Business Recovery Professionals
www.r3.org.uk

Association of Chartered Certified Accountants
www.acca.global.com

British Chambers of Commerce
www.britishchambers.org.uk

British Private Equity and Venture Capital Association
www.bvca.co.uk

Business in the Community
www.bitc.org.uk

The Chartered Institute of Patent Attorneys
www.cipa.org.uk

The Chartered Institute of Personnel and Development
www.cipd.co.uk

The Chartered Institute of Tax Advisers
www.tax.org.uk

The Confederation of British Industry
www.cbi.org.uk

The Department for Business, Innovation and Skills
www.bis.gov.uk

The Environment Agency
www.environment-agency.gov.uk

Federation of Small Businesses
www.fsb.org.uk

Financial Reporting Council
www.frc.org.uk

The Financial Services Authority
www.fsa.gov.uk

GOV.UK
www.gov.uk

Health & Safety Executive
www.hse.gov.uk

HM Courts and Tribunals Service
www.justice.gov.uk

HM Revenue & Customs
www.hmrc.gov.uk

HM Stationery Office
www.legislation.gov.uk

The Information Commissioner
www.ico.gov.uk

The Insolvency Practitioners Association
www.insolvency-practioners.org.uk

The Insolvency Service
www.insolvency.gov.uk

The Institute of Chartered Accountants in England and Wales
www.icaew.com

The Institute of Chartered Secretaries and Administrators
www.icsaglobal.com

The Institute of Directors
www.iod.com

The Institute of Risk Management
www.irm.org

The Institute of Trade Mark Attorneys
www.itma.org.uk

InterNIC
www.internic.net

The Law Society of England and Wales
www.lawsociety.org.uk

Nominet
www.nominet.org.uk

Office of Fair Trading
www.oft.gov.uk

Organisation for Economic Co-operation and Development
www.oecd.org

Public Relations Consultants Association
www.prca.org.uk

The Registrar of Companies for England and Wales (Companies House)
www.companies-house.gov.uk

UK Business Angels Association
www.ukbusinessangelsassociation.org.uk

UK Intellectual Property Office
www.ipo.org.uk

Index